Illustrated Encyclopedia of Medical Terms

Better Homes and Gardens

Illustrated Encyclopedia of Medical Terms

Edited by Donald G. Cooley

Artwork by Paul Zuckerman

MEREDITH PRESS

NEW YORK · DES MOINES

Table of Contents

Words Your Doctor Uses

When we say "I have a pain in a joint," we are using medical language. "Pain" describes a condition and "joint" tells where it hurts. Ordinary English is rich in simple words that express medical and anatomical ideas with admirable clarity. We use such words all the time, and perhaps some of us, if told that we are speaking medical language, would be as astonished as the man who discovered that he had been speaking prose all his life.

Long before they enter medical school, doctors learn everyday English like the rest of us. They know that a bone is a bone before they learn that it is also an *os*. Ordinary English is the language most doctors use in explaining matters to patients, and it is the language they usually expect to hear from patients. We might tell the doctor that we have "arthralgia," a ten-dollar word meaning "pain in a joint." There is little reason to do so, other than to toss around a little erudition or make the doctor suspect that we have been looking at a television ad for pain-relievers.

Any medical term can be translated into simple English. Doctors do it all the time in dealing with patients. But within their profession, technical language is a necessity. Doctors do not use jawbreaking medical terms to confuse the patient or hide the awful truth. They use it primarily for specific, concise professional communication—in medical journals, scientific reports, teaching, textbooks, clinical record keeping. In this they do not differ from other professions and occupations which have specialized language that is not at all secret, but which outsiders may not be privy to. Lawyers have their torts, printers their hellboxes, clergymen their epistemologies, loggers their wanigans, musicians their hemidemisemiquavers.

Specialized medical language, however, is rather exceptional. For one thing, it is enormously larger than other specialized languages. A complete medical dictionary has thousands upon thousands of entries, many of which are rarely referred to even by doctors. For another, medical language applies directly to *us*—our functions, organs, distempers, symptoms, health—and thus its presumed mysteries are of universal self-interest. A medical word we have never heard of or cared about may suddenly have some personal meaning.

Another exceptional thing about technical medical language is its almost total derivation from Greek and Latin. There are a few Arabic intrusions (*alcohol, elixir*) and a few Gallicisms (*tic douloureux*). But Greek and Latin predominate overwhelmingly. This gives medical words an arcane, scholarly, "it's Greek to me" formidability which we hope to show is deceptive. *Patella* is not a superior word for *kneecap*. It is just a different word.

Medical words insinuate themselves easily into the common tongue. Many words, originally quite technical, crop up in ordinary conversation—*antibiotic, Rh factor, hormone, hysterectomy, poliomyelitis, cholesterol, antihistamine, hypodermic, coronary*, and hundreds of others. A good deal of information about medicine (not implying any competence to practice it) is infused into the public mind by magazine and newspaper articles, "health columns," radio and television interviews, shows and novels about the tribulations of doctors, and dissemination of health and research findings by government and local agencies. Animated advertising may even inform us of things that do not exist, such as little hammers beating inside the skull to cause headaches.

Scientific progress continually adds new words to the language. Many of these new words are medical or have medical implications. In the present volume you will find listings under words such as *laser, nuclear medicine, ballistocardiography, tomography, Coxsackie virus, auto-immune diseases, hyperbaric medicine,* and others which did not exist a few years ago. Such words would surely have bewildered Hippocrates.

Indeed, much of the history of medical progress is embodied in words that have come down to us. Primitive ideas and misconceptions are memorialized in some of the most basic medical words. The *tibia* or shinbone got its name from its supposed resemblance to a flute. *Artery* traces back to the idea that the vessels were air-carriers. The *coccyx* or tailbone was named for a bird, the cuckoo. It was supposed to be shaped like a cuckoo's beak, a resemblance nowadays noted only by anatomists, if by them. The *pituitary* gland was thought to be the source of nasal mucus and its name bears the stamp of that humble secretion. A *hypochrondriac,* overly fretful of his health, would no doubt worry all the more if told that the word refers to the area under the rib cartilage of the upper abdomen, anciently thought to be the site of melancholy feelings.

Why a Special Language?

One of the virtues of technical language is compactness. "Tonsillectomy" says the same thing as "surgical removal of the tonsils" in fewer words. In a medical discussion of tonsil surgery, it is easier and more kindly to repeat the word "tonsillectomy" than its many-worded equivalent. Specific words take much of the sprawl out of communication.

A more important virtue of specialized language is precision of meaning. A patient may complain that he has a "stomach-ache." Diagnosis may disclose that he has *gastritis* or *duodenal ulcer* or even something as exotic as a *bezoar.* In fact, the doctor may discover that the ache isn't in the stomach at all. He is conditioned to suspect that some patients believe that the stomach encom-

passes the entire area between the nipples and the pubic bone.

A minor but not to be undervalued virtue of medical language is its wonderful treasury of euphemisms—respectable substitutes for words thought to be tainted by vulgarity. A lady does not *belch;* she may attain the same relief, in impeccable good taste, by genteel *eructation.* Untimely occurrence of *belly-rumbling* is much more embarrassing than a slight touch of *borborygmus.* A stomach-ache may actually be a *belly*-ache or a *gut*-ache. But *belly* is frowned upon in drawing rooms, and *gut*—a wonderfully terse Anglo-Saxon word for bowels—is even more disreputable. In descriptive emergencies, the easily defeated may resort to "tummy-ache," a term so arch as to be coyly vulgar. The more resourceful will seize upon *abdomen,* and can discuss "abdominal discomfort" with aplomb with practically anybody.

Curt Anglo-Saxon words for body parts and functions are not sharpened in meaning by euphemisms but necessary references may well be made more easily. Teaching the medical names of body parts to children tends to make bees-and-flowers instruction more comfortable for all concerned. Nothing makes a supposedly vulgar word more respectable than its equivalent borrowed from a foreign language.

Compound Words

Many medical words, like any new word, have to be looked up in a dictionary. Many of the oldest medical words are those which name body parts, and they must be accepted as arbitrary labels. There is no master design pattern to make us expect that the *jejunum,* the second part of the small intestine, should be called a jejunum. The word descends from a Latin word for "fasting" or "empty," and embodies the mistaken notion that the organ is always empty after death. Who would suspect that? Or who would suspect that mice have something to do with *muscles*? But flex a muscle, look at the moving ripples and bulges—obviously, little mice are running around under your skin, or so it seemed to those who gave us the word *muscle,* from the diminutive form of the Latin word *mus,* a mouse.

But there is a design pattern for hundreds of medical words, generally quite modern words—in fact, new ones of this sort are frequently added to the language. These are compound or put-together words, built of root-words butted together like alphabet blocks. They can be disjointed (or disarticulated) and if we know the root forms we can make a fair guess at the meaning, even if we have never seen the word before. There are hundreds of Greek and Latin roots, but a few dozen of the most common ones are quite enough to give us at least an inkling of the meaning of an unfamiliar medical word. Some root-forms are common in everyday language. The suffix *-itis,* meaning inflammation, is so familiar that words such as *appendicitis* and *tonsillitis* need no translation.

Some compound words are polysyllabic jawbreakers because they contain so much information. Breaking them into their parts cuts them down to size. Take *gastroenterocolostomy. Gastro* pertains to the stomach, *entero* to the intestines, *colo* to the colon, *stomy* to mouth, outlet or entrance. In one word, *gastroenterocolostomy* says "an operation in which a passage is formed between stomach, intestines and colon."

Not all compound medical words are that complicated. Many give the name of a part with a suffix indicating its condition or something that is done to it. Thus, *-ectomy,* a cutting out, preceded by *hyster-,* the womb, gives *hysterectomy,* surgical removal of the uterus.

For exact meaning of a word, consult the glossary. It is possible to make a wrong guess. Nevertheless, familiarity with a few root forms gives a modest amount of assurance and at least robs medical words of their mystery. A Roman speaking of his *genu* is no more mysterious than an American speaking of his *knee.* The list below gives root forms that occur most frequently in medical language. Roots may be prefixes, suffixes, or appear internally in a word. Combining forms may add or omit a vowel to connect syllables smoothly.

ROOTS OF MEDICAL LANGUAGE

a-, an-. Absent, lacking, deficient, without. An*emia,* deficient in blood.

aden-. Pertaining to a gland. Aden*oma* is a tumor of glandlike tissue.

alg-, -algia. Pain. A prefix such as *neur-* tells where the pain is (*neuralgia*).

ambi-. Both.

andro-. Man, male. An andro*gen* is an agent which produces masculinizing effects.

angi-, angio-. Blood or lymph vessel. Angi*itis* is inflammation of a blood vessel.

anti-. Against. An anti*biotic* is "against life"—in the case of a drug, against the life of disease germs.

arthr-. Joint. Arthro*pathy* is disease affecting a joint.

bleph-. Pertaining to the eyelid.

brady-. Slow. Brady*cardia* is slow heart beat.

bronch-, broncho-. Pertaining to the windpipe.

cardi, cardio-. Denoting the heart.

carp-. The wrist.

-cele. Swelling or herniation of a part, as *recto*cele, prolapse of the rectum.

cephal-. Pertaining to the head. *Encephal-,* "within the head," pertains to the brain.

cervi-. A neck.

chol-, chole-. Relating to bile. Chole*sterol* is a substance found in bile.

chon-, chondro-. Cartilage.

costo-, costal. Pertaining to the ribs.

cranio-. Skull. As in cranio*tomy*, incision through a skull bone.

cry-, cryo- Icy cold.

cyan-. Blue.

-cyst-. Pertaining to a bladder or sac, normal or abnormal, filled with gas, liquid, or semi-solid material. The root appears in many words concerning the urinary bladder (cysto*cele*, cyst*itis*).

-cyt-, cyto-. Cell. *Leuko*cytes are white blood cells.

dia-. Through.

dent-, dento-. Pertaining to a tooth or teeth; from the Latin.

-derm, derma-. Skin.

-dynia. Condition of pain, usually with a prefix identifying the affected part.

dys-. Difficult, bad. This prefix occurs in large numbers of medical words, since it is attachable to any organ or process that isn't functioning as well as it should.

-ectomy. A cutting out; surgical removal. Denotes any operation in which all or part of a named organ is cut out of the body.

endo-. Within, inside of, internal. The endo*metrium* is the lining membrane of the uterus.

-enter-, entero-. Pertaining to the intestines. Gastro*enter*itis is an inflammation of the intestines as well as the stomach.

eryth-, erythro-. Redness. Eryth*ema* is a redness of the skin (including a deep blush). An erythro*cyte* is a red blood cell.

eu-. Well and good. A eu*thyroid* person has a thyroid gland that couldn't be working better. A eu*phoric* one has a tremendous sense of wellbeing.

gastr-, gastro-. Pertaining to the stomach.

-gen-. Producing, begetting, *gen*erating.

glossa-. Pertaining to the tongue.

gnatho-. Pertaining to the jaw. *Micro*gnathia means abnormal smallness of the jaw.

-gogue. Eliciting a flow. A *chole*gogue stimulates the flow of bile.

gyn-, gyne-. Woman, female. Gyne*cology* literally means the study and knowledge of woman, a daringly ambitious enterprise, but useful in its common meaning: the medical specialty concerned with diseases of women.

-gram, -graph. These roots refer to writing, inscribing. They appear in the names of many instruments which record bodily functions on graphs or charts. The *-graph* is the instrument that does the recording; the *-gram* is the record itself. An *electrocardio*graph records the activities of the heart; an *electrocardio*gram is the record.

hem-, hemato-, -em-. Pertaining to blood. Hemat*uria* means blood in the urine. When the roots occur internally in a word, the "h" is often dropped for the sake of pronunciation, leaving *-em-* to denote blood, as in anox*em*ia (deficiency of oxygen in the blood).

hemi-. Half. The prefix is plain enough in hemi*plegia*, "half paralysis," affecting one side of the body. It's not so plain in *migraine* (one-sided headache), a word which shows how language changes through the centuries. The original word was *hemicrania*, "half-head."

hepar-, hepat-. Pertaining to the liver.

hyal-. Glassy.

hyper-. Over, above, increased. The usual implication is overactivity or excessive production, as in hyper*thyroidism*.

hypo-. Under, below; less, decreased. The two different meanings of this common prefix can be tricky. *Hypodermic* might reasonably be interpreted to mean that some unfortunate patient has too little skin. The actual meaning is *under* or *beneath* the skin, a proper site for an injection. The majority of "hypo" words, however, denote an insufficiency, lessening, reduction from the norm, as in *hypoglycemia,* too little glucose in the blood.

hyster-, hystero-. Denoting the womb. *Hysteria* perpetuates a Greek notion that violent emotional behavior originated in the uterus; when it occurred in men it must have been called something else.

-ia. A suffix indicating "condition," preceded by the name of the conditioned organ or system, as *pneumo*nia. A physician wishing to be more specific might call it pneumon*itis,* but a patient, hardly ever.

iatro-. Pertaining to a doctor. A related root, *-iatrist,* denotes a specialist— ped*iatric*ian, obst*etric*ian.

-iasis. Indicates a condition, as *trichin*iasis.

idio-. Peculiar to, private, distinctive. As in idio*syncrasy.*

inter-. Between.

intra-. Within.

-itis. Inflammation.

labio-. Pertaining to lips or lip-shaped structures.

leuk-, leuko-. White.

lig-. Binding. A liga*ment* ties two or more bones together.

lipo-. Fat, fatty.

-lith-. Stone, calcification. Lith*iasis* is a condition of stone formation.

mamma-, mast-. Pertaining to the breast. The first root derives from Latin, the second from Greek. *Mamma-* is obvious in *mammal* and *mammary* gland. The *mast-* root is usually limited to terms for diseases, disorders or procedures, as *mastectomy* (excision of the breast) and *mastoidectomy* (hollowing out of bony processes behind the ear). These lookalike words can be confusing. Is there breast tissue behind the ear? No, the root-key in mast-*oid*-ectomy is the three-letter insert "oid," meaning "like" or "resembling." Anatomists who named the bony *mastoid* process thought that its shape resembled a breast.

mega-, megalo-. Large, huge. The prefix *macro-* has the same meaning.

melan-. Black. The root usually refers in some way to cells that produce *melanin,* the dark pigment mobilized by a suntan. But it also endures in *melancholy,* "black bile," a gloomy humor anciently supposed to be the cause of wretchedness.

men-, meno-. Pertaining to menstruation, from a Greek word for "month."

metr-, metro-. Relating to the womb. Endo*metrium* is the lining membrane of the womb.

myelo-. Pertaining to marrow.

my-, myo-. Pertaining to muscle. Myo*cardium* is heart muscle.

nephr-, nephro-. From the Greek for "kidney." Also see *ren-.*

necro-. Deadness.

neur-, neuro-. Denoting nerves.

ocul-, oculo- (Latin) and **ophthalmo-** (Greek). Both roots refer to the eye, "ophth" words more often to diseases.

odont-, odonto-. Pertaining to a tooth or teeth. An ex*odont*ist extracts teeth (*ex-* or *ec-,* "out of," "out from.").

-oid. Like, resembling, Typh*oid* fever resembles typhus fever, or was supposed to when the name was given, but the two diseases are quite different.

olig-, oligo-. Scanty, few, little. Olig*uria* means scanty urination.

-oma. Denotes a tumor, not necessarily a malignant one.

onych-, onycho-. Pertaining to the nails of fingers or toes.

oo-. Denotes an egg. Pronounced oh-oh, not ooh. The combining form *oophor-* denotes an ovary. Oophoro*hyster*ectomy means surgical removal of the uterus and ovaries.

orch-. Pertaining to the testicles. Orchi*dectomy* has the same meaning as castration.

ortho-. Straight, correct, normal. Ortho*psychiatry* is the specialty concerned with "straightening out" behavior disorders.

oro-, os-. Mouth, opening, entrance. From the Latin, which also gives *os* another meaning, to complicate matters. See below.

os-, oste-, osteo-. Pertaining to bone. The Latin *os-* is most often associated with anatomical structures, the Greek *osteo-* with conditions involving bone. Osteo*gen*esis means formation of bone.

-osis. Indicates a condition of production or increase (*leukocyt*osis, abnormal increase in numbers of white blood cells) or a condition of having parasites or pathogenic agents in the body (*trichin*osis).

-ostomy. Indicates the surgical making of a mouth, opening, or entrance. The opening may be external, as in *colos*tomy, the creation of an artificial outlet of the colon as a substitute for the anus, or internal, as in *gastroenter*ostomy, establishment of an artificial

"mouth" or opening between stomach and intestine. Compare with *-otomy*.

ot-, oto-. Pertaining to the ear. Oto*rrhea* means a discharge from the ear.

-otomy. Indicates a cutting, a surgical incision (but not the removal of an organ; compare with *-ectomy*). *My-ring*otomy means incision of the eardrum.

pachy-. Thick. A pachy*derm* (not necessarily an elephant) is thick-skinned.

para-. (Greek). Alongside, near, abnormal. As in para*proct*itis, inflammation of tissues near the rectum. A Latin suffix with the same spelling, *-para*, denotes bearing, giving birth, as *mul-ti*para, a woman who has given birth to two or more children.

path-, patho-, pathy-. Feeling, suffering, disease. Patho*gen*ic, producing disease; *entero*pathy, disease of the intestines; patho*logy*, the medical specialty concerned with all aspects of disease. The root appears in the everyday word sym*pathy* ("to feel with").

ped-. A root with two meanings, requiring discrimination. The Latin root pertains to the foot, as in *pedal*. The Greek-derived root signifies children or child, as in ped*odontia*, dental care of children. Interestingly, a *peda-gogue* tries to elicit or stimulate a flow (*-gogue*), presumably of learning, from children (*ped-*).

-penia. Scarcity, deficiency, poverty, "starved of." As in *erythro*penia, deficiency in number of red blood cells.

peri-. Denoting around, about, surrounding. Peri*odontium* is a word for tissues which surround and support the teeth.

phag-, -phagy. Pertaining to eating, ingesting. As in *geo*phagy, dirt eating; *eso*phagus, the gullet; phago*cyte*, a cell capable of ingesting foreign particles.

phleb-. Denoting a vein. As in phleb*otomy*, cutting into a vein to let blood; phlebo*thrombosis*, a condition of clotting in a vein.

plast-, -plasia, -plasty. Indicates molding, formation. An objective of *plastic* surgery, as in *mammo*plasty, an operation for correction of sagging breasts.

-plegia. From a Greek word for stroke; paralysis. *Quadri*plegia means paralysis of both legs and arms.

-pnea. Pertaining to breathing. *Dyspnea* is difficult breathing.

pneumo- (Greek) and **pulmo-** (Latin). Both terms pertain to the lungs.

-poiesis. Production, formation. *Hematopoiesis* means formation of blood.

poly-. Many.

presby-. Old. As in presby*opia*, eye changes associated with aging.

proct-, procto-. Pertaining to the anus or rectum. Procto*plasty*, reparative or reconstructive surgery of the rectum.

psych-, psycho-. Pertaining to the mind, from the Greek word for "soul."

pur-, pus- (Latin) and **pyo-** (Greek). Indicates pus, as in *pur*ulent, sup*pura*tive, *pus*tulent, and pyo*derma*, suppurative disease of the skin.

pyel-, pyelo-. Pertaining to the urine-collecting chamber (pelvis) of the kidney.

pyr-, pyret-. Indicates fever.

-raphy. A suffix indicating a seam, suture, sewing together; usually describes a surgical operation, such as *herni*orraphy, a suture operation for hernia.

ren-. Latin for kidney; this root form is usually found in anatomical terms, such as *renal* and *supra*renal. The Greek-derived root, *nephr-*, usually occurs in words describing diseases or procedures. Custom dictates usage. *Nephritis* could as well be called *ren-itis,* but it isn't.

retro-. Backward or behind.

rhag-, rhagia-. Indicates a bursting, breaking forth, discharge from a burst vessel; usually denotes bleeding, as in *hemo*rrhage, with an aspect of suddenness.

-rhea. Indicates a flowing, a discharge, as in *oto*rrhea, discharge from the ear.

rhin-, rhino-. Pertaining to the nose.

scler-. Indicates hard, hardness. *Arterio*sclerosis is a condition of hardening of the arteries.

somat-, somato-. Pertaining to the body.

stom-, stomato-. Pertaining to the mouth or a mouth.

supra-. Above, upon.

tachy-. Indicates fast, speedy, as in tachy*cardia*, abnormally rapid heartbeat.

thromb-. Pertaining to a blood clot.

-ur-, ure-, ureo-. Pertaining to urine.

urethr-, urethro-. Relating to the urethra, the canal leading from the bladder for discharge of urine.

veni-, veno-. Relating to the veins.

xanth-. Yellow.

xero-. Indicates dryness, as xero*stomia*, dryness of the mouth.

ENCYCLOPEDIA
OF MEDICAL TERMS

The Encyclopedia is designed for reference with the Better Homes and Gardens Family Medical Guide. Numbers in parentheses refer to pages where a topic is discussed more fully or illustrations are given. SMALL CAPITALS in the text below indicate that the topic can be looked up under its own heading in the Encyclopedia.

A

Abduction. The moving of a part away from its midline or from the axis of the body; for example, moving the thumb away from the index finger.

ABO. Designates a classic blood group, the one most familiar to people who know their blood type. Blood groups are based on the presence or absence of "factors" or antigens in red blood cells, determined by heredity. Type A blood contains factor A; Type B blood contains factor B; Type AB contains both factors; Type O contains neither. These types are further subdivided by the presence or absence of anti-A or anti-B factors in red cells or serum, and by even more complicated factors.

Abortion. Expulsion of an embryo or fetus from the womb before it is capable of independent life. *Spontaneous* abortion is a not uncommon accident of pregnancy; the lay term is "miscarriage" (345). Some abortions of an embryo too malformed to live occur so early in pregnancy that they may not be recognized. *Induced* abortions may be therapeutic or criminal. Therapeutic abortions may be performed under safe and sterile conditions in a hospital if reputable physicians agree that the mother's life or health is endangered. Criminal abortions ("illegal operations") are usually performed under conditions of furtiveness, crudity, and haste which often lead to infection, invalidism, sterility and sometimes death.

Abrasion. A scraped skin surface, such as a skinned knee which oozes blood (797).

Abruptio placentae. Premature breaking off of the placenta, accompanied by hemorrhage, near the end of pregnancy. Causes may be mechanical or toxic.

Abscess. A collection of pus within a well-defined space in any part of the body. Treatment is by drainage and overcoming of infection.

Accommodation. Change in curvature of the lens of the eye to bring objects into sharp focus (530).

Accouchement. A French word for childbirth.

Acetabulum. The cup-shaped cavity in the hip bone in which the upper end of the thigh bone rests (596).

Achalasia. Inability to relax a hollow muscular organ; especially, a spasmodic tightening of the lower portion of the esophagus (*cardiospasm*), giving a feeling that swallowed food sticks at the entrance to the stomach (447).

Achilles tendon. The thickest and strongest tendon of the body, extending upward about six inches from the back of the heel. It binds the muscles of the calf of the leg to the heel bone.

Achlorhydria. Absence of free hydrochloric acid from the stomach. The condition is frequently a symptom of pernicious anemia, sometimes of stomach cancer or other diseases, but it may occur in elderly people who are quite healthy.

Acholic. Without bile. Clay-colored *acholic stools* indicate some obstructive or other disorder of the liver or bile ducts.

Achondroplasia. A form of dwarfism; the head and torso are of normal size but arms and legs are very short. The condition results from a congenital defect in the formation of cartilage at the growing ends of long bones which prevents normal lengthening.

Acid and Alkaline foods. There is no reason for a normal person to be in the least concerned about the acidity or alkalinity of foods. Doctors sometimes put patients who have acid kidney stones on a high alkaline ash diet, and patients who have alkaline kidney stones on a high acid ash diet. Persons with peptic ulcer should not drink large amounts of citrus or other acid juices on an empty stomach, because the immediate effect is to increase acidity and irritate the ulcer. But the ultimate effect of most acid juices and of foods which contain organic acids and taste sour is to leave an alkaline ash—that is, their ultimate reactions in the body are alkaline. Almost all fruits and vegetables, although they may taste acid, are alkaline-producing foods. The major acid-producing foods are cereals, meats, eggs and cheese, which don't taste very acid at all. An ordinary mixed diet provides perfectly adequate acid-alkaline ash balance, and even if doesn't, the body has remarkably efficient buffering systems.

Foods with alkaline ash:

All fruits except cranberries, plums, prunes, and rhubarb
All vegetables except corn and dried lentils
Milk
Almonds

Brazil nuts
Chestnuts
Coconut
Molasses

Foods with acid ash:

Bread
Cereals
Cranberries, plums, prunes, rhubarb
Bacon
Beef
Cheese
Chicken
Eggs
Fish
Ham
Lamb
Liver
Pork
Veal
Peanut butter
Peanuts
Popcorn
Walnuts
Corn
Lentils

Neutral foods:

Butter
Cornstarch
Cream
Lard
Oils
Sugar
Tapioca
Coffee
Tea

Acid-base balance. Blood is slightly alkaline; it is never acid during life. Mechanisms which maintain this delicate balance are remarkably efficient and do not require continued worry or attention except in presence of disease which a doctor is sure to recognize. Acid-base balance is kept constant by elimination of carbon dioxide from the lungs, excretion of acid by the kidneys (urine is normally acid), and buffer systems of the blood. The chief acid-maker is carbon dioxide which forms carbonic acid when dissolved in water. Sodium bicarbonate constitutes a large alkaline reserve in the blood. Interplay between carbonic acid and bicarbonate keeps the blood exquisitely balanced. *Acidosis* (reduced alkalinity of the blood, but not to the extent that it becomes acid) can result from disturbance of the balancing system by kidney insufficiency, diabetes (333), prolonged diarrhea with loss of bicarbonate, and other conditions that doctors are aware of. Significant acidosis practically never occurs except in diseases which are or should be under treatment. You can get a mild brief acidosis by holding your breath as long as you can, while carbon dioxide accumulates in the lungs; the main sensation is a wild desire to breathe. Strenuous exercise can also produce mild and harmless acidosis because breathing can't quite keep up with carbon dioxide accumulation. Colds and respiratory infections do not cause acidosis nor are such conditions made worse by a vague "acid condition" which is supposedly corrected by taking alkalis to "get on the alkaline side." Excessive intake of antacids or bicarbonate may in fact produce the opposite condition of *alkalosis*—slightly increased alkalinity of the blood. You can induce alkalosis by HYPERVENTILATION; overbreathing forces so much air into the lungs that carbon dioxide is diluted. The same type of alkalosis occurs in MOUNTAIN SICKNESS when overbreathing results from thinness of the air at high altitudes. Alkalosis can result from prolonged vomiting which removes much acid from the system.

Acidosis. Decreased alkalinity of the blood and other body fluids. See ACID-BASE BALANCE.

Acid stomach. Burning, gnawing pain in the upper abdomen is often self-attributed to "acid stomach," especially if distress is not continuous. The stomach is naturally acid and a reasonably normal stomach gets along contentedly with its acids. An acid-free stomach is abnormal and possibly belongs to a patient with pernicious anemia. It is possible for stomach contents to become too acid, from slow emptying, oversecretion, or other causes, but analysis of stomach juices is necessary to determine if acid abnormalities are truly involved. Self-diagnosed "acid stomach," encouraged by animated advertising which shows flaming acids dripping onto the cringing mucosa, is often the result of nervous squirming of the stomach, or inflation by gas-producing foods, or irritants, or too much smoking, or food allergy, or gorging, or a dozen causes other than a rain of red-hot acids. If distress persists, see a doctor; it is unwise to take antacids continuously over long periods to subdue symptoms while some possibly serious underlying condition gets a foothold.

Acne rosacea. A chronic disease, entirely unrelated to common acne, resulting from dilation of superficial blood vessels, giving an appearance of constant redness of the flush area of the middle part of the face (174).

Acne vulgaris. Common acne; a skin disorder, most conspicuously affecting the face, with pimples and blackheads as the most obvious lesions. Acne has nothing to do with "bad blood" or bad conduct; it is due to overactivity of oil-secreting glands and hair follicles. It is associated with the increase of sex hormones at puberty, and is in large degree a physiologic condition that most young people pass through on their way to sexual maturity. Acne usually subsides in the twenties, but in the meantime various treatments are beneficial (172). Severe cases particularly should have good medical care to avert possible scarring and pitting.

Acromegaly. A disorder of adults due to overproduction of growth hormones by the pituitary gland (305). The word means "giant extremities." There is gross enlargement of the bones and soft parts of the face and hands and feet. The face with its thickened tissues, enlarged jaw, nose, and bony ridges over the eyes, has a characteristic coarse appearance. Height is not increased. However, if the same hormone overproduction occurs in a young person before the growing ends of the bones have closed, he becomes a "pituitary giant" up to eight feet tall.

ACTH. Abbreviation of *adrenocorticotrophic hormone;* a hormone of the pituitary gland which stimulates the adrenal gland to produce cortisone-like hormones (305).

Actinomycosis (*lumpy jaw*). An infectious disease caused by fungi which produce lumpy, pus-draining abscesses, especially of the face and jaw (71).

Acupuncture. An ancient form of Chinese folk medicine, in which needles are stuck into parts of the body like golf course flags in hope of relieving pain or disease.

Adams-Stokes syndrome. Giddiness, fainting, sometimes convulsions, resulting from slowed heart action caused by heart block (106).

Addison's disease. A chronic disease characterized by weakness, easy fatigability, skin pigmentation, low blood pressure and other symptoms (319). The underlying cause is atrophy or disease of the outer layer of the adrenal gland, greatly reducing its output of hormones.

Adduction. The moving of a part toward another or toward the axis of the body: for example, moving the thumb toward the index finger. The opposite of ABDUCTION.

Adenoviruses. A group of viruses responsible for respiratory infections like the common cold (54), viral conjunctivitis, intestinal infections, and latent infections which may cause some swelling of tonsils, adenoids, and other glandular tissue, especially in children. There are more than 30 different types of adenoviruses. The or-

ganisms are widespread and sometimes give rise to epidemics of considerable extent. Most people have been infected by them. Except in small infants, adenovirus infections are rarely serious. They generally run their course in a week or less. Vaccines have been developed but their use is largely limited to military establishments where conditions are favorable for epidemics among young men in barracks.

Adhesions. Abnormal sticking together of tissues which should slip or slide freely over each other. Diseases may produce adhesions: in the chest cavity as a result of pleurisy, in injured joints restricted in movement, in other areas of inflammation. Adhesions in the abdominal and pelvic cavities may occur after surgical operations, particularly if pus has spilled from a ruptured abscess. It is not always or often desirable to do further surgery to free the adhesions unless they threaten to obstruct the bowel or interfere with other organs.

Adhesive tape removal. Ripping adhesive tape from the skin can be less ouchful if the patient is removed from the tape instead of the tape from the

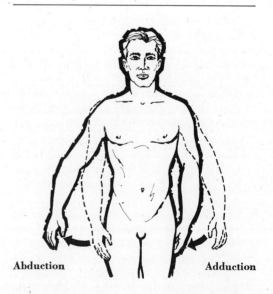

Abduction   **Adduction**

patient. Try it this way: Pick up a corner of the tape, lift it gently, and with fingers of the other hand press the skin that is just beneath the tape slowly away from it. In this way only a small area of skin is peeled down from the tape at a time, in contrast to the entire area which is pulled and lifted if the tape is rudely ripped.

Adipose tissue. Fatty connective tissue; commonly, the part of the body where fat is stored. Usually, "adiposity" is a polite way of saying "too fat."

Adiposis dolorosa. See DERCUM'S DISEASE.

Adolescence. The period of years between the beginning of puberty, when the reproductive organs become functionally active, and maturity.

Adolescent bent hip. A condition of older children resulting from disconnection of the upper end of the thighbone from its normal hip joint attachments, producing a wobbly, painful hip and limping (615).

Adrenalin. Proprietary name for *epinephrine*, the hormone produced by the inner portion or medulla of the adrenal gland (318).

Aerobic. Living or functioning in air or free oxygen.

Aero-otitis media. Inflammation of the middle ear caused by differences in air pressure within the chamber and outside of it. Also called "flyer's ear," since rapid changes of air pressure with changes in altitude tend to produce it. Normally, air pressure is equalized on both sides of the eardrum by the entrance or escape of air through the Eustachian tube which runs from the middle ear to the throat (571). This pressure-valve adjustment is what makes the ears "pop" during rapid ascent or descent of an elevator in a high building. Swallowing usually helps to "massage" a little air into or out of the tube. Infections or obstructions may block the free passage of air through the tube.

African sleeping sickness. A disease with a high fatality rate caused by organisms that get into the blood through the bites of tsetse flies indigenous to parts of Africa (71). It is not the same as sleepiness associated with some forms of encephalitis.

Afterbirth. The placenta and membranes discharged from the uterus a few minutes after the birth of a baby.

After-image. A visual image which remains for a few seconds after the eyes are closed or light has ceased to stimulate. An after-image can be produced by looking at a bright light or bright objects for a few seconds, then closing the eyes, or turning them on a dark surface, or fixing your gaze on a bright sheet of white paper. An image of the object will slowly float into view, become more distinct, and gradually fade away. After-images are either "positive" or "negative." A positive after-image shows the object in its correct shade of black or white or color. A negative after-image reverses dark and light parts and, if the object was colored, shows the complementary instead of the original color; for instance, a red object produces a green after-image.

Agammaglobulinemia. Blood deficiency of GAMMA GLOBULIN, protein molecules which produce protective antibodies against infections. The deficiency leaves the patient extremely susceptible to repeated infections. The condition may be congenital or acquired. The congenital form has an hereditary basis; it is a complex defect of IMMUNITY mechanisms of the body, manifested as undue susceptibility to repeated infections in infancy. It is important to avoid exposure of an affected infant to infections, as far as possible; to treat acute infections with antibiotics; to give monthly injections of gamma globulin.

Agranulocytosis. An acute, rare, frequently fatal illness associated with extreme reduction or complete absence of granular white blood cells (134) from the bone marrow. Absence of cells which protect against infection results in weakness, rapid onset of high fever, sore throat, prostration, ulcerations of the mouth and mucous membranes. The disease may arise from unknown causes, but usually it can be traced to some chemical or drug which injures the bone marrow; the agent may be a widely used valuable substance which is harmless to most people but to which the patient is peculiarly sensitive (166). Treatment aims to combat infection while the bone marrow becomes normal.

Air embolism. Plugging of blood vessels by air bubbles carried in the bloodstream, fatal if large numbers of bubbles reach the heart. Air can enter the bloodstream by accidental injection or through wounds of the neck. Air embolism is also a hazard of SCUBA DIVING; holding the breath while ascending from even relatively shallow depths may cause rupture of a part of the lung, forcing air bubbles into pulmonary veins and thence to brain arteries.

Air-swallowing (*aerophagia*). The habit, usually unconscious, of swallowing excessive amounts of air. The gas may escape via an embarrassing belch, or lead to FLATULENCE, or may from entrapment cause diversified distentions and twinges of the gut. A small amount of air is naturally swallowed with food or drink or conversation, but excessive intake may be promoted by gulping, chewing with the lips parted, swigging fluids from a narrow-necked bottle, talking while eating, chewing gum, smoking, and nervous swallowing. More often than not the air-swallower hasn't the slightest idea that he is indulging in pneumatic excesses, and he is usually able to overcome the habit if it is called to his surprised attention unless there is some neurotic basis for it.

Air travel. The Aerospace Medical Association and the American Medical Association agree that flying is not harmful to most ill patients and is the most desirable form of travel for those who have certain types of illnesses. This presupposes the availability of oxygen or medication that a particular patient may require, and evaluation by a doctor of some conditions such as severe anemia or recent eye surgery which may increase the hazard. Infants over six days old travel well by air. A very general rule is that "if a person is able to walk 100 yards and to climb 12 steps without manifesting symptoms, flight in pressurized aircraft is permissible."

Alastrim. A mild form of smallpox. See VARIOLA MINOR.

Albuminuria. Presence in the urine of albumin, a protein like egg white (281). The kidneys do not normally excrete albumin, which is a useful substance, and albuminuria suggests damage to the filtering apparatus, but this is not necessarily the case.

Aldosteronism (primary). A remediable form of high blood pressure (110); weakness, headaches, and other symptoms (320), due to excessive production of aldosterone, a hormone produced by the cortex of the adrenal gland. The hormone is a powerful regulator of salt and water balances. Excesses cause retention of sodium and loss of potassium. If the excess is caused by an adrenal gland tumor, its removal is indicated. All the manifestations of primary aldosteronism can be reversed in a few weeks by oral doses of an antagonistic drug, spironolactone.

Alkaline ash diet. A diet consisting mainly of fruits, vegetables and potatoes, with only small amounts of meat and cereals, sometimes prescribed for patients who have kidney disease or kidney stones of the uric acid type. Alkaline environment deters acid stone formation.

Alkalosis. Increased alkalinity of the blood. See ACID-BASE BALANCE.

Alkaptonuria. A rare hereditary disorder in which the body is unable to produce enzymes for proper utilization of certain AMINO ACIDS of protein foods. Byproducts of incomplete metabolism cause the urine to turn dark brown or black on long standing. The disorder does not affect life expectancy but in later life leads to discoloration of cartilage and possibly to a severe form of arthritis.

Allergy. An altered capacity to react distressfully to specific substances which cause no symptoms in most people (645); a general term for all kinds of hypersensitivities. "Atopy" is a general synonym for allergy.

Allopurinol. A drug which reduces the body's production of uric acid, used in treatment of GOUT.

Alopecia. Baldness; loss of head hair. Some types of hair loss are temporary, some are irreversible (186). Neither hair "tonics" nor any other medical measure known to dermatologists (not a few of whom have nude scalps) can overcome male pattern baldness. This type of baldness affects men who have a genetic predisposition, who produce adequate amounts of male hormone, and who have attained sufficient age (they do not become bald before puberty). New surgical techniques for transplanting hairs from an area of lush growth to the bare scalp have had some success but are not widely popular. The technique consists of punching plugs of skin containing four or five hairs out of the back of the neck and inserting them into the scalp in hope that they will take root and spread like plugs of zoysia grass. In time, after transplants of scores of tufts (about $5 per tuft), the plugs may grow into presentable confluence.

Altitude sickness. See MOUNTAIN SICKNESS.

Alveolus. A sac or chamber; a saclike dilation at the end of a passage; especially, an air cell of the lung (202), the bony socket of a tooth, or a honeycomb cell of the stomach.

Amaurotic familial idiocy (*Tay-Sachs disease*). An hereditary disease occurring in Jewish children, manifested early in infancy, characterized by muscle weakness, progressive helplessness, and blindness ("amaurosis" means blindness). A characteristic bright cherry spot can be seen at the back of the infant's eye with an ophthalmoscope. No known treatment can reverse the condition and life expectancy is short. Certain related diseases which occur later in life do not have a racial incidence.

Amblyopia. Dimness of vision without any organic lesion of the eye. Amblyopia may result from various toxins, or an eye, such as the "lazy" eye of a cross-eyed child, may lose its vision from long disuse (542).

Amebiasis. Amebic dysentery (69).

Amenorrhea. Absence of menstruation (326).

Amino acids. Building blocks of PROTEIN. There are about 20 important amino acids. An amino acid molecule has an acid group of atoms at one end and an amino (nitrogen-containing) group at the other. In between are carbon units with different side chains which give each amino acid its individuality. The acid end of an amino acid links with the amino end of another, a sort of chemical hook-and-eye arrangement. In this way amino acids form short chains (peptides) or large, complex molecules containing many hundreds of different amino acids in exact sequences (protein). Eight amino acids are called "essential" because the body cannot synthesize them and they must be obtained ready-made from protein foods (471, 479). The amino acids of protein foods are separated by digestion and go into a general pool from which the body takes the ones it needs to synthesize its own personal proteins; thus an amino acid which we may have obtained from a pork chop may become a part of a fingernail, skin, hair, of a hormone such as insulin, or of an enzyme that activates some vital chemical process of the body.

Amnion. The innermost of the fetal membranes, forming the BAG OF WATERS which surrounds and protects the embryo (357).

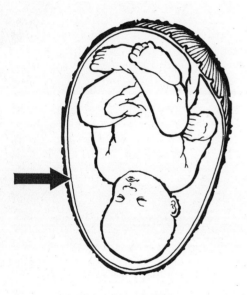

Arrow points to amnion

Amyotonia. Lack of muscle tone; a congenital form in infants is characterized by small undeveloped muscles and weakness of the limbs and trunk.

Amyotrophic lateral sclerosis. Progressive paralysis and wasting of muscles on both sides of the body; sometimes called "Lou Gehrig's disease" (252).

Anabolic steroids. Drugs related to male hormones, sometimes given for anabolic ("upbuilding") action, to stimulate growth, weight gain, strength and appetite. The drugs are more accurately called androgenic-anabolic steroids, since they are related to testosterone and retain some of the male hormone's masculinizing action. Although the maculinizing action has been minimized in some anabolic steroids, the separation is not complete and prolonged use will cause virilization. Testosterone itself has pronounced anabolic action but is not suitable for prolonged use in women and children.

Anabolism. The "building up" aspect of metabolism; constructive processes of body cells which build complex substances from simpler ones. The opposite of CATABOLISM.

Anaerobic. Living or functioning in the absence of free air or free oxygen. TETANUS and GAS GANGRENE organisms are anaerobic.

Such organisms thrive best if deprived of oxygen, as in deep puncture wounds, or cannot survive at all if oxygen is present.

Anaphylaxis. An acute reaction to a substance injected by a doctor or insect or inhaled or swallowed; a "super allergy." Anaphylaxis is an ANTIGEN-ANTIBODY reaction which occurs in seconds or minutes after a foreign substance has entered the body. The immediate, severe, and sometimes fatal reaction is manifested by hives, rhinitis, wheezing, shock, ANGIONEUROTIC EDEMA, difficult breathing, in varying combinations and degrees of severity. The most frequent causes of anaphylactic reactions are serums, drugs, and vaccines; next most common are insect stings (670). Skin tests may detect hypersensitivity to a substance but sometimes even the minute amount used in a test may provoke a reaction. If a doctor asks you to wait in his office 15 minutes or so after giving an injection, it's not a waste of time; he has emergency measures at hand if a dangerous reaction occurs. Because accident victims are often given routine injections of tetanus antitoxin or penicillin, persons who know they are sensitive to these substances should carry a warning card along with driver's license and identification papers where a doctor who is a stranger is sure to see it.

Anasarca. Generalized EDEMA.

Androgen. A substance which has masculinizing effects (323).

Android. Resembling a man; male-like.

Anesthesia. Loss of feeling. This can occur from natural processes or accidents; for example, nerve injury, frostbite, hysteria, blood vessel spasms, diseases. Ordinarily the word refers to obliteration of pain by anesthetic drugs, with or without loss of consciousness. There are many kinds of anesthetic drugs and gases, administered by inhalation, infusion or injection (746). Each anesthetic has specific properties, advantages and disadvantages; selection of the best agent or combination for a particular patient requires special knowledge. The safety and relative comfort of modern surgery, and the ability to perform complex prolonged operations without haste, depends no little upon the anesthesia team headed by an anesthesiologist who regulates the depth of anesthesia, chooses the most suitable anesthetics in consultation with surgeons, and keeps close watch on the patient's condition with the aid of a battery of monitoring devices.

Aneurysm. A blood-filled sac like a thin-walled balloon formed by dilation of artery walls; it is susceptible to rupture and hemorrhage (119, 125).

Angiitis. Inflammation of a blood or lymph vessel.

Angina. Any condition characterized by spasmodic attacks with sensations of strangling, pressure or suffocation; for example, *angina pectoris* (87).

Angiogram. X-ray visualization of blood vessels, usually accomplished by injecting a substance which is opaque to x-rays into the bloodstream. X-ray movies or large films taken in rapid succession may give important information about the condition of blood vessels in some types of heart trouble (755).

Angioma. A tumor composed of blood vessels.

Angioneurotic edema. Acute local swelling, like giant hives under the skin, frequently a result of food allergy (667). The swelling is most serious if it occurs around the tongue and larynx, threatening suffocation.

Anhidrosis. Abnormal deficiency of sweat.

Aniseikonia. A condition in which the image of an object as seen by one eye differs in size and shape from that seen by the other eye. The brain compensates for images of unequal size by suppressing one of them, and in time the eye which produces the suppressed image tends to become, for all practical purposes, blind. This type of blindness is called AMBLYOPIA; the affected person is essentially "one-eyed," and if the "good" eye is lost, the other is useless as a "spare tire." A complete eye examination of a child at about the age of three years can do much to prevent this insidious kind of damage.

Ankylosis. Stiffening or growing together of a joint; the fusion may be part of a disease process (640) or it may be a deliberate surgical immobilization of a part.

Antacid. A substance that counteracts or neutralizes acidity. Most commonly, an oral substance taken to reduce acidity of gastric juices.

Anthrax (*wool-sorter's disease*). A bacterial disease of herbivorous animals. Spores of the causative organisms sometimes infect persons who have close contact with raw wool, bristles, or hides (47).

Anomaly. Deviation from normal of an organ or part; abnormality of structure or location.

Anorexia. Loss of appetite. *Anorectic drugs,* sometimes prescribed for a short time for persons on reducing diets, tend to suppress appetite before a meal.

Anorexia nervosa. An emotional disturbance manifested by profound aversion to food, leading to extreme emaciation. The typical patient is a young single woman who rejects food in unconscious protection against an adult sex role she has difficulty in adjusting to. Usually she is not particularly concerned about her extreme skinniness and may even insist that she eats a lot. Management of the condition requires explanation, encouragement of eating, possibly hospitalization and psychiatric help.

Anoscope. An instrument for examining the lower part of the rectum; a SPECULUM.

Anoxemia. Deficiency of oxygen in the blood.

Anoxia. Oxygen deficiency in organs and tissues and disturbance resulting therefrom.

Antibiotics. Chemical substances produced by certain living cells, such as bacteria, yeasts, and molds, that are antagonistic or damaging to certain other living cells, such as disease-producing bacteria. Different antibiotics may kill disease germs or prevent them from growing and multiplying.

Antibody. A protein in the blood, modified by contact with a foreign substance (*antigen*) so that it exerts an antagonizing or neutralizing action against that specific substance. Antibodies are chiefly associated with GAMMA GLOBULIN in the blood and are key elements of IMMUNITY mechanisms of the body. Usually the antibody-antigen reaction is protective.

Measles virus is an antigen which stimulates the body to produce measles antibodies, so we don't have measles twice. But antibody-antigen reactions may also be distressing or harmful, as in allergies (645). So-called AUTO-IMMUNE DISEASES presumably result, at least in part, from harmful reactions of antibodies against normal proteins of the patient's own body.

Anticoagulants. Drugs which slow up the clotting process of the blood. Clots forming in blood vessels are potentially deadly (see THROMBOSIS, EMBOLISM). Anticoagulants are useful in reducing the clotting tendency. The doctor's problem is knowing when and when not to use them; administration requires frequent checks of the patient's blood since overdosage can induce hemorrhage. Anticoagulants are commonly given to patients for a few weeks after a heart attack caused by a blood clot in coronary arteries. Specialists generally agree that such short term use of anticoagulants is valuable. There is difference of medical opinion as to whether the drugs should be continued for preventive purposes for many months or years or the remainder of a lifetime. Some studies extending over a 10-year period indicate that the drugs are of little value in preventing subsequent heart attacks, but there is also evidence that selected patients having recurrent clot-formation problems or recurrent heart attacks or mild strokes benefit from the continued use of anticoagulants.

Anticonvulsants. Drugs which are used primarily to reduce the number and severity of chronic epileptic seizures. The physician's choice of drugs depends upon the type of seizure (264). Treatment must be individualized. Since the drugs must be used for a prolonged period of time, it is important that the patient be told of possible adverse effects and be instructed to report unusual symptoms promptly.

Antidiuretic hormone. A hormone produced in brain areas linked with the pituitary gland; it checks the secretion of urine (309).

Antiemetic. A drug or treatment which stops or prevents nausea or vomiting.

Antigen. Any substance which stimulates the production of ANTIBODIES.

Antihistamines. A large family of drugs which block some of the effects of histamine, a normal substance in body cells which plays a part in allergic reactions. Histamine, triggered by an antigen such as ragweed pollen, may escape from local groups of cells and cause symptoms of hay fever. Deliberate injection of histamine causes the walls of capillaries to become so permeable that fluids leak into nearby tissues. This leakage is characteristic of allergies. The effect may be superficial, as in weepy eyes or runny nose, or giant hives, or more deep-set as in dangerous swelling of the breathing passages.

Antihistamine drugs are most effective in treatment of acute urticaria and seasonal hay fever and generally give good results in subduing allergic tissue swellings (angioneurotic edema). They may often give symptomatic relief of allergic skin disorders and of itching not of allergic origin. The most widely prescribed preventives for motion sickness belong to the antihistamine family; they are effective against symptoms of dizziness, nausea and vomiting and have some sedative action. Although many attacks of bronchial asthma are allergic in origin, antihistamines have only limited value in prevention and treatment.

The drugs differ one from another in potency, effects, and duration of action; this is weighed by the physician in prescribing a specific drug. Some antihistamines have a pronounced tendency to cause drowsiness; others have very little sedative action. A person taking an antihistamine with somnolent action should reckon with its effects in driving a car. Some non-prescription sleeping pills and insomnia remedies contain small amounts of an antihistamine compound. These may cause some drowsiness but the effect is not uniform, most persons will acquire tolerance to the drug, and antihistamines cannot be considered reliable remedies against insomnia. Because of the depressant action of antihistamines, patients should not drink alcoholic beverages or take barbiturates during antihistaminic therapy.

Anti-Rh serum. Prevention of ERYTHROBLASTOSIS ("Rh disease") is a possibility for the near future. Pregnant women lacking a substance in their red blood cells (Rh factor) may develop ANTIBODIES against their own babies whose blood does possess the factor. These antibodies can cause severe anemia and damage to the unborn child. The risk increases with each pregnancy after the first, which usually is normal because the mother has not yet become sensitized. A preventive measure now being studied intensively in this country and abroad is treatment of the Rh-negative mother with a specially prepared anti-Rh serum after the birth of each Rh-positive baby, to destroy quickly any Rh-positive blood cells of the baby which might have entered into her circulation, thus greatly reducing the chance of her sensitization. Trials of anti-Rh serum in a number of medical centers have been encouraging. Wide use of the serum may in the future eliminate an important cause of stillbirth and serious birth defects.

Antitoxin. A substance which neutralizes a specific bacterial, animal or plant toxin. Most of the antitoxins injected by doctors for treatment or prevention of disease are prepared from serum obtained from a horse or other animal which has been immunized by gradually increased doses of a particular toxin. Harmful reactions may follow injection if a patient is sensitive to the serum component.

Antrum. See MAXILLARY SINUS.

Antivenin. An antitoxin to venom, especially snake venom (379, 809).

Anuria. Total suppression of urine secretion.

Aorta. The great vessel which arches from the top of the heart and passes down through the chest and abdomen (78). It is the main trunk line of the arterial system.

Aphakia. Absence of the lens of the eye, as after cataract surgery (552).

Aplastic anemia. A grave form of anemia due to progressive failure of the bone marrow to develop new blood cells; it may be triggered by chemicals which poison the cell-producing mechanisms of the marrow (166).

Apnea. Temporary cessation of breathing because of absence of stimulation of the breathing center, as by too much oxygen or too little carbon dioxide.

Appendicitis. Acute inflammation of the appendix (467, 701). It occurs in all age groups but is most common in children and young persons. Typically, pain is felt in the region of the navel before it moves down to the appendix area in the lower right quarter of the abdomen, but not all cases are typical. The early pain may be mistaken for colic. If a child's severe "stomach ache" persists more than an hour or two, a doctor should be called to diagnose the trouble, which more often than not isn't appendicitis, but if it is, prompt action is important because an inflamed appendix can reach the bursting point in a few hours.

Appetite depressants (*anorexiants*). These are drugs which tend to allay sensations of hunger and to make the early phases of adjusting to a reducing diet somewhat easier. Appetite depressants prescribed by physicians are quite potent and should not be confused with milder and sometimes du-

ARTERIES →

1. carotid sinus
2. vertebral
3. thyrocervical
4. axillary
5. internal mammary
6. brachial
7. pancreaticoduodenal
8. superior mesenteric
9. radial
10. interosseous
11. ulnar
12. volar
13. digital
14. deep femoral
15. femoral
16. plantar
17. digital
18. external carotid
19. internal carotid
20. common carotid
21. subclavian
22. pulmonary arteries
23. aorta
24. celiac
25. splenic
26. gastric
27. common iliac
28. external iliac
29. anterior tibial
30. peroneal
31. posterior tibial

biously effective products that can be bought without a prescription. Medically prescribed appetite depressants are drugs of the amphetamine family or other "sympathomimetic" amines which cause physiologic changes similar to those produced by the sympathetic nervous system (237). It has been suggested that the drugs act upon an "appetite control" center in the brain stem, although this has not been proved. Some of their effects may be due to mood elevation. The drugs should be used only for a short time as adjuncts to a low-calorie diet for overcoming obesity, as temporary "crutches." Permanent weight control requires re-education of eating habits.

Aqueous humor. Watery fluid which fills the chamber of the eye in front of the lens (529). Obstruction of drainage leads to glaucoma (549).

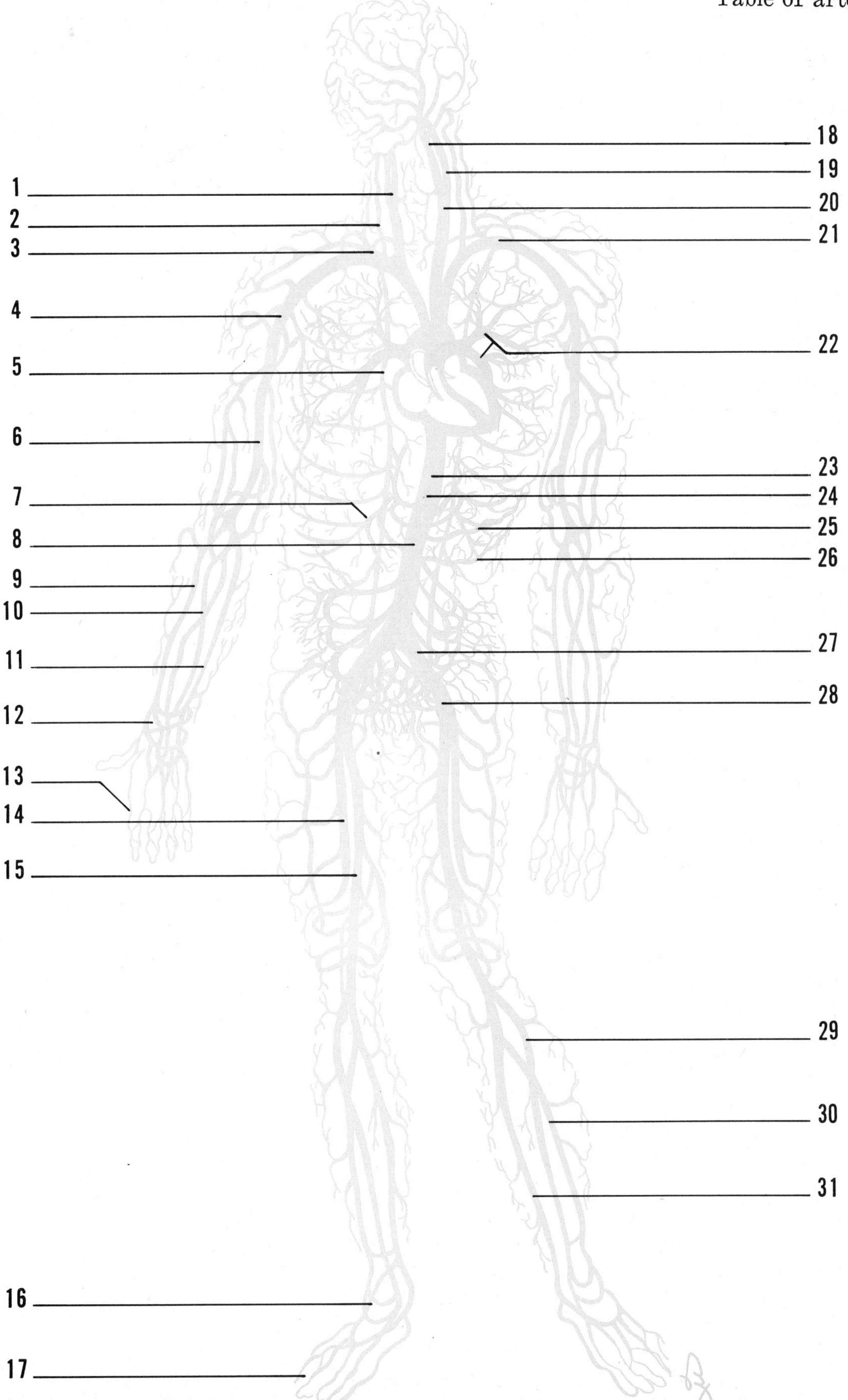

1 _____

2 _____

3 _____

4 _____

5 _____

6 _____

7 _____

8 _____

9 _____

10 _____

11 _____

12 _____

13 _____

14 _____

15 _____

16 _____

17 _____

18 _____

19 _____

20 _____

21 _____

22 _____

23 _____

24 _____

25 _____

26 _____

27 _____

28 _____

29 _____

30 _____

31 _____

Arcus senilis. A white ring around the outer edge of the colored portion of the eye, especially in the aged.

Areola. A pigmented ring surrounding a central point; for example, the pigmented area encircling the nipple.

Argyll-Robertson pupil. Excessively contracted pupils of the eye which do not react to light; a symptom of syphilis (48) of the central nervous system.

Ariboflavinosis. Deficiency of riboflavin, also called vitamin B₂, characterized by dryness of the skin, inflamed tongue, tiny blood vessels in the cornea giving a reddened appearance to the eye, and fissures at the angles of the lips (480).

Arrhythmia. Any departure from normal rhythm of the heartbeat (103).

Arteriosclerosis. A thickening and hardening of the walls of arteries and capillaries, leading to a loss of their elasticity. It is not the same condition as ATHEROSCLEROSIS.

Artificial heart. As body structures go, the heart is relatively simple—a four-chambered pumping device. It may some day be replaceable by an artificial heart. But the obstacles are formidable. Thus far, so-called "artificial hearts" used in a few human patients have been "heart assist" devices using compressed air power to augment the pumping force of the patient's own heart. In principle, the devices consist of a rigid outer shell containing elastic chambers which expand and contract rhythmically in response to pulses of compressed air entering through a tube in the chest. Their hopeful role is that of temporary auxiliaries to help hearts with enough reserves to recover if tided over a crisis. But more than a dozen varieties of artificial hearts have been developed, and many more experimental models will undoubtedly come out of current research. Some of the devices do not aim to assist the patient's own heart,

HEART-ASSIST PUMP →

Drawing shows principle of device developed by Dr. M. E. DeBakey and associates of Baylor University. Called "paracorporeal" (the pump itself is outside the body), its purpose as shown in the drawing is to by-pass and thus "rest" a diseased left ventricle by performing the ventricle's function of pumping arterial blood to the body. Numbered structures are: 1, axillary artery; 2, left atrium; 3, pump; 4 and 5, pump filling and pumping; 6, right atrium; 7, right ventricle; 8, pulmonary artery; 9, left atrium; 10, left ventricle; 11, aorta; 12 and 13, tubes to and from pump; 14; axillary artery.

but to replace it entirely. In fact, some artificial hearts have totally replaced the hearts of calves and pigs. The animals seem to function just as comfortably as if they had a heart of their own. But after a few hours, two or three days at most, the animals die. Scientists don't know why. Artificial hearts appear to cause mysterious physiologic changes which, if they exist, will have to be overcome if a mechanical organ is to serve for many months or years. The ideal artificial heart will have to be light in weight; its vibrations must not be harmful; it must be totally innocuous to surrounding tissues; its power source must be miniaturized and unfailing; and it must not induce blood clotting. The requirements are formidable but not insurmountable, in the opinion of eminent researchers who are tackling the problem whole-heartedly.

Artificial insemination. Mechanical introduction of semen into the vagina or uterus to induce pregnancy. If successful, conception, pregnancy, and childbirth occur in a perfectly normal way. The first recorded attempt at human artificial insemination was performed by the famous English surgeon, John Hunter, in 1799. Artificial insemination is widely employed in animal husbandry, but its availability to couples troubled by *infertility* (328) has largely come about in the

Drawing A shows pump in place. Arrows show path of blood, purified in the lungs, from the left atrium (2) to pump (3), and from pump to connection with arterial system via axillary artery (1). Tube from base of pump leads to compressed air power source.

A

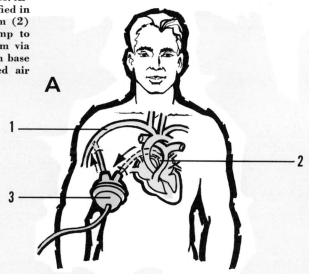

1

2

Drawing B. Air suction fills pump (4) with blood (diastole); air pressure (5) pumps blood to arteries (systole). Valves control flow direction.

3

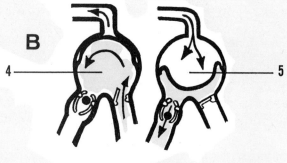

B

4

5

Drawing C, schematic diagram of normal circulation. Drawing D at right shows details: tube (12) connected to left atrium receives oxygenated blood from the lungs which fills pump; tube (13) delivers arterial blood to body, via axillary artery connection (14), when pump compresses by-passing the left side of the heart.

13

14

12

11

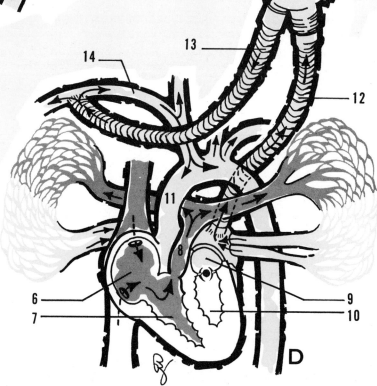

C

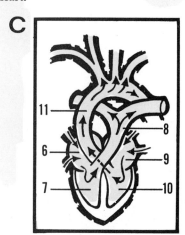

11

6

7

8

9

10

6

7

8

9

10

D

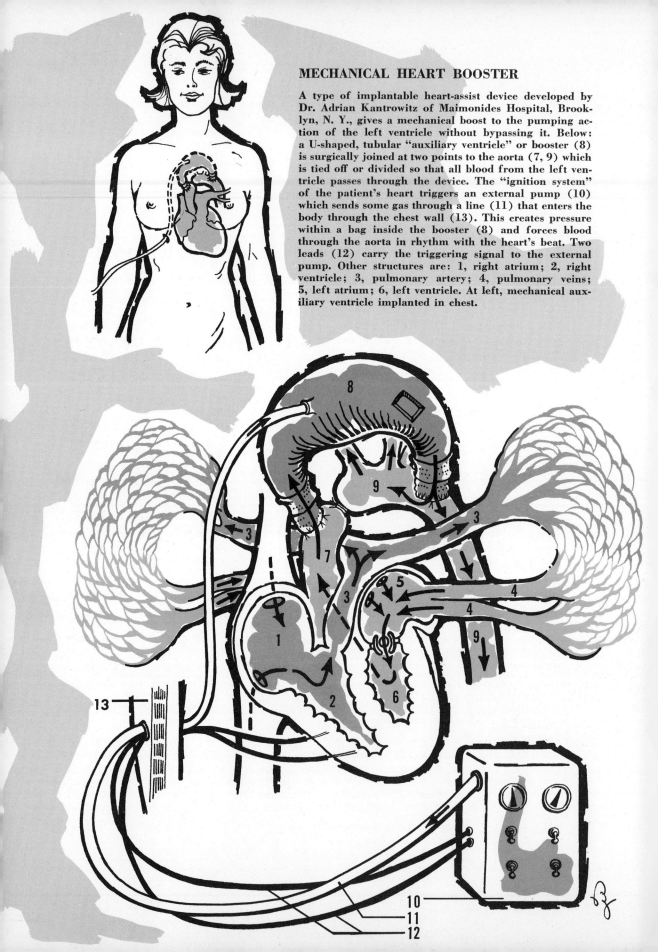

MECHANICAL HEART BOOSTER

A type of implantable heart-assist device developed by Dr. Adrian Kantrowitz of Maimonides Hospital, Brooklyn, N. Y., gives a mechanical boost to the pumping action of the left ventricle without bypassing it. Below: a U-shaped, tubular "auxiliary ventricle" or booster (8) is surgically joined at two points to the aorta (7, 9) which is tied off or divided so that all blood from the left ventricle passes through the device. The "ignition system" of the patient's heart triggers an external pump (10) which sends some gas through a line (11) that enters the body through the chest wall (13). This creates pressure within a bag inside the booster (8) and forces blood through the aorta in rhythm with the heart's beat. Two leads (12) carry the triggering signal to the external pump. Other structures are: 1, right atrium; 2, right ventricle; 3, pulmonary artery; 4, pulmonary veins; 5, left atrium; 6, left ventricle. At left, mechanical auxiliary ventricle implanted in chest.

past quarter century. Technically, there are two forms of artificial insemination: AIH, in which semen is furnished by the husband, and AID, in which semen is furnished by a donor. Because the husband's infertility is usually the dominant factor, AID is by far the most frequently used method. There are no exact figures on the number of children (popularly called "test tube babies") conceived by artificial insemination, but the number runs into the thousands and some of these children have become parents themselves.

Artificial kidney. A device, of which there are several types, which diffuses a patient's blood through a membrane outside of the body, to extract wastes and return cleared blood to the circulation (284).

Artificial pneumothorax. Surgical collapse of a lung for therapeutic purposes (211).

Asbestosis. Slowly progressing inflammation of the lungs resulting from inhalation of fine asbestos fibers (226). It occurs in miners and workers in construction trades exposed to asbestos-containing materials. The lungs cannot get rid of asbestos dusts and normal tissue is replaced by fibrous tissue; the incidence of cancer in persons with asbestosis is high.

Ascariasis. Infestation with species of roundworms which inhabit the small bowel (68).

Ascheim-Zondek test. The "mouse test" to confirm early pregnancy (341). Sex hormones in the urine of a pregnant woman cause telltale blood spots to appear in the ovaries of test animals.

Ascites. Painless accumulation of yellowish fluid in the abdominal cavity, indicative of impaired circulation often related to heart failure, cirrhosis of the liver, malignancy, or kidney disease.

Aspiration. Removal of fluids or gases from a body cavity by means of suction. Also, inhalation of foreign material.

Aspiration pneumonia. A form of pneumonia caused by foreign matter in the lungs. The foreign substance may be inhaled, it may trickle into the windpipe, or it may be forced into the windpipe by gagging, choking spasms, or difficulties of swallowing. Lipoid or "oil" pneumonia is the most common form in infants and elderly persons (227). It can result from oily nose sprays, animal oils, and mineral oils which accumulate in the lungs and remain there. It is best to avoid putting oils into an infant's nose, and to give oily substances such as cod liver oil when the child is in an upright position and can swallow properly.

Asthma. A condition of paroxysmal, difficult, labored, wheezy breathing. See BRONCHIAL ASTHMA and CARDIAC ASTHMA.

Astigmatism. Distortion of vision resulting from imperfect curvature of the cornea or lens of the eye (538). The defect may be so slight that nothing need be done about it, or severe enough to cause eye strain. A rotating chart with parallel vertical and horizontal lines is used in eye tests for astigmatism. The condition is corrected by using a lens that bends the rays of light in only one direction (axis).

Astragalus. The ankle bone.

Ataractics. "Peace of mind" drugs; see TRANQUILIZERS.

Ataxia. Loss of muscle coordination; groups of muscles cannot be brought into concerted action. *Locomotor ataxia,* also called *tabes dorsalis,* usually is a late consequence of syphilis. Degeneration of parts of the spinal cord causes excruciating "lightning pains," staggering gait, disturbances of the eyes, bladder, and other organs.

Atelectasis. A retracted or collapsed state of the lung which leaves all or part of the organ airless. The condition may arise from obstruction of bronchial tubes; gases in the affected part of the lung are gradually absorbed and the area collapses. *Fetal atelectasis* is a condition in which the lungs of an infant do not expand adequately immediately after birth as they normally should (199).

Atherosclerosis. Degeneration of blood vessels caused by a deposit of fatty materials along the lining of the wall of a blood vessel. CHOLESTEROL is one of these fatty materials. Many other factors play a part (82).

Athetosis. A condition usually occurring in children as the result of a brain lesion, characterized by constant slow movements of fingers, toes, or other body parts.

Atopy. A synonym for allergy (646).

Atresia. Closure or failure of development of a normal opening or channel in the body.

Atrial. Pertaining to the atria or auricles, the blood "receiving chambers" of the heart (74).

Atrophy. Wasting away or shrinking in size of a previously normal organ, tissue or part.

Atypical pneumonia. See PNEUMONIA.

Audiometer. An electrical instrument which emits pure tones that can be made louder or fainter (566). It is used in measuring acuity of hearing for sounds of different frequencies.

Aura. A peculiar premonitory sensation preceding an epileptic seizure (261), recognized by the patient.

Auscultation. Determination of the condition of organs, particularly the heart and lungs, by study of sounds arising from them.

Autoclave. An apparatus for sterilizing instruments by steam under pressure.

Autograft. A piece of tissue taken from one part of a patient's body and transplanted to another part, as in skin grafts to cover raw areas, burns, etc. Autografts "take" because they are not foreign tissues which would ultimately cause the body to cast them off.

Auto-immune diseases. Several diseases of unknown cause may reflect a strange inability of the body to "recognize" itself, so that mechanisms which normally create immunity to foreign invaders somehow establish a specific sensitivity to certain of the body's own tissues, like a "self allergy," with harmful consequences. The concept is complex, relatively new, and mechanisms are not fully understood but are the subject of much current research. Diseases now thought to be caused by auto-immune reactions include *acquired hemolytic anemia* (149) and *thrombocytopenic purpura* (151). Diseases apparently associated with auto-immune responses include *rheumatoid arthritis* (634), *glomerulonephritis* (281), *rheumatic fever* (99), *thyrotoxicosis* (310), *scleroderma* (641), *ulcerative colitis* (468). *Multiple sclerosis* (252) and several other diseases for which no causative agents have been found resemble auto-immune diseases in laboratory studies.

Auto-intoxication. Poisoning by toxins generated within the body; for example, uremic poisoning. To most laymen the word means a vague condition attributed to intestinal toxins resulting from constipation, although no such toxins have been satisfactorily identified and it is probable that distressing symptoms are produced by mechanical pressures.

Avascular. Without blood or lymphatic vessels; the nails, the cornea, and some types of cartilage are normally avascular.

Avulsion. The forcible tearing away of a part.

Axilla. The armpit.

Axon. A single long fine fiber which conducts impulses away from the body of a nerve cell (232). Most axons are covered with a sheath of whitish material called *myelin;* abnormalities of this covering occur in demyelinating diseases such as multiple sclerosis (251).

Azoospermia. Absence of sperm in the semen.

B

Babinski sign. Upward movement of the big toe and downward movement of other toes when the sole of the foot is stroked; an indication of nervous system disorder (240).

Bacillary dysentery (*Shigellosis*). Acute diarrhea, acquired by person-to-person contact, through eating contaminated food or handling contaminated objects, or through spread of contamination by flies (45). The causative germs are present in the excretions of infected persons. Infection is caused by rod-shaped bacteria called Shigella, of which there are several types of variable virulence. Good sanitary and hygienic practices prevent infections. In infants and small children, bacillary dysentery can cause serious loss of fluids and ELECTROLYTES in a short time; onset of severe diarrhea is cause for calling a doctor promptly.

Bacteremia. The presence of living bacteria in circulating blood.

Bacteria. Tiny, colorless, single-celled organisms of the vegetable kingdom (34). Bacteria can be seen with a good microscope. They are shaped like spheres, rods, spirals and commas. Most bacteria are harmless and even useful to man. Those which cause diseases are *pathogenic* bacteria.

Bagassosis. Chronic inflammation of the lungs caused by inhalation of bagasse, the material left from crushed sugar cane after its juices have been extracted.

Bag of waters. The fluid-filled sac which protects the fetus during gestation. During labor the bag of waters helps to dilate the outlet of the uterus for passage of the baby through the birth canal (359). Usually the bag of waters ruptures at the height of a strong pain and the fluid escapes with a gush, but rupture may occur even before labor pains begin (dry labor).

Baldness. See ALOPECIA.

Ballistocardiograph. An instrument for measuring the "kick" given by the heartbeat to the body (80).

Bamboo spine. A spine having the jointed appearance of bamboo, deformed by ankylosing spondylitis (640).

Balneotherapy. Bath treatment.

Banti's syndrome. Enlarged spleen and anemia, associated with cirrhosis of the liver and ASCITES (154).

Barber's itch (*tinea sycosis*). A fungus infection of bearded parts of the face, producing reddish patches covered with dry hairs and scales. A more severe condition, *sycosis barbae,* is caused by bacterial infection of follicles of the beard, producing crusts, pimples, and pustules perforated by hairs.

Barbiturates. The type of "sleeping pill" most commonly prescribed by physicians is some form of barbiturate. These constitute a large family of chemical compounds, most of which can be recognized by a name ending in "-al"; for example, *phenobarbital.* Properly used under medical direction, the barbiturates are safe and very effective sedatives and hypnotics. Small daytime doses may be given to reduce restlessness and emotional tension; in such use, the effect is much the same as that of TRANQUILIZERS, except that barbiturates tend to dull alertness and tranquilizers do not or do so to lesser degree. Adequate night-time doses of barbiturates usually induce sleep within fifteen minutes to half an hour.

Some barbiturates act rapidly but the effects do not last long (three or four hours). These may be prescribed for persons who have a hard time falling asleep but usually stay asleep after they have dropped off. Effects of long-acting barbiturates persist for up to eight hours, and there are forms of intermediate duration, selected by a doctor according to a patient's individual needs. Long-acting forms have some tendency to leave the patient with "barbiturate hangover," a feeling of grogginess and depression the morning after.

The "bad name" of barbiturates derives from gross abuse, quite unrelated to valuable medical uses. Unstable persons may obtain the drugs illicitly and take toxic doses for "kicks." Doses of sufficient size can cause excitement and intoxication somewhat similar to alcoholic intoxication. Gross misuse of barbiturates can result in addiction, with withdrawal symptoms very similar to those of narcotic withdrawal when the drugs are discontinued.

Occasionally, large doses of barbiturates may be taken with suicidal intent. A fatal dose is from ten to twenty times the normal dose. Death from a single ordinary dose of a barbiturate is unknown. The drugs when properly used, even daily for a considerable length of time, are quite safe. Nevertheless, as with all potent drugs, barbiturates should be treated with respect, be used only as directed, be kept in a safe place, and be identified by label or other means to avoid taking them by mistake. Sedatives depress the central nervous system. So does alcohol. A combination of barbiturates and alcohol is especially dangerous. Doses of either, which if taken alone would be well tolerated, can be extremely dangerous if the same doses of the two substances, which intensify each other's depressive actions, are taken close together.

A number of non-barbiturate sleeping pills with a somewhat greater margin of safety than the barbiturates have been developed. However, large doses are toxic and capable of causing stupor, coma, respiratory failure and death.

All of these drugs are sold only on medical prescription. Mild sedatives sold without a prescription do not contain them; many contain an ANTIHISTAMINE agent.

Barium meal. A suspension of insoluble barium sulfate in water, swallowed in preparation for a "G.I. series" (754). The barium has greater density to x-rays than surrounding tissues and thus defines structures clearly.

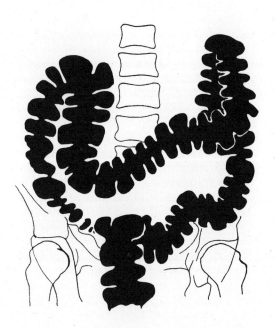

X-ray view of large intestine defined by barium.

Barrel chest. A rounded, bulging, barrel-shaped chest which does not move appreciably with the intake and output of air but is more or less fixed in a position of deep inhalation; characteristic of advanced emphysema (224).

Bartholin glands. Small glands on the floor and sides of the vaginal opening which secrete lubricating mucoid material. The glands are subject to infection and cyst formation.

Basal ganglia. Aggregations of nerve cells in the region of the base of the brain; Parkinson's disease is associated with abnormalities in this area (241).

Basal metabolic rate (*BMR*). A baseline of the minimal rate of energy expenditure for maintaining basal activities such as heart action, breathing, and heat production when the body is at rest; useful in diagnosis of certain diseases (315).

Baseball finger, also called *mallet finger*. It is a dislocation of the end joint of a finger, which drops down and can't be lifted, due to rupture or tearing of a tendon by a direct blow from a baseball or other object upon the end or back of the finger (612).

Basedow's disease. Hyperthyroidism (310).

BCG: Bacillus of Calmette and Guerin; a vaccine which gives immunity to tuberculosis for a variable time. The vaccine contains strains of live tubercle bacilli grown on ox bile for a long period to reduce their virulence. It is a safe vaccine, extensively used in Europe, but in the U.S. it has been mostly used in persons with special hazards of exposure to tuberculosis, such as doctors, nurses, and members of families of tuberculosis patients. BCG vaccination interferes with the interpretation of tuberculin tests (209), but proponents point out that there are other ways of detecting tuberculous infection.

Bearing down pains. Pains which occur in the second stage of labor (360) when the mother, feeling that some-thing must be expelled, makes powerful contractions of her abdominal muscles in coordination with contractions of the uterus.

Bed cradle. A frame to keep the weight of bedclothing off a patient's body (28).

Bedsores (decubitus ulcer). Sores or ulcers resulting from pressures on parts of the body in persons confined to bed for long periods; good nursing care can do much to prevent them (26).

Bedwetting. Enuresis (380).

Bejel. A non-venereal form of syphilis, transmitted by such means as contaminated eating and drinking utensils, chiefly occurring in the Middle East (50).

Bell's palsy. Paralysis of the facial nerve, usually temporary; it leaves the patient unable to move muscles of the mouth, eye, and forehead on one side of the face (255).

Bence-Jones protein. An abnormal protein in the urine, occurring most often in association with *multiple myeloma* (165). The substance is readily deposited in kidney tubules and leads to impaired kidney function.

Bends. See CAISSON DISEASE.

Benign. Mild; usually the word means that a tumor is not cancerous. Benign tumors are not necessarily harmless; they can cause a wide range of symptoms related to pressure, obstruction, twisting, and excessive production of potent substances such as hormones. Pregnancy has been described rather wryly as a benign self-limited tumor.

Beriberi. A deficiency disease, very rare in this country, chiefly the result of a deficiency of thiamine (vitamin B_1) in the diet (480). *Dry* beriberi chiefly affects the nerves of the extremities; *wet* beriberi is characterized by edema and congestive heart failure.

Berylliosis. Poisoning by beryllium, a metallic element. If beryllium particles are inhaled over a period of time, the lungs are seriously affected (226); growths in the skin occur if the material penetrates the skin.

Bezoar. A solid mass of compacted indigestible material in the stomach or intestines, found occasionally in mentally disturbed persons who swallow rags, rubber, hair, rope, and other inedible materials. Persimmons can produce bezoars. A "hair ball" is a *trichobezoar*.

B.i.d. Twice a day.

Bile. A yellowish or brownish fluid continuously manufactured in the liver; it is stored and concentrated in the gallbladder and released as needed into the duodenum (439). Bile helps to emulsify and absorb fats and to alkalinize the intestine. It is a complex, bitter-tasting fluid (gall) containing pigments, salts, fatty acids, cholesterol and other materials. Bile salts are sometimes used in medicine to stimulate the secretory activity of the liver.

Bilharziasis. Schistosomiasis (65).

Biliousness. A nondescript word for vague symptoms attributed, usually wrongly, to a fretful liver and maleficent activities of bile. Probably the word survives from ancient times when a "choleric" person was said to have an excess of yellow bile and a "melancholy" person an excess of black bile. Many symptoms, including jaundice, can indeed arise from deviations of bile, but it takes a doctor to determine what's wrong.

Bilirubin. The principal pigment of bile; a reddish substance derived from the breakdown of HEMOGLOBIN. Bilirubin tests are useful in determining the nature of certain blood and liver diseases, in distinguishing different types of jaundice, and in evaluating excessive destruction of blood cells.

Biologic "clocks." Some people can set a "mental clock" to awaken them before an alarm clock goes off. A few are confident enough to dispense with alarm clocks entirely. Many familiar physiologic rhythms recur approximately every 24 hours—sleep, waking, ups and downs of body temperature and heart rate. These are called *circadian rhythms*, from Latin words meaning "*about* a day." There are also multitudes of shorter rhythms, such as brain wave patterns, superimposed upon longer ones. All of these are rather like biologic clocks distributed through the body, ticking away at different speeds, some of their rhythms merging to augment others, some out of phase and dampening others.

Our built-in timepieces are a great challenge to physiologists who are giving a good deal of attention to mechanisms of which very little is known. Some rhythms are undoubtedly affected by external factors—light and darkness, heat and cold—but others appear to be built into individual body cells.

Better knowledge of our mysterious internal clocks may have practical applications. The timing of doses of medicine may be significant; test animals are more resistant or susceptible to certain drugs at different phases of their circadian rhythms. Passengers who cross many time zones in jet airplanes suffer lowered mental and physical efficiency for several days, not accountable for by ordinary fatigue. As of now there is no way of re-setting biologic clocks that have lost, or gained, many hours by jet-plane transport, other than to let the body re-set them in its own good time.

Glimpses into physiologic rhythms are tantalizing. Why should the number of certain white blood cells increase when we get up in the morning? Why should malaria parasites be released from a patient's red blood cells most frequently between 6 and 8 a.m.? Why should the peak frequency of epileptic seizures be between 10 and 11 p.m.? One study of 600,000 births showed that the peak frequency of spontaneous onset of labor is 1 a.m. and of births, 3 to 4 a.m. Asthmatic attacks and infarctions of the heart muscle are also most frequent around 3 to 4 a.m. Body temperature and heart rate, low in early morning, increase to a peak between 3 and 6 p.m., whereupon our biologic clocks begin to shut us down for bedtime. Sleep is not a smooth 8-hour rhythm; it has its own clock system which half awakens us and encourages dreams (see SLEEP).

Practical applications of knowledge that all organisms have their peculiar clocks are not extensive. But the U. S. Department of Agriculture has discovered that houseflies and cockroaches are especially vulnerable to insecticides around 4 p.m.

Biopsy. Removal of tissue from the living body for purposes of diagnosis, as in cases of suspected cancer. The tissue specimen may be subjected to biochemical tests; more often, it is set in a paraffin block, cut into very thin slices, stained, and studied under a microscope. If necessary, the procedure can be completed in a few minutes by quick-freezing the tissue. This is frequently done while the patient remains under anesthesia on the operating table and surgeons await the pathologist's verdict as to whether a tumor of the breast or other organ is or is not malignant.

Biotin. One of the 10 recognized vitamins of the B complex. Human deficiency has never been observed under usual conditions.

Birth control. See CONTRACEPTION.

Birth defects. About 2 per cent of live newborn infants have abnormalities recognizable at birth. Some defects such as a slightly twisted toe or a cleft lip are obvious *congenital malformations* (present at birth). Perhaps another 1 to 2 per cent of infants have abnormalities which are not recognizable at birth but which become apparent as they grow older. Many abnormalities are relatively minor, and about 80 per cent of birth defects, including the most serious forms such as congenital malformations of the heart, can be corrected and treated. Better than correction, of course, is prevention of abnormalities. To accomplish this, better knowledge of the causes of birth defects is a prerequisite.

Causes, if not the total mechanisms, of some birth defects are known. Some are hereditary, determined by parental CHROMOSOMES, and genetic counseling is helpful to prospective parents concerned about some real or fancied abnormality that "runs in the family" (see MEDICAL GENETICS). Some defects are *environmental,* quite unrelated to heredity. A disturbance of the environment of the fetus, its womb-nest, distorts its growth. The best-known example of environment-caused abnormalities is infection of the mother with German measles at a critical time of pregnancy. Some abnormalities are believed to be caused by a combination of hereditary and environmental factors, or by an accident at the time of delivery, as in cases of brain damage due to interruption of the oxygen supply to the newborn during delivery.

But at present, large numbers of birth defects simply have to be labeled "cause unknown." This situation is rapidly changing as concerted research casts more light on development of the embryo and possible agents that affect it. It is not yet feasible to prevent all birth defects, but there are at least a number of prudent precautionary measures to minimize their possibility.

Time of vulnerability. It is now well established that certain birth defects originate at a critical time of pregnancy; in general, at the time when cells and mere "buds" of the embryo are developing into arms and legs and vital organs. At this time the embryo is peculiarly vulnerable to inimical agents. Before then it is too young;

afterward, too old to be seriously affected. The period of danger is quite brief, but variable, and in animals used for testing drugs the period may be so short that it is difficult for researchers to pinpoint the effects of a specific agent—not to mention the fact that some drugs which produce abnormalities in the offspring of animals have no such effects on human beings, and vice versa. See TIMETABLE OF FETAL DEVELOPMENT.

It is also now well established that the PLACENTA is not a perfect barrier, protecting the fetus against all noxious agents. Cruel deformities of infants whose mothers took thalidomide, a supposedly innocuous sedative pill, made it very clear that substances that pass across the placenta can do grave harm to the fetus, and brought a vast amount of research to bear upon a previously neglected and largely unexplored area.

The role of specific drugs as *teratogenic* (malformation-producing) agents is by no means clearly defined. Harmful effects, if any, are produced during the first weeks of pregnancy, when a woman may not know that she is pregnant. Certain synthetic progestational agents (hormones) administered to women who habitually miscarry apparently have a masculinizing effect on female infants. Drugs given to treat thyroid disorders of a pregnant woman may pass across the placenta and cause goiter in her infant. Cortisone has been viewed with some suspicion, since it can regularly produce cleft palate in the fetuses of rats and rabbits, although it seems rarely to be associated with cleft palate in human infants.

Tetracycline, a widely prescribed antibiotic drug, may have undesirable effects on the fetus if administered to a pregnant woman late in pregnancy. The drug may be deposited in pigment form in growing bones of the fetus and temporarily delay growth, and it may be laid down in developing teeth and cause discoloration and abnormalities of the enamel when the teeth erupt. Certain sulfa drugs given to a woman late in pregnancy for treatment of urinary tract infection may increase the risk of development of KERNICTERUS in the infant. This is a serious form of jaundice with deposits of bile pigments in the brain. If the infant survives it may have all the symptoms of cerebral palsy, and possible deafness.

Drugs or other substances, harmless in themselves, may in combination have some effect in producing abnormalities if taken early in pregnancy. Little is known about this because of the obvious difficulty of incriminating common household medicines which are taken beneficially and harmlessly by millions of people. The public does not generally think of vitamins as medications but as substances which, if a little is good, a lot is better. There appears to be a relationship between excessive intake of Vitamin D by a pregnant woman and a condition in her infant known as *hypercalcemia*. High levels of blood calcium, resulting from high Vitamin D levels, are associated with abnormalities of the aorta and other major blood vessels. These infants have a fragile, elfin appearance, mental retardation, pallor, constipation, vomiting and failure of growth.

There is suspicion, but as yet no positive proof, that excessive intake of Vitamin C during pregnancy may result in infants who develop SCURVY despite ample amounts of orange juice or supplements, because their bodies are adjusted to excessively high intake of the vitamin.

During pregnancy, more than at any other time in a woman's life, it is important that no drugs be taken other than those prescribed by a physician who knows that she is pregnant.

If x-rays are essential during pregnancy, a radiologist will take precautions to protect the fetus against possible injury. But many women of child-bearing age do not know that a very early pregnancy is already established. Unless immediate x-ray of such a woman is imperative, it should be postponed to a time when she can be virtually certain that she is not pregnant: the first two weeks following the start of a normal menstruation.

Virus infections. In addition to German measles, other virus infections of pregnant women may pose a threat to unborn babies. There is reason to believe that the number of malformed babies resulting from the mother's infection by *cytomegaolviruses* (55) and *toxoplasmosis* (71) is as great as the number affected by German measles defects. Other virus infections of pregnant women, suspected of injuring the fetus, are mumps, influenza, and COXSACKIE VIRUS diseases (58). Some of these infections may cause no obvious disease in the mother (cytomegaloviruses and toxoplasmosis almost never do) though severely damaging the baby, and most birth defects due to inapparent infections are classed as of unknown cause.

Another way in which viruses may cause birth defects is by injuring the CHROMOSOMES of the germ cells of the parents. There have been reports of extraordinary frequency of chromosome defects in newborn infants occurring about 9 months after a virus epidemic. This suggests that parental egg or sperm cells which united were temporarily injured by a virus infection of one or both parents.

The hope is that as research closes in on causes, effective measures to prevent many kinds of birth defects will become available. In addition to research centers, the National Foundation has established two types of centers in a large number of states. One type is an Evaluation Center, consisting of diagnostic service by a team of specialists who determine each infant's medical problem and recommend specific treatment in consultation with the family physician and the parents. The second type is a Birth Defects Treatment Center, usually established in a teaching hospital or in affiliation with the medical school of a major university. In addition to diagnosis, these centers provide expert treatment and conduct teaching courses. Information about them can be obtained from the National Foundation, 888 Second Avenue, New York, N. Y. 10017.

Blackwater fever. An acute complication of MALARIA, especially in persons who have been treated with quinine. An attack is marked by high fever, shivering, profound anemia; the urine is very dark, hence the name (70).

Black widow spider. A small coal-black spider with a globe-shaped abdomen marked by a reddish design like an hourglass or dumbbell. Its bite is very painful and can be serious (810).

Blastomycosis. A group of diseases caused by yeastlike fungi, variously affecting the skin, lungs, or body as a whole (72).

Bleb. A small blister filled with blood or fluid.

Bleeder's disease. HEMOPHILIA (152).

Blepharitis. Inflammation of the eyelids, usually due to bacterial infection; sometimes associated with allergies or seborrhea of the face and scalp.

Blind spot. A small spot on the retina, where the optic nerve enters, which is insensitive to light (531). The blind spot can be recognized by closing one eye, fixing the other on a small black spot, and shifting the gaze of the open eye toward the nose until the spot disappears.

Blood-brain barrier. Some natural body substances, drugs, and chemicals circulating in the blood are unable to reach active brain cells. The apparent blood-brain barrier, serving as a selective traffic officer which permits some substances to "go" and directs others to "stop," is thought by some authorities to consist of a layer of cells around small capillaries in the brain. The barrier is presumably a natural protective mechanism.

Blood tests. Laboratory tests of blood can yield a vast amount of information. The extent of testing depends on what is being looked for. There are many special tests for special purposes. A "routine" blood test does not include unusual procedures, but does include standard studies, for which the following are normal physiologic values:

pH (acid-alkaline ratios; pH 7 is neutral, above 7 is alkaline) 7.35–7.45
Red blood cells (erythrocytes) . . . . . . 4,500,000–5,000,000 per cu. mm.
White blood cells (leukocytes) . . . . .5,000–10,000 per cu. mm.
Polymorphonuclear neutrophils. 60–70%
Lymphocytes 25–33%
Monocytes 2–6%
Eosinophils 1–3%
Basophils 0.25–0.5%
Platelets. 200,000–400,000 per cu. mm.
Hemoglobin . .14–16 Gm. per 100 ml.
Bleeding time . . . . .1–3 minutes
Coagulation time . . . . . .6–12 minutes
Serum cholesterol . . . . .150 to 250 mg. per 100 ml.
Glucose . . . . .80–120 mg. per 100 ml.
Albumin . . . .3.5–5.5 Gm per 100 ml.
Nonprotein nitrogen . . . . .25–38 mg. per 100 ml.
Urea nitrogen (BUN) . . . . .8–20 mg. per 100 ml.
Uric acid. . . . . . . .3–5 mg. per 100 ml.
(100 ml. (milliliters) is approximately one-tenth of a quart).

Blue baby. An infant with a congenital heart defect which allows venous and arterial blood to mix, resulting in insufficient oxygen in the blood and a bluish tinge of skin and mucous membranes (93).

Blood poisoning. A general term for the presence of germs or their toxins in circulating blood (38). See BACTEREMIA, SEPTICEMIA, TOXEMIA.

Body build. A general term for variabilities of height, weight, breadth, muscularity, boniness, limb length, etc., characteristic of individuals. Different proportions of bodily components can be measured scientifically; see SOMATOTYPING.

Boeck's sarcoid. See SARCOIDOSIS.

Bone age. An index of physiologic maturity, based on the fairly definite time schedule of development of bone from birth to maturity, independent of chronological age. Bone age is commonly estimated by taking x-rays of a child's hands and wrists and comparing these centers of ossification with standards appropriate to his age. There are normal variations; bone age may be advanced or retarded a year or so without necessarily being abnormal. Advanced bone age may be associated with overactivity of the adrenal or thyroid glands, retarded bone age with deficient thyroid activity or malnutrition. Tall children who reach sexual maturity at an early age usually have advanced bone age; probable late maturers, the opposite.

Bone banks. Stored collections of matchstick to pencil-sized pieces of human bone. When transplanted, the dead, sterile bone somehow stimulates the growth of new bone around it, eventually is incorporated into that new bone, and is slowly replaced. In the meantime the graft is a barrier which prevents soft fibrous tissue from filling the hole or defect in the patient's own bone. Bone grafts are used most frequently to correct curvature of the spine in children, and after fractures, if the bone ends fail to unite properly, to assist in mending.

Bone conduction. Bones of the head are natural channels for conduction of sounds to the ears. This can be demonstrated by stopping the ears and touching a vibrating tuning fork to the skull or teeth. Some types of hearing aids, in contact with bone behind the ear, make use of this phenomenon. Bone conduction explains in part why our own voices don't sound exactly the same to us as they do to others.

Bone marrow exam. Microscopic study of bone marrow tissue obtained by needle, used in diagnosing certain diseases of the blood.

Booster shot. Injection of a vaccine or immunizing agent given some time after an original vaccination, to enhance its effectiveness. Immunizations tend to wear off in the course of time; a timely booster shot rejuvenates them. Some primary immunizations are given in two or three spaced injections, several days or weeks apart, to produce maximum immunizing action.

Botulism. A violent form of food poisoning caused by toxins of botulinus organisms in improperly canned foods (42, 807).

Bougie. A slender cylindrical instrument introduced into a body orifice to explore or dilate a passage or act as a guide for other instruments.

Boutonniere deformity. Bending of the middle joint of a finger with extension of the other joints, resulting from a cut or rupture of a tendon (613).

Bowlegs (*genu varum*). Outward bowing of the knee joints; common in young children just "getting their feet on the ground," usually requiring no treatment unless bowing persists after five or six years of age (616).

Bowman's capsule. The cup-shaped capsule of a *nephron*, the minute filtering unit of the kidney (271).

Bradycardia. Abnormal slowness of the heartbeat, with a pulse rate of less than 60 per minute.

Brain waves. Minute electric currents of brain cells which, when amplified and transcribed, have the form of undulant, spiked, wavy lines. See ELECTROENCEPHALOGRAPH.

Breakbone fever. Sudden, acute high fever, called "breakbone" for the shattering pain it causes in muscles, bones and joints; also called *dengue* (57).

Breast support. A common source of breast pain, especially if the breasts are unusually large, is a poorly fitted brassiere which supports most of the weight from above by shoulder straps. Correct breast support sustains most of the weight of the breasts from *below*, by the portion of the brassiere which encircles the chest under the breasts; the main function of shoulder straps is to hold the garment in position.

Breath-holding. Crying of infants and small children so furious that they hold their breath until they turn blue or even lose consciousness for a moment. A breath-holding spell can be frightening the first time a parent is confronted with one, but the episode is just a blowoff of temper and anger, and nature has arranged that we can't hold our breath long enough to do serious harm; try it yourself.

Breech delivery. Presentation of an infant's buttocks instead of the head at the outlet of the birth canal (364).

Bright's disease. An old term for several diseases which fall under the general category of *glomerulonephritis* (280); sometimes used as a general term for kidney disease.

Brill-Zinsser disease. A mild form of typhus fever, occurring in persons who had an attack of typhus years before (63).

Bromhidrosis. Foul-smelling perspiration.

Bromism. Chronic poisoning from long continued use of bromides; these salts have sedative and sleep-inducing properties and are contained in many prescribed and non-prescription products. Symptoms of chronic bromide intoxication run the gamut from headache, sleepiness, cold hands and feet, worsening of acne, to toxic delirium, disorientation and hallucinations. Bromide salts accumulate in blood and body fluids over a period of continued intake. Treatment consists of stopping all intake of bromides; daily doses of table salt in amounts prescribed by a doctor help to speed their elimination.

Bronchial asthma. The common form of asthma; usually it has an allergic basis (658). Characteristic paroxysms of wheezy labored breathing are due to narrowing of bronchial passages, trapping inhaled air and making it very difficult to exhale.

Bronchial tree. The breathing passages which extend from the windpipe in finer and finer ramifications resembling the branchings of tree roots (201).

Bronchiectasis. Dilation of bronchial tubes, usually a result of pus-producing infections or obstruction by foreign bodies (216).

Bronchitis. Inflammation of the linings of bronchial tubes (214).

Bronchography. The taking of an x-ray film of the lungs after injection of iodized oil (753).

Bronchoscope. A thin tubelike instrument, inserted into the windpipe for purposes of inspecting tissues, withdrawing secretions or tissue samples, administering medicines, or extracting foreign bodies (219).

Bronze diabetes. See HEMOCHROMATOSIS.

Bornholm disease. See DEVIL'S GRIP.

Brucellosis (*Malta fever, undulant fever*). An infectious disease transmitted from animals to man, most commonly by contact with cattle or consumption of raw milk products (45). Also called *undulant fever,* from the up-and-down shifts of body temperature, down in the morning and up in the afternoon. Recovery from acute brucellosis is usually spontaneous but convalescence may be prolonged. Chronic brucellosis may be unrecognized and hard to diagnose; varied symptoms—obscure fever of long duration, weakness, fatigability, excessive sweating—may puzzlingly resemble those of infectious mononucleosis, tuberculosis, malaria, or rheumatic fever. Positive diagnosis is made by recovery of Brucella organisms from body excretions.

Bruxism. The habit of grinding the teeth (510).

Bubo. An inflamed, swollen lymph node, usually in the groin or armpit, caused by absorption of infective material; most often a concomitant of venereal disease.

Buccal. Pertaining to the cheek.

Buerger's disease. Inflammation of the inner walls of blood vessels with clot formation and interruption of blood supply. The legs, feet, and toes are especially affected. Shutting off of blood supply can lead to GANGRENE and amputation. The cause of the disease is unknown but it chiefly affects young males and is almost never seen in non-smokers. Absolute prohibition of smoking for the rest of the patient's life is an essential part of treatment; resumption of smoking can provoke renewed attacks and gangrene.

Bulimia. Insatiable appetite, requiring enormous meals for satisfaction.

Bulla. A large blister.

Buphthalmos. Enlargement of the eye.

Bursa. A sac between opposing surfaces that slide past each other. It is filled with lubricating fluid, something like the white of an egg, which permits free motion. Inflammation of a bursa causes painful *bursitis* (628).

Bunion (*hallux valgus*). Enlargement and thickening of the big joint of the big toe, bending the big toe toward the little toe (623). The deformity gets progressively worse if untreated. Surgical correction is not so simple as it seems, but is indicated for young persons. In older persons, a special shoe made to fit the deformity comfortably may be the most practical solution.

Butterfly suture. A strip of plastic or adhesive tape with a relatively thin "bridge" between wider ends, used to draw together the opposing edges of a minor laceration on a smooth skin surface.

Byssinosis. An occupational disease of textile workers caused by inhalation of dusts produced during certain processing stages in cotton, flax, and hemp mills. Initial symptoms are chest tightness, cough, wheezing, and shortness of breath, which occur predominantly on the first working days after absence from work, as over a weekend. The cause is thought to be a chemical substance in textile dusts which constricts the bronchi and causes asthma-like symptoms.

C

Cachexia. Profound weakness, emaciation, general ill health, resulting from serious disease such as cancer.

Cafe au lait spots. Multiple pigmented patches in the skin, the color of coffee with milk, associated with NEURO-FIBROMATOSIS.

Caffeine. A chemical substance contained in tea, coffee, and many cola-type beverages. Caffeine is a powerful stimulant of the central nervous system and tends to increase both mental and physical performance. A great variety of drug preparations contain caffeine, often in combination with other drugs.

Caisson disease. Diver's paralysis; cramping pain in the abdomen, legs and other parts, called "the bends" by divers. Symptoms are caused by nitro-gen bubbles in the blood which try to escape in much the same way that a rush of compressed gas escapes when a warm bottle of pop is opened. The nitrogen gets into the blood from air inhaled under pressure, as under water or in caissons or wherever surrounding pressure greatly exceeds that of the atmosphere. Attacks can be prevented by gradual ascent from a deep dive, or treated by putting the patient into a decompression chamber where high pressure is gradually reduced while nitrogen slowly dissipates from body fluids. "The bends" can affect Scuba divers who stay too long under water at depths of 100 feet or so and ascend too rapidly.

Calcaneus. The heel bone.

Calcification. The process by which tissues become hardened by deposits of calcium salts.

Calcium. A mineral element that is an essential constituent of bone and is essential for blood clotting, muscle tone, and nerve function.

Calculus. A stone formed in a duct, cyst, or hollow organ of the body, especially in the gallbladder (457) and kidney (275). Most calculi are composed of mineral salts, often with a mixture of organic matter. The composition of a stone may sometimes give a physician information of value in preventing future stone formation. Stones range in size from "gravel" like specks of sand to stones which fill the entire interior of the kidney. The stuff that stones are made of is somehow extracted and condensed from fluids of the body. Infection and stagnation of fluids play a part in stone formation, but exactly why some people form stones and others do not is not known. Drinking hard water has nothing to do with it. Stones may cause a few symptoms if they stay where they are, but excruciating pain ensues if a stone tries to squeeze through a passage too small for it. *Dental calculus* is tartar that accumulates on teeth (508).

Callus. A patch of hard, thickened skin, usually on the hands or feet; a protective reaction to pressure or friction. A callus is like a corn except that it is more diffuse and has no core, and it tends to disappear spontaneously when the cause is removed. Persons who stand a great deal often develop thick calluses of the heel or ball of the foot. The horny skin may be removed by rubbing with pumice stone, emery board, or a coarse Turkish towel after soaking the foot in hot water. Persistent calluses which cause a great deal of discomfort should have the attention of a podiatrist. "Callus" is also a word for the plastic bony material which exudes from and surrounds broken bone ends and plays a part in the healing of a fracture.

Calorie. A unit of heat. The unit used in measuring body metabolism and the fattening propensities of foods (471) is the "great calorie," the amount of heat necessary to raise the temperature of one kilogram (2.2 pounds) of water one degree Centigrade.

Calyx. One of the several small cuplike chambers which receive urine from kidney tubules and channel it into the funnel-shaped cavity of the kidney which merges with the ureter (272).

Canker sore (*aphthous stomatitis*). Little blisters on membranes of the mouth and cheeks which break and leave open sores. The painful ulcers usually heal spontaneously in a week or so, but attacks may be recurrent. It is no longer thought that canker sores are caused by viruses (the sores may appear at the same time as cold sores or fever blisters which are caused by herpes simplex virus). Scientists at the National Institute of Dental Health have isolated a bacterium which causes canker sores. Persons who have repeated or continuous crops of canker sores may be allergic to some substance in the bacterium's makeup. The organism is sensitive to tetracycline, an antibiotic; oral suspensions of the drug held in the mouth for two minutes and then swallowed (four times daily) shorten the healing time but do not prevent recurrences.

Cannula. A hollow tube for insertion into a body passage or cavity; within the cannula there is usually a *trocar*, a sliding instrument with a pointed tip, designed to puncture a cavity and release fluid, after which the trocar is withdrawn and fluid drains through the cannula.

Canthus. The angle formed where the eyelids meet at the outer or inner side.

Carbohydrate. The primary fuel of muscular activity, the major source of energy we need for moving, working, acting, living. Carbohydrates occur as sugars and starches, in many complex forms; the starches are converted to sugar in the digestive processes (472). Cereals, vegetables, and fruits are inexpensive carbohydrate foods which are major sources of food for much of the world's population. Carbohydrate is necessary to burn fats efficiently, and it "spares" protein, which can be burned for energy if necessary but is more valuable for other purposes. Cellulose, the indigestible matter in many carbohydrate foods, supplies useful bulk in the intestines. Most of the carbohydrates in the body are stored in the liver and muscles in the form of glycogen (animal starch), but not much more than a half day's needs are held in storage. As the supplies become depleted, hunger pangs remind us that it is time to replenish our energy reserves.

Carbon dioxide snow. Extremely cold snow-like particles (about 100 degrees below zero) formed by rapid evaporation of liquid carbon dioxide. Application of the snow freezes the skin instantly. It is used in treatment of various skin lesions, such as birthmarks (184).

Carbon monoxide. A colorless, odorless gas which is the most frequent cause of fatal poisoning except alcohol. Immediate first aid is imperative (778). Carbon monoxide kills by depriving tissues of oxygen; it combines 200 times more readily than oxygen with HEMOGLOBIN of the red blood cells. The gas is produced by any incompletely burned fuel. Common belief that a fire in a closed space is dangerous because it "burns up all the oxygen" is erroneous; it is dangerous because it emits carbon monoxide. Most of us know that it is dangerous to let a car run in a closed garage even for seconds. It is not so well known that gas can seep into a car in bumper-to-bumper traffic or from a leaky muffler or exhaust pipe. Relatively small amounts of the gas in a car driven with windows closed can dull a driver's senses or cause him to "fall asleep" at the wheel. It is wise to drive with one window at least partly open and to have the exhaust system checked for leaks during routine inspections.

Carbuncle. A deep-seated infection of the skin, like several boils joined together; pus is discharged from a number of points on the tight, reddened skin surface (38).

Carcinogen. Any agent which produces cancer.

Carcinoma. Cancer comprised of epithelial cells, the type that cover the skin and mucous membranes and form the linings of organs. Carcinomas may arise in almost any structure of the body; many forms are curable if proper treatment is begun early.

Cardia. The valve of ringlike muscle at the junction of esophagus and stomach (430).

Cardiac. Pertaining to the heart; a person with heart disease.

Cardiac asthma. Paroxysms of difficult breathing, often occurring at night, characteristic of congestive heart failure (96).

Cardiac catheter. A slender tube which is threaded into a vessel of the arm and pushed into the heart to obtain several kinds of important diagnostic information (84, 89).

Cardiac pacemaker. A device which electrically stimulates the sympathetic nerves to the heart, triggering the "beat" and producing contractions at near the normal rate when the organ itself cannot do so reliably (107). There are several varieties of pacemakers. The type most widely employed for permanent use is "implantable." The "package" with its electronic components is implanted under the large muscle on the left side of the chest. Electrodes in contact with the heart muscle are wired to the implanted unit which is powered by mercury batteries. Usually a new electronic pack is spliced in place every two years.

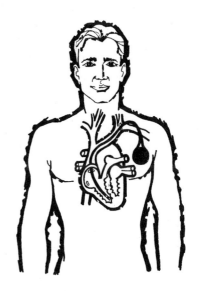

Implanted cardiac pacemaker, electrodes in right ventricle.

Cardiospasm. See ACHALASIA.

Cardiovascular. Pertaining to the heart and blood vessels.

Carotid. The principal artery that runs up either side of the neck (117). At approximately the middle of the neck it divides in a Y-formation; one branch continues as the external carotid artery and the other as the internal carotid artery which goes directly to the brain. Some strokes are caused by obstruction of the artery at the crotch of the Y; the structure is close to the surface, readily accessible to a surgeon, and an operation may give dramatic improvement of the patient's symptoms (118). Overstimulation or compression of nerves at the point where the artery divides can cause dizziness and loss of consciousness.

Carpal. Pertaining to the wrist. The *carpal tunnel* through which a large nerve passes from the wrist to the hand may become constricted and cause tingling and numbness of the fingers (611).

Car sickness. See MOTION SICKNESS.

Caries. Decay of bone; the dentist's word for tooth decay (dental caries).

Carotene. A yellow pigment occurring in sweet potatoes, carrots, leaves, yellow vegetables, egg yolk and other foodstuffs. The body converts it into Vitamin A. Excessive intake over a long period of time of carrots or other carotene-rich foods may raise the blood's content of carotene to such an exaggerated level that the skin takes on a yellowish hue, sometimes mistaken for jaundice. This condition, known as *carotenemia,* is harmless but fairly spectacular.

Cartilage. Gristle; white, elastic connective tissue. It is the substance of soft parts in infants which later become bone. It forms part of the skeleton. Pads of cartilage cushion the opposing surfaces of joints; thinning or wearing away of cartilage is associated with some forms of arthritis (630). The stiff but flexible substance of the external ear is cartilage, the most convenient article of cartilage to touch or squeeze. Cartilage does not have a blood supply and if injured cannot

heal. Tearing or other injury of cartilage is quite common among athletes and often requires surgical removal (618).

Caruncle. A small, non-malignant, fleshy growth; a type which causes pain and bleeding (urethral caruncle) occurs at the urinary outlet of women, most frequently at the menopause.

Castration. Removal of the testicles or ovaries. Functional powers of the ovaries can be destroyed by radiation, sometimes necessary in treatment of disease; this is called non-surgical castration.

Casts, *renal.* Castoff particles in sediments of urine, sometimes indicative of latent forms of kidney disease (274). There are three forms of casts, *hyaline* (glassy), *red cell,* and *epithelial,* from which inferences concerning the nature of kidney lesions may be drawn.

Catabolism. The "tearing down" aspect of METABOLISM; the breaking down of complex substances by cells is often accompanied by release of energy. The opposite of ANABOLISM.

Catamenia. Menstruation.

Catarrh. A flowing down; a rather old-fashioned term for inflammation of mucous membranes, especially of the nose and throat, with free-flowing discharge, as in a cold.

Cataract. An opacity of the lens of the eye (552). A cataract is not a foreign substance or something to be peeled off the lens, but a biochemical change in structure. Babies may be born with cataracts and some of these cases are on an hereditary basis. Increasing age, physical injury, chemical injury from certain drugs and industrial chemicals, diabetes and other endocrine diseases, are associated with cataract formation, but the great majority of cataracts seem to be a part of the aging process. The only way to restore useful vision is to remove the lens surgically (742) ; this permits light waves to enter the eye once again. Of course the light-bending powers and power of ACCOMMODATION of the absent lens are lost. The patient has to wear heavy spectacle lenses to substitute, somewhat inefficiently, for the missing lens. He can see quite well again—a wonderful reprieve from partial or total blindness—but it takes some adjustment and reeducation. Many improvements have been and are being made in cataract glasses but they do not restore normal ease of seeing completely. Contact lenses have been improved and come closer to restoring normal visual function but they are not suitable for everyone. Attempts to insert a permanent plastic lens inside the eye in place of a removed cataractous lens are being made but are still in experimental stages of development.

Catatonia. A phase of schizophrenia in which the patient stands or sits in some awkward fixed position for hours on end and resists all attempts to get him to speak or move.

"Cat cry" syndrome. A peculiar condition of infants who give a cry like that of a cat, because of defective development of the larynx. It is an inherited abnormality, resulting from lack of a short arm on one of the infant's CHROMOSOMES.

Caterpillar dermatitis. Are caterpillars dangerous? Not very, but they can be offensive in more ways than one. Some varieties have tiny hollow hairs containing irritating material. These minute hairs can penetrate the skin and cause an itchy rash, usually mild. The rash may be puzzling because caterpillars are not usually thought of as the source. There may even have been no direct contact with caterpillars. A few mothers have acquired caterpillar dermatitis from contact with invisible hairs trapped in children's clothing. As a general rule, it is prudent to regard caterpillars as untouchable.

Cathartic. A purgative medicine; a substance that increases evacuation of the bowels. Regular use of carthartics is unwise; they can be habit-forming, and do not correct an underlying condition. Cathartics or laxatives should not be used if abdominal pain is present, and powerful cathartics such as castor oil or epsom salts should only be used as a physician directs.

Catheter. A hollow tube for insertion through a narrow canal into a cavity to discharge fluids, especially of the urinary bladder (274). The heart may also be catheterized for diagnostic purposes (94).

Cat scratch disease. An infection characterized by painless swelling of lymph nodes, acquired from a scratch by a cat (62). The offending cat usually shows no sign of disease.

Caul. The head of a baby born with a "caul" is covered with a fetal membrane, the AMNION, which has become detached.

Canities. Gray hair.

Causalgia. Excruciating, burning pain caused by injury to sensory nerves, especially of the palms and soles; often associated with poor circulation to the part and discoloration, clamminess, and coldness of the skin. Blocking the affected nerves with procaine may give relief.

Cautery. Application of heat or a chemical to destroy tissue. Anciently, a red hot iron was applied to wounds to stop bleeding and infection. Today the most common form is *electrocautery,* in which a wire loop heated by electric current is used to seal bleeding vessels or destroy tissue.

Cecum. The blind pouch in which the large bowel begins; the appendix projects from it (467).

Celiac disease. A disorder, believed to have an hereditary basis, in which the small intestine is unable to absorb fat from foods. See MALABSORPTION SYNDROME.

Cellulitis. Diffuse, pussy inflamation of soft, loose connective tissue beneath the skin.

Cementum. The bone-like substance which covers the roots of teeth (498).

Centigrade (C). A thermometer scale, widely used in science and medicine, in which water freezes at 0 degrees C. and boils at 100 degrees C. To convert to Fahrenheit degrees, multiply degrees Centigrade by nine-fifths and add 32. Average body temperature, 98.6 degrees Fahrenheit, is 37 degrees Centigrade.

Centipede bites. Ugly multi-legged creatures of the southern U.S. occasionally "bite," injecting a little venom into a puncture wound. The bitten area may swell, cause burning pain and turn red, but it generally doesn't last long —three or four hours—and there is no danger of serious poisoning. Wet dressings applied to the area are comforting; if pain is very severe, a doctor may give a sedative. Tropical centipedes are bigger, uglier, produce more venom, and their bites may cause vomiting, fever, headache, and inflammation of lymphatic vessels. Innocent visitors to the tropics would do well to shake out their shoes, turn back the bed covers, watch their step, and exhibit total inhospitality to centipedes.

Central nervous system (*CNS*). The brain and nerves of the spinal cord 236). The system is "central" because all of the nerves of the body, except the cranial nerves which connect directly with the brain, enter or leave the spinal cord.

Cephalalgia. A fancy name for headache.

Cephalic. Pertaining to the head. Turning the fetus so that the head presents is called *cephalic version.*

Cerebellum. A specialized part of the brain, about the size of an orange, tucked under the CEREBRUM at the back of the head (239, 253). It is concerned with equilibrium and coordination of movements.

Cerebral palsy. A form of paralysis manifested by jerky, writhing, spastic movements, resulting from damage to brain center controls of muscles (258). Cerebral palsy is not a single disease but a group of syndromes with a common denominator, some form of injury to motor control centers in the brain. It is not always possible to determine the cause of brain damage. It may result from birth injury, from infections of the mother or embryo, from errors of development, and other causes.

Cerebrum. The main part of the brain; the great mass of nerve tissue that occupies the entire upper part of the skull. *Cerebration,* by general human assent, means the most profound sort of thinking. *Cerebral* refers to phenomena that occur in the cerebrum; for example, cerebral hemorrhage.

Cerebrospinal fluid. Clear, colorless fluid that surrounds the spinal cord and is continuous with the same fluid in ventricles of the brain. Examination of cerebrospinal fluid assists in diagnosis of various diseases (such as meningitis, polio, brain tumor) which cause changes in the fluid. The fluid may contain blood, pus and other substances which do not belong there; it may be given chemical, microscopic and bacteriologic tests and may be cultured to determine the presence and identity of germs.

Cerebrovascular accident. A stroke, resulting from interruption of blood supply to the brain (117). The "accident" may be obstruction by a clot of a vessel supplying the brain, or rupture of a vessel with bleeding into brain tissue.

Cerumen. Ear wax (574).

Cervical rib. An extra rib in the cervical or neck region, in addition to the usual 12 on each side. It can be felt as a bony projection at the root of the neck. The spare rib may cause no trouble, but if pressures or other disturbing symptoms develop, it is as dispensable as the appendix.

Cervical effacement. Thinning of the outlet of the uterus preceding the onset of labor (359).

Cervicitis. Inflammation of the neck of the uterus (412).

Cervical erosion. A rough spot in the membrane lining the opening of the cervix, looking much like a child's skinned knee (709).

Cervix. A neck; the word applies to any neck-like or constricted part of the body; especially, the tapering neck of the pear-shaped uterus (406). Also, the neck of the urinary bladder. The seven cervical vertebrae (592) occupy the topmost part of the spine; cervical lymph nodes occur in the neck region.

Cesarean section. Delivery of a baby through an incision in the abdomen and uterus. Legend has it that Julius Caesar was born in this way, but legend is unreliable. The operation in Caesar's time was done only on dead women, and Caesar's mother survived his birth by many years. Julius was a dutiful son who wrote often to his mother during his wars. The word probably derives from the Latin *caedere,* to cut.

Chadwick's sign. A blue discoloration around the entrance to the vagina and on the neck of the uterus; an early indication of pregnancy (343).

Chancre. The primary lesion of syphilis; a hard sore or ulcer at the site where syphilis germs gained entrance to the body.

Chancroid (*soft chancre*). A non-syphilitic venereal disease caused by a specific bacillus, *Hemophilus ducreyi.* Initially a soft sore appears, usually on the genitals. In a few days it breaks down into a painful, pus-discharging ulcer (41).

Chafing. See INTERTRIGO.

Chagas' disease (*American trypanosomiasis*). A disease related to African sleeping sickness, caused by protozoa which enter the body through an insect bite contaminated by the insect's feces (69). The disease is characterized by fever, enlarged lymph nodes, and various complications; it can be fatal but is frequently mild. It occurs in Central and South America.

Chalazion. A painless small tumor or cyst of the eyelid due to an obstructed drainage duct; dammed-up secretions cause the swelling. Hot compresses can be applied, together with an antibacterial medicine if the doctor so directs. If the tumor does not disappear spontaneously, incision and curettage may be necessary.

Charleyhorse. A term most often used by athletes for tenderness and soreness of muscles, commonly of the thigh, incurred by some heroic sports effort. Pain and swelling result from rupture or strain of muscle or tendon fibers. Torn tissues may bleed, producing black-and-blueness or a charleyhorse of another color. Tenderness and stiffness usually disappear in a few days as the affected part is gradually returned to use. The healing process, following the acute stage of injury, may be encouraged by gentle applications of heat, massage, and comforting bandages.

Cheilitis. Inflammation of the lips.

Chemotherapy. Treatment with chemicals which favorably alter the course of disease but do not seriously injure the patient.

Cheyne-Stokes respiration. An abnormal form of breathing in some patients with heart, kidney, or vascular diseases. Intensity of breathing gradually decreases until no breath at all is taken for a few seconds or longer than half a minute. This is followed by increase in breathing and shortage of breath. The pattern occurs in repeated cycles. One of the causes is thought to be a decrease in blood supply to the brain.

Chilblain (*pernio*). An acute or chronic form of cold injury, less severe than frostbite, characterized by inflammation of the skin, itching and swelling, frequently followed by blisters. The immediate cause is exposure to cold, to which some persons have an exaggerated sensitivity; it is advisable for them to stay indoors or wear heavy garments and fleece-lined gloves and overshoes during cold weather. Such persons should begin to wear protective clothing early in the cold season when the environmental temperature drops below 60 degrees.

Chloasma. Discoloration of the skin with yellow-brown spots and patches. The condition is often associated with some endocrine disturbance. Chloasma frequently occurs in pregnancy as a result of increased secretion of a pituitary hormone, MSH (305), which stimulates pigment-producing cells. Hormone production returns to a normal level soon after delivery and the pigmented areas fade, though not always to the previous degree of lightness.

Chocolate cysts. Cysts of the ovary filled with chocolate-colored material, characteristic of *endometriosis* (415).

Choked disk. See PAPILLEDEMA.

Cholangitis. Inflammation of the bile ducts.

Cholecyst. The gallbladder.

Cholecystitis. Inflammation of the gallbladder. It may occur in acute or chronic forms (457).

Cholelithiasis. Stones in the gallbladder or its ducts (458).

Cholera (*Asiatic*). An epidemic infectious disease with a high fatality rate caused by comma-shaped germs, transmitted in bowel discharges of carriers to food and water. It is characterized by profuse watery diarrhea, cramps, vomiting, prostration, and suppression of urine. The principal mechanism by which cholera weakens and kills is through extreme losses of body fluids and ELECTROLYTES. The disease virtually never occurs in the U. S., but travelers going to regions where cholera outbreaks occur (India, Pakistan, Southeast Asia) should be vaccinated with a cholera vaccine which gives immunity for about six months.

Cholesteatoma. A tumor of the middle ear, like a bag of skin in the wrong place. The first sign may be a scanty discharge from the ear when the tumor liquefies and perforates the drum. The wall of the bag causes erosion of bone which may extend dangerously into neighboring structures. In most cases, surgical removal of the cholesteatoma is considered the best treatment (572).

Cholesterol. A waxy substance resembling fat in its properties, closely related to the sex hormones and Vitamin D. It is present in brain tissue, bile, nerve sheaths, all animal tissue. It regulates the passage of substances through cell walls, keeps us from becoming waterlogged when we bathe, and prevents us from drifting away as a cloud of vapor from evaporation of body water. It is so important to the body that it is manufactured by the liver and other tissues whether we get cholesterol in our diets or not. Despite these virtues, cholesterol has become something of a scare word, blamed for degenerating the walls of arteries and setting the stage for heart attacks. However, most specialists are reluctant to indict cholesterol as the primary, predominant, most vicious villain in heart and blood vessel diseases (85). One reason for cholesterol's bad publicity is that it is easier for doctors to measure than other fatty components of blood serum. Clinically, such measurement is useful as an index of the overall pattern of fatty substances in the blood. The normal range of serum cholesterol is about 125 to 265. It tends to rise in later years, and changes can be caused by variations in thyroid activity, diabetes, kidney insufficiency, and stress. Moderation of fat intake, reduction of overweight if obese, and substitution of polyunsaturated fats for some of the "hard" fats in the diet (85), would appear to be prudent measures in the present state of knowledge.

Chondroma. A tumor with the structure of CARTILAGE, usually benign, but with a tendency to recur after removal.

Chorea. A disease of the nervous system manifested by involuntary, irregular, rapid, jerky movements of muscles of the face, legs, and arms. Its common form (also called *St. Vitus' dance* and *Sydenham's chorea*) is a disease of childhood, often a manifestation of rheumatic fever (100). The jerky movements and facial grimaces subside in a few weeks. Signs of rheumatic disease may never appear, but about half of patients with chorea develop or have rheumatic fever. HUNTINGTON'S CHOREA is an entirely different hereditary disease.

Chorion. The outermost of the fetal membranes (352). The fetal part of the placenta develops from it.

Choroid. The middle coat of the eye, continuous with the iris in front; a thin, pigmented layer composed largely of interlaced blood vessels, vital to the eye's nutrition (529).

Christmas disease. An hereditary "bleeder's disease," having the same symptoms as classic hemophilia but resulting from deficiency of a different blood-clotting factor (153). Named for the family in which it was discovered.

Chromosomes. Threadlike bodies in the nucleus of a cell; they contain the GENES and DNA (see HEREDITY). The chromosomes separate during a stage of cell division. Stained and prepared specimens can be studied under a microscope. Normally, a human cell contains 46 chromosomes in 23 pairs. Each parent contributes a chromosome to the pair. One of the pairs contains the sex chromosomes. A mother contributes an X (female-determining) chromosome to the pair. A father contributes *either* an X or a male-determining Y chromosome. If the sex chromosome pair is XX, the child is female; if XY, male. Genes in chromosomes are too small to be seen, but some gross abnormalities of chromosomes can be detected and related to disease or malformations, such as MONGOLISM, KLINEFELTER'S SYNDROME, TURNER'S SYNDROME. Some chromosome "errors" are compatible with life, but some are lethal; as many as one-half of spontaneous abortions are estimated to be due to chromosomal aberrations. Accidents occurring to the egg or sperm or during stages of division of the fertilized egg may produce various abnormalities—too few chromosomes, too many, or wrong reunitings of broken chromosomes. Not all genetic abnormalities can be related to visible gross changes in chromosome specimens, but some of them can. Inspection of chromosomes has been too costly, time-consuming, and cumbersome a process for routine use in hospitals and laboratories. However, newly developed automatic processes employing a programmed computer to count, measure, and tick off intricate structural differences of chromosomes have greatly speeded and simplified the inspection process. (See illustration, page 862).

Chronic. Long continued, persistent, continuous ill health as opposed to *acute* illness.

Chromosomes

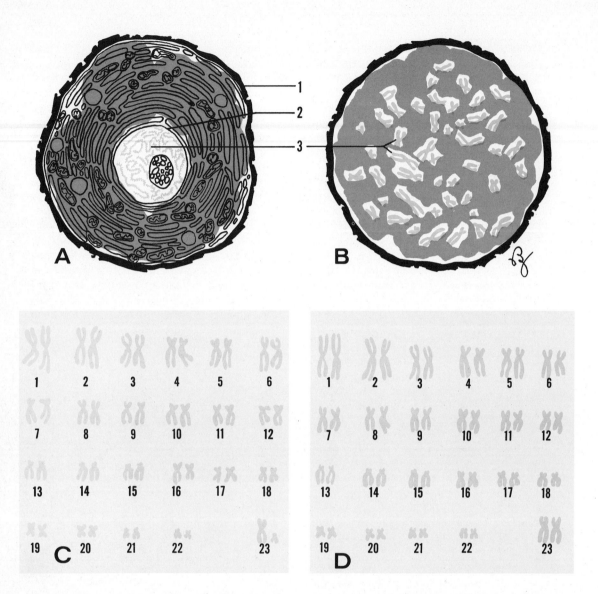

← CHROMOSOMES

Drawings A and B show: 1, cell wall; 2, nucleus; 3, chromosomes. Delicate filaments (A) contract, segment, form "arms" during a stage of cell division (B). The "package" of chromosomes characteristic of a particular organism is called the *karyotype*. The normal karyotype of human beings contains 23 pairs of chromosomes. For purposes of study and systematic identification, researchers usually arrange the pairs according to descending order of size and position of the *centromere*, the constriction between "arms." The 23rd pair of chromosomes determines sex. It contains either a large X chromosome and a small Y chromosome (male) or two X chromosomes (female). Drawings C through F show normal and abnormal human chromosome patterns. (C), normal male karyotype. (D), normal female karyotype. (E), abnormality characteristic of *mongolism*; chromosome 21 is not a normal pair but a triplet (*trisomy*). (F), abnormal chromosome with part of a long arm missing (*Philadelphia chromosome*), found in a high percentage of patients with chronic myelogenous leukemia.

Cilia. Minute hairlike processes of specialized cells which beat rhythmically and keep debris-laden fluids flowing in one direction; for example, out of the lungs. The word also means "eyelashes."

Ciliary body. The part of the eye which suspends the lens and secretes aqueous humor (529).

Circadian rhythms. Cycles and rhythms of body processes that recur approximately every 24 hours; "circadian" means *"about* a day." See BIOLOGIC "CLOCKS."

Circumcision. Removal of the foreskin or prepuce.

Cirrhosis of the liver. Chronic, progressive inflammation of the liver, with increase of non-functioning fibrous tissue, distortion of liver cells, enlargement or shriveling of the organ, and various eventual complications and symptoms such as edema, digestive complaints, weight loss, jaundice, bleeding veins of the esophagus (455).

Cisternal puncture. Puncture of a "cistern" at a point beneath the skull in the back of the neck to withdraw CEREBROSPINAL FLUID.

Claudication. Lameness, limping. *Intermittent claudication,* characterized by cramplike pain in the legs which comes on when walking, may be a symptom of obliterative arterial disease (123).

Clavicle. The collarbone (593).

Clavus. A corn.

Cleft lip, -palate. Congenital malformation of structures of the lip, palate, or both, which fail to fuse properly during fetal development (590). The bilateral parts of the lips and palate fuse at about the eighth week of pregnancy. See TIMETABLE OF FETAL DEVELOPMENT.

Cleft lip and stage in its repair.

Climacteric. The change of life. See MENOPAUSE and MALE CLIMACTERIC.

Clinical. Pertaining to the bedside; by extension, observation and treatment of patients, results and experience thus gained, as opposed to theoretical, laboratory, or experimental medicine.

Clitoris. The small erectile sex organ of the female situated above the vagina (408); homologue of the penis.

Clonorchis. A chronic Asiatic disease caused by liver flukes transmitted by raw, smoked or pickled fish (65).

Clonic. Spasmodic muscular contractions and relaxations which succeed each other alternately and jerkily. It may be combined with *tonic* contractions which are continuous.

Clubbed fingers. Short, broad, bulbous finger ends with overhanging nails. The condition results from local deficiency of oxygenated blood and almost without exception is associated with abnormalities of the heart and respiratory system such as congenital heart malformations, emphysema, bronchiectasis, chronic diseases of the heart and chest.

Clubfoot (*talipes*). A foot twisted out of shape so that the sole does not rest flat on the floor when standing; there are several types (621). Heredity has little if anything to do with the condition. The principal causative factor is thought to be a fixed position of the fetus in the uterus, maintained for a long period of fetal life; scantiness of amniotic fluid possibly inhibits free movement of the fetus. Pressures of long-maintained fixed posture tend to modify the development of body parts in a mechanical way.

Co-arctation of the aorta. Congenital constriction of the great vessel which carries arterial blood from the heart. The constricted area resembles the narrowed section in the casing between two link sausages (715).

Coagulation time. The time it takes a sample of blood to form a clot, determined by laboratory procedures. This information is useful in treating patients with a tendency to hemorrhage, and as a guide to treatment of patients receiving anticoagulants.

Cobalt bomb. In medicine, not really a bomb but a device employing RADIOISOTOPES of cobalt for powerful irradiation of patients.

Coccidioidomycosis. An infectious disease, most prevalent in the southwestern U. S., caused by inhalation of certain fungi (72). The infection may be so mild that no symptoms occur, but a progressive form can be disabling and serious.

Coccus. A sphere-shaped bacterium. Some types, such as those which cause gonorrhea and pneumonia, occur in pairs; other types form chains; still others cluster in irregular masses like a bunch of grapes (34).

Coccyx. The tailbone (595).

Cochlea. A bony pea-sized structure of the inner ear, shaped like a snail shell, lined with fine hairs and nerve endings which are the essential organs of the sense of hearing (561).

Coenzyme. A partner needed by some enzymes to accomplish a biochemical change. Many vitamins are coenzymes.

Coffee-ground vomit. Dark brown or blackish granular vomited material, somewhat resembling coffee grounds; the color comes from changed blood and indicates bleeding in the upper alimentary tract (376).

Coitus. Sexual intercourse.

Colchicine. A drug prepared from roots of the meadow saffron which is remarkably specific in relieving acute attacks of GOUT (632).

Collagen. Fibers of connective tissue which supports the body; it constitutes 40 per cent of the body's protein. In ways not fully understood, it is associated with rheumatic and other diseases collectively called collagen or connective tissue diseases (634). Collagen fibers vary greatly in structure and function. Some, as in the cornea of the eye, are as transparent as water. Collagen is the cushioning material of cartilage in the joints, the matrix on which minerals are laid down to form bones, the inelastic stuff of tendons which transfer muscle movements over joints, the elastic stuff of skin, a part of webs and struts which hold the body together, a substance which when boiled yields glue or gelatin. Once laid down in the body, collagen is not renewed or replaced. "Old" collagen is less elastic than young collagen. It is related to stiffness of joints and leatheriness of skin with increasing age, and may be a fair index of a person's biological rather than chronological age.

Collapsed lung. Pneumothorax (223).

Colles' fracture. A common fracture of the end of the forearm bone (*radius*) near the wrist joint on the thumb side. It is usually a consequence of falling with an arm thrust out and hand bent backward to break the fall.

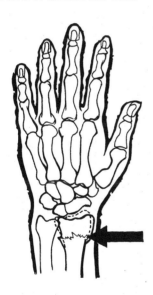

Colles' fracture.

Colloid baths. Soothing baths for excessively dry, sensitive, or itching skin, prepared by adding corn starch, bran, or oatmeal to the bath water (175).

Colloid goiter. Soft, smooth, symmetrical enlargement of the thyroid gland, usually a result of iodine deficiency; "simple goiter" (314).

Colon. The large bowel (437).

Colorado tick fever. Aching, fever, nausea, produced by the bite of a virus-infected woodtick (57). The disease is not limited to Colorado but occurs in all western states where the woodtick is found.

Color blindness. Inability to distinguish colors. There are many types and degrees of color blindness, some so slight that an affected person may never know it. Color blindness does not affect keenness of vision and is no great handicap except in occupations where safety or fine color discrimination is a factor. A color blind man may choose a shirt, necktie, jacket, socks and slacks of violently clashing hues, and think his costume quite sedate, but this does no harm to society and may even win him a good deal of surprised attention. Total color blindness in which everything is seen as shades of gray is extremely rare. The most common type is red-green color blindness, which may range from ability to see only the brightest hues of red and green to inability to see the two colors as other than shades of gray. Injury of the retina or ocular disease may produce color blindness in a person not disposed to it, but this is very rare. Color blindness is almost always inherited; a few women are partially color blind but the condition predominantly affects males. Common red-green color blindness is a sex-linked trait, transmitted to her sons but not her daughters by a mother who herself is not color blind. The inherited defect is in the structure of the CONES, the color-sensitive nerve cells of the retina (532). Nothing can be done to change the defect, although some improvement in discrimination of shades may be attained by training.

Colostomy. A surgically created opening of the colon (artificial anus) in the wall of the abdomen (704). A colostomy may be temporary, to divert intestinal contents while a portion of the colon is healing, or it may be permanent, as is usually the case if a large section of the bowel must be removed because of disease. A *colostomy bag* is a container which covers the artificial opening and receives excretions.

Arrow points to colostomy, outlet through abdomen.

Colostrum. The "first milk" secreted by the mother's breasts shortly after the birth of a child. Colostrum is not "true" milk but a clear or slightly cloudy fluid containing fats and sugars which have a slight laxative effect on the newborn baby. Colostrum also con-

tains IMMUNOGLOBULINS which pass on to the baby some of the immunities acquired by the mother; passive immunity thus transmitted is not long lasting.

Colpotomy. Any surgical cutting of the vagina.

Coma. Unconsciousness so deep that it is impossible or extremely difficult to arouse the patient. Many different conditions are associated with coma: advanced liver and kidney disease, diabetes, poisoning, head blows, tumors, strokes, to mention a few.

Comedo. Blackhead.

Comminuted fracture. One in which the broken bones are crushed into small pieces (626).

Compound fracture. One in which the broken bone breaks through the skin or into an open wound.

Concussion. Violent jarring, shocking, shaking, or the resulting condition. *Concussion of the brain* (790) may result from a fall or violent blow on the head. The injured person may not be "knocked out cold," but may be dizzy, stuporous, nauseated, or he may lose consciousness and have a feeble pulse, cold skin and pallor. Medical help should be sought immediately, even though the person seems to have "recovered" or to be only slightly dazed. A physician treating a concussion may wish to keep the patient under observation, or to make tests, to be sure the skull has not been fractured.

Conduction deafness. Failure of airborne sound waves to be conducted efficiently through and over the external and middle ear structures, so that adequate messages do not reach the nerves of the inner ear (564).

Condyloma. Warty growths on the skin around the anus and external sex organs; usually removed by electrocoagulation (411).

Cones. Specialized cells of the central part of the retina which distinguish colors and are responsible for finely detailed seeing (532).

Congenital malformations. Abnormalities that are present at birth. See BIRTH DEFECTS.

Conization. Reaming out of a cone-shaped piece of tissue by high-frequency current; usually a gynecologic procedure performed on a diseased cervix (709).

Conjunctiva. A thin mucous membrane which covers the insides of the eyelids and is reflected over the front of the eye (544). *Conjunctivitis* is an inflammation of this tissue resulting from infection, allergies, irritation, or inflammation from within the eye itself.

Consanguinity. Blood relationship.

Contact dermatitis. Skin eruption, redness, inflammation, resulting from contact with any of hundreds of commonplace substances in the world around us (175, 655).

Contact lenses. Plastic lenses worn invisibly over the cornea of the eye (539). Meticulous fitting to eye contours is essential. The lenses must have proper sanitary care. Serious complications are rare, minor ones not uncommon. The most painful complication appears to result from wearing the lenses too long. They should not be worn while sleeping, or when the eye is infected, or when there are cold sores on the face (the cold sore virus can infect the eyes dangerously). Flush-fitting contact lenses which cover the white of the eye permit a thin layer of tears to circulate beneath them and have special medical uses as healing aids. Such lenses improve the healing of chemical burns of the cornea, ulcerations, corneal transplants and other conditions. Plastics which are hard when dry but absorb as much as 60 per cent of their weight of water and become soft when placed

on the eye are being experimented with in a search for better materials for contact lenses.

Contraception. Prevention of conception or impregnation (331). See ORAL CONTRACEPTIVES, INTRAUTERINE DEVICES, VASECTOMY, TUBAL LIGATION.

Contrast medium. A substance which has greater density to x-rays than tissues which are objects of study. Contrast media are given by injection or other means to obtain clearly outlined x-ray or fluoroscopic images of structures being examined.

Contusion. A bruise (798). An experienced mother's prescription for the best treatment of trivial contusions of childhood is, "kiss them."

Cool enema. An enema of cool water with a small amount of baking soda, useful in reducing fever (373).

Cooley's anemia (*thallassemia*). A congenital form of anemia which occurs primarily in people bordering on the Mediterranean Sea or their descendants (149).

Coombs' test. An antibody test on blood, used in determining the compatibility of bloods for transfusion and in diagnosis of certain anemias.

Cor pulmonale. A form of heart disease secondary to chronic disease of the lungs.

Cornea. The curved, transparent tissue over the iris and pupil on the outside of the eye; the "window" of the eye (529).

Corneal transplant. The cornea (529) may become scarred or clouded, obstructing vision as if a curtain were pulled down. If the rest of the eye is in good condition, sight may be restored by transplanting a disk taken from the cornea of a recently deceased person. It is like replacing an opaque pane of glass with a clear, transparent one. The procedure requires a supply of donor eyes, and "eye banks" have been established in many cities to receive and preserve donated eyes, which must be removed promptly after death of the donor. It is futile to donate one's eyes in a will, because of legal delays. Anyone wishing to donate his eyes after death should do so through his physician or an eye bank.

Corns. Horny skin thickenings about the size of peas which occur principally on or between the toes. "Soft corns" between the toes are softened by sweat. The common hard corn has a cone-shaped core which presses on nerves to cause dull discomfort or sharp pain. Corns are caused by continued pressure and friction, as from too tight or ill-fitting shoes and stockings. Pressure can be lessened by wearing softer shoes with ample toe-room and by foam rubber pads and inserts. The hard tissue of a corn usually must be removed occasionally for comfort's sake. Soaking the feet in hot water and paring the surface of the corn with a razor blade often relieves friction and pressure, but there is risk of cuts and infection. Superficial hard tissue may be removed with an emery board, nail file, or pumice stone. The core may be sufficiently loosened by soaking to be lifted out by sterilized tweezers. Corn plasters and medicines usually contain salicylic acid which softens the hard growth. Diabetics should be especially circumspect in care of the feet because of the risk of gangrene (339).

Coronary thrombosis. Commonly called a "heart attack"; a blood clot in coronary arteries that nourish the heart muscle (84, 89).

Corpuscle. Any small round body; the word used to be a synonym for "cell." Technically, a cell has a nucleus; the mature red blood cell does not, and is sometimes called a corpuscle.

Corpus luteum. The "yellow body" which develops from a follicle of the

ovary after a ripened egg has been discharged. The yellow body produces progesterone, a hormone which prepares the lining of the uterus to receive a fertilized egg (327). If fertilization occurs, the corpus luteum enlarges and continues to produce pregnancy-sustaining hormone for several months. If conception does not occur, the corpus luteum shrinks and degenerates.

Cortex. The surface layer of an organ such as the brain, kidney, adrenal gland. The cortex of an organ has different functions from its inner part (medulla); for example, the adrenal cortex produces hormones entirely different from those of its inner part. The thin surface layer of the brain (*cortex cerebri*) consists of gray matter, largely composed of small-bodied nerve cells with rich interconnections, interspersed with larger neurons which send AXONS into underlying white matter.

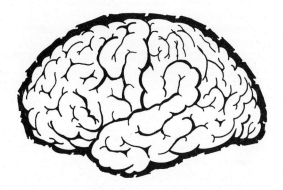

Cortex of the brain.

Corticosteroids. Substances having the properties of hormones secreted by the cortex of the adrenal glands (318). Cortisone, hydrocortisone, prednisone, and many other corticosteroids have important medical uses.

Coryza. An old word for the common cold.

Cosmetic dermatitis. Inflammation of the skin, usually allergic, produced by contact with cosmetic creams, dyes, lotions, perfumes and the like (179).

Cowper's glands. Two small glands of the male which secrete lubricating fluids into the urethra (290).

Cowpox. A disease of cattle so closely related to smallpox, but insignificantly mild in man, that inoculation with vaccine containing cowpox virus has long been the standard method of immunizing against smallpox.

Coxsackie viruses. A family of viruses named for a community in New York whose ill townsfolk furnished excretions from which the viruses were first isolated and identified. A score or more of different Coxsackie viruses cause diseases such as HERPANGINA, DEVIL'S GRIP, and forms of *meningitis* (58).

"Crabs." Infestation by pubic lice (191).

Cradle cap. Patchy areas of greasy crusts on an infant's scalp, arising from secretions of oil glands (386).

Cranial nerve. A nerve attached directly to the brain, leaving it through a perforation in the skull. There are 12 pairs of cranial nerves, with names that suggest their function or location: transmission of the sense of smell (*olfactory*), sight (*optic*), hearing (*acoustic*); control of movement —of the eyeball (*trochlear*), a muscle of the eyeball (*abducens*), the pupil (*oculomotor*), muscles of the upper throat and taste sensations from the back of the tongue (*glossopharyngeal*), sense of taste, salivary glands and muscles of the face (*facial*), muscles of the larynx and throat (*accessory*), the tongue (*hypoglossal*); sensory nerve of the face and front part of the scalp (*trigeminal*); "wandering" sensory and motor nerve branching to the heart, stomach and esophagus (*vagus*).

Craniotomy. Surgical opening into the skull cavity (731).

Cranium. The skull; the brain-containing part.

Creeping eruption (*larva migrans*). An odd parasitic infection of the skin: thin, red, tortuous lines creep ahead at one end an inch or more a day while fading at the other end. The moving lines mark the progress of larvae burrowing under the skin. The burrowers, often immature forms of cat or dog hookworm, get into people who go barefoot at beaches, children in sandboxes, gardeners, repairmen who work under porches or houses. Freezing the larvae in the skin with an ethyl chloride spray usually stops their migrations cold.

Creeping ulcer. One which creeps slowly outward from its center.

Cremaster. The muscle which retracts the testicle.

Cretin. A child born with impaired function of the thyroid gland (312).

Cross-eye. Eyes that do not work as a team in holding the gaze straight upon an object, because of imbalance of muscles that control movements of the eyeballs (542). An eye that turns in or out in young children may lose its vision completely unless the condition is corrected before it is too late.

Crohn's disease. See REGIONAL ILEITIS.

Croup. Difficult, laborious, raspy breathing and barky coughing of a child. *Spasmodic croup* is more frightening than serious; another type, *laryngotracheobronchitis*, is one of the most serious conditions of infancy and constitutes a medical emergency (386).

Croup tent. An arrangement that confines vapors for inhalation by an infant with croup (29).

Crowning. The stage in childbirth when the crown or top of the infant's head first becomes visible, as wrinkled scalp in the dilated outlet of the womb.

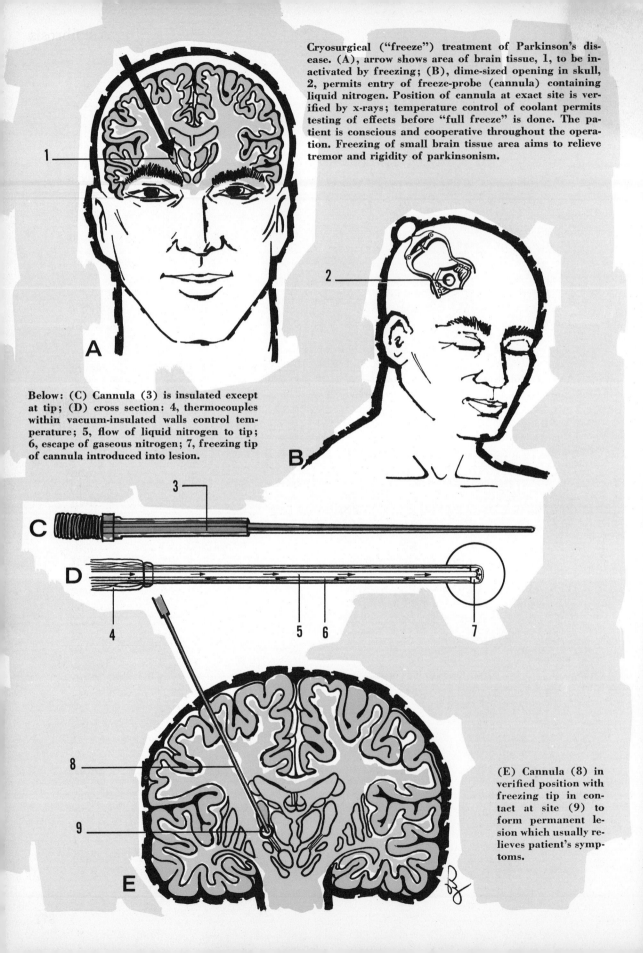

Cryosurgical ("freeze") treatment of Parkinson's disease. (A), arrow shows area of brain tissue, 1, to be inactivated by freezing; (B), dime-sized opening in skull, 2, permits entry of freeze-probe (cannula) containing liquid nitrogen. Position of cannula at exact site is verified by x-rays; temperature control of coolant permits testing of effects before "full freeze" is done. The patient is conscious and cooperative throughout the operation. Freezing of small brain tissue area aims to relieve tremor and rigidity of parkinsonism.

Below: (C) Cannula (3) is insulated except at tip; (D) cross section: 4, thermocouples within vacuum-insulated walls control temperature; 5, flow of liquid nitrogen to tip; 6, escape of gaseous nitrogen; 7, freezing tip of cannula introduced into lesion.

(E) Cannula (8) in verified position with freezing tip in contact at site (9) to form permanent lesion which usually relieves patient's symptoms.

Cryosurgery. Use of extreme cold to destroy or to freeze and later revive tissues. Instruments which apply extreme cold quite precisely to tissues are usually supercooled by liquid nitrogen. Pioneering cryosurgical work was done in the field of brain surgery, especially in surgical management of *Parkinson's disease* (249). Complete destruction of tissue by super-freezing has been used to relieve benign or malignant obstruction of the *prostate* gland (295). The "freeze treatment" for *gastric ulcer* does not permanently destroy stomach tissue, but tends to decrease acid production; long term benefits are considered disappointing by many specialists. A newer application of cryosurgery (more exactly, cryotherapy, since tissue is not destroyed) is in treatment of *glaucoma* (547). The purpose is to decrease production of fluid in the eye. Cryotherapy is a reserve method if drugs or surgery fail to stop the advance of glaucoma.

Cryosurgical treatment of Parkinson's disease was pioneered by Dr. Irving S. Cooper of St. Barnabas Hospital, New York; see illustration at left.

Crypt. A cavity, pit, or follicle; as, the natural depressions in the tonsils.

Cryptorchidism. Failure of the testicles to descend into the scrotum during fetal development; the undescended organs remain in the abdominal cavity or groin (299, 325).

Curettage. Scraping out of a body cavity with a spoon-shaped instrument called a *curet*.

Curling's ulcer. An ulcer of the stomach or duodenum associated with severe and extensive skin burns.

Cushing's disease, -syndrome. Disorders resulting from excessive output of certain adrenal gland hormones (320).

Cuspid. A canine tooth (500).

Cuticle. The horny outer layer of skin; popularly, the skin surrounding the nails, notoriously the site of "hangnails."

Cyanosis. A bluish tinge of the skin and mucous membranes resulting from insufficient oxygen in the blood. There are many different causes; for example, congenital heart defects (93), congestive heart failure, emphysema, mountain sickness, respiratory and blood disorders.

Cyesis. Pregnancy.

Cyst. A normal or abnormal sac with a definite wall, containing liquid or semisolid material.

Cystic fibrosis. An inherited disease of the *exocrine* glands which pour secretions into or out of the body rather than into the blood; for example, pancreas, biliary, intestinal and sweat glands. Thick, viscid secretions obstruct or depress the functioning of many different organs and tissues and produce a great variety of symptoms; respiratory distress is prominent (387). Cystic fibrosis was "discovered" in 1938, at which time it was thought to be a disease of the pancreas gland; it is now known that nearly all of the exocrine glands are affected to some degree. The earliest symptom of cystic fibrosis in a newborn infant is MECONIUM ILEUS. Prompt recognition and treatment of cystic fibrosis, with aerosol aids to breathing, postural drainage, digestive enzymes, antibiotics to combat infection, have carried affected infants through critical periods of childhood. The disease is being increasingly recognized in adults who have had it from infancy without knowing it. Specialists think it likely that many patients treated for BRONCHIAL ASTHMA or various chronic lung conditions actually have cystic fibrosis. The disease is transmitted as a recessive trait (the mother and father are carriers but do not have the disease themselves). An abnormal protein in the blood serum of cystic fibrosis patients and of blood-related persons is the possible basis for a test to detect carriers of the trait; if two carriers marry, the chance that each of their children will have cystic fibrosis is one in four.

Cystic kidney. A congenital condition in which the kidneys are filled with bubble-like cysts (278).

Cysticercosis. Infestation of the body with a form of tapeworm, sometimes present in raw beef. Beef should be cooked at least to the rare stage (140 degrees F.) to avoid danger.

Cystinuria. An inherited disease in which cystine, a sulfur-containing amino acid, is excreted in large quantities in the urine. The poorly soluble cystine tends to form recurrent kidney stones (275); alkalinizing the urine and drinking large amounts of water may help to reduce the likelihood of cystine stone formation.

Cystocele. Sagging of the base of the bladder into the vaginal canal (416).

Cystoscope. An instrument for examining the interior of the urinary bladder (276).

Cytology. Scientific study of the structure, elements, and functions of cells.

Cytologic diagnosis. Microscopic study of cells shed by body tissues to detect abnormalities; especially, the presence of cancer cells. The "PAP TEST" for detection of cancer of the cervix is the most widely used cytologic screening test (418), but the technique is applicable to "smears" obtained from the lungs, stomach, bladder and other organs.

Cytoplasm. The substance of a cell outside of its nucleus. Transformations of energy, synthesis of proteins, and uncountable chemical exchanges that keep us alive go on incessantly in the cytoplasm.

D

Dander. Minute skin particles shed by animals. Inhalation of danders is a frequent cause of allergic reactions, the reason why cats make some people weep and sneeze (653).

Dandruff. Fine, whitish, somewhat greasy scales formed upon the scalp (178); the condition is controllable but rarely curable.

Deaf-mutism. Inability to hear and speak. The two disabilities are interrelated. A totally deaf child cannot learn to speak in the normal way because he cannot hear sounds to imitate. Various signs may arouse suspicion of deafness in an infant as young as six months (567). While the child is still young, he can be taught "unnaturally" to speak, by difficult training techniques used in special schools for the deaf.

D & C. Dilation and curettage, a common minor operation on women; the canal of the uterus is dilated and the lining of the uterus scraped with a spoon-shaped instrument called a curet (708).

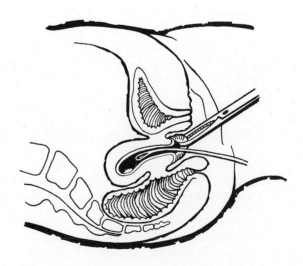

Dilation and curettage.

Debridement. Surgical cleaning of a wound; removal of foreign material and devitalized tissue.

Decalcification. The withdrawal of calcium from the bones where it has been deposited. It may be caused by an inadequate supply of calcium in the diet so that calcium has to be taken from the bones, or it may be caused by hormonal imbalances.

Decibel. The unit of measurement of the loudness of sound, used in tests of hearing (566). A whisper is about "20 decibels loud."

Decidua. That part of the lining of the uterus which is modified during pregnancy and cast off after delivery.

Deciduous teeth. Baby teeth; the teeth which are shed when the permanent teeth erupt.

Decubitus ulcer. A bedsore (26).

Defecation. Passage of feces; evacuation of the bowels.

Deficiency diseases. Those caused by insufficiency of some constituent of the diet, such as vitamins, minerals, protein, fatty acids (479).

Deglutition. The act of swallowing.

Dehiscence. A splitting open, as of a sutured wound that "comes apart at the seams."

Dehydration. Drying out of the body; loss of more water than is taken in. Dehydration may be induced for medical reasons, but often it is an aspect of disease or injury, characterized by dry mucous membranes, fever, scanty urine, tight abdominal skin, possible shock. Treatment, which may present an emergency, requires recognition of underlying circumstances, calculation of water and ELECTROLYTE deficits, and usually replacement of water and salts (sometimes of plasma or blood) by infusion into a vein.

Déjà vu. "Already seen"; an illusion that a present experience has occurred before.

Delirium. A state of mental confusion, excitement, incoherent talk, restlessness, hallucinations. Delirium may be associated with high fever, poisoning, drug intoxication, infections, and metabolic disturbances. Treatment is directed to the underlying condition while the patient is kept in a quiet room, closely watched to prevent injury. Calming medications may be prescribed. Reassurances by a close member of the family help to allay fears.

Delirium tremens (*D.T.'s*). A serious, sometimes fatal form of delirium, most often occurring in persons with a long history of alcoholism, but occasionally associated with other poisonings of the brain cells, senile brain changes, and psychoses. The patient has vivid visual hallucinations, often of moving colored animals—he may actually "see" pink elephants—but the hallucinated creatures may be very tiny and frequently he feels as well as sees them crawling over his skin. Anxiety, fear, coarse trembling of the hands, mental confusion, and sleeplessness are other manifestations. Physical restraints may be necessary but skilful attendants can often avoid this. The delirium lasts for a couple of days to a week or more and usually terminates in profound sleep. The patient is often malnourished and run down physically. Appropriate calming medication and large doses of B vitamins are commonly a part of treatment. KORSAKOFF'S PSYCHOSIS may begin as delirium tremens.

Deltoid. Triangular in shape, like the Greek letter *delta;* specifically, the muscle which covers the shoulder joint and extends the arm out from the side.

Dementia. A general term for mental deterioration, usually implying serious impairment of intellect, irrationality, confusion, stupor, "insane" behavior.

Dementia may result from poisons, physical changes in the brain, toxins produced by disease, or psychoses of which the basic cause is unknown.

Dendrites. Fine, branched fibers, somewhat in the pattern of tree roots, which accept and convey incoming impulses to the central body of a nerve cell (232).

Dengue fever. See BREAKBONE FEVER.

Dentalgia. A superfluous word for toothache.

Dental implants. Replacement of lost teeth, as by re-implantation of a knocked-out tooth (524). The space left by extraction of a decayed molar of a young person may sometimes be filled successfully by transplantation of one of the patient's own immature wisdom teeth. The root of the wisdom tooth does not mature until late adolescence and if it is transplanted before age 18 it may anchor itself permanently in its new position.

Dental plaque. A thin, transparent film that builds up on the teeth. It is made up of material from saliva. The plaques contain bacteria which are thought to be a factor in tooth decay.

Dentin. The ivory-like material, harder and denser than bone, which underlies the enamel of the teeth (498).

Denture. The set of natural teeth; also, a set of artificial teeth; "plates," "false teeth" (515).

Denture stomatitis. Sore mouth due to ill-fitting dentures or allergy to substances in the plates (664).

Depilation. Removal of hair. Permanent removal of unwanted hair is best accomplished by ELECTROLYSIS, which inactivates the follicle so the hair does not grow again.

DeQuervain's disease (*stenosing tenovaginitis*). Thickening of sheaths covering tendons of the thumb, resulting in pain at the base of the thumb radiating to the nail and into the forearm (610).

Depot desensitization. A "one shot" technique for desensitization to allergies, using oily emulsions (679).

Dercum's disease (*adiposis dolorosa*). A rare disease of middle-aged and older women. Firm fat nodules, slightly sensitive or exquisitely painful, are distributed over various parts of the body except the face, lower arms and lower legs; overlying skin is red and shiny. There is pronounced muscular weakness and degrees of psychic disturbance. The cause is not known. Non-specific methods of treatment include measures to relieve pain, reduce weight, and combat psychic disturbances.

Dermabrasion. A method of removing layers of skin with an abrasive instrument, usually a rapidly rotating wire brush, for cosmetic improvement of scars or blemishes (173).

Dermatitis. Inflammation of the skin; often called eczema (175). Its causes are manifold, its symptoms varied. Chemicals, plants, common household agents, cosmetics, drugs, x-rays, and almost numberless things can produce a dermatitis; allergies are often involved.

Dermatoglyphics. The study of ridges, whorls, lines and creases which form highly individual patterns of the skin of hands and feet. Readers of detective stories know all about fingerprints for identification; medical uses are new and different. Skin patterns determined by GENES begin to form in the fetus at about the fourth month of pregnancy. Several abnormal patterns, such as a single crease instead of the usual two which run across the top of the palm, are characteristic of infants with congenital diseases. Some disorders such as MONGOLISM and KLINEFELTER'S SYNDROME result from abnormal CHROMOSOMES. Others, such as malformations associated with the mother's infection by German measles, result from unfavorable environment of the fetus at the time when skin patterns as well as organ systems are developing. It is not yet possible to identify specific diseases by abnormal palmprints, but they usually indicate some congenital abnormality. Palmprint studies may give early warning of a congenital disorder, or confirm some suspected condition, such as mongolism, without the need of analyzing chromosomes.

Dermatome. An instrument for cutting thin layers of skin for grafts.

Dermatomyositis. An ill-defined disease of unknown cause, affecting connective tissue structures, manifested principally in the skin and voluntary muscles; characterized by pain and swelling in muscles, weakness, inflammation and swelling of skin of the face, upper trunk, and extremities (641).

Dermatophytes. Fungi which produce blistery, scaly, crusty lesions of the skin; most notoriously, those responsible for *dermatophytosis* or "athlete's foot" (190).

Dermis. The "true skin"; the *corium;* a dense, elastic layer of fibrous tissue underlying the topmost epithelial layers (167).

Dermoid cyst. A congenital cyst (often of the ovary) which contains fragments of skin appendages such as strands of hair, sweat and oil glands, and sometimes cartilage, bone, and teeth.

Dermographia. "Skin writing"; a condition in which a tracing made on the skin by a fingernail or blunt instrument produces a pale streak bordered on each side by a reddened line. The marks disappear after a few minutes. The condition may be associated with URTICARIA but in itself is not injurious to health. Dermographia occurs in persons whose mechanisms for expanding and constricting blood vessels are hypersensitive to any irritation.

Desensitization. Reduction of a person's allergic reaction to a specific substance such as pollen or house dust. Sensitivity is reduced by spaced injections of small amounts of extracts of specific allergens; "hay fever shots" are a familiar example (679).

Desquamation. Shedding of the skin in scales or sheets, as after scarlet fever or severe sunburn.

Detached retina. Separation of the light-receiving layer of the back of the eye from its underlying layer (553-54). In the majority of cases, the detached filmy structure can be "spot-welded" into its proper place by various surgical procedures.

Deviated septum. Diversion from a straight line of the wall that divides the nose into two equal parts, usually a result of injury but sometimes congenital (586). The deformity may not be obvious from the outside. Depending on its nature, a deviated septum may partially obstruct air passages, deflect air currents, and lead to mouth-breathing and excessive postnasal drip.

Devil's grip (*Bornholm disease, epidemic pleurodynia*). An infectious disease of sudden onset, produced by COXSACKIE VIRUSES, marked by knifelike pains in the chest or abdomen (58).

Devil's pinches (*purpura simplex*). Bruises or black-and-blue spots caused by bleeding under the skin without apparent cause. The purplish spots range from pinhead size to rather large patches. The condition, which seems to "run in families," seems to be harmless and there is no effective treatment.

Dextrocardia. Congenital transposition of the axis of the heart toward the right side of the chest.

Dextrose (*glucose*). A sugar, often called "blood sugar," since it is an essential constituent of blood, a source of energy, and necessary for combustion of fats. The liver converts dextrose into *glycogen* ("animal starch") and stores it. This reservoir is drawn upon for dextrose, reconverted from glycogen, as energy needs of the body require. Dextrose solutions are often infused into the veins of patients.

Dhobie itch. See JOCKEY ITCH.

Diabetes. The word comes from a Greek term for "syphon," "to flow through," referring to excessive flow of urine and excessive thirst. Used alone, diabetes means *diabetes mellitus* or "sugar diabetes" (333). There are other forms of diabetes, such as *diabetes insipidus* (309), a hormone imbalance causing enormous thirst and compensating urinary outflow, and *bronze diabetes*, associated with HEMOCHROMATOSIS.

Diagnosis. The art and science of identifying a patient's disease, a prerequisite to treatment; fraught with hazard if applied by the untrained in reckless self-diagnosis. Some diagnostic tools are as old as Hippocrates: the patient's history, symptoms, physical signs; thumping and listening, feeling, inspecting, applying all the trained senses. Modern tools project the perceptions of physicians into occult chemical and electrical processes of the body. Instruments amplify and transcribe minute currents of the heart and brain and muscles; "scopes" of many kinds carry educated eyes into caverns of the body; a film of tissue yields secrets to a pathologist; x-rays probe hidden structures; scores of complex tests give clues to what is going on in the infinitesimal world of the body's molecules. The diagnostician gains all possible and necessary information, interprets it, often arrives at a firm diagnosis, but sometimes can only make a tentative diagnosis subject to change by later information and developments.

Dialysis. Separation of substances in solution by passing them through a porous membrane; this is done naturally by the kidney and mechanically by an artificial kidney (283).

Diaper rash. An ammonia burn resulting from breakdown of urine (389).

Diaphragm. The transverse, dome-shaped muscle which separates the chest from the abdomen; the chief muscle of breathing (204). Contraction of the diaphragm expands the chest cage and lungs and air rushes in; relaxation allows the chest cage and lungs to collapse partially, and air is exhaled. A *vaginal diaphragm* is a ringed latex cup which covers the cervix for contraceptive purposes.

Diaphragmatic hernia (*hiatus hernia*). Protrusion of part of the stomach through a weak spot in the DIAPHRAGM (446, 696).

Diarrhea. Abnormal frequency and liquidity of stools (376, 466). In young infants, profuse diarrhea (and vomiting) can cause serious loss of fluids and ELECTROLYTES and the baby should be under care of a physician.

Diastole. The "resting" stage of the heart during which relaxed chambers are filling with blood (76). Diastolic pressure is the lower of the two figures (such as 120/80) by which doctors express blood pressure readings (see SYSTOLE). Diastolic pressure gives the doctor significant information about the condition of blood vessels and the injurious effects of sustained hypertension (110).

Diathermy. Generation of heat in body tissues by passing high-frequency electric currents through them. Resistance of tissues—like the resistance element in an electric toaster—produces the heat, which is very penetrating and can build up to dangerous intensity unless treatment is supervised by an experienced operator. In surgical diathermy, heat is sufficient to destroy tissues or to cut tissues with little or no bleeding.

Diathesis. Inborn, constitutional susceptibility to a certain disease or condition.

Digitalis. A drug derived from the foxglove plant which is a powerful stimulant of heart muscle contractions. "Whole" digitalis contains a number of active agents called *glucosides;* some of these, such as *digitoxin,* are prepared pharmaceutically in pure form. *Digitalization* is the procedure of administering digitalis until a desired concentration of the drug is built up in the patient's body, after which maintenance doses suffice. The toxic effect of digitalis is close to the therapeutic effect and expert medical supervision of dosage is necessary.

Diopter. The unit of measurement of the refractive (light-bending) power of a lens, including the lens of the human eye, which has a power of about 10 diopters. Abbreviated as "D" in prescriptions for glasses; +D (plus D) indicates a convex lens for a farsighted person, —D (minus D) a concave lens for a nearsighted person (538).

Diphtheria. An acute contagious disease, once responsible for many deaths of children, but no longer a threat to the child who is properly immunized (398).

Diplegia. Paralysis of like parts on both sides of the body.

Diplopia. "Seeing double"; one object is seen as two. The condition may be temporary or persistent and can be caused by a number of diseases and disorders, including head injuries, alcoholism, and poisoning. The double vision effect is the result of paralysis or improper functioning of muscles that control eyeball movements, or paralysis of one of the nerves controlling action of the eye muscles. Persistent double vision may be the result of a nervous system ailment such as multiple sclerosis, myasthenia gravis, meningitis, tabes dorsalis, or a brain tumor affecting nerves running between the brain and eye muscles. Treatment of persistent diplopia may require surgery, the use of special corrective lenses, or both.

Dipsomania. Compulsion to drink alcoholic beverages to excess.

Dislocation. Displacement of a bone from its normal position in a joint, usually the result of a severe blow, fall, or twisting force; often there is an accompanying sprain (625, 801).

Diuretic. An agent which increases the output of urine; especially, a drug prescribed for this purpose. Along with other treatment, physicians prescribe diuretics for a variety of conditions associated with excessive retention of water; for example, congestive heart failure (98); hypertension (114); premenstrual tension (332); toxemia of pregnancy (356); cirrhosis of the liver (456).

Diverticula. Small pouches like thinwalled balloons opening from a hollow organ. They can occur anywhere along the alimentary tract from the esophagus to the terminus, but the most common site is the colon (466). A person with these superfluous little pockets has *diverticulosis* but may never know it; they may not cause symptoms. It is estimated that 10 per cent of people over 40 years of age have diverticulosis. Chances that existing pockets may become infected, inflamed, or ruptured, resulting in *diverticulitis,* increase with advancing age. Diverticulitis is sometimes called "left-sided appendicitis" because the patient's symptoms are quite similar to those of appendicitis except for reversal of position. Many patients with diverticulitis are well controlled with medical measures. A soft diet with cooked fruits and vegetables and avoidance of irritating foodstuffs such as coarse fibers and seeds is often prescribed to lessen the risk of flareups. Sometimes surgery is necessary to remove a diseased portion of the bowel (702).

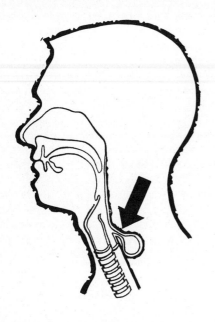

Diverticulum of the esophagus.

Dizygotic. Developed at the same time from two fertilized eggs; fraternal twins (358).

Dizziness. A whirling, head-swimming feeling of unsteadiness and of the world revolving about one (257). The disturbance may be primarily in the inner ear (574A), in nerves serving this area, in reduced blood supply to the brain, in nervous messages from the heart, eyes, or stomach, or in association with many other conditions. An ordinary mild bout of dizziness can usually be abated by sitting or lying down. Dizziness is not always or often a symptom of serious disease but recurrent attacks should be investigated.

DMSO. Dimethyl sulfoxide. A solvent which can penetrate intact skin and carry drugs or chemicals with it. This unique property may prove useful in administering drugs, relieving pain, easing arthritis, but the substance is still under experimental investigation.

Dominant eye. The eye unconsciously preferred in visual tasks such as sighting a rifle (see test, 528).

Dorsum. The back; any part of the body corresponding to the back, as the back of the hand.

Double-blind study. A technique most often used in studying the effects of drugs. Neither the administering physician nor the patient knows whether a given medicine contains an active drug or totally inert ingredients. Presumably this eliminates unconscious bias in knowing that a drug "should" or "should not" have some effect.

Double vision. See DIPLOPIA.

Douche. A stream of water directed against or into a part of the body; used alone, the word usually means *vaginal douche* (410).

Down's syndrome. MONGOLISM.

DPT. Vaccine combining immunizing agents against *diphtheria, pertussis* (whooping cough), and *tetanus*, administered in a single injection instead of separate injections for each disease.

Draining ear. Chronic discharge from an ear, a warning that serious infection may erupt at any time (571).

Dreams. See SLEEP.

Dropsy. An old term for EDEMA.

Dry labor. See BAG OF WATERS.

Dry socket. Failure of a protective blood clot to develop in the socket left after extraction of a tooth, or premature loss of a clot, causing pain and delay in healing (518).

Drug addiction. Certain drugs (including alcohol) have an effect on body cells, particularly those of the nervous system, called *tissue tolerance*. Body chemistry is upset and the cells adjust

1

their metabolism to accommodate the drug. The tissues become physically dependent upon the drug to maintain their normal functions.

Over a period of time, increasingly large doses of the drug are necessary to obtain the same original effect and the body, in turn, constantly alters its chemistry to accommodate the larger doses. Eventually the addict is able to tolerate doses of drugs which would be fatal to a non-addict. When an addict suddenly stops using drugs, he experiences severe WITHDRAWAL SYMPTOMS because of physical dependency; he also has psychological dependency. Because "addiction" and "habituation" are often used interchangeably, the World Health Organization has adopted a more general term, "drug dependence," to banish confusion. Dependence is defined as "a state arising from repeated administration of a drug on a periodic or continuous basis." This is subdivided into "dependence of the morphine type," "cocaine type," "barbiturate type," "marihuana type," "amphetamine type," and "alcohol type," applying to all types of drug abuse.

Physical dependence, independent of psychological dependence, is demonstrated by babies who are "born drug addicts." These unfortunate infants receive morphine or heroin before birth from the blood of a mother who uses the drugs. About 24 hours after birth the baby becomes extremely agitated, yawns frequently, perspires profusely and crawls around the crib as though in pain. His skin becomes flushed, his cry high-pitched, and he may develop tremors, convulsion, and death unless withdrawal symptoms are recognized and treated as in an adult by decreasing doses of the drug until he is "weaned" from it.

Dry ice. Frozen carbon dioxide or "dry ice" gives off carbon dioxide gas when it sublimes (passes from a solid to a gaseous state without going through a liquid phase). Carbon dioxide gas is not directly poisonous—we exhale it constantly—but in heavy concentra-

tions it can displace oxygen and cause unconsciousness or asphyxiation. This never happens with ordinary amounts of dry ice used to pack a gallon or so of ice cream, but it can occur if a large quantity of dry ice is kept in an occupied confined space without ventilation. Some motorists use dry ice to keep a car cool while driving with windows closed in hot weather. Several accidents have resulted from drivers being made unconscious by this practice. The National Safety Council reports that a 10 per cent concentration of carbon dioxide is sufficient to cause unconsciousness.

Ductus arteriosus. In the fetus, a channel which short-circuits blood from the pulmonary artery to the aorta; normally it closes and ceases to function at birth (95). In certain "blue babies," the channel fails to close.

Duodenum. The first part of the small intestine; a tubular organ shaped like a horseshoe (433). Here, just beyond the acid stomach, the intestinal environment begins to become alkaline. Highly alkaline bile and digestive juices of the pancreas flow into the duodenum in the general area of its horseshoe bend. *Duodenal ulcer* is the most common type of peptic ulcer (453, 494).

Dupuytren's contracture. Thickening of connective tissue (FASCIA) of the palm of the hand, pulling one or more fingers down into the palm (612).

Dumping syndrome. Symptoms of bloating, diarrhea, vomiting, distress, occurring soon after eating in persons whose stomachs have been partially removed (452).

Dura mater. The outermost membrane of tough connective tissue which covers the brain and spinal cord (253).

D.V.M. Doctor of Veterinary Medicine.

Dyscrasia. Abnormal state, especially of the blood.

Dysentery. Inflammation of the colon with severe diarrhea, abdominal cramps, painful and ineffectual rectal straining; the stools may contain blood and mucus. Chemical poisons and various irritants of the bowel can cause dysentery, but there are two major forms of the disorder: BACILLARY DYSENTERY produced by certain bacteria (45) and AMEBIC DYSENTERY produced by protozoa (69).

Dysfunction. Abnormality or impairment of the normal activities of an organ or bodily process.

Dyslexia. Inability to read efficiently. The child may have simple incapacity to learn, but about 90 per cent of "retarded readers" are children of normal or superior intelligence. The reading difficulty is secondary to emotional, physical, or educational factors. Remedial reading measures are usually successful in this group of children when the specific cause is found and remedied. About one out of ten "reading problem" children has an eye muscle imbalance (542) detectable by an ophthalmologist. Many children with eye muscle imbalances do not have a reading problem; they use their "good" eye and function as one-eyed persons. But some of these children evidently work hard to "fight" eye muscle imbalance and achieve binocular vision; their effort to control the defect is thought to create reading difficulties. In this special group of children, some of whom have been labelled mentally retarded, have failed one or more years of school, and whose reading has not been improved by various forms of training, surgery to correct the eye muscle imbalance has produced prompt improvement in reading skills and comfort. Eye muscle surgery is not recommended as a cure-all for all children with reading problems, but is advised when a muscle imbalance, no matter how small, can be elicited, and when no other factor exists.

Dyslogia. Impairment of speech.

Dysmenorrhea. Difficult, painful menstruation (409). For helpful exercises, see PAINFUL MENSTRUATION.

Dyspareunia. Painful or difficult sexual intercourse; the cause may be physical, psychic, or both.

Dyspepsia. Disturbed digestion; indigestion. There are several disorders (see MALABSORPTION SYNDROME) in which foods are inadequately digested or assimilated. But the terms "dyspepsia" and "indigestion" are often rather casually applied to symptoms which do not arise primarily from incomplete digestion of food but which originate, or seem to, in the alimentary canal or organs adjacent thereto. Inaccurate use of the word does no harm if it sends one to a physician to find out what the trouble is.

Dyspnea. Difficult breathing, distress, often associated with heart or lung disease.

Dystocia. Painful or difficult labor or birth.

Dystrophy. Degeneration, wasting, abnormal development.

Dysuria. Difficult or painful urination.

E

Eaton pneumonia. A form of atypical pneumonia. See PNEUMONIA.

Ecchymosis. Bleeding into the skin and discoloration of skin so produced, as, a black-and-blue bruise which fades from purple to green to yellow as blood trapped in tissues is absorbed.

Echinococcus cyst. Multiple fluid-filled cysts, particularly in the liver or lungs, produced by tapeworm larvae; *hydatid disease* (67).

ECHO viruses. The initials mean "Enteric Cytopathic Human Orphan," the "orphan" indicating that the viruses are not associated with known diseases. The designation has become less appropriate since some of the viruses have been identified as the causative agents of certain diseases (58).

Eclampsia. Convulsions. A serious form occurs in late pregnancy or even during or after delivery; it is an extreme manifestation of *toxemia of pregnancy* (356), often associated with kidney disorders. Early signs of impending eclampsia are practically always evident to the attending physician, in ample time to institute effective preventive measures. Eclampsia is rare in women who receive proper pre-natal care.

Ectopic. In wrong position, out of place; for example, *ectopic pregnancy* (353) in which the embryo is implanted in a Fallopian tube or elsewhere outside of the uterus.

Ectropion. Out-turning of an eyelid, drooping away from the eyeball.

Eczema. Inflammation of the skin (175, 393).

Edema. Excessive accumulation of watery fluid in body cavities and spaces around cells. The fluid produces puffy, boggy swelling of waterlogged tissues. Edema is not a disease but a symptom of little or great significance. The waterlogging may be mild and localized, such as the puffiness around a bruise or a slight swelling of the ankles after standing all day, or it may inflate almost all of the body like a balloon. The underlying cause may be trivial, as in PREMENSTRUAL TENSION, or quite serious. "Pitting edema," the kind which leaves a little pit or depression when pressed, is often associated with heart or kidney disorders. Edema results from some disturbance of mechanisms of fluid exchange in the body, of which there are many causes: allergy, protein deficiency, salt and water retention by the kidneys (see ELECTROLYTES), congestive heart failure, obstruction of lymphatic drainage (see LYMPHEDEMA), inflammation, injury, liver and kidney disease, tumors. Modern diuretic drugs which increase the output of urine and get rid of excess fluid are helpful in management of edema while underlying disease is treated.

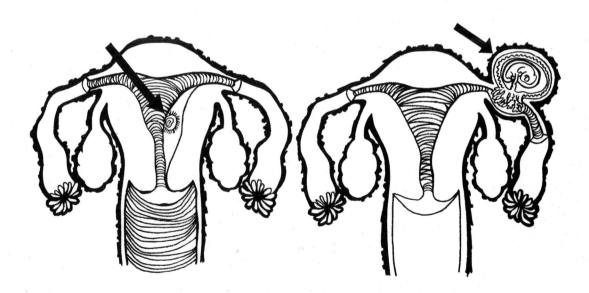

Normal pregnancy. Ovum rests in wall of womb, fetus grows in womb.

Ectopic pregnancy. Drawing shows embryo growing in Fallopian tube.

Edentulous. Toothless.

EEG. An electroencephalogram; a brain wave record. See ELECTROENCEPHALO-GRAPH.

EENT. Eye, Ear, Nose and Throat.

Effleurage. A stroking movement used in massage.

Effusion. Outpouring of fluid into a body part or tissue.

Ejaculation. Ejection of semen.

EKG. An electrocardiogram. See ELEC-TROCARDIOGRAPH.

Elective treatment. Postponable treatment, not immediately urgent. *Elective surgery* can be put off until a more convenient or desirable time.

Electric knife. A surgical instrument employing electric current to cut and seal vessels bloodlessly (731).

Electrocardiograph. An instrument which amplifies tiny electric charges in contracting heart muscle and records these on paper in the form of squiggly lines; the written record is an *electrocardiogram* (EKG). Electric impulses are conveyed to the machine from surfaces above several areas of the heart. Skilled interpretation of electrical events within the heart muscle, recorded in an EKG, gives valuable information in diagnosis of heart disease and in following the progress of a patient after recovery from a heart attack (80, 89, 105).

Electroencephalograph. An instrument which amplifies minute electric currents from brain cells and transcribes them by means of an inked arm to a moving strip of paper. This record, called an *electroencephalogram* (EEG), shows aspects of brain activity, popularly called "brain waves," in the form of undulant, spiked, wavy lines (265). Disk electrodes taped to the subject's scalp pick up tiny currents from brain cells near the surface of the skull. The brain has several characteristic rhythms; "brain writings" from different areas of the scalp may vary considerably. Modern electroencephalographs have a score or more channels, each recording changes in electric potential between two electrodes taped to different areas of the scalp. The instrument is useful in diagnosing various disturbances of brain function, such as epilepsy, and is a valuable research tool for investigating the manifold mysteries of the brain. Recent advances in studies of SLEEP and dreams have been greatly aided by the electroencephalograph's ability to identify rhythms characteristic of different levels of consciousness.

Electrolytes. We rarely give the slightest thought to our electrolytes, or need to, but in certain disease states a doctor gives a great deal of attention to electrolyte balances. Electrolytes are dissolved salts or ions in body fluids, analogous to electrolytes in an automobile storage battery. Our electrolytes conduct electric currents; they participate in countless chemical processes of life; they are bearers of electrical energy within our cells; they are in constant motion and exert outward pressure; they are vital regulators of acid-base balance. The principal regulator of water and electrolyte balance is the kidney (272). The major electrolytes are sodium, chlorine, potassium and bicarbonate. Numerous conditions affect or reflect the critical composition of the sea within us: vomiting, diarrhea, kidney or liver disease, congestive heart failure, dehydration, severe burns, diabetes, drug treatments, surgery, edema, to name a few. There may be excessive loss or excessive retention of electrolytes. Sodium (salt) locks considerable amounts of water in the body. This is the rationale for *low-sodium diets* (32), designed to ease waterlogged tissues of their burden. But a gross deficiency of sodium may produce leg cramps and other distresses. Correction of electrolyte deficits or excesses is an important part of management of many ills. Delicate electrolyte imbalances are never a matter of self-diagnosis or self-treatment; they may be of a chronic or emergency nature; they are secondary to disorder which is or should be treated; they are considerations in preparation for surgery, and it is enough to know that physicians are well aware of them.

Electrolysis. Permanent removal of superfluous hair by means of an electric needle which renders the hair follicle incapable of further growth. The word also means decomposition of a salt or chemical compound by means of an electric current.

Electromyography. Tracings of electric currents produced by muscle action, in tests of neurologic disorders (240).

Electroshock. A physical treatment for some forms of mental illness; harmless electric current is passed from temple to temple through the patient's brain, producing unconsciousness (690). The patient has no memory of the shock, but competent supervision is necessary to prevent convulsive injuries or fractures.

Elephantiasis. Gross enlargement of a body part (legs, scrotum) due to fluids in tissue spaces under the skin, dammed back by obstruction of lymphatic drainage channels. See LYMPHEDEMA. The most extreme forms of elephantiasis are seen in persons in tropical countries who have FILARIASIS.

Elimination diets. Menus which start with a few foods that rarely cause allergic reactions, and then add one new food at a time to determine which one a patient reacts to (657).

Embolism. Obstruction of a blood vessel by an EMBOLUS. Consequences vary according to the size of the blocked vessel and the part of the body deprived of blood. The lungs, brain, and heart are frequent sites of embolism. *Pulmonary embolism* which can cause sudden death results from blockage of the pulmonary artery (75) or its large branches. *Fat embolism* results from a crushing injury of bone or fatty tissue which disperses fat into the bloodstream, whence it is disseminated to many organs. Fat embolism is often fatal.

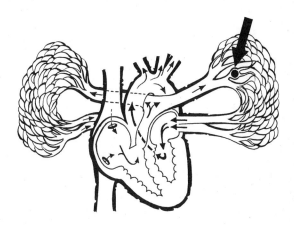

Pulmonary embolism. Embolus in lung (arrow) blocks flow of blood (small arrows).

Embolus. Any foreign substance—a blood clot, fat globule, air bubble, clumps of cells—which is swept along in the bloodstream until it lodges in a vessel and blocks the flow of blood beyond that point (118).

Embryo. The developing human being in the uterus through the third month of pregnancy, after which it is known as a fetus.

Emetic. Productive of vomiting.

Emmenagogue. An agent which stimulates menstrual flow.

Emphysema. Overinflation of air sacs of the lungs or tissues between them with air which cannot readily escape (224). Long-continued pressures stretch and rupture delicate walls of air sacs, reducing the surfaces on which gases are exchanged. The affected person develops a BARREL CHEST, shortness of breath, an overworked heart.

Empyema. Accumulation of pus in a body cavity, especially in the pleural cavity (222).

Encephalitis. Inflammation of the brain. Some forms of encephalitis are caused by viruses (59), others are complications of other diseases or conditions.

Encephalogram. An x-ray of the contents of the skull.

Endarterectomy. Surgical removal of a clot or plaque from the inner wall of an artery (119).

Endarteritis. Inflammation of the innermost layer of an artery.

Endemic. "In the people"; occurring constantly or repeatedly in the same locality.

Endocarditis. Inflammation of the lining of the heart, especially attacking the heart valves (39).

Endocrine. Inpouring, internally secreting; ductless glands which secrete hormones into the circulation (301).

Endodontics. A branch of dentistry concerned with disease and treatment of inner structures of the teeth; pulp, root canal filling, etc. (513).

Endogenous. Originating within or inside the cells or tissues.

Endometriosis. Presence in abnormal locations of fragments of the membrane which lines the cavity of the uterus (414). The displaced tissue "menstruates" where it shouldn't and tends to form "chocolate cysts."

Endoscopy. Visual examination of hollow parts of the body by insertion of a lighted instrument through a natural outlet. There are many types of "scopes" (sigmoidoscope, bronchoscope, cystoscope and others) named for the inspected organs. Some have systems of lenses and auxiliary devices for removing foreign objects or bits of tissue for examination.

Endotoxin. A toxin produced by internal processes of a germ, liberated when the cell of the germ is destroyed.

Enteric coating. A coating of drug tablets which permits them to pass through the acid stomach without dissolving and to liberate their dose in the alkaline intestine.

Enteritis. Inflammation of the intestine, particularly of the small intestine (470).

Enterobiasis. Pinworm infection (69).

Enteroviruses. Viruses, such as polio and ECHO viruses, whose preferred habitat is the intestinal tract.

Enucleation. Removal of the eyeball.

Enuresis. Bedwetting; involuntary discharge of urine (287, 380).

Eosinophils. Certain white blood cells which accept a rose-colored stain called eosin. Large numbers of eosinophils are present in nasal and other secretions during allergic attacks. It is not known for sure whether the eosinophils protect against allergic reactions or accentuate them.

Epidemic. Rapid spread of disease attacking large numbers of people in the same locality at the same time.

Epidemic pleurodynia. See DEVIL'S GRIP.

Epidermis. Popularly, the skin; technically, the outermost part of the skin consisting of four layers without blood vessels (168).

Epididymitis. Inflammation of that part of the semen-conducting duct which lies upon and behind the testicle (299).

Epigastrium. "Upon the stomach"; the upper middle abdomen. A hand stretched across the lower end of the breastbone just about covers the epigastrium.

Epiglottis. A structure like a hinged lid above the voice box; it opens to admit air and snaps shut like a trapdoor when swallowing to prevent food from going down the windpipe (200).

Epilation. Removal of hair by the roots. See ELECTROLYSIS.

Epilepsy. A nervous disorder of varying severity, marked by recurring explosive "discharge" of electrical activity of brain cells, producing convulsions, loss of consciousness, or brief clouding of consciousness (261).

Epinephrine. The hormone produced by the medulla of the adrenal gland (318). It stimulates heart action, constricts blood vessels, relaxes small bronchial tubes, inhibits smooth muscle, and has many medical uses in allergic and other disorders. Also known as adrenaline.

Epiphysis. The end part of a long bone which in children is separated from the shaft of the bone by a layer of cartilage. As growth progresses, the cartilage layer disappears, the epiphysis is said to have "closed," and the bone does not grow longer. When this process is complete, ultimate height has been attained.

Episiotomy. An incision in the margin of the vulva to enlarge the area through which the baby's head passes in childbirth; the purpose is to prevent or minimize injury to the mother (362).

Epispadias. A malformation of the penis in which the urinary canal remains open on the upper side of the organ (290). The problem is to restore urinary control and then to form a new tube by plastic surgery.

Epistaxis. Nosebleed (784).

Epithelial. Refers to those cells that form the outer layer of the skin, those that line all the portions of the body that have contact with external air (such as the eyes, ears, nose, throat, lungs), and those that are specialized for secretion, as the liver, kidneys, urinary and reproductive tract.

Epithelium. Specialized tissue which covers all free surfaces of the body, forms the EPIDERMIS, lines hollow organs, glands, respiratory passages; it does not possess blood vessels.

Epizootic. Epidemic disease in animals.

Eponym. The name of a person applied to a disease, syndrome, or theory which it is presumed he was the first to discover or describe; for example, *Bright's disease, Addison's disease.* This form of honorific has become a little less common since more precise and specific descriptions of disease have been made possible by scientific advances. Physicians generally prefer a scientific name for a condition unless they happen to have discovered it first.

Equinovarus. A form of clubfoot (621).

Ergotism. Poisoning with *ergot*, a substance contained in a fungus that grows on rye and other grains. Ergot has powerful constrictive action on small blood vessels; chronic poisoning may produce closure of blood vessels, resulting in gangrene of the extremities. Various ergot drugs and combinations have medical uses, as in prevention of migraine headaches. It is interesting that ergot is closely related chemically to LSD.

Eructation. A belch.

Erysipelas. An acute bacterial infection of the skin and underlying tissue (38).

Erythema. Abnormal redness of the skin. The pattern, intensity, distribution, duration, and appearance of the reddened areas give clues to disease, which may be trifling, or a disease of childhood manifested by a rash, or an allergy or systemic disorder.

Erythroblastosis (*"Rh disease"*). A disease of newborn infants associated with the Rh blood factor (356). ANTIBODIES of an Rh-negative mother whose blood does not possess the factor react with the Rh-positive blood of the baby which does possess the factor, resulting in destruction of some or many of the baby's red cells. The anemia may be mild or severe enough to require total blood replacement by EXCHANGE TRANSFUSION.

Erythrocytes. Red blood cells; elastic, jelly-like disks containing HEMOGLOBIN (132).

Erythrocytosis. A condition of too many red blood cells crowding the circulation; *polycythemia* (145).

Erythropoiesis. The process of red blood cell formation.

Eschar. Sloughed-off tissue produced by a burn or corrosive substance.

Escutcheon. The pattern of pubic hair growth, different in male and female; from the Latin word for "shield."

Esophagoscopy. Direct examination of the esophagus with an *esophagoscope*, a hollow-tubed instrument with a light and lens (441).

Esophagus. The gullet; the muscular tube through which swallowed food is "milked" into the stomach by muscular action (429).

Esophagitis. Inflammation of the lining of the esophagus (445).

Estrogen. A general term for female hormones; technically, substances which produce changes in the uterus (and psyche) corresponding to activities of the ovaries and endocrine glands (327).

Eunuch. A castrated male; a boy or man whose testicles have been removed. In origin the word means "guardian of the couch." Eunuchs cannot produce SPERMATOZOA or father children, but if only the testes are removed, and this operation is done after sexual maturity, some eunuchs retain a degree of sexual potency. *Eunuchoidism* is a natural condition in which the sex organs are malformed or physiologically inactive (302).

Ethmoid. A sieve-like bone of the upper nose behind the frontal sinus; nerve fibers of the sense of smell pass through perforations in it (580).

Etiology. The study of causes of disease or disorder. "Etiology" is not a word for "causes," but for the *study* of causes.

Euphoria. Feeling of well-being; often implies exaggerated elation.

Eustachian tube. A tubular passage about an inch and a half long which leads from the middle ear to the throat (571). Air passing through it equalizes pressures on both sides of the eardrum, enabling the drum to vibrate freely. Infectious material can enter the middle ear through the tube.

Exanthem. A skin eruption or the disease which causes it. *Exanthem subitum* (also called *roseola infantum*) is a disease of childhood; fever comes on suddenly, persists for three or four days, then drops, a skin rash appears, and the child is well (401). The skin eruption of scarlet fever or measles is an exanthem.

Exchange transfusion. Replacement of all of a baby's blood with suitable whole blood of a donor; resorted to in some instances to save the life of a baby with severe blood-destroying anemia resulting from a clash of the mother's and baby's Rh blood factors. See ERYTHROBLASTOSIS.

Excision. The act of cutting out.

Excoriation. A scratch mark of the skin, usually deep enough to bleed or become crust-covered, produced by scraping or scratching.

Exfoliation. Peeling or shedding of surface skin in scales or sheets.

Exocrine. Outpouring; glands which do not deliver their secretions to the bloodstream but through ducts and channels to organs and surfaces; for example, sweat glands, oil glands, digestive juices of the pancreas gland. Inherited disabilities of the exocrine glands are the fundamental defects in CYSTIC FIBROSIS.

Exogenous. Originating from outside the cells or tissues.

Exostosis. Projection of a bony growth from the surface of a bone; a bony spur.

Expectorant. A substance that softens or increases bronchial secretions and helps to "bring up" phlegm from the chest.

Exophthalmos. Bulging eyes, "pop eyes," characteristic of thyroid disease (311).

Exstrophy of the bladder. A congenital malformation in which the bladder has no abdominal covering and urine comes out to the surface of the body (287).

Extensor. A muscle which straightens or extends a body part.

External cardiac massage. A first-aid measure to make a stopped heart start to beat, used in conjunction with mouth-to-mouth resuscitation (774); the latter supplies fresh oxygen. With the victim on his back, place the heel of one hand on the lower part of his breastbone (over the heart), and the other hand on top of the first one. Press down with your weight on the breastbone to force blood out of the heart into vessels. Relax the pressure; blood flows into the heart chambers. Repeat at intervals of about one second. Too much pressure can hurt the heart or break ribs; if the patient is a child, pressure of one hand may be sufficient. Ideally, one person gives mouth-to-mouth resuscitation while the other applies external heart massage. If one person must do it all, he can give external massage for half a minute, then mouth-to-mouth breathing for ten seconds or so, and repeat.

Extrasystole. A premature beat of the heart; a contraction that is triggered too soon and is followed by a compensating delay in the next beat (104). The pause between the premature beat and the succeeding one, which is likely to come with a thump, gives a feeling that the heart has skipped a beat. The phenomenon is quite common and almost never serious.

Extravasation. Escape of fluids from a vessel, especially a blood vessel, into surrounding tissues. A black eye looks the way it does because of extravasated blood.

Extrinsic asthma. A form of bronchial asthma in which the provoking substance enters the body from the outside world (660). *Intrinsic asthma* which has its source within the body can co-exist with extrinsic asthma.

Extrinsic factor. Literally, a constituent from outside; medically, the term commonly refers to Vitamin B_{12} which prevents pernicious anemia (142). The vitamin is assimilated from food in conjunction with a substance secreted by the stomach called INTRINSIC FACTOR.

Exudate. Anything that is exuded, oozed, trickled, pushed out. One exudes sweat as well as confidence. Although many exudates are entirely normal, in medical usage the word often refers to pus or other materials of pathologic interest.

Eye bank. See CORNEAL TRANSPLANT.

Eye tooth. A canine tooth (500).

Eye wash. A simple and effective eye wash can be made by adding a level teaspoonful of salt to a pint of boiled water (541).

Eyegrounds. The interior of the eye that can be seen with an OPHTHALMOSCOPE.

F

Face lift. An operation to remove wrinkling caused by loose skin and to tighten fatty tissues which tend to sag in the face and neck with advancing years. Results vary, depending on the condition of the patient. In time, tissue tends to sag again, but the operation can be repeated. In some cases, improvement may last from five to ten years; in the heavy-faced, improvement tends to be more short-lived. Scarring is not conspicuous, being concealed by hair or crease lines. Face-lift surgery usually takes four to five hours and the patient is hospitalized for three days to a week.

Face presentation. Appearance of the face of the fetus at the outlet of the uterus during delivery, instead of the top of the head, as is normal.

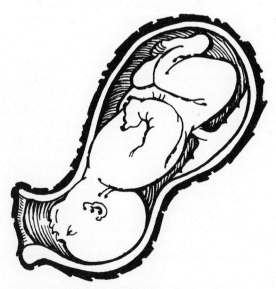

Face presentation.

F.A.C.P. Fellow of the American College of Physicians; a qualified medical specialist.

F.A.C.S. Fellow of the American College of Surgeons; a qualified surgical specialist.

Fahrenheit (F.). The thermometer scale generally used outside of scientific circles. It marks the freezing point of water at 32 degrees F. and the boiling point at 212 degrees F. See CENTIGRADE.

Fainting (*syncope*). Brief loss of consciousness due to diminished blood supply to the brain. Usually self-corrected; the fainting person droops to the floor and blood flows more easily to the brain. Blood vessels in the abdominal area have immense capacity to hold blood, almost the body's entire blood volume, when fully dilated. Shock or strong emotion may cause these vessels to dilate and fill with so much blood that blood pressure drops and fainting results. Rarely is fainting due to heart trouble. A soldier standing at attention for some time may faint, not from want of military ardor, but because of lack of muscular movement to aid the return flow of blood through veins. Oncoming faint may be prevented by lying down.

Fallen womb. Prolapse of the uterus; sagging of the organ into the lower vagina, due to weakness, stretching, or tearing of supporting structures (415).

Fallout. RADIOISOTOPES from nuclear explosions which settle out of the atmosphere.

Fallopian tubes. See OVIDUCTS.

False pregnancy (*pseudocyesis*). Signs and symptoms of pregnancy occurring without conception. The woman herself is usually deceived, and even an able obstetrician may be deceived for a while. The patient is usually a woman with an overpowering, obsessive desire to have a child who through autosuggestion is somehow able to mimic the signs of pregnancy—cessation of menstruation, breast changes, "morning sickness," enlargement of the abdomen at the rate of normal pregnancy—to perfection. Careful examination and tests can determine that no pregnancy exists, but in some instances it is difficult to convince the woman until the expected date of delivery passes unfruitfully.

Fanconi's syndrome. Multiple inherited abnormalities which impair kidney function and progressively depress blood cell formation in the bone marrow (165).

Farmer's lung. An inflammatory disease of the lungs which principally affects agricultural workers exposed to moldy hay, grain, fodder or silage. The disease resembles pneumonia but does not respond to antibiotics as bacterial pneumonias do. Symptoms of chills, fever, cough, headache, and chest tightness are thought to be caused by allergy-like sensitivity to inhaled mold dusts, and may appear a few hours after heavy exposure. Total avoidance of moldy vegetable matter is most important during the illness and after recovery.

Farsightedness (*hyperopia*). A condition in which light from near objects is focused behind rather than upon the retina, usually because the eyeball is too short (538). Close objects are blurred but distant ones are distinct. Farsighted persons may read and do close work with fair success through ACCOMMODATION, but this effort of ciliary muscles (530) can give rise to complaints of "eye strain," "tired eyes," and distaste for tasks of close seeing. With increasing age, the lens of the eye loses flexibility and farsighted people tend to hold their newspapers at arm's length to read them. Glasses for reading, or a reading segment in bifocal glasses, can do much to give comfort and may even minimize the appearance of wrinkles.

Fascia. Tough sheets of connective tissue which give support under the skin, between and around muscles, blood vessels, nerves and internal organs.

Fat embolism. Plugging of a blood vessel by fatty particles carried in the bloodstream; this can occur from crushing injuries of fatty tissue or bone, or injection of oily solutions.

Fatty acid. A compound of carbon, hydrogen, and oxygen which combines with glycerol to make a fat.

Favism. Acute anemia with red blood cell destruction caused by eating fava beans. The condition occurs only in genetically susceptible persons who do not possess an enzyme that is important in red blood cell metabolism. Certain drugs, such as aspirin and sulfas, may produce the same symptoms in susceptible persons. Oddly, absence, of the enzyme seems to give some protection against malaria.

Febrile. Feverish.

Feces. Contents of a bowel movement; the stool. Feces are not simply unabsorbed food residues. The greatest part of the solid matter is made up of materials excreted from blood and cells shed by lining membranes of the intestines; about 10 per cent is bacteria (see INTESTINAL FLORA). Practically all of the protein, fat, and carbohydrate that is eaten is absorbed. Unabsorbed food residues consist largely of indigestible vegetable cellulose, the amount of which varies with the diet. This indigestible "roughage" stimulates activity and secretions of the bowel. Large amounts of undigested food elements in feces are associated with diseases which impair assimilation.

Felon. See PARONYCHIA.

Felty's syndrome. Chronic infectious arthritis with enlargement of the spleen and decreased numbers of certain white blood cells (154).

Femur. The thighbone (593).

Fenestration. An opening (literally, "a window") in a part of the body, or the act of making one. The *fenestration operation* for improving the hearing of persons with OTOSCLEROSIS creates a bony window for passage of sound waves to the inner ear (727).

Fertile period. The period of about one week around the midpoint of the menstrual cycle when conception can occur. The period cannot be pinpointed precisely, but occurs approximately through days 11 to 18 counting from the onset of menstruation (327).

Festination. The taking of hurried short steps to prevent falling, characteristic of *Parkinson's disease* (242).

Fetal growth. See TIMETABLE OF FETAL DEVELOPMENT.

Fetus. The unborn child after the third month of pregnancy; before that it is called an embryo.

Fever. Abnormally high body temperature. Normally, body temperature varies slightly through the day, is higher in the evening than in the morning, higher internally than at the skin surface, and is increased by such commonplace things as eating and exercising. The most common fevers accompany infections, but disturbances of heat-regulating centers of the brain, as in heat stroke, and other non-infectious conditions can produce fever. Experienced people can often recognize significant fever by the "feel" and look of the patient's hot, dry, flushed skin. Accurate fever-reading, however, requires use of a clinical thermometer (18). Different forms of fever (50) are helpful in diagnosis and following the course of disease. That is why "fever charts" are kept of hospitalized patients, and may be desired by the doctor for patients under home nursing care. Mothers should have a little knowledge about fevers in children (373).

Fever increases the body's rate of metabolism about seven per cent for each degree Fahrenheit of temperature elevation. The heart's ability to contract decreases and it beats more rapidly in an attempt to move more blood to the skin to increase heat loss. Excessively high (*hyperthermic*) fever of 105 degrees F. and more cannot be endured for a long period; the very high fever of SUNSTROKE is so quickly lethal that immediate efforts to bring it down must be made by immersing the patient in an ice bath or applying a stream of cold water to the body. Young children react to the slightest infection with fever, sometimes as high as 104 degrees; the height of the fever does not necessarily parallel the seriousness of the infection. If a doctor cannot be reached promptly, a small child's very high fever can be reduced by an alcohol sponge or cool enema (373).

Whether or not fever is part of nature's treatment to cure infection is an unsettled question. In tissue cultures, temperatures of feverish degree inhibit the multiplication of some viruses. There is some evidence that fever increases the production of INTERFERON. But fever-producing organisms in patients survive the temperatures they produce and many authorities doubt that fever has any direct effect on the patient's resistance to infection. All agree, however, that fever is an important guide to the progress of an illness; sometimes it is the only important diagnostic clue. The fever is not the disease. The doctor may very well decide to leave the fever alone while he treats the infection.

Fibrillation. Tremor of a muscle, especially the heart muscle. Individual muscle fibers act independently, uncoordinated, out of rhythm, causing rapid, irregular, ineffective heartbeats. The condition may affect the *atria* (102) or *ventricles* (106) of the heart. Defibrillating devices that administer an electric shock are used to restore normal rhythm.

Fibrinogen. A protein manufactured in the liver and distributed into the bloodstream where it acts as a clotting agent when a blood vessel is cut or injured. Fibrinogen combines with another substance, *thrombin*, to yield long, threadlike crystals of *fibrin* which form a mesh to entrap blood corpuscles in a clot.

Fibroids. The word commonly refers to muscle and connective tissue tumors of the uterus (413).

Fibrositis. Inflammation of connective tissue (628); often, combined inflammation of muscle and connective tissue (*fibromyositis*), producing pain, tenderness, and stiffness. A form of rheumatism.

Fibula. The slender bone on the outer aspect of the lower leg (593).

Filariasis. A chronic disease caused by the presence of threadlike worms (*filaria*) in the body (69). The organisms get into the blood through the bites of mosquitoes. The adult worms live in the lymphatic system and cause overgrowth of fibrous tissue which obstructs drainage. Obstructed fluids accumulate in tissue spaces and cause the affected part to swell (LYMPHEDEMA). The result is some degree of ELEPHANTIASIS. The most extreme forms of the disease occur in long-time residents of tropical countries who are frequently re-infected from mosquito bites.

Fimbria. A fringelike structure; especially, fimbriae of the opening of the OVIDUCTS, close to the ovary (326, 351). The fringelike projections are covered with *cilia,* minute hair-like processes which wave back and forth and set up rhythmic currents in surrounding peritoneal fluid. Their function is to "catch" a mature egg cell released by the ovary and sweep it into the tube which is where fertilization usually occurs. An engineer would consider this method of bridging a small gap to be poorly designed

but it has worked pretty well for a good many years.

Fish skin disease. See ICHTHYOSIS.

Fissure. A break or crack in the skin or a membrane, most frequent in the rectal area (384, 468).

Fistula. An abnormal channel between body parts, or leading from a hollow organ to a free surface, which usually discharges fluids or material from an organ. A fistula may be caused by disease, injury, or an abscess which bores an abnormal drainage channel for itself. Many fistulas are named for the body parts they connect; for example, *vesicovaginal* fistula (bladder and vagina). Some fistulas never heal by themselves because of continual infection and surgical correction is necessary.

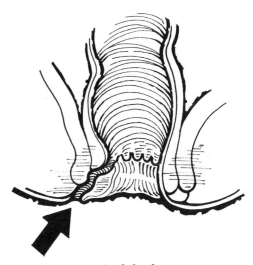

Anal fistula.

Flank. The fleshy outer part of the body between the ribs and hip.

Flash blindness. Visual disturbance resulting from an intense light source, such as an atomic blast.

Flat foot. Ordinarily, if a print of a bare foot on a piece of paper shows that the sole has made flat contact all around, without an open space under the middle inside part of the foot, it is construed as a sign of flat feet caused by "fallen arches." This is not always true. Babies' feet are always flat. Some people have naturally flat feet which are perfectly efficient and comfortable. When feet become *flattened*, and hurt, troubles arise and treatment is necessary (620).

Flatulence. Excessive gas in the stomach or intestines. A normal bowel always contains some gas; balance is maintained by unostentatious gas exchange mechanisms. Excessive "gassiness," vented by belching or passing wind, may result from indiscretions of diet or some disorder of the digestive tract which should be looked into by a physician. Frequently, excessive belching (*eructation* is a more seemly word) is often a consequence of unconscious AIR SWALLOWING.

Fletcherism. A food fad of the late nineteenth century, promoted by Horace Fletcher of Lawrence, Mass., who advocated that each mouthful of food be chewed 50 to 60 times, reducing it to a liquid state before swallowing. Fletcher ultimately went on a one-meal-a-day diet with an alternate day of fasting, spit out all food that did not liquefy after thorough chewing, developed permanent constipation, and his death from chronic bronchitis was speeded by malnutrition.

Flexor. A muscle which bends a limb or part, as in flaunting the biceps.

"Floaters." Cells or strands of tissue which float in the VITREOUS HUMOR and move with movements of the eyeball, casting shadows on the retina (557). The floaters, particularly when seen against a bright background such as open sky, look like moving spots, "clouds," threads and swirls of diverse shapes. Floaters are most prevalent in nearsighted and older persons. Usually they are more annoying than serious, but if very worrisome or exag-

gerated, an eye examination is indicated.

Floating kidney. A loose, somewhat wandering kidney, abnormally movable from its normal location because of slack attachments and inadequate support from surrounding fat.

Flora (intestinal). Bacteria and other small organisms found in the intestinal contents.

Flukes. Parasitic flatworms, rarely encountered in the U. S., which cause infections of the intestines, liver, and lungs (65).

Fluorides. Salts of fluorine, a gaseous element. The role of fluorides in helping to lessen tooth decay is well known (506). Recent studies have furnished evidence that fluorides contribute importantly to sturdy bones as well as teeth and may play a part in treatment and prevention of *osteoporosis* (624), a condition of abnormal porousness, thinning, and easy fracturing of bone, common in women after the menopause and in old persons. One study of more than a thousand persons over 45 years of age has shown osteoporosis to be much less frequent in those who lived most of their lives in areas of relatively high fluoride content of drinking water than in those who lived in low-fluoride areas. There was also much less hardening of the AORTA in those who lived in high-fluoride areas. It appears that fluoride helps to keep calcium deposited in hard tissues of the body and not in soft tissues. If such action is confirmed, fluorides may assume an important preventive role in osteoporosis and hardening of the arteries, two of the main diseases of aging.

Fluoroscope. A device for viewing x-ray images on a fluorescent screen. The patient stands behind the screen and x-rays passing through the body make structures visible to the radiologist. The digestive tract, heart, lungs and other organs can be viewed in action, and the progress of a BARIUM MEAL can be followed through the alimentary tract.

Flutter. Rapid, fluttery, but rhythmic beats of the heart auricles, resembling fibrillation (105).

Flying. See AIR TRAVEL.

Folacin. The name officially selected to replace the term *folic acid,* a vitamin of the B complex. Also known as *pteroylglutamic acid.* It is a bright yellow compound needed in very small amounts in the diet of animals and man. A deficiency results in poor growth, anemia, and other blood disorders.

Foley catheter. A tube inserted through the urethra into the bladder for drainage of urine; it has a small balloon at the bladder end which is inflated after insertion to hold the catheter in place (274).

Folic acid. A vitamin important for blood formation.

Folie a deux. Mental disorder communicated from a person who has it to a closely associated person so suggestible that he is persuaded that he has it too.

Follicle. A small sac or cavity which produces secretions or excretions. Hair grows from a follicle linked with sebaceous glands which produce skin oil (170).

Fontanel. The "soft spot" on the top of a baby's head. The area, which is covered by a very tough membrane that is by no means so fragile as some mothers fear, will be filled with bone as the skull grows. It takes anywhere from one to two years for the soft spot to close.

Food diary. A complete record of everything that is eaten for a period of time, a guide to detection of food allergies (658).

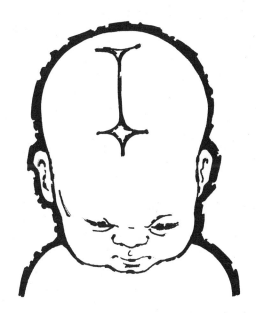

Fontanels ("soft spots") of an infant's head.

Food groups. Four basic groups of common foods, each group of similar nutritive value; useful in planning balanced diets (475).

Food poisoning. Intestinal infection caused by bacteria or their toxins in foods. Many attacks of food poisoning are not recognized for what they are. Even severe attacks with nausea, vomiting, violent diarrhea, perhaps abdominal cramps, fever, and dizziness, may be blamed on "intestinal flu" or a "24-hour virus" unless several people who attended the same banquet or picnic are simultaneously stricken. The most common causes of food poisoning are strains of *salmonella* bacteria (43) which are widespread in the animal kingdom, and *staphylococci,* readily spread by human carriers. An originally slight population of salmonella in pies, eclairs, egg dishes, cakes, custards and salads can multiply enormously if such foods are left to incubate for a short time at room temperatures. Violence of food poisoning symptoms varies with the "dose" of bacteria and with individual susceptibility. Attacks two or three hours after eating suggest that the poisoning was caused by bacterial toxins rather than by live bacteria. Thorough cooking destroys bacteria and some toxins (see BOTULISM) but heat must be sufficiently high, penetrating, and long continued. A large turkey may not be thoroughly cooked because the stuffing acts as a sort of internal insulation. Proper refrigeration and sanitation guard against food poisoning (807).

Foot drop. Drooping of the foot, due to paralysis or injury of muscles or tendons that extend or lift it.

Foot supports. Simple arrangements of bedding or accessories to keep the weight of blankets off a bedridden patient's upturned feet (16).

Foramen. A perforation or opening in a body part. There are many such perforations, especially in bones, to permit passage of blood vessels and nerves. Some are abnormal, such as openings in congenitally malformed hearts of "blue babies" (93).

Forceps. An instrument with two opposing blades and handles, on the general principle of pliers, for grasping, compressing, or holding body parts or surgical materials. *Forceps delivery* is extraction of the fetus from the birth canal with the mechanical aid of OBSTETRIC FORCEPS of special design (363).

Foreskin. The fold of skin covering the head of the penis; the part removed in circumcision.

Formication. Sensation that ants are crawling over the skin.

Fornication. Sexual intercourse of unmarried persons.

Fortify. To add one or more nutrients to a food so that it contains more of the nutrients than was present originally before processing. Milk is often fortified with Vitamin D, margarine with Vitamin A, beverages with Vitamin C, various cereal products with thiamine and riboflavin. Foods with vitamins added to replace lost values are said to be "restored."

Fossa. A pit or trench-like depression in a body part.

Fovea. A pit, cup or depression in a body structure; especially, the *fovea centralis*, a pinhead-sized depression near the center of the retina which is the area of sharpest, most finely detailed seeing (532).

Fraternal twins. Twins of either sex originating from two separate eggs; they are no more closely related genetically than brothers and sisters (358).

Free grafting. Transplantation of a completely detached piece of skin from one part of a patient's body to another (741).

Frenum. A fold of tissue which partially limits the movement of an organ, like a checkrein. A small frenum can be seen as a band of tissue connecting the underside of the tongue with the floor of the mouth.

Frigidity. Sexual coldness in women. There may be some physical cause, but more often the aversion has a psychologic origin which may be difficult to recognize and overcome. Frigidity which occurs after the menopause, in women who have previously had normal sex drive, may respond to judicious hormone treatments (332).

Froelich's syndrome. Excessive fat deposits in the pelvic area and lack of genital development in young males, often with retardation of growth, somnolence, and other symptoms. The condition results from impairment, as by a tumor of the pituitary gland, of functions of the *pituitary* and *hypothalamus* (303). Careful diagnosis is necessary because most obese, genitally underdeveloped adolescent boys do not have this specific disorder.

Frog test. A pregnancy test, employing frogs, which gives a verdict in three to five hours (342).

Frozen section. A piece of tissue removed from the body which is quickly frozen by carbon dioxide spray, sliced, and examined immediately under a microscope. This is most often done when cancer is suspected and the patient is on the operating table, while surgeons await the verdict which will determine the extent of the operation.

Frozen shoulder. Pain, stiffness, and limitation of movement in the shoulder and upper arm (608).

Frozen sperm. SPERMATOZOA frozen at very low temperatures with a small amount of glycerol added "come alive" when thawed and are capable of fertilization. Normal pregnancies with delivery of normal babies have followed ARTIFICAL INSEMINATION with frozen sperm of the husband. The method has been used to enhance the fertility of husbands with a poor sperm count, by adding several specimens together.

FSH. Follicle stimulating hormone (305).

Fulguration. Destruction of tissue by electric sparks.

Fulminating. Sudden in onset, explosive, severe, rapid in course.

Functional disease. Disease without any discoverable organic disorder.

Fundus. The part of a hollow organ farthest from its opening; for example, the back part of the eye; the top part of the uterus farthest from its outlet.

Fungi. Low forms of plant life, including molds and yeasts, some of which are capable of causing annoying or serious infection. See the *mycoses* (71); *ringworm* (189), *otitis externa* (570); *thrush* (397); *yeast infections* (412).

Funnel chest (*pectus excavatum*). A congenital deformity in which the breastbone is depressed toward the spine, forming a more or less funnel-shaped cavity. The deformity rarely affects the heart and lungs adversely unless unrelated diseases are present. Surgical correction is rarely necessary for reasons of health, but may be desired to improve the appearance.

Funny bone. It isn't the bone that's funny, but a nerve which tingles crazily when the elbow is banged just right. The ulnar nerve which runs down the arm from the shoulder to the hands passes over bones and is quite close to the surface at the inner side of the elbow; a bump there causes the fingers to tingle and feel "funny."

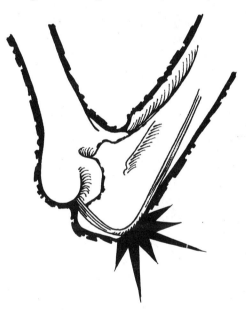

Blow on nerve at elbow causes "funny" tingling.

Furuncle. A boil (38).

Fusiform. Spindle-shaped.

Fusion. Union, cohesion, merging together; for example, *spinal fusion*, the uniting of two vertebrae by disease or by surgical procedures to improve some painful condition of the back. Also, the fusion of images from the two eyes for efficient binocular vision.

G

Galactosemia. An hereditary condition of infants who cannot handle milk sugars (*lactose, galactose*) because their bodies lack a necessary enzyme (488). Milk feedings lead to toxic accumulations of galactose in the blood, injuring the lens of the eye, the brain, and kidneys, with formation of cataracts and mental retardation unless all milk and milk products are immediately and stringently removed from the infant's diet. The outlook with strict dietary control is good and children who survive early infancy are often normal. Galactosemia is inherited as a recessive trait (see HEREDITY). If a galactosemic infant is born into a family, the physician will test later offspring of the same parents and institute a galactose-free diet immediately after birth if the diagnosis is established.

Galactagogue. An agent that promotes the flow of milk.

Gallbladder. The saclike organ underlying the liver in which bile is stored, concentrated, and delivered to the digestive tract as needed (440).

Gallstones. Stones in the gallbladder; they may or may not cause symptoms (458).

Gallop rhythm. Sounds of the heart resembling the gallop of a horse, indicative of failing heart muscle.

Gamete. A germ cell; an egg or sperm.

Gamma globulin. An IMMUNOGLOBULIN; a protein in the blood which gives immunity to certain diseases through ANTIBODY production. Gamma globulin injections containing specific antibodies are sometimes given in hope of preventing an infection in a person who has been exposed to it, or making it milder. Antibodies which protect against bacterial and viral infections are mostly in gamma globulin circulating in the blood; other closely related immunoglobulins occur in internal and external secretions outside of the blood, as in saliva, tears, nasal, bronchial, and intestinal fluids.

Ganglion (of the wrist). A cyst of a tendon sheath on the back of the wrist, traditionally treated by striking a bursting blow with the family Bible (610). A *ganglion* is also a cluster of nerve cells which serves as a center of nervous influence.

Ganglionic blocking agents. Potent drugs, prescribed for some patients with high blood pressure, which reduce the actions of ganglia (clusters of nerve cells) that transmit impulses which constrict blood vessels and increase pressures. Ganglionic blockers produce the greatest fall in blood pressure when the patient is standing, relatively little change when the patient is lying down. Sometimes a patient who has been lying down may feel faint when he suddenly rises to a sitting position.

Gangrene. Death of tissue due to failure of blood supply to the area. There are many precipitating causes: vascular disease, frostbite, burns, crushing injury, pressure, obstruction of blood vessels, too tight a tourniquet. *Wet gangrene* has an offensive watery discharge and becomes infected so that complications of infection are superimposed upon the gangrene. Amputation of the part may be necessary to save the patient's life. *Dry gangrene* does not become infected but the part becomes shriveled and mummified. Small areas of dry gangrene may sometimes be saved by appropriate treatment, but amputation may be necessary. Diabetics are especially prone to gangrene of the feet and legs and preventive measures are very important (339).

Gargoylism. An hereditary condition characterized by opacities of the cornea, protruding abdomen, large head, short arms and legs, mental deficiency.

Gas endarterectomy. A recent technique for removing a clot from an artery by using a jet of carbon dioxide gas to separate the outer coat of the artery from the inner core containing the clot. Gas pressure is applied by means of a needle inserted into the wall of the artery; the separated inner core is then pulled out and amputated.

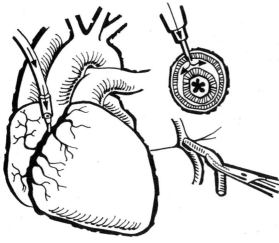

Gas endarterectomy: Gas jet separates clot from inner wall of artery (small drawing, upper right). Loosened clot is withdrawn.

Gas gangrene. An infection of injured tissues with bacilli which produce bubbles of foul-smelling gas in the wound (42).

Gastrectomy. Surgical removal of all or part of the stomach.

Gastric analysis. Analysis of stomach juices for acidity, presence of cells, organisms, and other elements. The juice, obtained after the patient has fasted 12 hours, is withdrawn by a syringe connected to a tube passed through the nose or mouth into the stomach.

Gastric freezing. A treatment for peptic ulcer; the patient swallows a balloon which is cooled by passing freezing agents through it (451). The treatment gives transient pain relief, stops gastric bleeding, but long-term benefits are questionable and freezing has not superseded conventional treatments. Initial enthusiasm for gastric freezing has waned somewhat, but experimental improvements benefiting from experience are being made.

Gastric resection. Removal of the lower part of the stomach (697).

Gastritis. Inflammation of the stomach (449).

Gastrocnemius. The long muscle of the inner side of the lower leg which bends the leg and extends the foot.

Gastroenteritis. Inflammation of the stomach and intestine, producing such symptoms as diarrhea, abdominal cramps, nausea, vomiting, fever. There are many causes: infections, food poisoning, parasites, allergies, bacteria, viruses, toxins, to mention a few.

Gastroenterostomy. Joining the stomach to a loop of intestine to bypass the duodenum (699).

Gastrointestinal. Pertaining to the stomach and intestines.

Gastroscope. An instrument which permits the examining physician to see into the inside of the stomach (441).

Gastrostomy. A surgically created outlet of the stomach onto the skin surface (696).

Gaucher's disease. A disorder of LIPID metabolism, transmitted as a recessive trait (see HEREDITY). It is characterized by enlarged spleen and liver, bone and joint pains, brown pigmentation of the skin, due to accumulation of abnormal fat-like substances.

Gavage. Feeding of liquid nutrients into the stomach via a tube.

Genes. The ultimate units in transmission of hereditary characteristics, contained in the CHROMOSOMES.

Genitalia. The reproductive organs.

Genitourinary. Pertaining to genital and urinary organs—kidneys, ureters, bladder, urethra, prostate, testes—which are interrelated (269).

Genetic counseling. See MEDICAL GENETICS.

Geophagia. Dirt-eating. See PICA.

Geographic tongue. Fancied resemblance of the surface of the tongue to a relief map gives this disorder its name. Thickened patches like miniature islands, seas, and continents occur on the tongue and shift positions from day to day. This odd appearance is the only symptom. The cause is not known. The disorder usually occurs in children and adolescents; debilitated persons appear to be more susceptible.

Geotrichosis. An infection caused by species of fungi, affecting mucous membranes of the mouth, lungs, or intestinal tract. Chronic cough is a common symptom. The condition responds well to proper treatment.

Geriatrics. The medical specialty concerned with care of old people.

German measles (*rubella*). A mild viral infection producing a pink rash which spreads all over the body, sometimes with symptoms of headache and slight fever, sometimes with symptoms so slight that the infection passes unnoticed (398). The great threat of German measles is to the unborn child of a woman who has the disease during the first three months of pregnancy when organs of the embryo are in a vulnerable stage of development. In such case the risk of giving birth to a child with multiple abnormalities (brain damage, severe heart disease, blindness, deafness) is high. It is estimated that a woman infected during the first month of pregnancy has about a 50-50 chance of giving birth to a malformed child; infection during the second month carries about a 25 per cent risk of malformation; during the third month, about 15 per cent. Injections of GAMMA GLOBULIN may give some protection to pregnant women exposed to German measles, but better measures are urgently sought. Experimental German measles vaccines of the live virus type, giving permanent immunity, reached a high state of development in 1967, at which time large scale tests were under way to make sure that vaccinated persons would not spread viruses to the unvaccinated. A simple new blood test which can determine in three hours if a pregnant woman is susceptible to German measles has been developed by a unit of the National Institutes of Health. If the woman is already immune to German measles—she may well have had the disease and gained lifetime immunity without knowing it—the test gives assurance that her unborn child, or a child conceived in the future, will not be harmed.

Gestation. Pregnancy.

G.I. Gastrointestinal.

Giant hives. Larger, deeper swellings than ordinary superficial hives, life-threatening if air passages are affected (667).

Giantism. Abnormal tallness, most often a result of excessive secretion of GROWTH HORMONE by the pituitary gland before the growing ends of the bones have closed, but other factors may produce excessive height (306). Boys up to six feet six inches tall and girls up to six feet are not considered to be giants; they fall at one extreme of a normal bell-shaped distribution curve of height in the population, with unusually short people at the other extreme.

Gibraltar fever. See BRUCELLOSIS.

G. I. series. X-ray films and fluoroscopic observations of the gastrointestinal tract; details are defined by a BARIUM

MEAL, opaque to x-rays, swallowed prior to examination (754).

Gingiva. The gum. *Gingivitis,* inflammation of the gums, is the most common form of *periodontal disease* (508).

Gland. A cell or organ which makes and releases hormones or other substances used in the body. *Endocrine* glands secrete their products into the bloodstream; *exocrine* glands, to body surfaces or elsewhere, via ducts or channels.

Glandular fever. INFECTIOUS MONONUCLEOSIS.

Glaucoma. The most common cause of blindness in adults, produced by intensive destructive pressure of fluids inside the eye (547). An acute form may come on suddenly and cause intense pain; a chronic form may cause no symptoms that the patient is aware of although his vision is being insidiously stolen away. Measurement of internal pressures of the eye with a *tonometer* (553) is an important part of an eye examination.

Gleet. Chronic gonorrheal discharge.

Glia. Supporting cells and fibers of nervous tissue, sometimes called "nerve glue." *Glioma* is a tumor of glial tissue, occurring principally in the brain and spinal cord.

Globe. The eyeball.

Globus. A "lump in the throat" which does not disappear on swallowing; also called *globus hystericus* when no disease or organic cause can be discovered. (447). The condition, most common in women, is associated with anxiety and tightness or spasm of throat muscles. The feeling may also be caused by a foreign object in the throat, or swelling of lymphoid tissues such as tonsils or adenoids. The complaint if persistent calls for medical examination to rule out possible physical causes.

Glomeruli. "Little balls"; tufted networks of capillaries which bring blood to chambers of the kidney for filtration of wastes (271). A normal kidney contains about one million glomeruli.

Glomerulonephritis. Acute or chronic inflammation of fine blood vessels of the glomeruli, usually preceded by a streptococcic infection (280).

Glossitis. Inflammation of the tongue.

Glottis. The aperture between the vocal cords, including parts of the voice-box concerned with sound production.

Glucagon. A hormone produced by cells of the pancreas gland, comparable to insulin but opposite in action. Glucagon's function is to correct LOW BLOOD SUGAR levels by stimulating the liver to convert more GLYCOGEN into sugar.

Glue-sniffing. The dangerous, perverted practice of inhaling volatile intoxicating fumes of airplane glues and similar cements, indulged in by some teenagers for "kicks." Intoxicating effects of the fumes have in some instances led to mental upsets and accidents, and there is risk of serious injury to the bone marrow and liver.

Glucocorticoids. Cortisone-like hormones of the adrenal gland which influence carbohydrate, protein, and fat metabolism (318).

Glucose tolerance test. A test for early diabetes and other metabolic disorders. It measures the patient's ability to reduce blood sugar levels at a normal rate. After fasting, a blood sugar level is taken as a baseline and the subject is given a measured amount of dissolved sugar to drink. Blood sugar levels are then taken at hourly intervals. Abnormal rise or persistence of blood sugar is indicative of diabetes. The test is used in borderline cases.

Gluteal. Pertaining to the *gluteus* muscles of the buttocks.

Gluten-free diet. A regimen which excludes wheat, rye, oats, and their products from the diet of patients with *celiac disease.* See MALABSORPTION SYNDROME.

Glycerol. Same as glycerin. Serves as the framework of a molecule for attachment of fatty acids to make a fat.

Glycogen. "Animal starch," quite similar to vegetable starch; the form in which carbohydrate is stored in the liver and released as energy needs demand. The liver manufactures glycogen from DEXTROSE (glucose), a sugar, and re-converts glycogen to blood sugar as needed.

Glycogen storage disease. An hereditary disorder of infants; survival beyond the second year of life is rare. The infant lacks certain enzymes necessary for converting glucose to GLYCOGEN and vice versa. This leads to abnormal deposits of glycogen in various tissues of the body, with progressive slowing down of body processes.

Glycosuria. Presence of sugar in the urine.

Goiter. Enlargement of the thyroid gland. There are several types of goiter (309).

Goitrogens. Substances such as are contained in plants of the cabbage family and some other vegetables, which in excessive amounts induce goiter (314).

Gold salts. Rather toxic compounds of gold, used in progressive, crippling *rheumatoid arthritis* (636) with hope of suppressing the active inflammatory disease and decreasing bone and cartilage destruction.

Golf ball hazard. Liquid-center golf balls are made by freezing liquid material into a solid and wrapping windings around it. When the center thaws, it exerts tremendous pressure against its covering. This is good for long drives down the fairway, but not without hazard to curious children who may cut into a nicked old ball to see what is in it. A golf ball can explode in the face when its liquid center is cut into, spraying white sticky material that can penetrate the skin.

Gonads. The primary sex glands, ovaries or testes.

Gonioscope. An instrument for studying angles of the eye where fluids drain (537).

Gonorrhea. The most common venereal disease, an infection produced by sphere-shape bacteria (40). Recovery from gonorrhea does not give significant future immunity; re-infection is frequent. Incidence of the disease has increased in recent years. The reservoir of symptomless gonorrhea in women is far greater than most medical textbooks indicate, according to authorities of the government's Venereal Disease Research Laboratory in Atlanta. Research at this center indicates that a gonorrhea vaccine may eventually be developed.

Gonorrheal arthritis. A specific form of arthritis associated with gonorrhea, responsive to treatment with penicillin (641).

Gonorrheal ophthalmia. Blinding eye disease of newborn infants, acquired in passage through the birth canal of a mother who has gonorrhea. Obstetricians are required by law to put drops into the baby's eyes at birth to prevent the infection.

Gooseflesh. Little skin bumps induced by chill or shock, almost but not quite hair-raising. The bumps arise around hair follicles in response to vestigial muscles which attempt to raise the hair but can't quite make it.

Gout. An hereditary disorder of body chemistry resulting in too much uric acid in the blood, with chalk-like deposits of urate crystals (derived from uric acid) in cartilage of the joints and sometimes elsewhere (631). *Uricosuric* drugs increase the excretion of uric acid through the kidneys to lessen the accumulation of hurtful urate deposits. Zyloprim (allopurinol), an oral drug made available to the medical profession in 1966, inhibits an enzyme necessary for uric acid production and prevents the body from making too much of it. It is the first drug which actually cuts down the production of uric acid inside the body. There is also evidence that allopurinol may prevent the formation of urate stones, a common type of kidney stone.

GP. General practitioner.

Graafian follicles. Tiny, round, transparent "blisters" imbedded in the ovary (327). Each follicle contains an immature egg cell. Under the influence of the follicle-stimulating hormone of the pituitary gland, one of the blisters is stimulated to grow, and its egg matures in preparation for fertilization. The follicle bursts at about the fourteenth day of the menstrual cycle and releases the "ripened" egg; this is called *ovulation*.

Gram-positive, -negative. Classification of bacteria according to whether they do or do not accept a stain named for Hans Gram, a Danish bacteriologist. Different life processes and vulnerabilities of germs are reflected by their Gram-positive or Gram-negative characteristics. For instance, an antimicrobial drug effective against certain Gram-positive germs may be ineffective against Gram-negative ones, or vice versa.

Grand mal. Severe epileptic seizure; convulsions, loss of consciousness, jerking and stiffening of the body (261).

Granulation tissue. Tiny red, rounded, fleshy masses having a soft pebbly surface and granular appearance; the type of tissue that forms in early stages of wound healing. Each granule has new blood vessels and reparative cells. "Proud flesh" is an excessive overgrowth of granulation tissue.

Granulocytes. White blood cells containing granules that become conspicuous when dyed (134). They are manufactured in red marrow of the bones. One of their functions is to digest and destroy invading bacteria.

Granuloma. A tumor, new growth, or chronically inflamed area in which GRANULATION TISSUE is prominent.

Granuloma inguinale. A mildly contagious venereal disease produced by rod-shaped bacteria (41). It is named for the *inguinal* region (groin) where lesions with a base of GRANULATION TISSUE appear.

Gravel. Fine, sandlike particles of the same substance as kidney stones, often eliminated in the urine without incident.

Graves' disease. Hyperthyroidism, toxic goiter (310).

Gravid. Pregnant. In obstetrician's language, a *gravida* is a pregnant woman; a *primagravida*, one who is pregnant for the first time; a *multigravida*, one who has had several pregnancies.

Greenstick fracture. An incomplete fracture of a long bone, usually in children whose bones are quite pliable (626). The break does not go all the way through the bone, which is splintered on one side only, in much the same way that a green stick splinters on the outside if you hold an end in each hand and bend it inward until it breaks.

Gristle. CARTILAGE.

Grippe. Influenza (54).

Groin. The lowest part of the abdomen where it joins the legs; the groove at this junction. Also called the *inguinal* area, a common site of hernia (710).

Ground substance. Semi-fluid material which fills spaces between connective tissue fibers and cements them together (634).

Growing pains. Pain in a child's legs or arms may be associated with subacute rheumatic fever and the complaint should be investigated by a doctor, but there are other quite harmless causes of what grandma called "growing pains." Non-rheumatic muscle pains at night are quite common in normal healthy children. These pains may possibly be due to normal growth, but more probably are an after-effect of vigorous if not violent playtime activities. The harmless pains usually occur in muscles of the legs and thighs at the end of the day or soon after the child goes to sleep; there is no pain on motion and the child does not limp; he is vague in pointing out where it hurts and is free of pain in the morning.

Growth hormone. A hormone of the anterior pituitary gland which stimulates growth (305).

G.U. Genitourinary.

Guaiac test. A dye test, usually of a stool specimen, for the presence of blood; the blood takes on a blue color if present.

Gullet. The esophagus; the muscular tube through which food passes from mouth to stomach and sometimes vice versa (445).

Gumboil. A swelling of the gum produced by an abscess at the root of a tooth.

Gumma. A firm, rubbery mass of tissue resembling GRANULATION TISSUE, occurring almost anywhere in the body but most frequently in the skin, heart, liver or bones. It is a characteristic lesion of late syphilis (48).

Guthrie test. A blood test to determine whether an infant has *phenylketonuria* (488, 766).

Gynecoid. Resembling a woman; female-like.

Gynecologist. A physician who specializes in diseases of women.

Gynecomastia. Abnormal enlargement of either or both male breasts. It may result from therapeutic use or unintentional absorption of female hormones, from glandular abnormalities, from drugs such as digitalis, amphetamine, or reserpine, or it may be associated with conditions which have little in common, such as thyroid disease, adrenal or testicular tumors, cirrhosis of the liver. Gynecomastia frequently occurs in perfectly healthy adolescent boys and usually disappears in a few weeks; this form is a transient phase of the body's coming into mature hormonal balance.

H

Hairy tongue. A rare condition which may occur after use of antibiotics, or from unknown causes; intertwining hairlike filaments form black or brownish patches on the tongue. The disease, if it may be called such, is harmless. The hairy patches may disappear quickly or persist for months.

Hallucinogenic drugs. Chemical agents which produce hallucinations and distortions of the mind. The best publicized and most potent of these is LSD-25 (*lysergic acid diethylamide*). Others are *mescaline*, derived from buttons of a cactus plant; *psilocybin*, a mushroom poison; *bufotenine*; DMT (*dimethyltryptamine*). *Marijuana* is a mild hallucinogen which can produce panic reactions and acute mental derangement. LSD is a potent analgesic which, under careful medical supervision, has been used to relieve suffering in patients with terminal disease; it has been used experimentally in treatment of alcoholism and forms of mental illness but accumulated evidence is meager. Serious scientific research has been handicapped by the aura of mystery and magic created by cultists who take self-administered drugs to "expand consciousness," give new insights and powers, and invoke mystical experiences. The dangers of illicitly taken LSD have been amply documented; there is no doubt that the drug can induce acute psychosis in an apparently healthy person, and worsen the condition of some mental patients. Reactions to LSD may not be beautiful images but profound terror and violence. Only a single experience with LSD may produce delayed, permanent brain changes; panic reactions and hallucinations have occurred as long as two years after taking a single dose of the drug. There is no convincing proof that LSD stirs the mind to feats of creativity; the drug may simply give an illusion of creative potency. It is thought that LSD acts on centers of the brain where incoming impulses from the senses are sorted and organized, and that in some way the drug distorts normal associations. Hallucinogenic drugs seem to appeal most strongly to neurotic and unstable persons who are most likely to be harmed by them.

Hallux. The big toe.

Hallux valgus. See BUNION.

Hammer toe. A toe which is bent upward like an inverted V and cannot flatten out, usually caused by cramping the toes into too small a shoe (623).

Hamstring. Tendons above the back of the knee. A person crippled by cutting of the hamstring tendons is "hamstrung."

Hand-Schuller-Christian disease. An insidiously developing disease in the first decade of life, manifested by bulging eyes, excessive thirst, deposits of CHOLESTEROL in bones and tissues under the skin (164).

Hansen's disease. See LEPROSY.

Hashimoto's disease. A form of chronic thyroiditis occurring most frequently in middle-aged women (315). It is thought to be an AUTO-IMMUNE DISEASE.

Haverhill fever. See RATBITE FEVER.

Hay fever. Pollinosis; an allergic reaction to inhaled pollens, characterized by reddened, weepy eyes, runny nose, sneezing, nasal stuffiness. (662).

Hearing aids. Choice of the right hearing aid requires hearing tests by an ear specialist, since there are many kinds of hearing impairment, improved by different types of instruments (569). The ear specialist will suggest which type of hearing aid is suitable. The decision depends upon the type of hearing loss, its severity, and other factors. The specialist may suggest a brand-name of hearing aid or make general recommendations.

In selecting a hearing aid:

Compare for clarity and quality of sound. Listen to familiar voices with different aids.

Compare how well you understand speech with each of the aids. Listen in noisy places as well as in quiet. Try the aids outdoors a well as indoors.

Compare for comfort and convenience. Controls should be easy to operate. Batteries, parts and minor repairs should be available locally.

Compare costs. A low-priced aid may be just as satisfactory as a high-priced aid, depending on your needs. Does the price include the ear mold, the cord and the receiver and the battery? Ask about the costs of batteries.

Compare extra services. Does the dealer give you a convenient repair and replacement service? Will the dealer help you to learn to use your aid?

Hearing and Speech Centers can make thorough non-medical study of hearing problems. The centers do not have a commercial interest in hearing aids, but they do have the staff and instruments to help you decide whether an aid will be of benefit. The non-medical tests describe how well you hear at different levels of loudness, under different noise conditions and for different speech sounds. Hearing and speech centers will compare how well you hear when using different models and makes of hearing aids. The centers can help you make better use of whatever hearing you have. This is done by lessons in auditory training and lip-reading. You can get a list of Hearing and Speech Centers near you from the Speech and Hearing Service in your State Department of Health or from your State Vocational Rehabilitation Service.

Heart attack. Common term for *coronary thrombosis* (89).

Heartburn. Mild to severe burning sensations in the upper abdomen or beneath the breastbone, usually resulting from backing-up of stomach contents into the esophagus. Heartburn typically occurs after a heavy meal containing fatty foods, often occurs when the patient is lying down, or sitting with feet slightly elevated, as in watching television, and is relieved by sitting up. Occasional heartburn associated with dietary orgies is not uncommon and does not necessarily require treatment. Weight reduction, antacids, diet regulation, and sleeping with the head of the bed elevated are helpful measures. Persistent or severe heartburn, or pain thought to be heartburn, may be associated with disease requiring medical diagnosis. Heartburn is the most common symptom of *hiatus hernia* (446). It is frequent in the middle and later months of pregnancy (346).

Heart-lung machine. A device which infuses oxygen into a patient's venous blood (a lung function) and pumps the freshened blood to the circulation (a heart function). Several types of such devices make open heart surgery feasible (103, 714).

Heart murmurs. Various sorts of soft, swishing sounds murmured by the heart to a physician's discriminating ears. The mere presence of murmurs does not necessarily indicate serious disease. Some murmurs are congenital, some are acquired (as from rheumatic fever), some are functional and of no great significance. Murmurs are heard in many healthy children and adults. The meaning of murmurs, as of all symptoms, must be interpreted by a physician; some indicate a need for tests and studies leading to corrective treatment (389).

Heat cramps. Painful muscle spasms of legs and abdomen resulting from loss of salt through profuse, prolonged sweating (815).

"Heat hives." Wheals and "blush patches" on the skin produced by external warmth or internal warmth (as by vigorous jitterbugging) in sensitive persons, especially red-headed young women (676).

Heatstroke (*sunstroke*). A very serious reaction to exposure to extreme heat. The heat-regulating centers in the brain are paralyzed; the victim's extremely high temperature must be reduced immediately with ice packs or streams of cold water (814).

Heberden's nodes. Knobby lumps at the end joints of a woman's fingers, occurring usually after the menopause (631). The condition is a form of osteoarthritis which does not progress to severe crippling. The classic description by William Heberden, an English physician, is as valid today as when he published his account in 1802: "... little hard knobs, about the size of a small pea, which are frequently seen upon the fingers, particularly a little below the top, near the joint. They have no connection with the gout, being found in persons who never had it; they continue for life; and being hardly ever attended by pain, or disposed to become sores, are rather unsightly than inconvenient, though they must be of some little hindrance to the free use of the fingers."

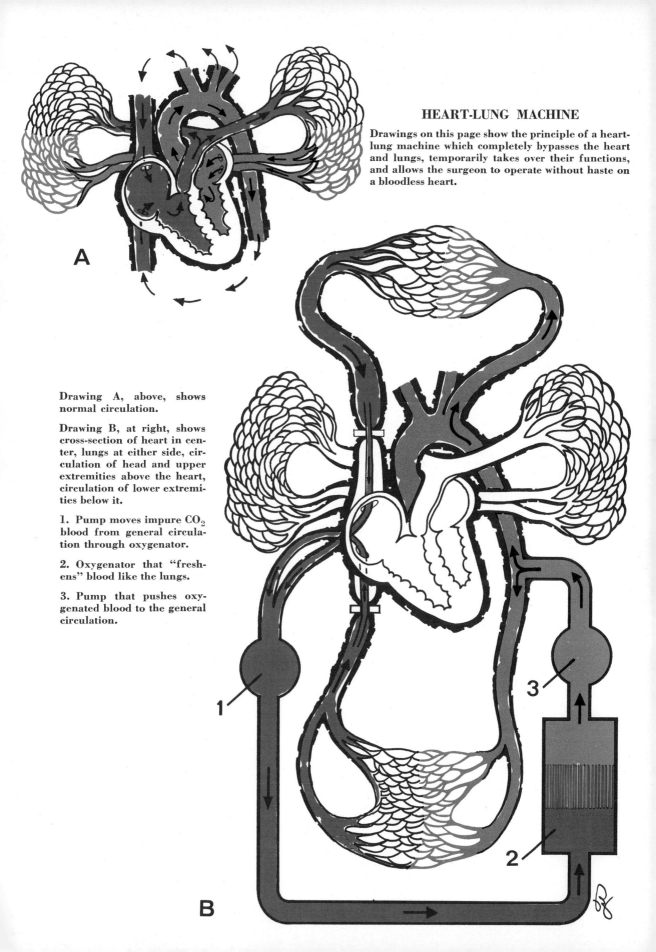

HEART-LUNG MACHINE

Drawings on this page show the principle of a heart-lung machine which completely bypasses the heart and lungs, temporarily takes over their functions, and allows the surgeon to operate without haste on a bloodless heart.

A

Drawing A, above, shows normal circulation.

Drawing B, at right, shows cross-section of heart in center, lungs at either side, circulation of head and upper extremities above the heart, circulation of lower extremities below it.

1. Pump moves impure CO_2 blood from general circulation through oxygenator.

2. Oxygenator that "freshens" blood like the lungs.

3. Pump that pushes oxygenated blood to the general circulation.

1

3

2

B

Helminthiasis. Infestation with *helminths,* parasitic worms (65).

Hemangioma. A red, often elevated birthmark; "strawberry mark." It may or may not be present at birth. Only superficial blood vessels are involved. The mark often disappears of itself after some months, but some cases may require treatment (184, 382).

Hematemesis. Vomiting of blood.

Hematocele. A swelling produced by effusion of blood into a cavity.

Hematocrit. The percentage of red blood cells in whole blood, by volume; a reading is obtained by whirling whole blood in a centrifuge to pack the cells.

Hematoma. A swelling filled with blood which clots to form a solid mass. The blood accumulates from vessels injured by a blow or disease. A *subdural hematoma* is one that occurs under the skull. The "cauliflower ear" of boxers results from a neglected hematoma.

Hematuria. Blood in the urine. *Occult* blood in the urine is not visible but can be detected by tests. Hematuria may occur from relatively harmless causes (for example, prolonged marching, and severe stresses of physical contact sports), but it may portend serious disease and always requires medical investigation (279).

Hemocytometer. A device for counting blood cells.

Hemianopsia. "Half vision"; blindness for one half of the field of vision. One or both eyes may be affected.

Hemiplegia. Paralysis of one side of the body, due to a clot or rupture of a brain artery (stroke, 117), or a lesion or injury of a part of the nervous system.

Hemochromatosis (*bronze diabetes*). A progressive disease characterized by abnormal deposits of iron in many organs of the body, associated with bronzing of the skin, diabetes, and impaired functioning of the liver and pancreas. Mild forms of the disease with few if any clinical symptoms may require liver biopsy to make the diagnosis. Just why enormous amounts of iron are stored in tissues is not fully understood. It is thought that the patient has an abnormal capacity to absorb iron, rather than lessened ability to excrete it, and that the trait is genetically determined. A key treatment of severe hemochromatosis is frequent bloodletting (PHLEBOTOMY) as often as once a week, to deplete the stores of iron.

Hemodialysis. Separation of waste materials from blood by passage through a semipermeable membrane, especially as performed by an artificial kidney (284).

Hemoglobin. The coloring matter of red blood cells. The molecule contains a protein part (*globin*) joined with an iron-containing pigment, *heme* (from which comes the prefix *hem-* for many medical words denoting some relationship to the blood). *Heme* is the oxygen-carrying portion of hemoglobin. The molecule functions like a pickup truck for oxygen and a dump truck for carbon dioxide. Hemoglobin picks up oxygen in the lungs, holds it loosely, carries it in arterial blood and delivers it as a fuel to cells. In exchange, it picks up carbon dioxide which cells must get rid of and carries it to the lungs where it is dumped and exhaled while a fresh load of oxygen is taken on. Iron is the key element of this remarkable gas-transporting molecule but the protein part is vital too; not all anemias are benefited by merely taking iron.

Hemolysis. Dissolution, breakdown of red cells with release of HEMOGLOBIN. Red cells are constantly being broken down and replaced; the process balances out in healthy persons (134). Excessive hemolysis may result from chemicals, incompatible transfusions, snake venom, and congenital or acquired conditions leading to hemolytic jaundice and anemia (147).

Hemophilia. Bleeder's disease (152). Hope that hemophilia may be conquered received great impetus in 1967 with development of a concentrated anti-hemophilic protein (*globulin*) which may lead to a dosage form that the patient can inject daily to prevent bleeding episodes.

Hemoptysis. Spitting of blood from the chest.

Hemorrhage. Bleeding. The only normal form of bleeding is menstruation. Otherwise, bleeding is a sign of something wrong, often the major symptom to be dealt with immediately in giving first aid (780). *Arterial bleeding* comes in spurts and jets of bright red blood with each beat of the heart, unless blood wells up into a wound from a deep artery. *Venous bleeding* is indicated by a continuous flow of dark blood. *Capillary bleeding* is a general oozing from a raw surface such as a skinned knee. *Internal bleeding* is to be suspected if the patient has suffered severe blows, crushing, falls, penetrating injuries which may lacerate internal organs. Disease, such as erosion of a peptic ulcer, may cause hemorrhage into closed body cavities, with signs of impending shock (784).

Hemorrhoids (*piles*). Dilated, overstretched, varicose veins in and around the rectal opening. The condition is common, often is tolerated quite well for years, sometimes is temporary, as in pregnancy (347), and frequently responds to medical treatment and improvement of bowel habits (468). Hemorrhoids may shrink of themselves, or get worse. There may be no symptoms, or mild occasional discomfort, eased by a hot SITZ BATH or prescribed ointment, or there may be complications of infection, bleeding, distressing pain, formation of a clot in a vein. Hemorrhoids do not become cancerous, but rectal bleeding should be investigated because hemorrhoids and cancer may co-exist. Continued slight blood losses may lead to anemia. Some hemorrhoids can be injected with a solution which hardens and obliterates the vein. Some are best removed by a common surgical operation, *hemorrhoidectomy* (738).

Hemostat. An instrument which stops bleeding by clamping a blood vessel, or an agent which stops bleeding.

Henoch-Schoenlein purpura. An allergic form of hemorrhage into the skin, beginning with pain in the abdomen and joints. Recovery is usually spontaneous unless the kidneys are affected. The condition may be associated with streptococcal infection or rheumatic fever or food allergy (665).

Hepatitis. Virus-caused inflammation of the liver (60, 398). There are two forms, *infectious hepatitis*, transmitted by contaminated food or water or direct contact with an infected person, and *serum hepatitis*, associated with blood transfusions, injections, contaminated needles. Presumably the two forms are caused by different viruses, although there are respected authorities who suggest that viral hepatitis may be an occasional complication of a general viral disease caused by a variety of agents, rather than a primary disease of the liver caused by one or two specific viruses. The actual incidence of viral hepatitis is probably far higher than has been estimated; for every diagnosed case there may be as many as 30 symptomless, undiagnosed cases.

Hepatolenticular degeneration. See WILSON'S DISEASE.

Hepatoma. A tumor of the liver (456).

Heredity. Great unravelings of structures in cells which transmit hereditary characteristics from ancestors to progeny have been made in recent years. The "gross stuff" of heredity, the CHROMOSOMES, can be seen under a microscope and have long been known to scientists. The finer, infinitesimal structures of heredity—molecules invisible to man—have only recently yielded some of their age-old secrets. Stupendous, coded, message-carrying molecules in the chromosomes are called *deoxyribonucleic acid* (DNA). A long DNA molecule consists of two intertwining chains coiled around a common axis, roughly like a spiral ladder with thousands of connecting rungs or steps. These rungs (bases) are of four kinds of rather simple chemical units known as adenine, guanine, cytosine, and thymine. Call these by their initials, A, G, C, and T, and you have a four-letter "alphabet" with which to write the genetic codes for chemical processes of organisms from bacteria to man. Thousands and millions of the four "letters" in a DNA molecule can be arranged in almost infinitely different sequences. There are about 100 million of these sequences in a chromosome.

It is thought that GENES which determine particular traits (eye color, or differences between mice and men) are sites of specific sequences of a few A, G, C, T "letters" on the DNA molecule. How can a non-living molecule write the blueprints of life? The "one gene, one enzyme" theory postulates that a gene directs the body to synthesize a specific enzyme to catalyze some vital chemical process of life. All enzymes are proteins, constructed of some 20-odd simple AMINO ACID units in different sequences. Each enzyme must have its scores or hundreds of amino acids in exactly the right sequence; if not, some life process may go awry and be manifested as disease.

According to present knowledge, DNA directs the synthesis of enzymes, and hence of myriads of life processes, in this way: In the cell nucleus, DNA imprints its base-code upon a slightly different form of nucleic acid, ribonucleic acid (RNA). The imprinted RNA moves out from the nucleus into the cytoplasm of the cell where it serves as a template for linking different amino acids in directed sequence. Assembly of amino acids into proteins takes place on the surface of minute particles called *ribosomes*. A different form of RNA, called transfer RNA, picks up an amino acid, carries it to the template, deposits it in its ordained place, and goes back for another load. There is a specific transfer RNA for each kind of amino acid.

Thus, in sketchy outline, the genetic code is expressed in synthesized molecules which give us our uniqueness, regulate and control incessant chemical transactions of the body, become parts of structures, and expedite processes of thought and feeling. Increasing knowledge of these marvelous chemical mechanisms has profound implications for the future of medicine. Some diseases (for example, PHENYLKETONURIA, GALACTOSEMIA, ALKAPTONURIA) are now known to result from lack of an enzyme for which the patient did not inherit the necessary gene. Many diseases of presently unknown cause may be shown to have a similar basis, to be the ultimate result of a "disorder" of molecules. It may some day be possible to "treat" molecules instead of symptoms. See MEDICAL GENETICS.

Hermaphrodite. A person with the sex organs of both sexes. True hermaphrodites are rare. More common are *pseudohermaphrodites*, examples of *intersex* (298, 321). Such persons, "assigned" to the wrong sex at birth, may in later life be candidates for SEX REVERSAL operations, which do not actually change the basic sex, but give it better expression. Assignment of true sex at birth can be very difficult because of great variation in external and internal structures. Males with HYPOSPADIAS and UNDESCENDED TESTICLES may be assigned a female role; females may be mistaken for males with these abnormalities. Surgical exploration is often necessary in doubtful cases, and it may be possible for surgery to correct the condition, if not completely, at least to a degree of sat-

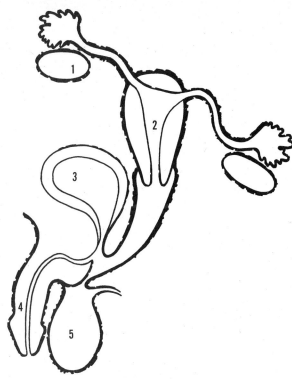

Schematic drawing of true hermaphrodite with organs of both sexes: 1. ovary; 2. uterus; 3. bladder; 4, penis; 5. testicle.

isfactory adjustment. But the varieties of hermaphroditism are far too numerous and complex for any single "rule" of sex assignment. Even the genetic sex may be "wrong." "Girls" with testicular feminization have internal testes and are genetically male, but they have a body of normal female appearance, with a vagina but without a uterus or menstruation; their hormones at puberty are exclusively feminizing and their entire psychic outlook is feminine. Cases of doubtful sex require individual study and technical knowledge. If the sex of an infant is in doubt, appropriate steps, surgical or otherwise, should be taken at an early age, not only that the child may identify with its appropriate sex, but because in some cases an endocrine disturbance detrimental to health may underlie the condition.

Hernia (*rupture*). Protrusion of an organ or part of an organ through a weak spot in tissues which normally contain it. There can be herniations of the brain, lung, or other organs, but the most common herniations are of

organs contained by the abdominal wall. A natural weak spot in the groin area, especially in men, who have an opening through which the spermatic cord passes, is the site of *inguinal* hernia, the most common type in both men and women. It is repairable by a common surgical operation (709), as indeed are other forms of hernia (391, 446, 697).

Herniorraphy. Any operation for repair of hernia which includes suturing.

Herpangina. A COXSACKIE VIRUS infection, usually of infants and children, producing fever, sore throat, loss of appetite, sometimes nausea and vomiting (58).

Herpes simplex. The cold sore or fever blister virus (55).

Herpes zoster. See SHINGLES.

Hiatus hernia. DIAPHRAGMATIC HERNIA.

Hiccups (hiccough). The annoyance is known to all; its definition—spasmodic contraction of the DIAPHRAGM and sudden closure of the glottis—is rather formidable. Irritation of nerves that control the diaphragm (203) causes spasm, and the glottis, the chink between the vocal cords, snaps shut, causing a peculiar sound. The hiccup trigger may be an overloaded stomach, trapped gas, something that went down the wrong way, swallowing hot foods or irritants, gulping, or unknown trifling provocations. Virtually all of the popular cures for hiccups (rebreathing from a paper bag, holding the breath as long as possible, taking a dozen swallows of water without stopping to breathe) increase the carbon dioxide content of the lungs and thus help to stabilize the breathing center. Severe hiccups which continue for hours or days may be associated with liver, abdominal, or intestinal disease or lesions of the breathing center; temporary surgical interruption of the phrenic nerve may be necessary to stop incessant spasms.

Hip dislocation, congenital. Spontaneous dislocation of the hip shortly after or before birth (613).

Hippocratic oath. A statement of ethics traditionally demanded of the young physician on entering practice. It contains some anachronisms—mention of freemen and slaves, and apparent ruling out of operations for bladder stone (*lithotomy*) as beneath the dignity of reputable men of medicine. Anciently, through the Middle Ages and beyond, the operation of "cutting for stone" was usually attempted by itinerant operators who acquired some skill through trial and error at the expense of patients. Surgery was necessarily crude and dangerous, devoid of aseptic techniques, reliable anesthesia, and other supports of modern surgery, and mortality was high. If the patient survived, the operator benefited from word-of-mouth advertising; if the patient died, the operator was usually long gone to some other community. But the ethical precepts of the Oath endure. The Oath bears the name of Hippocrates, the famous Greek physician, born about 460 B.C., who is called the "Father of Medicine" for his sound and close observations of patients and diseases which began to give the medical arts a scientific foundation, but whether or not Hippocrates himself wrote the Oath is not known; more likely it is a collective expression of his followers. There are several English translations of the Oath; the wording that follows is best known:

"I swear by Apollo the physician, by Aesculapius, Hygeia, and Panacea, and I take to witness all the gods, all the goddesses, to keep according to my ability and my judgment the following Oath:

"To consider dear to me as my parents him who taught me this art, to live in common with him and if necessary to share my goods with him, to look upon his children as my own brothers, to teach them this art if they so desire without fee or written promise, to impart to my sons and the sons of the master who taught me and the disciples who have enrolled themselves and have agreed to the rules of the profession, but to these alone, the precepts and instruction.

"I will prescribe regimen for the good of my patients according to my ability and my judgment and never do harm to anyone. To please no one will I give a deadly drug, nor give advice which may cause his death. Nor will I give a woman a pessary to procure abortion. But I will preserve the purity of my life and my art. I will not cut for stone, even for patients in whom the disease is manifest. I will leave this operation to be performed by specialists in this art.

"In every house where I come I will enter only for the good of my patients, keeping myself far from all intentional ill-doing and all seduction, and especially from the pleasures of love with women or with men, be they free or slaves. All that may come to my knowledge in the exercise of my profession or outside of my profession or in daily commerce with men, which ought not to be spread abroad, I will keep secret and will never reveal.

"If I keep this oath faithfully, may I enjoy my life and practice my art, respected by all men and in all times, but if I swerve from it or violate it, may the reverse be my lot."

Hirschsprung's disease. See MEGACOLON.

Hirsutism. Abnormal hairiness of body parts not normally hairy (328).

Histamine. A normal chemical of body cells which plays a part in allergic reactions (648).

Histoplasmosis. Systemic infection due to inhalation of dusts containing spores of a species of fungi (72).

Hives. Urticaria (666).

Hoarseness. Generally a trivial (and socially benevolent) symptom resulting from using the voice at the top of the lungs too long; if it persists more than a couple of weeks, a doctor should be consulted to determine the cause (589).

Hookworm. Infestation of the carelessly barefooted who tread upon soils contaminated with eggs of the responsible worm (67).

Hobnail liver. A liver studded with small nodules which somewhat resemble hobnails; characteristic of the most common form of CIRRHOSIS OF THE LIVER (455).

Hodgkin's disease. Malignancy of the lymph nodes (162). The pessimistic view that the disease is incurable (stemming from crude diagnostic methods and primitive radiation equipment of the past) is just not true, in the light of results with intensive high-energy x-rays which give apparently permanent cure to 80 to 90 per cent of patients with only a few lymph nodes affected by the disease.

Horseshoe kidney. Kidneys linked at their lower ends by a band of tissue instead of being separate; their shape somewhat resembles a horseshoe (279).

Hordoleum. A stye (544).

Hot flashes. See MENOPAUSE.

Household pets. The family dog, cat, or other pet is a pleasure-giving member of the household—if the animal is healthy and well cared-for. Most pet-owners realize the importance of having a veterinarian vaccinate an animal against RABIES. Less well known are some of the discomforts, and even serious diseases, which may arise from animals that do not get the veterinary or loving care that they deserve. Puppies and kittens in particular should be de-wormed by a veterinarian to prevent contamination of soil and materials with worm eggs in their excretions. Children and puppies make a pretty intimate team. Ingested eggs of the common dog roundworm can enter the bloodstream and larva

can reach many parts of the body. Mysterious cases of SCABIES, "the itch," have occurred in persons who never dreamed that the family dog carried the mites. Animals may be hosts to ticks which can cause disease. Animals with fur or feathers (even stuffed toy ones) are suspect inhabitants if someone in the family has allergies, even though skin tests may not show sensitivity to a particular animal. Allergic persons have a tendency to become sensitized to danders. Pets that give a lot deserve a lot, and should have veterinary attention if they show any of the following symptoms: Abnormal behavior, sudden viciousness or lethargy; abnormal discharges; abnormal lumps or difficulty in getting up or lying down; loss of appetite, marked weight loss or gain, or excessive water consumption; excessive head shaking, scratching, and biting any part of the body.

Housemaid's knee. Bursitis of the knee joint (628).

Housewife's eczema. A more dignified term than "dishpan hands" for dermatitis associated with soaps, detergents, and water (177).

Humor. Any fluid or semi-fluid of the body; for example, aqueous and vitreous humors of the eye (529). No connection with the ancient humoral theory of disease, which held that sickness results from lamentable disproportions of four body humors—blood, phlegm, yellow bile and black bile—respectively associated with sanguine, phlegmatic, choleric, and melancholic temperaments. Our word "melancholy" literally means "black bile."

Hunner's ulcer. An ulcer of the lining of the urinary bladder, associated with chronic interstitial cystitis (shrinkage of the bladder wall, splitting, decreased capacity).

Huntington's chorea. A rare hereditary disease, appearing in middle life or later; there is progressive deterioration of the nervous system, manifested in jerky, involuntary movements of the arms, legs, and face; personality changes, speech defects, difficulties of walking and swallowing. Profound nervous degeneration ultimately leads to idiocy and death. The disease is transmitted as a dominant trait (see MEDICAL GENETICS). Members of families in which the disease has appeared should have the benefit of genetic counseling; if they are carriers of the defective genes, half of their children, statistically, will have the disease, and for that reason they may choose to forgo parenthood.

Hutchinson's teeth. Widely spaced, narrow-edged upper central incisors with notching at the biting edge; a sign of congenital syphilis, though not always of that origin.

Hyaline membrane disease. A condition of pronounced respiratory distress which affects newborn infants, especially premature infants, at birth, and may be fatal in a day or two. It is the most common cause of death of live-born premature infants. The affected infant can't get enough oxygen because ducts leading to tiny air sacs in the lungs are lined with hyaline (glassy) material, probably derived from the baby's own secretions. Breath is rapid and labored almost from the moment of birth; CYANOSIS appears; the tiny heart works desperately to push enough blood through the lungs. Absence of a substance which reduces surface tensions and normally lines the air sacs seems to be the most important abnormality. Treatment consists of measures to avoid premature delivery if possible, rapid resuscitation at birth of premature infants, care in an incubator to maintain high humidity and prevent heat loss. Babies who survive beyond the third day almost always recover.

Hydatid disease. Infestation with animal tapeworms which produce clusters of fluid-filled cysts in the lungs and other organs (67).

Hydatidiform mole. A rare complication of early pregnancy, resulting from degeneration of membranes which would normally become a part of the placenta. The mass resembles a bunch of grapes of irregular size.

Hydramnios. An excess of fluid produced by the innermost of the fetal membranes (*amnion*) which forms the BAG OF WATERS that surrounds the fetus. *Acute hydramnios* is rare; it begins during mid-pregnancy and rapidly expands the uterus to enormous size. The condition terminates in spontaneous abortion or abortion induced to save the mother's life. *Chronic hydramnios* is a more common and less threatening form, does not often terminate in miscarriage, but frequently provokes premature labor.

Hydrocele. Swelling of the scrotum from accumulation of fluid in the sac of the membrane that covers the testicle (300). It is painless but weight of the fluid causes a dragging sensation. Usually only one side is involved. The condition may be related to some injury but in most cases the cause is obscure and the testicles function normally. Chronic hydrocele, most frequent in middle-aged men, is relieved by withdrawal of fluid (TAPPING) but the swelling tends to recur.

Hydrocephalus. "Water on the brain"; actually, water *in* the brain—abnormal amounts of CEREBROSPINAL FLUID in brain cavities, exerting destructive pressure on brain substance (260).

Hydronephrosis. Swelling of the cavity of the kidney because of obstruction to outflow of urine, as from a stone, stricture, or tumor, in the kidney itself or in a ureter or within the bladder (285, 286).

Hydrophobia. A common word for RABIES. The literal meaning of the word is "fear of water."

Hydrotherapy. Treatment by means of water.

Hymen. A membranous partition which partially blocks the external orifice of the virginal vagina (408).

Hyperbaric therapy. Treatment by inhalation of oxygen at greater than atmospheric pressure; an auxiliary to other appropriate treatment. The patient, physicians, and nurses occupy a large, long pressure chamber wherein the atmospheric pressure is increased to about three times the sea level pressure. The patient breathes pure oxygen to increase the amount delivered to body cells. The technique has been employed experimentally in treatment of carbon monoxide poisoning, tetanus, and infections caused by bacteria which do not thrive in the presence of oxygen.

Hyperchlorhydria. Excessive hydrochloric acid in gastric juices.

Hypercholesteremia. Excessive amounts of CHOLESTEROL in the blood.

Hyperemesis gravidarum. Vomiting of pregnancy, more severe than simple MORNING SICKNESS which clears up by itself; may require hospitalization.

Hyperhidrosis. Excessive sweating.

Hyperinsulism. A condition of abnormally low blood sugar resulting from an excess of insulin or deficiency of sugar; similar to insulin shock.

Hypernephroma. A malignant tumor of the kidney which occurs primarily in persons over 40 years of age (283).

Hyperopia. Farsightedness.

Hyperplasia. Overgrowth of an organ or tissue from an increase in the number of its cells which are, however, in normal arrangement.

Hypertension. Abnormally high arterial blood pressure (108).

Hypertensive heart disease. A form of heart disease associated with high blood pressure which forces the heart to work harder to pump blood against resistance (81).

Hyperthyroidism (*thyrotoxicosis, toxic goiter.*) Overactivity of the thyroid gland (310).

Hypertrophy. Increase in size of an organ because of overgrowth of cells, without an increase in the number of cells. It is usually a response to increased activity or functional demands; voluntary, as when a robustly exercised muscle increases in size, or involuntary, as when the body enlarges one kidney to compensate for a deficiency of its partner.

Hypnotic. Inducing sleep; a sleeping-pill. BARBITURATES are hypnotics most often prescribed by physicians.

Hypnosis. There is no black magic about medical hypnosis, and its purpose—to assist in treatment of patients—is quite different from the entertaining art of the stage hypnotist. Hypnosis is not a curative treatment, but at times it can be helpful to a physician in undertaking procedures he is qualified to undertake without hypnosis. The American Medical Association recognizes that there is a significant place for hypnosis in modern medical practice. Medical hypnosis first of all requires that the practitioner be trained as a physician. The hypnotic trance itself is harmless but it can be misused by the medically untrained; a headache which can be temporarily "hypnotized away" may result from a low-grade brain tumor. The major medical uses of hypnosis are for relief of pain and anxiety; for example, in childbirth (351), dentistry, psychological preparation for anesthesia and surgery. Hypnosis may reduce the amount of an anesthetic that is needed, and is especially useful when anesthetics and sedatives are for some reason undesirable. Unreasonably high hopes for medical hypnotic miracles are not justified. A physician who occasionally uses hypnosis treats his patients as usual but sometimes uses hypnosis as an adjunct. A principal disadvantage of hypnosis is the amount of time required. It may be difficult to find a physician who employs hypnosis; if found, he is not necessarily more skilled in treatment of disease than physicians who do not. About one physician in 40 or 50 uses hypnosis more or less regularly in his practice. A dozen medical schools now offer courses in hypnosis as a part of medical training.

Hypodermic. Under the skin; commonly refers to hypodermic injection, or the needle which effects it, or to the "shot" itself.

Hypoglycemia. Deficiency of sugar in the blood. *Hypoglycemic shock* due to an overdose of insulin is the same as *insulin shock.*

Hypoovarianism. Inadequate functioning of the ovaries (326).

Hypophysis. The pituitary gland (304).

Hypospadias. A congenital malformation in which the urethra, the urinary outlet, fails to fuse completely, but takes the form of an open trough-like channel on the underside of the penis (291). A similar malformation in the female permits urine to escape into the vagina.

Hypotension. Low blood pressure; sometimes significant, but usually harmless, not warranting treatment or concern, and perhaps even a promise of longevity (116).

Hypothalamus. A part of the "old brain" concerned with primitive functions such as appetite, procreation, sleep, body temperature; closely associated with the pituitary gland (303).

Hypothyroidism. Deficiency of thyroid hormone, leading to a slowing down of mental and physical processes. If the deficiency occurs in an infant before birth, it is known as *cretinism;*

if it occurs in an adult, it is known as *myxedema* (312).

Hysterectomy. Surgical removal of the uterus (421), either through an abdominal incision, or through the vagina, which leaves no abdominal scar (706).

I

Iatrogenic diseases. Those unintentionally induced by words or actions of a physician. A patient may misconstrue a doctor's remark or ominous look and be convinced that he has a grave disease which doesn't exist or is not nearly so grave as he fears. Iatrogenic heart disease is not uncommon; a doctor's casual mention of a murmur or premature beat may send a fearful patient to his rocking chair with iatrogenic invalidism, although he would be much better off if he remained active. A sort of pseudo-iatrogenic disease can be induced by "recognizing" in one's self the horrendous symptoms of exotic maladies described on television or in the press; in such case the obvious cure is to consult a doctor and believe his reassurances. Some iatrogenic disease is unavoidable, the side effects of drugs nevertheless necessary for the patient's welfare.

Icterus. Same as JAUNDICE.

Ichthyosis (*fish skin disease*). Dry, fishlike scaliness of the skin, a congenital abnormality (196). There are two forms of ichthyosis, both of which are hereditary. The commoner form is transmitted as a dominant trait; the other is determined by a sex-linked recessive gene. The latter type affects males only but is tranmitted by apparently normal females. See MEDICAL GENETICS.

Identical twins. Twins, always of the same sex and having the same heredity, developing from a single fertilized egg (358).

Idiopathic. Originating spontaneously from unknown causes, not the result of any other disease; peculiar to the self.

Idiosyncrasy. Peculiar personal capacity to react differently than most people to drugs, foods, or treatment.

Ileitis. Inflammation of the ILEUM (702).

Ileum. The lower portion of the small intestine, a tube about ten feet long in which major processes of digestion and assimilation take place (429). It is continuous with the *jejunum,* a section of the small intestine which lies above it, and joins the colon at the *cecum,* a bulgy, dilated pouch from which the appendix dangles. The *ileocecal valve* at this junction controls the admission of semi-liquid contents into the colon.

Ilium. The broad upper part of the hipbone (595).

"Immediate" dentures. Artificial dentures worn immediately after extraction of the front teeth, the other teeth having been removed previously. While the gums are healing, the denture is prepared and is worn as soon as the front teeth are removed. This saves the patient the embarrassment of being conspicuously toothless for a while (516).

Immunity. Complex body mechanisms which create immunities to disease germs and foreign substances are not at all well understood, but a continuing ferment of research in this area has produced exciting bits of knowledge which may ultimately be relevant to cancer, arthritis, and other diseases which many authorities think may be related to the inability of immunity mechanisms to cast out abnormal cells and substances. The role of the thymus in producing protective ANTIBODIES has only recently been clarified (see THYMUS GLAND). It now seems probable that the human body has two immunity systems. The second system has not been pinpointed, and its existence is debated by specialists, but it is known that chickens have two immunity systems. In addition to a thymus, chickens have an organ at the end of the intestinal tract (bursa of Fabricius) which controls antibodies. While researchers are hopefully looking for something comparable in the human appendix, intestines, tonsils, spleen, and other tissues, present methods of immunizing against diseases (374) give certain protection to all except a very few unfortunate persons who have defective immunizing mechanisms (and whose deficiencies have given scientists an invaluable tool for prying out secrets of the mechanisms). There are two kinds of immunity. *Passive immunity* is the kind borrowed from someone else, when a doctor injects GAMMA GLOBULIN or some other substance containing preformed antibodies made by another person or animal, or when a mother's antibodies are transferred to her unborn child. These donated antibodies wear out in a few weeks. *Active immunity* is the kind produced by vaccination or exposure to disease germs; the body is stimulated to produce its own antibodies, continues to do so for a long time, and steps up antibody production when renewed by a booster shot or another contact with germs it "recognizes" immediately.

Immunization. Procedures by which immunities to diseases are produced in a person; especially, by vaccines and toxoids. See IMMUNITY, *active* and *passive.*

Active Immunizing Agents (1966)

Diphtheria toxoid
Tetanus toxoid
Pertussis (whooping cough) antigen
Poliomyelitis
Measles
Vaccinia (smallpox)
BCG (tuberculosis)
Yellow fever
Rabies
Typhoid

Influenza
Mumps
Tularemia
Typhus
Rocky Mountain spotted fever
Cholera
Plague
Adenovirus

Schedule for Active Immunization and Tuberculin Testing of Normal Infants and Children

(as recommended by Committee on Control of Infectious Diseases, American Academy of Pediatrics)

DTP = combined diphtheria and tetanus toxoids and pertussis vaccine
OPV = Oral Polio vaccine
TD = tetanus and diphtheria toxoids
Frequency of TUBERCULIN TESTS depends on risk of exposure and prevalence of tuberculosis in the population group.

Age	
2–3 months	DTP, OPV
3–4 months	DTP, OPV
4–5 months	DTP, OPV
9–11 months	Tuberculin test
12 months	Measles vaccine
15–18 months	DTP, OPV, smallpox vaccine (initial smallpox vaccine may be given at any time between 12 and 24 months of age)
2 years	Tuberculin test
3 years	DTP, tuberculin test
4 years	Tuberculin test
6 years	TD, smallpox vaccine, tuberculin test
8 years	Tuberculin test
10 years	Tuberculin test
12 years	TD, smallpox vaccine, tuberculin test
14 years	Tuberculin test
16 years	Tuberculin test

After age 12, as in adults, smallpox vaccine is recommended every five years and tetanus toxoid booster every ten years.

Immunoglobulins. Substances in the blood and in certain body fluids other than blood which build immunities to various diseases; loosely synonymous with ANTIBODIES.

Impacted. Firmly lodged, wedged in place; as, an impacted wisdom tooth, imbedded in the jawbone so it can't erupt (502).

Imperforate hymen. Complete closure of the membrane at the opening of the vagina (405).

Implant dentures. Artificial dentures with projecting buttons which snap into metal receptacles implanted in the jawbone, like snap-fasteners of a garment. The purpose is to prevent dentures from wobbling if the gums are too flabby to hold them firmly (515).

Impotence. Incapacity of the male to have a penile erection and perform the sexual act. Impotence is an impediment of delivery rather than of production of SPERMATOZOA; it is not the same as infertility, which may affect perfectly potent males. Anatomical defects, injuries or disorders of the nervous or endocrine systems, and systemic diseases may cause impotence, and the possibility should first be investigated. But the great majority of cases have a psychic basis; the affected male may be impotent with one sexual partner but not with another; emotional factors are varied and complex and counseling or psychiatric help may be required.

Incisors. The four cutting teeth at the front of the jaw, upper and lower (*central incisors*). Each pair is flanked by *lateral incisors*. (499).

Incontinence. Inability to restrain feces or urine.

Incubation period. The time between infection with disease organisms and the first appearance of symptoms (398). The period varies for different diseases, as short as a day or two for influenza and as long as 50 days for infectious hepatitis.

Incus. A tiny anvil-shaped bone, the middle bone in the chain of *ossicles* of the middle ear which conduct sounds to the inner ear (560).

Indigestion. A general lay term for abdominal distress with such symptoms as heartburn, bloating, gas, cramping, "fullness" (449).

Indolent. Slow to heal, as an indolent ulcer.

Induction of labor. Artificial stimulation of labor before it starts naturally; accomplished by rupturing the BAG OF WATERS or use of drugs such as *oxytocin* (364).

Indurated. Hardened.

Infant sleep patterns. Newborn infants don't actually sleep most of the time. They sleep about 16 hours out of the 24, and can sleep only about 4 hours at a stretch. One study of newborn infants showed only a gradual decrease in amount of sleep per day over a 16-week period. By the time they were four months of age they slept about 14½ hours a day, while increasing the length of a single sleep period to a little more than eight hours. Waking periods of newborn infants are more frequent from 5 p.m. to 3 a.m. than during the day. Long intervals between feedings may account for nighttime wakefulness. At two to three weeks of age, CIRCADIAN RHYTHMS (24-hour cycles) of sleep and wakefulness begin to develop. At three years of age a child has generally consolidated his sleep time and sleeps about ten hours a night. "Sleep problems" may be aggravated about the fifth year when daytime naps are given up. There is no arbitrary time for giving up afternoon naps, but generally they should be tapered off when a nap delays the onset of sleep in the evening and keeps the child awake after going to bed.

Infantile eczema. An eruptive skin disorder of infancy, frequently due to food sensitivities (393).

Infarct. An area of dead tissue resulting from complete blockage of its blood supply. This frequently occurs in *coronary thrombosis* when a clot in a coronary artery stops the supply of blood to a portion of the heart muscle, producing *myocardial infarction* (89). "Infarction" is easily misspelled or misread as "infraction."

Infectious jaundice. See LEPTOSPIROSIS.

Infectious mononucleosis. Presumed to be a viral infection, but no specific virus has been identified (61). The name comes from involvement of *mononucleocytes,* a type of white blood cell. The disease is quite benign, rarely causes complications, and needs no treatment other than bed rest, aspirin, and perhaps gargling. Occasionally the disease causes temporary and usually harmless liver changes; some of the fear that infectious mononucleosis is a very serious disease may arise from confusing minor liver changes with the much more serious changes of infectious hepatitis. Reports from several college infirmaries indicate that "mono" lasts about two weeks, patients with the most acute symptoms require on the average only four days of bed rest, for the majority no bed rest is required, and that patients who have symptoms for several weeks and drop out of school probably have symptoms induced by too much physical restriction.

Infertility. Barrenness (329).

Inflammation. In origin the word means "to set on fire"—an admirable description. Inflammation is a defensive reaction to all sorts of tissue injury. The names of hundreds of inflammatory processes are designated by the suffix "-*itis,*" preceded by the name of the affected tissue—for example, *appendicitis, arthritis.* The four characteristics of inflammation are reddening, swelling, pain, and heat (in classic medicine, *rubor, tumor, dolor, calor*). Reddening results from increased blood supply to the affected part; white blood cells whose job it is to trap and destroy germs are also increased. Concentration of fluids causes swelling. Increased local metabolism produces heat. Pain is a warning not to abuse the part and to get something done about it. These are signs of reparative processes. They may not suffice in themselves. A doctor is needed if inflammation is at all serious, to find out what is wrong and what to do about it.

Influenza (*grippe, flu*). An acute, highly contagious viral infection tending to occur in epidemics (54). The causative viruses, photographed in an electron microscope, have the look of innocent fluffy cottonballs.

Infusion. Introduction of fluid into a vein.

Ingrown hairs. Curled, corkscrew-like hairs that burrow into the skin particularly affect the bearded area. Shaving may cut such hairs more or less longitudinally, leaving a sharp point which turns upon its master. The ingrown hair may cause inflammation of the follicle, and usual treatment is to pull it out with antiseptic precautions. A better method which also tends to prevent ingrown hairs is recommended by some dermatologists. Brush the affected areas briskly at night with a stiff-bristled nail brush, brushing against the direction of beard growth.

Inguinal. Pertaining to the GROIN. A frequent site of hernia.

Inkblot test (*Rohrschach test*). A test sometimes used by psychologists and psychiatrists. Formalized figures used in the test are weird, splotchy, irregular silhouette patterns of the sort obtained by splashing a drop of ink on a piece of paper and folding the blot in the middle. What a person says he sees depicted in the patterns gives, it is believed by believers, profound information about his state of mind.

Inkblot; standardized designs are used in tests. What one sees in figure (bird, airplane?) gives clues to thought patterns.

Inoculation. Introduction of a disease agent into the body to produce a very mild form of disease giving immunity; for example, cowpox vaccination for smallpox.

Insemination. Introduction of semen into the vagina, by natural means or by artificial insemination.

In situ. In a normal place.

Inspiration. Inhaling, breathing in.

Inspissated. Thickened, from absorption or evaporation of fluid.

Insufflation. Blowing gas or powder into a body cavity, as the lungs or vagina.

Insulin. A hormone produced by islet cells of the pancreas gland, essential for metabolism. Insulin in treatment of *diabetes* (335) must be given by injection, since it is a protein molecule broken down by digestion. Pharmaceutical companies prepare insulin in a number of different forms from animal sources. The structure of insulin was worked out by Frederick Sanger, a British biochemist. Insulin is a rather small protein molecule composed of 51 amino acids in two chains held together by a sulfur-containing link. Human and animal insulins have the same properties but differ in a sequence of three amino acids in one of the chains. Some diabetics become sensitized to insulin from a certain animal source. This complication may be averted, and insulin may be obtained independently of animals, if laboratory methods of synthesizing insulin become practicable. Scientists have already synthesized insulin by laborious mechanical methods, not commercially feasible. Some progress has been made in developing computer-controlled machines to perform synthesizing operations automatically. If "protein-making machines" become practicable for large scale production, a great many enzymes and protein substances of vital medical importance may roll off the assembly lines in pure form.

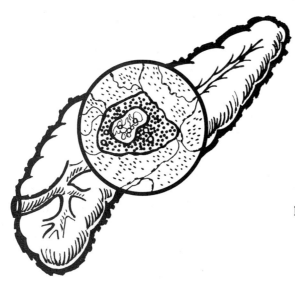

Islet cells of the pancreas gland secrete insulin. Magnified cell in center of circle; tiny black granules indicate insulin production; pancreas in background.

Integument. The skin.

Intention tremor. Involuntary trembling triggered or intensified when some voluntary movement is attempted.

Intercostal. Between the ribs.

Interferon. Infection caused by one virus may prevent concurrent infection by a different virus. This phenomenon, called viral interference, has been recognized for a quarter of a century. An apparent mechanism which gives this protection has recently come under intensive study. It is now known that body cells invaded by a virus produce a substance called *interferon* which diffuses out of the cells and into neighboring cells. The cells then become resistant to infection by viruses. Interferon is a complex protein. Its production by the body is a generalized phenomenon occurring when cells are exposed to viruses. Its unique properties suggest that it might be developed into a powerful agent for treatment of viral diseases, but great practical difficulties stand in the way. Interferon is too complex for synthetic manufacture and difficulties of producing large amounts of the pure substance are formidable. Even if large amounts of interferon become available, medical uses may be limited. Interferon must be absorbed into cells to block the multiplication of viruses, and means must be found to get interferon into cells in time to produce a curative or beneficial response. It is possible that some chemical agent (a drug) may be found, which triggers the production of interferon by body cells without exposure to viruses.

Intermenstrual pain. A usually brief attack of moderate to severe cramping pain which some women experience about midway between menstrual periods, coincidental with OVULATION, rupture of an egg-sac of the ovary and release of a mature ovum (327). Primary DYSMENORRHEA never occurs in absence of ovulation; intermenstrual pain of this nature is a rough guide to the time of ovulation and the fertile period. Discovery as long ago as 1940 that ovulation is essential for menstrual cramps, and that administration of estrogen early in the cycle could eliminate the cramps, was an aspect of studies which later led to the development of oral contraceptive pills. For physical exercises which help to relieve menstrual cramps, see PAINFUL MENSTRUATION. The right ovary lies near the appendix and midmenstrual pain in that region may be mistaken for a symptom of appendicitis. A physician can distinguish between intermenstrual pain and appendicitis on the basis of laboratory tests and dates of the menstrual cycle.

Intermittent claudication. Pain in the calf muscles and limping, occurring while walking, due to inadequate blood supply (123).

Intersex. See HERMAPHRODITE.

Intern. A graduate M. D. who serves in a hospital for a year or more, taking care of patients under supervision of the medical staff, preparatory to his being licensed to practice.

Internist. A specialist in internal medicine; that is, diseases of internal organs. Allergy, cardiovascular disease, gastroenterology, and pulmonary disease are subspecialties of internal medicine.

Intertrigo (*chafing*). Redness, abrasion, and maceration of opposing skin surfaces that rub together. Common sites are the armpit, groin, anal region, and beneath the breasts. Moisture and warmth with friction of adjacent skin parts set the stage for chafing, which may be complicated by bacterial or fungus infection. Regular use of a dusting powder and reduction in weight if obese are helpful preventives. Diabetes increases the susceptibility to intertrigo.

Intervertebral disks. Cartilaginous cushions between vertebrae (593, 603).

Intestinal flora. Bacteria which normally inhabit the intestine, do no harm and even some good. Various species of intestinal flora which we have grown accustomed to normally get along together like a happy family. Varieties of intestinal bacteria vary somewhat with diet. Diseases or antibiotics or other circumstances sometimes incapacitate one or more floral species, permitting others to thrive disproportionately from lack of competition; this may cause disturbing symptoms. A few kinds of bacteria may get through the stomach, but most kinds do not survive a bath in highly antiseptic, acid gastric juices. The floral population flourishes increasingly from the stomach downward. Some intestinal bacteria synthesize all the vitamin K we need, some synthesize other B vitamins but not all are well absorbed.

Intestinal juices. Digestive juices secreted by the intestinal walls, in contrast to gastric juices secreted by the stomach and pancreatic juices secreted by the pancreas gland. Intestinal juices contain enzymes which complete the final stages in digestion of protein, fat, and carbohydrate.

Intestine. The digestive tube from the outlet of the stomach to the outlet of the rectum. Although it is a continuous structure, different sections have different functions. See DUODENUM, JEJUNUM, ILEUM, CECUM, COLON, RECTUM.

Intubation. Introduction of a tube into a hollow organ such as the larynx, to keep it open.

Intima. The inner lining of an artery; the innermost of its three coats or layers.

Intracutaneous test. Introduction of allergens into the skin; a positive reaction indicating sensitivity to a test substance occurs in a few minutes in the form of an itching skin eruption somewhat resembling a mosquito bite (657).

Intradermal. Into or within the skin.

Intramuscular. Into or within a muscle. Many drugs are injected into muscles. A doctor's favorite site for intramuscular injection into somebody else is the buttocks.

Intrauterine transfusion. An emergency method of preventing death in the womb of an infant with severe ERYTHROBLASTOSIS, "Rh disease" (356). Appropriate blood is transfused via needle through the mother's abdomen into the peritoneal cavity of the fetus, whence it enters the fetal circulation. This makes it unnecessary to deliver the baby so prematurely that it might not survive or at best would have the additional hazard of premature birth.

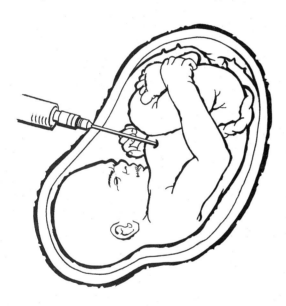

Intrauterine transfusion.

Intrauterine contraceptive devices (IUD, IUCD). Flexible devices of stainless steel, silkworm gut, or plastic, inserted by a physician into the uterus and retained there indefinitely for prevention of conception. Various devices are shaped like a bow, spiral, ring, or loop; some have a "tail" which protrudes from the cervix, to facilitate removal and enable the wearer to feel that the device is in place. The devices are alternatives to oral contraceptives which must be taken daily. Just how the devices prevent conception is not certainly known. They do not inhibit the migration of fertilizing sperm, or expel an already implanted ovum. The most generally accepted theory is that the devices increase the movements of the Fallopian tube, so that the fertilized egg is impelled through it so rapidly that it enters the uterus before it is ready for implantation. It is also possible that the lining of the uterus is affected in a way to prevent "nesting" of the fertilized egg. The devices are effective contraceptive agents, but sometimes are unknowingly expelled; a small percentage of women cannot retain them. (See page 922).

Intravenous (*I.V.*). Into or within a vein; as, *intravenous feedings* (695).

Intrinsic asthma. Bronchial asthma which has its origin within the body, from such a source as chronic sinusitis (660).

Intrinsic factor. A substance produced by the stomach for the transport of vitamin B_{12} across membranes into the blood. The fundamental defect in *pernicious anemia* (142) is absence or deficiency of intrinsic factor so that vitamin B_{12}, necessary for normal development of red blood cells, cannot be absorbed from foods. Intrinsic factor is a very elusive substance which has not yet been isolated in a pure state.

Introitus. The entrance to the vagina.

Intussusception. Sliding of a part of the intestine into its hollow interior; "telescoping," like the pushed-in finger of a glove (394, 461).

In vitro. In glass; pertaining to studies done in test tubes or laboratory hardware, outside of the living body. *In vivo* studies are done with living bodies.

Ionizing radiation. The effect of radiation (x-rays, radium, radioisotopes,

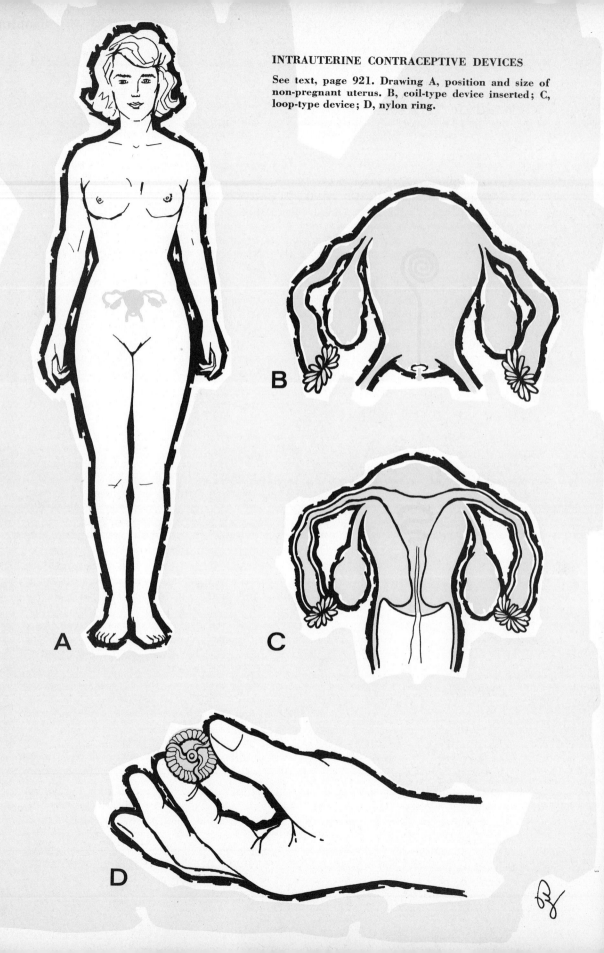

INTRAUTERINE CONTRACEPTIVE DEVICES

See text, page 921. Drawing A, position and size of non-pregnant uterus. B, coil-type device inserted; C, loop-type device; D, nylon ring.

etc.) is to drive electrons out of atoms; the electrons become attached to other atoms or molecules, forming chemical units called *ions*. Such alteration of the electron patterns of components of living cells, changing their functional capacities, is the basis for the therapeutic use of x-rays (749).

Iontophoresis. Passing medication through the skin by electric current.

Iridectomy. Excision of a piece of the iris to open drainage channels for relief of *glaucoma* (745).

Iris. The circular, pigmented structure of the eye, perforated by the pupil (531). The iris controls the amount of light entering the eye and gives the eyes their color. *Iritis* is an inflammation of the iris (547).

Iron. The essential mineral of HEMOGLOBIN. The body preserves its iron reserves quite tenaciously, constantly re-uses iron salvaged from broken-down red blood cells. The small amount lost each day is easily replaced from the diet, but if reserves are depleted, food alone will not restore them. Infants and children particularly need good sources of iron; milk, which may constitute a large proportion of their diet, is relatively low in iron and a pediatrician's advice about addition of solid foods or possible supplements should be followed. Pregnancy increases a woman's requirements for iron.

Chronic blood loss, dietary deficiencies, or disorders of absorption may result in iron-deficiency anemia (141). It is very easy for a physician to determine if iron-deficiency anemia exists in a patient. Unless it does, iron will do nothing to correct fatigue or a possibly serious underlying disease of which fatigue is a symptom. In men, iron-deficiency anemia leads the physician to look for some cause of chronic blood loss, such as bleeding ulcer or hemorrhoids. Women of childbearing age are somewhat more susceptible to iron-deficiency anemia because of

monthly blood losses, but the loss normally is very small in terms of iron.

Good food sources of iron:

Whole grain and enriched cereals
Dried beans and peas
Greens
Eggs
Apricots
Meats and Poultry
Liver and organ meats
Prunes and raisins
Molasses
Dried figs and peaches
Bouillon cubes
Brewer's yeast
Wheat germ
Oysters
Nuts

A once important source of iron has all but vanished from American kitchens: iron cooking utensils. Considerable amounts of iron are dissolved into foods, especially acid foods, prepared in iron cookware. An iron cooking pot may not be very handsome but its occasional use can contribute very significantly to a family's iron intake.

Iron lung. Popular name for a machine which expands and contracts the chest, so that a person with paralyzed respiratory muscles can breathe; a respirator.

Iron poisoning. Common "iron pills" or tablets, prescribed for iron-deficiency anemias and very commonly for pregnant women, are dangerous and even deadly to small children who get hold of a bottle and swallow the pills which sometimes have a candy-like appearance. Children have died from swallowing as few as a dozen of the tablets, usually five-grain tablets of ferrous sulfate. Symptoms of poisoning develop in an hour or so, with signs of shock, coma, vomiting, diarrhea. Iron poisoning is an acute emergency requiring immediate medical treatment. Iron pills, like all other tablets and medicines, should not be kept in a purse or on an open bathroom shelf or anywhere else where an inquisitive small child can lay hands on them.

Irradiation, medical. Treatment or diagnosis of disease with x-rays, RADIOISOTOPES, or other sources of IONIZING RADIATION. The body normally contains a certain amount of radioactive potassium and is subject to radiation from rocks and other unavoidable background sources.

Irreducible. Incapable of being put back in normal position; said of a hernia.

Irrigation. Washing out of a cavity.

Irritable colon. Over-reaction of the colon to emotions or other stimuli, without discoverable organic cause (464). Symptoms include cramping pain in the lower abdomen, bloating, "gassiness," distention, generalized abdominal ache.

Ischemia. Local deficiency of blood supply, due to spasm or obstruction of an artery. A frequent concomitant of *coronary heart disease* (81).

Ischium. The bone we sit on when sitting (595).

Islet cells. The cells of the pancreas gland which produce INSULIN (459). Also called *islands of Langerhans.*

Isometric exercise. A form of exercise in which a muscle group exerts utmost force without moving a part. No special equipment is needed. Muscles of the abdomen or other parts of the body can be held at maximum tension while sitting or standing; arms can push against the sides of a doorway while standing in the opening; the palms of the hands can strain upward under the kneehole space of a desk while one sits in front of it. Isometric exercise builds strength up to a plateau. After the plateau is reached, increasing frequency of exercise does not increase strength further. Mild effort is useless. Strength increases only if absolutely maximum effort is maintained for at least six seconds.

I.V. Intravenous.

J

Jacksonian seizure. A *focal* epileptic seizure, so called because the spasm or convulsion originates in a local part of the brain and its effects are limited to one part of the body; for example, a twitching arm or leg (262). The patient usually remains conscious.

Jactitation. Extreme restlessness, tossing about in bed.

Japanese encephalitis. A virus-caused infection, occurring in eastern Asia, transmitted by the bites of mosquitoes (59).

Jaundice. Yellowish discoloration of skin and tissues by bile pigments in the blood (454). The skin is usually very itchy and the urine dark yellow or brown. The whites of the eyes have a yellowish tinge; in skin discolorations which might be mistaken for jaundice, the whites of the eyes remain clear. The symptom indicates that something has happened to cause bile pigments to back up into the blood. The underlying abnormality may be in the liver, in bile drainage channels outside the liver, or in the blood itself. *Hemolytic jaundice* is due to increased destruction of red blood cells; the stools are dark. A harmless form of hemolytic anemia occurs in newborn babies, lasts three or four days; the baby has an excess of red cells which are destroyed during the first few days after birth. *Toxic* or *infective jaundice* reflects injury to liver cells by some agent which interferes with their ability to eliminate bile pigment. *Obstructive jaundice* results when bile channels are blocked by disease, inflammation, gallstones, infection, tumors, causing pigments to spill over. In this type of jaundice the discoloration of skin and mucous membranes is intense, the stools clay-colored, the urine deeply colored. Underlying causes of jaundice are numerous. Various laboratory tests help to pinpoint what is wrong.

Jejunal ulcer. A peptic ulcer occurring near the opening between the stomach and jejunum, after a surgical operation to establish a direct connection between the organs (*gastrojejunostomy*).

Jejunum. An arbitrarily designated portion of the small intestine, eight to ten feet long, continuous from the DUODENUM to the ILEUM (429). Absorption of food elements is practically limited to the small intestine. Digestion is accelerated in the jejunum which receives gruel-like materials from the stomach after thorough mixing with bile and pancreatic juices in the duodenum.

Jellyfish stings. See PORTUGUESE MAN-OF-WAR.

Jet injection. A technique for vaccinating without a needle or the stab thereof. A volume of liquid is suddenly compressed and forced through a very fine orifice at such speed that it penetrates the skin painlessly and delivers a cone-shaped spray of material into tissues under the skin. Various types of jet injectors have been developed; some have reservoirs holding enough material for several hundred "shots." The devices have been used principally for speedy, mass vaccination of large numbers of people.

Jiggers (*chiggers*). Sand fleas; pregnant females of the species bore into the skin, causing itching and inflammation.

Joint mice. Small loose fragments of bone that have become separated within a joint, often the knee (617).

Jockey itch (*tinea cruris*). Ringworm of the groin; a fungus infection of the skin of the upper thighs near the genital organs (190). It is caused by the same group of organisms responsible for athlete's foot. Because the symptoms are similar to those of psoriasis and other skin diseases, a physician should be consulted.

Jugular veins. Veins of the side of the neck which drain blood from the head and neck toward the heart. The internal jugular veins are deep-lying; the external ones are near the surface.

K

Kahn test. A blood test for syphilis.

Kala-azar. An infection transmitted by the bites of sandflies, occurring in Mediterranean, tropical, and oriental regions (71). It is characterized by fever, anemia, enlarged spleen, emaciation, and has a high fatality rate if untreated but responds well to treatment.

Kaposi's disease. See XERODERMA PIGMENTOSUM.

Keloids. Irregular ridges, nodules, and cordlike bands of skin like raised scars, at first rubbery and later very dense and hard (196). The growths tend to occur on the site of previous scars. The cause of such effusive growth is not known. Keloids can be removed by surgery but have a tendency to recur.

Keratin. The hard, horny protein which is the chief structural stuff of the outermost layer of the skin, of hair and nails, and in animals lower than man, of claws, horns, hoofs, and feathers.

Keratitis. Inflammation of the cornea (549).

Keratoconjunctivitis. Acute inflammation of the cornea and conjunctiva, tending to occur in epidemics, caused by a specific virus (adenovirus Type 8).

Keratoconus. Cone-shaped projection of the cornea; vision is impaired by the bending of light waves in distorted ways. Good vision may be restored by contact lenses (539).

Keratoplasty. Surgical procedures on the cornea, such as CORNEAL TRANSPLANT.

Keratosis. Overgrowth of the horny layer of the skin; for example, a wart or callus.

Kerion. Fungus infection of the beard or scalp, producing deep pustules (189).

Kernicterus. A severe form of JAUNDICE characterized by deposits of bile pigments in parts of the brain and degeneration of nerve cells, occurring in infants with ERYTHROBLASTOSIS.

Ketogenic diet. A diet high in fat relative to carbohydrate, deliberately designed to produce KETOSIS. In the past, ketogenic diets were sometimes used in treatment of epilepsy and urinary tract infections, but since the advent of effective drugs, such diets are rarely resorted to.

Ketosis. A condition produced when more fat is eaten than can be burned completely by the body. The unburned fats produce acid chemical substances called *ketone bodies*. An excess of ketones produces a form of ACIDOSIS to which some diabetics are especially susceptible; acetone derived from incomplete combustion of fats gives a characteristic vinegary odor to the breath of diabetics with *keto-acidosis* (337).

Kidneys. Paired organs in the small of the back behind the abdominal cavity. Evolution of the kidney permitted primitive creatures of the sea to live on dry land by carrying with them an internal sea quite similar to the sea they took leave of. The kidneys regulate the volume and composition of body fluids, filter out impurities, keep ELECTROLYTES and blood composition in balance, and secrete substances which modify blood pressure. The kidneys are subject to infections, stone formation, tumors, malformations, circulatory and other underlying diseases (269).

Kimmelsteil-Wilson disease. A specific form of kidney disease (sclerosis of structures of the GLOMERULI) associated with diabetes of long duration.

Kinesia. MOTION SICKNESS.

Kinesthesia. "Muscle sense"; we all have it in addition to the standard five senses. It is the sense by which we perceive weight, position, movement, resistance, and rapidly integrate countless muscle-registered stimuli—from a grasped steering wheel, baseball bat, bicycle handlebars, or from muscles that tell us an arm is outstretched or bent without our looking at it.

Kinins. Miniature proteins associated with rheumatism and allergic reactions (648).

Kissing ulcer. One that appears to result from parts that press upon or "kiss" each other.

Klebsiella pneumonia. A type of pneumonia caused by a type of bacteria other than the common pneumococci (36). It tends to produce chronic lung abscesses.

Klinefelter's syndrome. Undeveloped testes and female characteristics such as breast enlargement in males, due to an abnormality of the sex-determining pair of CHROMOSOMES. A normal female has two X chromosomes (XX), a normal male, an X and a Y (XY). A person with Klinefelter's syndrome has an extra and harmful X chromosome (XXY), triplets instead of a normal pair of chromosomes.

Kline test. A blood test for syphilis.

Knee jerk. The patellar reflex; sudden jerking forward of the lower leg when tapped below the kneecap. A test of the integrity of nerves.

Knock-knees (*genu valgum*). Inward bending of the knees at the joint; in young children it usually corrects itself spontaneously (616).

Knockout drops. Chloral hydrate, a potent hypnotic drug, poured into a victim's drink to cause rapid blackout; a Mickey Finn.

Koplik's spots. Small bluish-white spots on mucous membranes of the cheeks and lips, present shortly before the rash of MEASLES appears.

Korsakoff's psychosis. This severe mental disturbance usually, but not always, follows a bout of DELIRIUM TREMENS which blends into it. The outstanding manifestation is loss of memory for recent events, and falsifications of memory, such as "remembering" things that never happened. The psychosis is associated with chronic alcoholism and chronic malnutrition; treatment is much the same as for delirium tremens. Some patients recover their memories after weeks or months, but some never do.

Kraurosis. Progressive drying and shriveling of the skin, due to atrophy of glands, often accompanied by severe itching; especially, kraurosis of the vulva in elderly women (419).

Krukenberg tumor. Cancer of the ovaries which has spread from the stomach.

Kwashiorkor. A PROTEIN deficiency disease occurring most often in children in subtropical countries who are raised on exclusive cereal diets after weaning. Affected children have pot bellies, apathy, muscular wasting, edema, and fail to grow. It is an extreme form of disease which may occur in lesser degree in persons whose diets are severely curtailed in protein. The basic deficiency is lack of AMINO ACIDS for synthesis of proteins.

Kyphosis. Humpback, backward curvature of the spine. A mild form is "round shoulders." Kyphosis may result from poor posture or from diseases such as rickets, tuberculosis, osteoarthritis, and rheumatoid arthritis, which affect the spine.

L

Labia. Lips or liplike organs. *Labia majora*, folds of skin on either side of the entrance of the vulva; *labia minora*, folds of tissue covered with mucous membrane within the labia majora (408).

Labor. Childbirth. There are three stages: dilation of the cervix; expulsion of the child; expulsion of the placenta (360).

Labyrinth. Intricate passageways, intercommunicating canals; especially, structures of the inner ear (562).

Laceration. A wound caused by tearing of tissue; for example, lacerations of the perineum in childbirth.

Lacrimal. Pertaining to tears, produced by the *lacrimal gland* in the upper outside region of the eye socket (535).

Lactation. Secretion of milk (492). Interacting hormones initiate and sustain this complicated process. The milk-duct system of the breast enlarges during pregnancy under the influence of *estrogen*, an ovarian hormone. Milk-secreting lobules also proliferate under the influence of a different hormone, *progesterone* (422). During labor, OXYTOCIN, a hormone which has the property of "letting down" milk (and of stimulating contractions of the uterus) takes effect. Shortly after the baby is born the breasts secrete COLOSTRUM, which is not true milk but a secretion containing protective antibodies of the mother. True milk appears when *prolactin*, a pituitary gland hormone, acts upon breasts already prepared by estrogen and progesterone. Lactation can be suppressed by giving hormones.

Lactose. A sugar that occurs in milk.

Lactovegetarian. A person who lives on a diet of vegetables, cereals, fruits, and dairy products.

Laennec's cirrhosis. The most common form of cirrhosis of the liver; portal cirrhosis (455).

Laminectomy. Surgery of the wall of the spinal canal to expose underlying structures (732).

Lancet. A short, pointed, double-edged surgical knife, used for *lancing*—that is, cutting open.

Lancinating. A description of sharply cutting, shooting pain.

Lanugo. Fine downy hair on the body of the fetus and on the adult body, except the palms and soles.

Laparotomy. Opening of the abdomen by an incision; a variety of surgical procedures may be used subsequent to the opening.

Larva migrans. See CREEPING ERUPTION.

Laryngectomy. Surgical removal of all or part of the voice box, usually because of cancer. There is a high rate of cure if the cancer is discovered early. The patient is left without vocal cords, but with persistence and encouragement can learn to speak again by "burping" air and manipulating it with muscles of the tongue and mouth. "Laryngectomees," as persons who have lost their voice boxes are called, have formed "Lost Chord Clubs" in many cities to teach and reassure recent laryngectomees that they too can learn to speak again.

Laryngitis. Inflammation of the LARYNX (voice box). Acute laryngitis is often associated with a common cold, infection, or overuse of the voice. The throat is dry, swallowing may be affected, it is not possible to speak above a hoarse whisper if at all. Absolute rest of the voice is an essential part of treatment (589).

Laryngoscope. A hollow metal tube with a light inserted into the throat for examining the LARYNX.

Laryngotracheobronchitis. An acute, very serious, "croupy" condition of children, rapid in onset, requiring immediate medical care (386). The outstanding symptom is extreme difficulty in breathing, due to thick mucus and fluid which can quite rapidly plug the breathing passages.

Larynx. The vocal apparatus, located between the base of the tongue and the windpipe (584). It includes the vocal cords and muscles which modify the vibrations of air passing through them, to produce controlled sounds.

Laser. A remarkable device which gets its name from the initial letters of Light Amplification by Stimulated Emission of Radiation. Essentially, a laser multiplies the triggering energy of a light source, such as the flash of a photographic bulb, into a tremendously powerful emission of parallel light waves of the same wave length, all in step. The original "ruby laser" employed a ruby crystal about the size of a cigarette, impregnated with chromium atoms, with a reflective mirror at one end and a semi-transparent mirror at the other. Setting off a high-powered flash bulb excites atoms in the crystal to higher energy levels; they drop to normal levels and in doing so excite other atoms, trapped between mirrored ends of the tube, rebounding, intensifying, until an extremely intense burst of coherent (non-diffuse) light is emitted from the semi-transparent end of the tube. For a very brief time, hundredths of thousands of a second, a laser beam is more brilliant than the sun and its parallel rays can be focused on a spot no wider than a millionth of a millimeter. Medical uses of a laser are still experimental and many problems remain to be solved. Laser beams have successfully destroyed pigmented skin cancers in human patients, have been used to remove portwine stains and tattoos, and have been employed to "weld" *detached retinas* (554) firmly into position. Many new types of lasers are being developed.

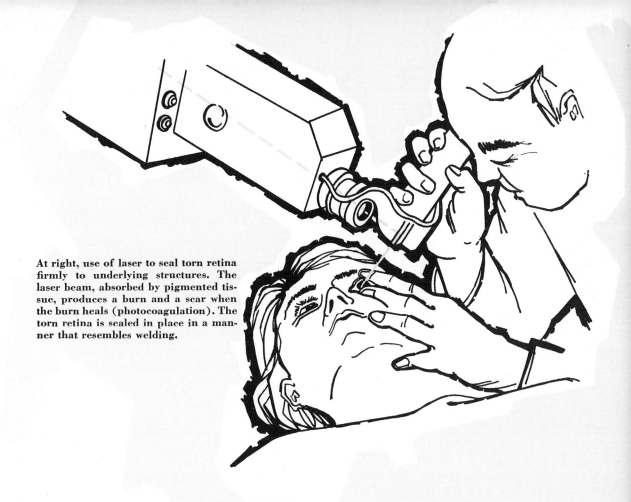

At right, use of laser to seal torn retina firmly to underlying structures. The laser beam, absorbed by pigmented tissue, produces a burn and a scar when the burn heals (photocoagulation). The torn retina is sealed in place in a manner that resembles welding.

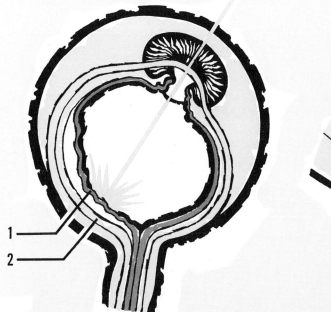

Below: torn retina (1) is shown separated from choroid layer (2) to which it normally adheres. Laser beam enters through pupil of eye to make contact with very tiny area of retina.

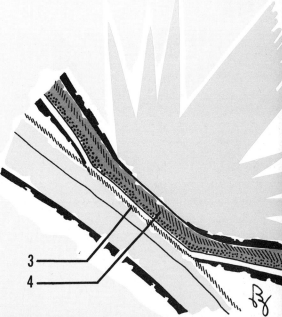

Magnified representation of "spot welding" effect of laser beam inside eye. Beam at retina (3) causes formation of scar tissue that "welds" retina to choroid (4).

1

2

3

4

Laurence-Moon-Biedl syndrome. A genetic disorder of the pituitary gland producing obesity, mental retardation, degeneration of the retina, webbed fingers or toes, and underdevelopment of the genital system.

Lavage. Washing out of a hollow organ such as the stomach or a sinus.

Lead poisoning. Intoxication from absorption of lead or its salts into the body; *plumbism*. Mild lead poisoning may produce no apparent symptoms but the metal can accumulate in the body over a period of time and produce chronic poisoning. Some of the signs of lead poisoning are abdominal pain, constipation, pallor, drowsiness, mental confusion, a "blue line" on the gums. It has been suggested that the use of lead pipes to carry water may have hastened the decline of the Roman empire; continued ingestion of small amounts of lead may have led to lassitude and mental torpor in the population. Lead poisoning occasionally occurs in young children who nibble on materials containing paints with a lead base. Insidious lead poisoning is not rare in children who live in old, poorly maintained houses with flaking paint and plaster. Infants explore the world by putting all sorts of things into their mouths. Around the time when they begin to walk and have a few teeth, they may develop a depraved appetite for non-food substances (see PICA). It is a dangerous habit which should be sternly corrected by teaching the child what should and should not go into his mouth.

L. E. cell. A white blood cell which has undergone changes characteristic of *lupus erythematosus* and related diseases (643).

Left-handedness. When a left-handed child appears in a right-handed family there may be some consternation. "Lefties" suffer unjustly in a right-handed world. Words originating from the left, such as "sinister" and "gauche," have denigrating meanings, while those originating from the right, such as "dexterous," are complimentary. Perhaps it is such considerations that lead some parents to force a naturally left-handed child to favor his right hand. The consensus of authorities is that if a child wants to use his left hand, let him. Some things we learn to do with either the right or left hand because it's most convenient. A left-handed person shakes hands with his right hand because that's the way the world shakes. A right-handed person holds a telephone receiver with his left hand (and uses his left ear) to leave his right hand free for writing. We are left- or right-eyed as well as handed; it's easy to determine one's dominant eye (528). Teachers and parents never make any effort to change eye dominance. If handedness is to some extent hereditary, the mode of transmission has not been elucidated. Some investigators think that a left-handed person is the mirror-image of a right-handed twin who did not survive the early stages of cell division.

Left-sided appendicitis. See DIVERTICULA.

Leishmaniasis. A parasitic disease transmitted by sandflies; it has several forms (71).

Leprosy (*Hansen's disease*). A chronic disease, often very painful, which inflicts cruel deformities and mutilations, caused by bacteria closely related to those that cause tuberculosis. Biblical references to lepers probably concerned various repulsive skin diseases rather than leprosy as it is known today. About 12 million persons suffer from leprosy today. Most of them live in tropical or subtropical countries, but leprosy still occurs in Hawaii, Puerto Rico, and the southern United States. The disease affects the skin and nerves of all patients, but is usually classified according to which tissue is predominantly involved. Patients with "nerve" leprosy develop discolored skin areas, devoid of feeling because nerves are deadened. Ultimately, fingers, toes, or other parts may shrivel and drop off. Patients with "skin" leprosy develop thick, knobby growths which grossly distort the features. Drugs known as sulfones seem to prolong the lives of some patients but others appear to get worse after chemotherapy is begun. Close skin contact with a patient who has leprosy seems a likely route of entry of organisms into the body. Leprosy is generally thought not to be very "catching." Husbands and wives of patients with leprosy may remain apparently uninfected after living many years together. Some investigators feel that leprosy is a highly contagious disease but only to a few people who are highly susceptible.

Leptospirosis (*infectious jaundice; spirochetal jaundice*). An infectious disease caused by certain spirochetes (*leptospira*). The germs are spread in the urine of infected animals—rats, mice, dogs, cows, pigs—and most people who acquire the infection have had contact with animals or with water or moist soil to which animals have access. The disease is not exceptionally rare in the United States. Several local outbreaks have been traced to swimming or wading in ponds or slow-moving streams in rural areas where waste disposal is not properly screened. The germs enter the body through mucous membranes or minute breaks in the skin. Typically, the infection produces sudden fever, chills, headache, and muscle pains. In some cases there may be few if any symptoms; in others, jaundice may develop. Usually leptospirosis is a brief self-limited illness, but *Weil's disease* (50) is a severe form in which jaundice, kidney failure, hemorrhage, anemia and heart damage may become threatening complications.

Lesion. Alteration of tissue or function due to injury or disease. A pimple, fracture, abscess, scratch, wart, or ingrown toenail may be referred to as a lesion.

Leukemia. Malignant disease of the blood-forming organs, sometimes called "cancer of the blood." The characteristic abnormality is gross overproduction of white blood cells. There are several acute and chronic forms of leukemia, so diverse that the word does not refer to a single specific disease but to a variety of "leukemic states" (155).

Leukocytes. White blood cells (134).

Leukocytosis. Abnormal increase in numbers of white blood cells. The cell count normally increases slightly after eating and in pregnancy, but the word implies an abnormal increase, often associated with bodily defenses against infection and inflammation. For instance, a high count may help to confirm a diagnosis of appendicitis. Disorders of the blood-forming organs may also induce leukocytosis.

Leukoderma. See VITILIGO.

Leukopenia. Abnormal scantiness of white blood cells. The condition may result from allergies, drug reactions, irradiation, certain infections or anemias.

Leukoplakia. Whitish, leathery patches on mucous membranes of the mouth (520) or vulva (419). No specific cause is known, but continued irritation is considered to be a factor. Patients with oral leukoplakia are forbidden to smoke and the white patches may regress if this and other irritations are removed. Leukoplakia by no means progresses inevitably to cancer, but it is considered to be a precancerous lesion and requires competent medical care and followup.

Leukorrhea. Whitish discharge from the vagina. Increased flow of mucus about midway between menstrual periods often accompanies OVULATION. The discharge is sometimes called "the whites." It may result from yeast or protozoal infection. See TRICHOMONIASIS and MONILIASIS.

Leydig cells. Interstitial cells of the testes which produce testosterone, the male hormone (and small amounts of female hormone). The cells are separate structures from those that produce SPERMATOZOA (323). Thus, infertile males whose production of spermatozoa is impaired may produce adequate amounts of male hormone and be entirely potent.

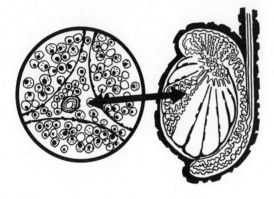

In circle, Leydig cells of the testis (right).

LH. Luteinizing hormone of the pituitary gland. It causes a GRAAFIAN FOLLICLE which has released a "ripened" egg to become a yellow body which produces *progesterone,* a hormone which helps to prepare the lining of the uterus for implantation of a fertilized egg (327).

Libido. Sexual drive; in Freudian psychology, the sum total of psychic energy.

Lichenification. Leathery thickening and hardening of the skin, usually the result of long-continued irritation from scratching and rubbing.

Lichen planus. An itching eruption of unknown cause; dull purplish-red spots appear on thin-skinned areas of the body (182).

Ligament. A band of tough, flexible fibrous tissue which connects bones or supports organs.

Ligate. To tie up; for example, a bleeding blood vessel. In surgery, a *ligature* is a thread of silk, catgut, wire, or other material used for tying vessels.

Lightening. The time around the middle of the last month of pregnancy when the baby's head settles more deeply into the pelvis preparatory to birth. This slightly decreases the mother's feeling of abdominal distention, "lightens" the load (354).

Limbus. A border; the edge of the cornea where it joins the white of the eye.

Lipids. A broad term for fats and fat-like substances. Lipids contain one or more fatty acids. Lipids include fats, cholesterol, phospholipids, and similar substances which do not mix readily with water.

Lipoid pneumonia. See ASPIRATION PNEUMONIA.

Lipoma. A compressible tumor composed of fat tissue, occurring chiefly on the trunk, back of the neck, forearms or armpits. Lipomas must be distinguished from other tumors by a physician. Lipomas usually stop growing after they reach a certain size and remain at that size indefinitely. True lipomas are painless, harmless, never become malignant, and are best left untreated unless they are so large and objectionable as to justify surgical removal.

Lithiasis. Stones where they don't belong (gallstones, kidney stones); the condition of having stones.

Lithotomy. Cutting into the bladder to remove a stone (275). Structures are close to the surface, and because of this accessibility the operation has an ancient history. Mortality was high in the centuries before antiseptic surgery, but some patients did recover, notably Samuel Pepys, who spent a few shillings for a box "to hold the stone that I was cut of." Wandering surgeons who "cut for stone" in ancient times were not highly regarded by contemporary physicians, as is evidenced by a sentence from the Hippocratic Oath: "I will not use the knife, not even on sufferers from stone." This Hippocratic prohibition has long since fallen into desuetude.

Little's disease. Cerebral palsy of children affecting both sides of the body.

Liver. The largest organ of the body and the most versatile chemically (438, 454).

"Liver rot." A disease acquired by ingesting food or water contaminated with cysts of sheep liver flukes, a species of flatworm (65).

Lobotomy. Cutting into a lobe of an organ, especially a lobe of the brain. See PSYCHOSURGERY.

Lochia. The discharge from the vagina which continues for a week or two after childbirth. It is a normal aftermath of childbirth and ceases when the uterus returns to its pre-pregnancy state.

Locked knee. A painfully swollen knee joint which cannot be extended fully, due to torn CARTILAGE. Surgical removal of the injured cartilage is usually necessary (618).

Lockjaw. See TETANUS.

Locomotor ataxia. See ATAXIA.

Lordosis. Exaggeration of the normal forward curve of the spine at the small of the back. The general aspect is that of an abdomen thrust forward and shoulders thrust back. Lordosis usually reflects a feat of balancing abdominal weight to bring it into comfortable alignment with the body's center of gravity. The characteristic posture of late pregnancy, called "pride of pregnancy" because of the seemingly flaunted abdomen, is a temporary lordosis. Abnormalities of the hip joint sometimes cause lordosis.

Low blood sugar (HYPOGLYCEMIA). Less than normal amounts of GLUCOSE (sugar) in circulating blood. Blood sugar naturally drops if we go a long time between meals. Mild transient symptoms of hunger, weakness, faintness, are perfectly normal and no surprise at all to anyone who skips food long enough to deplete his reserves; a square meal restores the balance. *Chronic* hypoglycemia may be associated with various endocrine and other disorders. Insulin, which reduces abnormally high blood sugar levels, is only one agent in nature's complicated balancing scheme. A companion hormone, *glucagon*, also produced by the pancreas gland but by different cells than those which produce insulin, stimulates the liver to convert GLYCOGEN to blood sugar. Glucagon is an essential corrective mechanism for low blood sugar, comparable to insulin's action against high blood sugar.

Low-calorie soft drinks. The insignificantly few calories in these popular beverages for weight-watchers come from coloring and flavoring agents. Most cola-type drinks contain caffeine, limited by Federal regulation to 6 mg. of caffeine per ounce. Low-calorie cola drinks contain approximately half as much caffeine as the standard types. Artificial sweeteners used in low-calorie drinks are usually a combination of sodium cyclamate and saccharin. There is no evidence that any of the ingredients in these beverages is harmful. The required labeling statements that non-nutritive sweeteners should be used only by persons who must restrict their intake of ordinary sweets does not in any way mean that there is danger to others. The statement means that the user should be aware that the artificial sweeteners do not contribute any calories or nutritional values.

LSD. Lysergic acid diethylamide. See HALLUCINOGENIC DRUGS.

Lues. Syphilis.

Lumbago. A general term for pain in the middle of the back, the lumbar region (594). Lumbago is not a specific disease but a symptom to be investigated.

Lumbar puncture. Withdrawal of CEREBROSPINAL FLUID through a hollow needle inserted between lumbar vertebrae of the small of the back (592). Withdrawal may be done for purposes of diagnosis, to relieve pressures, or the puncture may be made to introduce medication, as an anesthetic.

Lumen. The open space inside a tubular structure such as an intestine or blood vessel; the "hole of a tunnel" through which traffic passes.

Lumpy jaw. See ACTINOMYCOSIS.

Luxation. Dislocation.

Lymphangitis. Inflammation of lymph vessels due to spread of an infection, producing swelling and burning pain. Irregular, wavy red lines mark the path of inflamed vessels. There is danger of bacteria getting into circulating blood. Treatment is directed to overcoming the original infection.

Lymphedema. Swelling of a part of the body, especially the legs or arms, from a "back-up" of fluids because of obstruction or inadequacy of the lymphatic drainage system (135). The condition may cause huge enlargement of a part (ELEPHANTIASIS). Lymphedema of the arm sometimes occurs after breast removal surgery. Obstructive lymphedema is secondary to other conditions such as tumors or FILARIASIS. A less frequent, sometimes congenital form results from primary defects in the functioning of lymphatic channels in the skin and its deep layers. This type of lymphedema manifests itself as a grossly swollen leg in the teens or middle life. The unsightly swelling may be controlled to some degree by rest in bed, elevation of the limb to promote drainage, and wearing a firm rubber bandage over a white stocking when up and about.

However, this does not cure a chronic condition which tends to worsen with time, and surgery to remove the diseased tissue before extensive changes occur may be advisable.

Lymphogranuloma venereum. A disease produced by viruses transmitted by sexual contact (56).

Lymphosarcoma. A malignant tumor of lymphatic tissue (161). *Lymphogranulomatosis* is sometimes a synonym for HODGKIN'S DISEASE.

Lysozyme. A natural antibacterial substance contained in many bodily secretions, such as tears (534).

M

Maceration. Sodden; softening and deterioration of tissue soaking or in confined contact with fluids.

Macula lutea. A small, round, yellowish spot near the center of the retina, the area of color perception and most distinct vision (532).

Macule. A flat discolored spot on the skin.

Madura foot (*mycetoma*). A chronic fungus infection of the feet, occurring in tropical regions. The swollen foot becomes filled with connecting cystlike areas from which fungus-containing pus drains. In the course of time the disease destroys muscle and bone and amputation may be necessary.

Magenstrasse. "Stomach street"; a groove along which food passes to the outlet of the stomach.

Maidenhead. The HYMEN.

Malabsorption syndrome. A descriptive term for several disorders resulting from defective absorption of foodstuffs in the small intestine (463). Certain diseases or surgical procedures may disturb previously normal assimilative processes, but the most common forms of the syndrome (variously called *celiac disease, sprue, idiopathic steatorrhea*) seem to involve hereditary defects in the absorptive surface of the small intestine, and deficient activity of intestinal enzymes. Large amounts of unabsorbed fat produce frequent, pale, loose stools (steatorrhea). *Celiac disease* in children is the same as *nontropical sprue* in adults. Symptoms in adults—diarrhea, weakness, loss of weight, anemia deceptively like pernicious anemia—are insidious and require careful diagnosis. Young children with celiac disease commonly have poor appetite, various signs of malnutrition, stunted growth, bulging abdomen, and frequent frothy stools containing excessive amounts of fat. Gluten, a wheat protein, has a toxic effect on the small bowel of many patients with malabsorption syndromes. Strict elimination of gluten from the diet often restores bowel function to normal and maintains it even though there is no structural improvement in the bowel. A gluten-free diet prohibits wheat, rye, oats, and their products such as bread, cookies, and crackers, as well as foods such as gravies and soups which have wheat flour added to them.

Malacia. Softening of part of an organ.

Malar. Pertaining to the cheek; the cheekbone, the *zygoma*.

Malaria. An infectious disease characterized by chills and intermittent or remitting fever, caused by parasites transmitted to man by the bites of mosquitoes (70).

Mal de mer. Seasickness; a form of MOTION SICKNESS.

Male climacteric. An indefinite "change of life" state in elderly men, analogous to the menopause in women but without a clearcut sign comparable to cessation of menstruation which marks the female climacteric. Some physical changes occur with age as the hormone output of the sex glands diminishes; it may be difficult to separate physical factors from psychological reactions to fears, worries, boring environment, retirement, decreased sexual function and opportunity, unrecognized illness, depression, apprehensive brooding on the passage of time. Vague symptoms self-attributed to the male climacteric call for a physical checkup by a physician, who may decide that hormone treatment is worth a trial, or who may find some condition that requires quite different treatment. Symptoms associated with diminished male hormone production (restorable to normal maintenance levels by replacement therapy) are decreased sexual potential, irritability, depression, lack of concentration, diminished growth of beard and body hair.

Malaise. Listlessness, tiredness, irritability, depression, distress, general feeling of illness and of being "under par"; often precedes some feverish infection.

Malignant. Life-threatening; the usual medical meaning is "cancerous."

Malingering. The feigning of illness. The motive may be to avoid work, collect damages, escape military service, or gain sympathy. The deception can usually be exposed by tests and observations not understood by the malingerer.

Malleus. One of the three tiny bones (*ossicles*) of the middle ear which amplify vibrations of the eardrum and conduct them to the inner ear (560). "Malleus" means "hammer"; the "handle" of the hammer, attached to the eardrum, amplifies vibrations which are hammered onto the adjacent anvil-bone.

Malocclusion. Inharmonious meshing of the upper and lower teeth; poor "bite"; bad alignment of teeth and jaws (519).

Malpresentation. Any position of the fetus in the birth outlet other than the normal head-down position at childbirth; for example, breech, forehead, foot presentation.

Mammography. X-rays of the breast; several views are taken, to improve accuracy in detecting very small lesions (425, 753).

Mammoplasty. Plastic surgery of the breast; especially, an operation to correct sagging breasts. It is performed by excising tissue and fixing the glands in their normal position.

Mandible. The lower jawbone (521).

Manic-depressive psychosis. A severe form of mental illness (685). It is characterized by swings from intense elation and hyperactivity to blackest depression; between swings the patient may act quite normally. In the manic phase, the patient is enormously optimistic, overtalkative, physically busy, always on the go; his thoughts skip wildly from one subject to another; he is excited by grandiose projects. In the depressive phase, he may be hopelessly discouraged, have feelings of utter worthlessness, hear "voices" which nag him unmercifully, and have difficulty in performing the simplest mental and physical tasks.

Mantoux test. See TUBERCULIN TEST.

Manubrium. The uppermost handle-like part of the breastbone (593).

Marasmus. Wasting and emaciation of infants from no discoverable cause.

March foot. Painful swelling, even fracture of bones of the foot, not produced by acute injury but by excessive strain, as in marching.

Marfan's syndrome. A rare hereditary disorder, characterized by unusual flexibility of joints, disproportionately long legs, flabby tissues, funnel chest or pigeon breast, spider fingers, flat foot, displacement of the lens of the eye, and heart defects (94). The fundamental defect appears to be in connective tissue which breaks down or fails to produce normal amounts of strong fibers to support body structures.

Marginal ulcer. A peptic ulcer occurring at the junction where the stomach and jejunum have been surgically united.

Marie-Strumpell disease (*ankylosing spondylitis*). A progressive disease of joints of the spine, related to but not identical with rheumatoid arthritis (640).

Marrow. Soft material which fills the cavities of bones. Formation of blood cells takes place in the *red marrow* of certain bones of adults and of all bones in early life. *Yellow marrow* is fatty material which does not perform any blood-making function.

Masseter. A "chewing" muscle that moves the lower jaw.

Mastectomy. Surgical removal of the breast, usually because of cancer (425, 728). In *simple* mastectomy, only the breast tissue is removed and underlying muscles are preserved. Usually, if cancer is present, *radical* mastectomy is performed, to remove not only the breast but lymph nodes near the collarbone and armpit, and sections of arm and chest muscles.

Mastitis. Inflammation of the breasts, from bacterial infection or other causes. The most common disease of the female breast is *chronic cystic mastitis;* the breasts contain nodules and small cysts of rubbery consistency, usually painful. Most patients with this condition can be treated satisfactorily by a physician in his office. A "lump" in the breast is not necessarily cancer, but it is imperative to have a physician determine its nature (423).

Mastodynia. Pain in the breast.

Mastoid. "Breast-shaped"; refers to mastoid air cells which surround the middle ear. Infection reaching these cells from the middle ear may require *mastoidectomy,* surgical removal of affected cells (573).

Materia medica. Substances used in medicine, and the science concerned with the origin, preparation, dosage and administration of such substances.

Maxilla. The upper jawbone.

Maxillary sinus. A pyramid-shaped cavity, largest of the nasal sinuses, located in the front of the upper jaw on either side of the nose (582). Also called the *antrum.* The floor of the cavity is close to the root of the eye-tooth.

Measles (*rubeola*). An infectious disease caused by viruses (398). Although most children recover from a natural attack of measles without suffering serious after-effects, the disease is treacherous and can be fatal. It can lead to ENCEPHALITIS and mental retardation. Immunizing vaccines of the live-virus type make it unnecessary for any child to be exposed to such risk. One injection of live-virus measles vaccine gives long-lasting, probably lifetime immunity. The U. S. Public Health Service recommends immunization against measles of all infants at one year of age, and immunization on entering school of all children not given measles immunization in infancy.

Meat grades. Except for products produced and sold within a state, all meat and meat products are inspected by experts of the U. S. Department of Agriculture. The inspection begins with the live animal and continues through the slaughtering operation. It applies to the meat through its many stages of processing and manufacture and to the many ingredients that are used and the processes employed. After the production of clean disease-free meat in the slaughtering department, production-control inspectors see that the clean meat stays wholesome and that it is handled under sanitary conditions. Recent legislation extends the protection of Federal inspection to meat and meat products produced within a state.

Meat *grading* by Federal inspectors is not compulsory. This is an evaluation of quality; some processors establish their own grading systems. Federal grades, however, give a uniform designation of quality of beef, veal, and lamb, useful to livestock dealers and consumers. About half of the beef, one-third of the lamb and mutton, and one-sixth of the veal produced by commercial slaughterers is Federally graded. There are six Federal grade marks stamped on the carcass: USDA Prime, USDA Choice, USDA Good, USDA Standard, USDA Commercial, and USDA Utility. A large part of the limited supply of Prime beef goes to hotels and restaurants and these cuts are not often available in retail stores. The top grade generally available from retailers is USDA Choice. USDA Good, the next grade, has less fat and less taste appeal. The lowest grades, Standard, Commercial, and Utility, may sometimes be found in retail markets but much goes into the preparation of meat product specialties. The lowest grades are perfectly wholesome but tougher and less flavorful, and they need additional care in cooking.

Meatus. An opening or passage, such as the external opening of the urethra.

Meckel's diverticulum. An outpouching from the small intestine, a blind tube two to five inches long (461). It is normally obliterated in the course of fetal development, but in some people it remains as a vestigial remnant. It may become inflamed and cause symptoms resembling appendicitis.

Meconium. Pasty, greenish material which fills the intestines of the fetus before birth and forms the first bowel movement of the newborn. *Meconium ileus,* obstruction of the intestines by sticky, viscid meconium, is the earliest manifestation of *cystic fibrosis* (387).

Mediastinum. The space in the middle of the chest between the lungs, breastbone, and spine, containing the heart, great blood vessels, esophagus, windpipe and associated structures.

Medicaid. Medical Assistance, sometimes referred to as Medicaid, is a program that pays medical care costs for people with low incomes. It differs from Medicare in that it is a State-administered program, aided by Federal funds. Each State decides for itself if it wants the program. Status of the program in a particular State can be learned by checking with the Department of Welfare of the State. More than half the States have initiated programs. Medicaid is designed to provide medical care for needy persons of all ages under a definition of need defined by each State. Eligibility of the individual or family is determined by State provisions. There are State by State differences in who is eligible and for what benefits.

Automatically eligible groups are (1) all persons who receive financial assistance from the federally aided public assistance programs for the aged, the blind, the disabled, and families with dependent children; (2) all persons who would be eligible for financial assistance except that they do not meet certain State conditions—durational residence requirements, for example; (3) all persons under age 21 who, except for a State age or school-attendance requirement, would be eligible for assistance through the program of aid to families with dependent children. A State may also include persons whose income is too high to permit eligibility for financial assistance to meet their daily living expenses but not high enough to meet their medical bills.

Anyone who wishes to apply can get full information about State regulations from the local public welfare agency.

Medical genetics. Birth of a malformed or abnormal child always worries parents who wonder if a subsequent child will have the same defect. Couples planning to marry may worry about some condition in one family line or the other, rightly or wrongly assumed to be hereditary. The science of genetics is not sufficiently far advanced to give hard-and-fast answers to every such question. But advances in knowledge of mechanisms of HEREDITY enable a physician or a genetic counselor recommended by him to give reliable information that is often reassuring. Some birth defects are accidental, do not arise from any defects in the parents' own chromosomes, and are no more likely to be repeated than any other rare accident. Some birth defects and diseases are truly genetic, transmitted by abnormal GENES of one or both parents. Defects such as MONGOLISM and KLINEFELTER'S SYNDROME result from abnormal chromosomes of the child; the parents' chromosomes are normal but some environmental circumstance of unknown nature presumably distorts the complicated division, shifting, and uniting of chromosomal material in the fertilized egg. A number of such disorders can be recognized through chromosome analysis. Many more subtle, and numerous, genetic disorders cannot be identified by chromosome analysis; the defect is in parental genes, too small for direct analysis, and the transmitted disorder is truly genetic, an error in the genetic code which dictates hereditary characteristics. The abnormal gene may have been present in the parent's ancestors, or it may have arisen in the parent by mutation. Genetic traits are said to be "dominant" or "recessive." A dominant trait is transmitted by an abnormal gene of only one parent—a "single dose." Recessive traits require a "double dose" —the same defective gene from both the mother and father. The chance of this occurring is not overwhelmingly great. In two-child families, with one child affected by a given recessive disorder, the other child will be normal in 86 per cent of instances. Genetic counseling usually involves study of family pedigrees. Often, the chance of a given disorder occurring in offspring of given parents can only be expressed as a mathematical probability—say, the probability that one out of four of the parents' offspring will be affected. But *none* of their successive children may be affected, or *all* of them; the one-in-four risk applies to each pregnancy. Genetic counselors often can give great peace of mind by banishing worrisome misconceptions. The non-hemophilic brother of a hemophiliac cannot transmit the disease to his children, but he may not know it unless a genetic counselor informs him. The more complex the genetics of a given condition, such as cleft palate, the less likely it is to appear in later offspring.

Medicare. This broad system of health insurance, administered by the Social Security Administration, is for all citizens who have passed their 65th birthday. It is not necessary to have earned wages under Social Security. Persons over 65 who receive a Social Security pension automatically receive a Medicare card; other eligible persons must apply at an office of the Social Security Administration.

There are two parts to Medicare: *Hospital Insurance* (HI) and *Supplementary Medical Insurance* (SMI). HI is free. SMI coverage is voluntary; the subscriber must enroll for it and pay $4 a month.

HOSPITAL INSURANCE provides up to 90 days of hospitalization for one illness. The patient pays the first $40 of the hospital bill; after 60 days, he pays $10 a day. The limit is 90 days. But if another illness requiring hospitalization occurs 60 days or more after discharge from a hospital or nursing home, another 90-day period of benefits begins again.

What is covered: hospital room and board in a semi-private room; regular services of nurses, interns, resident physicians; operating room charge; drugs and appliances furnished by the hospital; diagnostic and therapeutic services.

Not covered: Private room, private duty nurses, cost of first three pints of blood for transfusions, extras such as room phone or TV.

Nursing home care. If a Medicare patient is transferred to a qualified nursing home after a hospital stay of at least three days, the cost of semi-private room, board, nursing and other care ordinarily furnished is paid for the first 20 days. For the next 80 days Medicare pays $5 a day. The limit for one illness is 100 days.

There are comparable benefits for hospital outpatients, covering diagnostic services, and for home care after a hospital stay.

SUPPLEMENTARY MEDICAL INSURANCE helps to pay medical bills. The subscriber pays premiums of $4 a month, matched by the government. It is important to apply for coverage several weeks before the 65th birthday.

What is covered: Reasonable charges of physicians and surgeons; services, tests, and supplies related to treatment; drugs not administered by the patient; home health services even if the patient is not hospitalized first. The patient pays the first $50 of medical expense in any calendar year; SMI pays 80 per cent of any additional doctor bills for covered services and the patient pays 20 per cent.

Not covered: Eyeglasses, hearing aids, drugs the patient can administer, dentures, routine physical checkups, routine dental care, immunizations, services of chiropractors, naturopaths, chiropodists or optometrists.

Regulations are subject to change and latest information should be obtained from a Social Security office well in advance of one's 65th birthday. Medicare does not cover every penny of hospital and medical expense. Blue Cross and many commercial insurance companies offer policies to take care of costs that Medicare does not pay. These policies are paid for by the individual who must decide if they fit his needs and budget.

Medulla. The inside parts of certain organs, such as glands and bones, as distinguished from the cortex or surface layer. The word also means "marrow-like."

Medulla oblongata. The lowest part of the brain, where it merges with the spinal cord (231). It resembles a bulb at the end of the spinal cord. It contains vital nerve centers which control such functions as heart action, breathing, and swallowing.

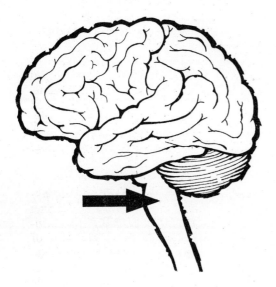

Medulla oblongata.

Megacolon. Gigantic colon. In a congenital form known as *Hirschsprung's disease,* the colon lacks nerve cells necessary for its emptying (464). The symptoms are a greatly enlarged abdomen and intractable constipation; days may go by without a bowel movement. An acquired type of megacolon usually has a psychologic basis; the child refuses to have a bowel movement and the rectum and colon become greatly distended from retained feces.

Megakaryocyte. A giant cell of the bone marrow. Fragments of this "mother cell" are blood PLATELETS, essential for normal coagulation of blood (151).

Meibomian glands. Sebaceous glands of the eyelid, subject to infection (*sty*) and obstruction (CHALAZION).

Melanin. A yellow to black pigment which is a factor in skin color. It is derived from an AMINO ACID, tyrosine, through the action of an enzyme; if the enzyme is missing the person is an albino. Its production is stimulated by a hormone of the pituitary gland (305). Suntan, freckles, and flat brown spots on the skin of elderly people are examples of melanin deposits.

Melanoma. A dark mole colored by melanin granules. The word often means *malignant melanoma,* a dangerous form of cancer, arising from pigment-producing cells. Many physicians recommend that blue or black moles be removed as a preventive measure. Moles that darken or increase in size or appear after age 30 can be dangerous and should be removed (184).

Melena. Black, tarry stools discolored by presence of blood altered in the intestinal tract, as in bleeding from the stomach or intestines. Melena of the newborn occasionally occurs from seepage of blood into the alimentary tract and is rarely a symptom of disease. Otherwise, passage of tarry stools calls for medical investigation.

Membrane. A thin layer of tissue which lines a part, separates cavities, or connects adjacent structures.

Memory drug. Theories that memory is an aspect of PROTEIN synthesis by nervous tissues have led to much investigation of the nature of memory and to chemical efforts to improve it. One drug, *magnesium pemoline,* a mild central nervous system stimulant, has shown some capacity to increase the synthesis of brain protein elements in rats. Trials of the drug in some elderly persons with memory defects have been reported to be "encouraging." Investigations of the chemistry of memory are highly experimental, and current theories of how we remember, based on very limited knowledge, may or may not prove to be correct.

Menarche. The time of first occurrence of menstruation (407). The periods may be irregular while the menstrual cycle (327) is becoming established. In the U. S. the average age at onset of menses is about 13 years; variations of a year on either side of the average are not unusual. If menstruation is not established before or shortly after the sixteenth year, the cause should be investigated.

Meninges. Membranes which cover the brain and spinal cord (238).

Meningitis. Inflammation of the MENINGES (41, 398).

Menopause. Cessation of menses; the milestone which marks the end of a woman's reproductive years (331). The average age at menopause in the U. S. is 48 years, but it is not unusual for women to continue to menstruate up to or beyond 50 years of age. At menopause, menstruation may cease abruptly, or there may be a gradual increase in the number of days between menstrual periods over a year or two. The final menstrual cycles are usually *anovulatory*—that is, no egg cells are produced by the ovaries. Many cycles which occur long before the menopause are probably anovulatory, but this cannot be relied on as assurance against conception. The average menstrual life span is about 33 years, during which a mature egg cell is released from the ovaries every month. Over the years, fewer and fewer cells which develop into ova remain in the ovaries. Along with the dwindling numbers of such cells there is progressive decrease in production of ovarian hormones. "Hot flashes" and other symptoms of the menopause reflect this decline. Most women adjust to the menopause with little difficulty. Perhaps one out of four seeks medical attention for symptoms which are likely to be more annoying than incapacitating. However, symptoms occurring at this time may be wrongly blamed on "the change" and should be investigated to determine the cause, which may be quite unrelated to the menopause.

Menorrhagia. Excessive menstrual bleeding (328).

Merycism. Deliberate regurgitation, rechewing, and reswallowing of food; an innocent habit of some infants and a pernicious one of some mentally ill persons.

Mescaline. See HALLUCINOGENIC DRUGS.

Mesentery. The flat, fan-shaped sheet of tissue which carries nerves and blood vessels and supports the intestine, from the "handle" of the fan attached to the back wall of the abdomen (436, 700). The arrangement allows considerable freedom of intestinal movement.

Metabolism. The sum total of all the physical and chemical activities by which life processes are organized and maintained; the breakdown and buildup of complex substances by body cells, assimilation of nutrients, and transformations which make energy available to the living organism. *Basal metabolism* is the minimal amount of heat (energy) needed to sustain activities when the body is in a state of rest about 18 hours after eating.

Metaplasia. Alteration of one kind of tissue into another.

Metastasis. Spread of disease from one part of the body to an unconnected part, by transfer of cells or organisms via blood and lymph channels. Ability to metastasize is characteristic of invasive cancer.

Metatarsalgia. Foot pain in the instep area (621), usually due to weakness of muscles and ill-fitting shoes.

Metatarsals. The five long bones of the

foot, overlying the longitudinal arch, between toe joints and heel structures (619).

Meteorism. "Gassiness"; inflation of stomach or intestines with gases. The term comes from a Greek word meaning "to lift off the ground," fairly descriptive of ballooning sensations.

Metritis. Inflammation of the uterus.

Metrorrhagia. Abnormal bleeding from the uterus at times other than the menstrual period.

Microtome. An instrument which cuts extremely thin slices of tissue which are placed on slides, stained, and studied by pathologists.

Micturition. The act of passing urine.

Middle ear. The air-filled bony box between the eardrum and the inner ear. It contains the chain of three tiny bones over which sound vibrations are conducted (559, 571).

Miliaria. Prickly heat, heat rash (180). Obstruction of sweat glands traps sweat under the skin, producing small pricking, burning, tingling, itching pimples. The condition disappears when the stimulus to sweating is removed, as by a cool environment.

Milk leg. A form of THROMBOPHLEBITIS which occasionally occurs a week or two after childbirth. The affected leg swells and the tensed skin has a white appearance, hence the name. Getting out of bed and moving around soon after delivery helps to prevent clot formation in veins. There is very little risk of EMBOLISM in this condition.

Milk line. "Extra" breasts or nipples are congenital anomalies that occur occasionally in men and women. Supernumerary nipples with little or no underlying breast tissue are more common than miniature out-of-place breasts. In some instances, superfluous breasts of women may attain con-

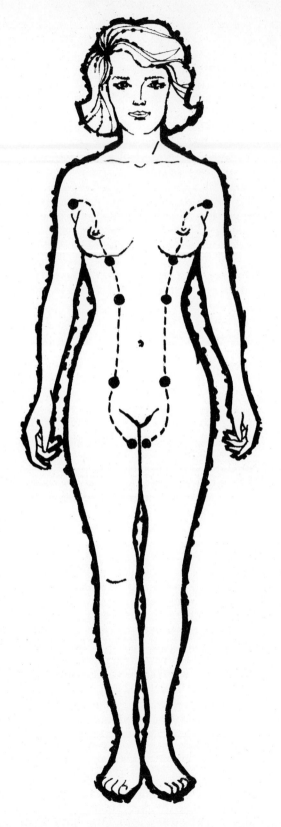

Milk line.

siderable size and even produce milk. The most frequent site of accessory breasts is about three inches below the normal pair, but they may occur anywhere along an imaginary line running from the armpit to the groin on either side. This is called the "milk line," and marks the course of structures which permit the development of multiple breasts in mammals other than man. Development of accessory breasts along this line is determined early in fetal life when traces of cells which will develop into distinct parts first appear.

Miller-Abbott tube. A double-channeled tube for insertion through the nose into the stomach to relieve distention of the small bowel. One channel has a small balloon at the end which is inflated in the stomach; peristaltic movements carry the tube farther down. Intestinal contents are withdrawn through the other channel.

Mineralocorticoids. Hormones of the cortex of the adrenal gland which regulate salt and water balances (318).

Miscarriage. Expulsion of the fetus before it is capable of independent life. See ABORTION (345).

Mitochondria. Infinitesimal sausage-shaped particles in body cells; "power plants" of the cell which contain the chemical machinery for generating energy. A typical mitochondrion has an outside membrane and numerous connecting internal folds. The outer membrane extracts energy from molecules derived from food and shunts it to inner membranes which make ATP (*adenosine triphosphate*), the form of energy we draw on to keep life processes going.

Mitral valve. The valve on the left side of the heart which admits oxygenated blood to the main pumping chamber, the left ventricle (99). The valve has two peaked flaps shaped somewhat like a bishop's miter. The valve may be damaged by rheumatic fever so that it leaks, or is scarred and thickened and cannot open widely enough (102). An operation to slit the scarred valves open is called *mitral commisurotomy* (716).

Mittelschmerz. A sign of OVULATION; lower abdominal pain produced by escape of blood into the peritoneal cavity as a result of ovulation, about midway in the menstrual cycle. The nature of the pain is usually identified by absence of any signs of pelvic disease and onset of menses about 14 days later.

Molar pregnancy. See HYDATIDIFORM MOLE.

Molluscum contagiosum. A contagious viral infection of the skin, producing yellowish pulpy pimples containing cheesy material (183).

Mongolian spot. A bluish-dark spot or spots in the region of the lower back, seen in some newborn infants. The congenital spots usually disappear by the fourth or fifth year. Not related to MONGOLISM.

Mongolism. A congenital abnormality which gets its name from the somewhat Oriental appearance of the child (395). Mongoloid babies tend to have upward slanting eyes, broad face, flattened skull, short hands, feet and trunk, stubby nose. The average mongoloid seldom achieves a mental capacity beyond that of a 3 to 7-year-old child, but is often lively and lovable. Life expectancy is not great. Placement in an institution is often recommended, especially if there are other children in the family. Mongolism results from a specific defect in CHROMOSOMES, called *trisomy*. One set of chromosomes (No. 21) is not a normal pair, but a triplet. The extra "mongolism chromosome" causes defects of physical and mental development. The mongoloid child has 47 instead of the normal complement of 46 chromosomes. The parents are in no way responsible for this accident, which occurs sporadically. The only known predisposing factor is advanced maternal age. In some very rare moagoloids, no chromosome abnormality can be detected.

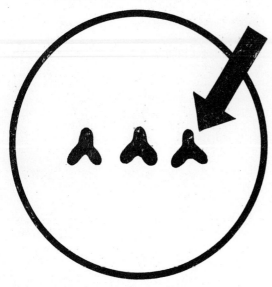

Three instead of the normal two chromosomes in a set (No. 21). This abnormality, called *Trisomy*, is characteristic of mongolism.

Moniliasis. Infection caused by yeastlike organisms, usually *Candida albicans*, which have a predilection for mucous membranes. Common sites of infection are the skin, nails, mouth, vagina, gastrointestinal tract. See vaginal yeast infections (412), in pregnancy (347), thrush (397).

Monocyte. A type of large white blood cell with a single central mass or nucleus (159). *Infectious mononucleosis* gets its name from an excess of such cells.

Mononucleosis. See INFECTIOUS MONONUCLEOSIS.

Monosodium glutamate. A substance used to enhance the flavors of foods. It is a concentrated source of sodium and would not be permitted in diets in which sodium intake must be kept low.

Monozygotic. Developed from a single fertilized egg, as identical twins (358).

Mons veneris. The rounded prominence of fatty tissue above the external female sex organs.

"Montezuma's revenge." A flip name for tourist diarrhea, the gastrointestinal upset of undetermined cause which frequently afflicts visitors to foreign countries until they become adapted.

Morning sickness. The simplest form of nausea of pregnancy (342, 491). Nausea and vomiting usually occur around breakfast time, then subside, only to recur the next morning. The symptom usually persists for two or three weeks and clears up without treatment. The cause is not known, but nothing serious can be afoot since it is estimated that 50 per cent of pregnant women experience a few episodes of morning sickness. A more serious form of vomiting of pregnancy (*hyperemesis gravidarum*) may go on for weeks, produce serious weight loss, and require medical treatment or hospitalization.

Morphinism. Addiction to morphine.

Morton's toe. A form of METATARSALGIA; there is acute pain in the region where the fourth metatarsal bone, next to the little toe, joins the toe joint.

Motion sickness. Nausea and vomiting induced by forms of motion which rotate the head simultaneously in more than one plane (sea sickness, car sickness, train sickness, air sickness). The trouble originates in the labyrinth of the ear where organs of equilibrium are located (562). Confusing impulses reach the vomiting center in the brain. Motion sickness may sometimes be prevented or minimized to some extent by not overeating or overdrinking; by lying down; by taking a position where motion is least exaggerated, as amidships in a vessel; by not reading or looking out a car window or watching a rolling horizon from a boat. A number of drugs help to prevent or lessen motion sickness if taken according to a physician's directions.

Mottled enamel (*dental fluorosis*). Dappled yellow-brown discoloration of enamel of the teeth, produced by high concentrations of fluorides naturally present in drinking water in some parts of the country.

Mountain sickness. A temporary condition brought on by diminished amounts of oxygen in the air at high altitudes. Persons who live at high altitudes adapt to the thin air; their red corpuscles increase in number. Acute mountain sickness is most likely to affect persons who are suddenly transported to high altitudes and do strenuous work. Edward Whymper, the first man to climb the Matterhorn, described an attack of mountain sickness which overcame him and his companions on a trip to the Andes: "I was incapable of making the least exertion. We were feverish, had intense headaches, and were unable to satisfy our desire for air except by breathing with our open mouths. There was no inclination to eat. All found smoking too laborious and ceased the effort in a sort of despair." The symptoms usually abate in a few days.

Mouth breathing. The habit of breathing through the mouth instead of the nose has a drying action on mouth tissues, which become inflamed, sometimes swollen and painful. Habitual mouth breathers may develop abnormal positions of the teeth because the upper teeth get no muscular support from the tongue and lower lip if the mouth is held open continually. Another risk of mouth breathing is an uncommon type of tooth decay, associated with large whitish spots around the gum line of the front teeth, a result of drying of foreign material that collects about the necks of the teeth. Mouth breathers usually have a high incidence of colds and upper respiratory infections because they do not have the normal protection of the filtering, warming, air-conditioning functions of the nose. Some children with short upper lips may keep their mouths partly open while breathing, although they actually breathe through the nose and are not true mouth breathers. Physical factors may encourage mouth breathing. Children with narrow nasal passages, easily "stuffed up" by a minor cold, tend to breathe through the mouth. Enlarged adenoid or tonsil tissue, which normally grows in excess up to about 10 years of age and then diminishes, may obstruct the airway and force the child to breathe through the mouth, which can easily become a habit. A physician or dentist can diagnose mouth breathing easily, determine if there is a physical cause, and help parents to help a child to overcome a harmful habit.

Mucous colitis. Not an organic disease, but the overreaction of an easily irritated colon to various stimuli such as emotions or foods (464). Passage of large amounts of mucus with bowel movements is quite harmless.

Mucous membrane. Mucus-secreting tissue lining the inner walls of body cavities and passages which contain or may contain a certain amount of air and hence could dry out if not moistened. Mucous membranes are quite similar in general design but perform somewhat different functions in various parts of the body. Mucous membranes of the nose warm and moisten air before it reaches the lungs. Membranes of the windpipe are equipped with fine hairlike processes which sweep a thin film of mucus containing trapped particles of dust and dirt outward from the lungs. Membranes of the stomach have special glands concerned with digestion; the membrane of the uterus undergoes periodic changes linked with the menstrual cycle.

Mucus. Watery material secreted by mucous membranes, normally thin and unobtrusive, profuse in the presence of colds, and subject to thickening and stickiness if it becomes dehydrated.

Multipara. A pregnant woman who has previously given birth to children.

Multiple births. The statistical chance of a mother's giving birth to twins is about one in 90 and the odds against triplets, quadruplets, or quintuplets are very much greater (357). But averages are not very dependable; twins are more frequent in countries with high birth rates and more frequent among Negroes than white people. There is some tendency for fraternal (two-egg) twins to run in families. Women under age 20 have the lowest incidence of twins and women 35 to 39 the highest. Likelihood of having twins is greater if a woman has already borne children, and greater yet if any of those children were twins. Treatment with gonadotropin hormones to stimulate fertility seems to increase the likelihood of multiple births. Several women so treated have given birth to septuplets; all died within minutes of birth.

Mummification. Drying and shriveling of tissue to a mummy-like mass, a result of dry GANGRENE.

Mumps skin test. A test for susceptibility to mumps, carried out by applying mumps ANTIGEN to the skin of the forearm. It is helpful in determining whether persons in a family exposed to the disease are likely to catch it. A surprising percentage of adults who have no history of having had mumps are in reality immune to the disease.

Mumps vaccine. A new addition to the vaccine family. It is of the attenuated live virus type (see VACCINE) which gives durable and lasting immunity.

Muscae volitantes. "Spots before the eyes"; floating specks like flitting flies (557).

Muscle. About half the body's weight is muscle, remarkable tissue which has one pre-eminent ability: to contract, shorten its length, pull its ends together. Muscle is not like iron, but

MUSCLE CHART →
1. frontalis
2. orbicularis oculi
3. orbicularis oris
4. mylohyoid
5. sternocleidomastoid
6. trapezius
7. deltoideus
8. pectoralis major
9. brachialis
10. triceps brachii
11. biceps brachii
12. obliquus externus
13. rectus abdominus
14. pronator teres
15. brachioradialis
16. flexor carpi radialis
17. flexor carpi ulnaris
18. flexor digitorum superficialis
19. flexor digitorum sublimis
20. tensor fasciae latae
21. gracilis
22. sartorius
23. vastus lateralis
24. rectus femoris
25. vastus medialis
26. patella (bone)
27. tibialis anterior
28. gastrocnemius
29. extensor digitorum longus
30. flexor digitorum longus pedis
31. tendon of extensor hallucis longus
32. tendon of tibialis posterior
33. temporalis
34. zygomaticus
35. masseter
36. buccinator
37. digastric
38. scalenus medius
39. scalenus anterior
40. scalenus posterior
41. omohyoid
42. sternohyoid
43. subclavius
44. pectoralis minor
45. subscapularis
46. coracobrachialis
47. latissimus dorsi
48. serratus anterior
49. intercostal
50. supinator
51. obliquus internus
52. lumbodorsal fascia
53. flexor pollicis longus
54. flexor digitorum profundus
55. head of femur (bone)
56. obturator internus
57. adductor magnus
58. flexor pollicis brevis
59. adductor brevis
60. adductor longus
61. vastus intermedius
62. quadriceps tendon
63. tibia (bone)
64. peroneus longus
65. peroneus brevis
66. extensor hallucis longus
67. soleus

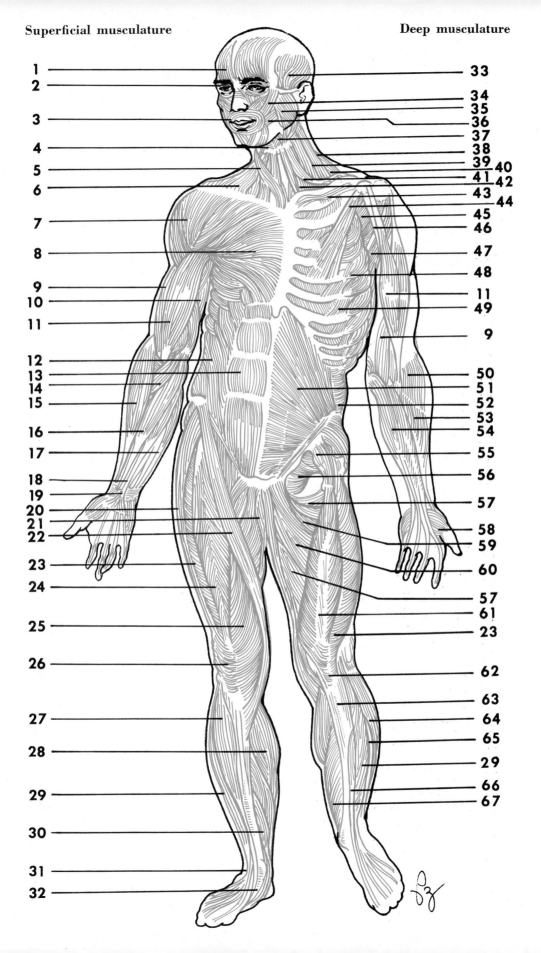

1
2
3
4
5
6
7
8
9
10
11
12
13
14
15
16
17
18
19
20
21
22
23
24
25
26
27
28
29
30
31
32

33
34
35
36
37
38
39 40
41 42
43
44
45
46
47
48
11
49
9
50
51
52
53
54
55
56
57
58
59
60
57
61
23
62
63
64
65
29
66
67

more like jelly; it is about 80 per cent water and most of the rest is protein. We have three types of muscle, different in function and visibly different under a microscope. Muscles we are most aware of are the big ones that move our bones and make it possible to chew, walk, and execute all manner of graceful or clumsy movements. This type is called *striped, voluntary,* or *skeletal* muscle. It has dark and light crossbands giving a striped appearance. Voluntary muscles move when we will them to; their ends are connected to the parts they move. (The only notoriously voluntary muscle that is not attached at both ends is the tongue). Another type of muscle is called *smooth, visceral,* or *involuntary.* It has no cross-striping. It is present in the walls of the digestive tract, blood vessels, bladder, uterus, windpipe and other tissues, where it works without our conscious command. The pupil of the eye changes its size involuntarily; we are propelled into the world by the involuntary contractions of smooth uterine muscles. A third type of muscle is unique. It constitutes the heart muscle (*myocardium*). It is a firm network of fibers connected to one another to function as a unit, in continuous operation. Muscle contraction requires energy, produces heat, and is responsible for most of the body temperature. Even when "resting," muscles are in a constant state of mild contraction (*tonus*). *Muscle cramps* result from too-continuous nerve impulses which keep a muscle in a painful state of contraction. A "pulled muscle" results from tearing or stretching by some massive effort. Exercise increases the size of muscles by enlarging individual cells, not by adding more cells.

Mutation. A change in the hereditary material of an organism, producing a change in some characteristic of the organism; especially, alteration of the character of a GENE. Mutations may occur spontaneously or they may be induced by some external stimulus, such as irradiation.

Myasthenia gravis. A chronic debilitating disease characterized by rapid fatigue of certain muscles, with prolonged time of recovery of function. Muscles of the eyes and throat are most often affected, producing such symptoms as inability to raise the eyelids, difficulties of swallowing and talking, loss of chewing power, impairment of breathing. The muscles do not waste away. It is thought that the patient lacks some chemical concerned with nerve transmission. A drug called *neostigmine* acts at nerve and muscle fiber junctions to restore considerable muscle power quite rapidly. Many myasthenia gravis patients have an enlarged *thymus gland* (302) or tumors of the thymus. X-ray treatment or surgical removal of the gland has produced some remissions, but results for individual patients are not predictable.

Mycetoma. See MADURA FOOT.

Mycoses. Infections caused by fungi (71).

Myelin. White, fatty material which covers most nerve AXONS, in the manner of insulation around an electric wire; it is essential to proper transmission of nerve impulses. Degeneration or disappearance of the myelin sheath is the characteristic lesion of *demyelinating diseases* (251).

Myelitis. Inflammation of the spinal cord or bone marrow. *Poliomyelitis* is inflammation of gray matter of the cord.

Myelogram. An x-ray film of the spinal canal made after injecting a contrast medium.

Myeloma, multiple. Malignant tumors of the bone marrow (165).

Myiasis. Infestation with larvae of flies which develop in the skin, eyes, or passages of the ear or nose.

Myocarditis. Inflammation of the heart muscle (101).

Myocardium. The heart muscle; a highly specialized, cross-layered, very powerful involuntary muscle (78). Shutting off of blood supply to a portion of the muscle, as in coronary thrombosis, results in local death of tissue (*infarction*).

Myocyte. A muscle cell.

Myoglobin. A form of HEMOGLOBIN, slightly different from that of blood, which is present in muscles and serves as a short-time source of oxygen to tide muscle fibers from one contraction to another.

Myoma. A tumor composed of muscle elements; it is a rather common benign tumor of the uterus (413).

Myometrium. The muscle of the uterus.

Myopathy. Any disease of muscle.

Myopia. Nearsightedness (537).

Myositis. Inflammation of muscle.

Myringitis. Inflammation of the eardrum.

Myringoplasty. Surgical repair of a damaged eardrum.

Myringotomy. Incision of the eardrum to relieve pressure of pus and fluids behind it (571).

Myxedema. Thyroid deficiency, *hypothyroidism* in adults (312). Congenital thyroid deficiency in children is known as *cretinism*. The patient with untreated myxedema has dry, thick, puffy skin, thinning hair, low basal metabolism, is sensitive to cold, thick of speech and mentally sluggish. Hormone replacement corrects the condition very satisfactorily.

Myxoma. A tumor derived from connective tissue.

Myxomatosis. A fatal virus disease of rabbits.

N

Narcissism. Self-love, undue admiration of one's own body; a psychologic term indicating self-admiration fixed at a level appropriate to infants but not to adults. The word comes from a character in Greek mythology who saw his image reflected in a pool and was forever after enamored of it.

Narcolepsy. Irrestible attacks of sleep, often with transient muscular weakness. Attacks occur during normal waking hours, not only under conditions conducive to drowsiness—after a heavy meal, during a dull lecture, riding on a train—but in inappropriate and even hazardous circumstances, as in driving a car. The affected person usually sleeps a few minutes, wakes refreshed, but may fall asleep again in a short time. The sleep does not differ from normal sleep except in its untimeliness; there are no signs of disease or physical abnormality. Treatment with amphetamine drugs is usually successful in warding off attacks of somnolence during the day.

Narcosis. A state of deep sleep, unconsciousness, and insensibility to pain. *Narcotics* are drugs that produce such effects. Such drugs are very important in medicine, but if misused can lead to true drug addiction.

Nares. The nostrils.

Narcosynthesis. A method of treating psychoneuroses by intravenous injection of a hypnotic drug which induces the patient to dredge up suppressed emotional material.

Nasopharynx. The top part of the throat behind the nasal cavity (583).

Nates. The buttocks.

Nausea of pregnancy. See MORNING SICKNESS.

Near point. The point closest to the eye where an object, such as fine print, is seen distinctly. The near point is too far away when a newspaper has to be held at arm's length to read it, at the time of life when the lens of the eye has lost some of its flexibility and glasses for efficient close vision become desirable.

Necropsy. Autopsy; a post-mortem examination.

Necrosis. Death of a localized portion of tissue that is surrounded by living tissue.

Negri bodies. Round or oval particles in certain cells of animals dead of *rabies* (55). Their presence is proof that the animal had rabies.

Neisserian infection. Usually means infection with gonorrhea germs, *Neisseria gonorrhoeae* (40).

Neonatal. Newborn; the first two or three days of life.

Neoplasm. Any abnormal new growth; a tumor which may be malignant or benign. "Neoplastic disease" is a common term for cancer.

Nephrectomy. Surgical removal of a kidney.

Nephritis. Inflammation of the kidney, not as a direct result of infection (280).

Nephrolith. Kidney stone.

Nephroma. Malignant tumor of the cortex of the kidney.

Nephron. The urine-forming unit of the kidney (271). It consists of a double-walled cup-shaped structure (*Bowman's capsule*) within which a tuft of tiny blood vessels (*glomerulus*) exudes blood constituents which pass as a dilute filtrate into the tubule of the capsule. Most of the water and some essential materials in the filtrate are reabsorbed and the remainder is concentrated as urine.

Nephropexy. Surgical anchoring of a "loose" or floating kidney.

NERVE CHART →

1. facial
2. great auricular
3. spinal cord
4. dorsal scapular
5. suprascapular
6. axillary
7. subscapular
8. medial antibrachial cutaneous
9. ulnar
10. median
11. radial
12. lateral cutaneous femoral
13. sciatic plexus
14. femoral
15. sciatic
16. superficial peroneal
17. deep peroneal
18. cerebrum
19. cerebellum
20. great occipital
21. vagus
22. supraclavicular
23. phrenic
24. anterior thoracic
25. musculocutaneous
26. long thoracic
27. sixth intercostal
28. ilio-inguinal
29. genitofemoral
30. obturator
31. lumbosacral
32. lumbo-inguinal
33. external spermatic
34. common peroneal
35. tibial

Nephrosclerosis. Nephritis due to hardening of kidney blood vessels (281).

Nephrosis. Degeneration of the kidney without signs of inflammation; usually refers to nephrotic disease of children (281).

Nephrotoxic. Poisonous to the kidneys.

Nerve deafness. Impairment of hearing from partial or complete failure of auditory nerves to transmit impulses to hearing centers in the brain (565).

Nettlerash. Hives, urticaria (666).

Neuralgia. Severe pain in a nerve or along its course, without demon-

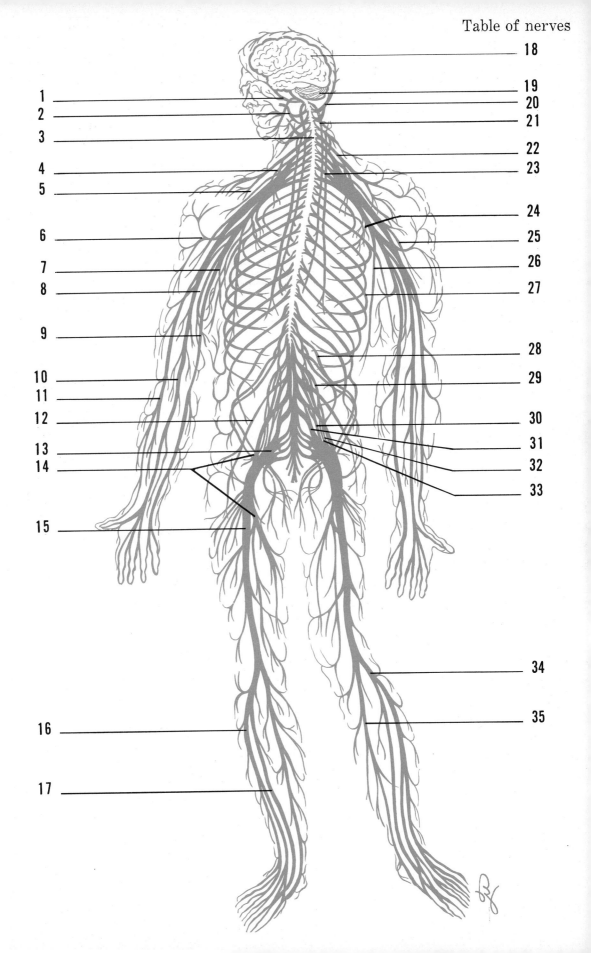

strable change in the structure of the nerve (255). The pain is typically sharp, stabbing, excruciating, short-lasting.

Neurasthenia. A somewhat out-of-fashion term for a state of great fatigability, listlessness, aches and pains, once attributed to depletion or exhaustion of nerve centers, but without any demonstrable abnormality of the nervous system. Nerves do not become screamingly twisted or come apart like frayed ropes, although such misbehavior is popularly attributed to them. Neurasthenic symptoms may have some organic cause and medical examination may disclose some treatable condition quite unrelated to nerves. If not, the label "neurasthenia" indicates a functional disorder with a psychic basis.

Neuritis. Inflammation of a nerve or its parts due to infection, toxins, compression, or other causes.

Neurodermatitis. A chronic skin condition of unknown cause, not related to infection or allergy. It occurs most frequently in nervous women and may have a neurotic basis. Itchy patches of thickened skin (see LICHENIFICATION) occur especially on the neck, the inner surface of the elbows, and the back of the knees. Treatment to relieve itching and discourage rubbing of the skin helps to alleviate the condition.

Neurofibromatosis. A condition of multiple, painless soft tumors in the skin along nerve pathways. The tumors, mainly composed of fibrous material, tend to increase in size and number. The growths are not cancerous, but very rarely may undergo malignant transformation. Frequently the tumors can be removed surgically, often permanently, although in some cases they have a tendency to recur. The disorder is thought to be of hereditary origin.

Neurogenic. Of nervous origin.

Neuron. The complete nerve cell, including the cell body, *dendrites* which bring incoming impulses to the body, and the *axon* which carries impulses away from it (232).

Neuropsychiatry. The medical specialty concerned with both nervous and mental disorders and their overlappings.

Neurosis. See PSYCHONEUROSIS.

Neurosyphilis. A late stage of syphilis affecting the central nervous system (48).

Neutrophil. A type of white blood cell stainable by neutral dyes (134). *Neutropenia* is a condition of scarcity of such cells in the blood (154).

Nevus. A local area of pigmentation or elevation of the skin; a mole, a birthmark.

Nictitation. Winking.

Nidation. "Nesting"; implantation of a fertilized egg in the uterus.

Nidus. A nest; a point of origin or focus.

Niemann-Pick disease. A rare hereditary condition occurring almost exclusively in children of Jewish families (164). It is a disorder of LIPID metabolism (inability to handle fat-like substances) which progresses to anemia, emaciation, mental retardation, blindness and deafness. Affected children rarely survive their second year. There is no treatment. The disease is inherited as a recessive trait (see HEREDITY).

Night blindness (*nyctalopia*). Imperfect vision at night or in dim light; reduced dark adaptation. The symptom may result from deficiency of vitamin A, which is necessary for regeneration of nerve cells of the retina (rods) which do most of the work of seeing when light is poor (480, 532). Certain diseases of the retina can also cause night blindness.

Nitrogen balance. An expression of the body's PROTEIN balance, determined by measurements of its nitrogen constituents. If nitrogen intake exceeds excretion, the balance is positive. Excessive retention of nitrogen may indicate kidney disease or other conditions. Negative nitrogen balance may indicate inadequate dietary protein, excessive loss of protein due to toxic goiter, burns, draining wounds, etc., impaired absorption of protein, or defective metabolism of protein as in some liver diseases.

Nitrogen mustard. A drug used to destroy malignant cells in lymphomatous diseases.

Nitrous oxide. Laughing gas; an inhalant for producing brief anesthesia, as for tooth extraction.

Nocturia. Excessive urination at night.

Node. A small protuberance, swelling, rounded knob, knot of cells. A *nodule* is a small node.

Nodular goiter. Enlargement of the thyroid gland characterized by lumpy masses on the surface or in the substance of the gland (314).

Nonviable. Incapable of living.

Normotension. Normal blood pressure.

Nosocomial. Pertaining to a hospital.

Nuchal. Pertaining to the nape of the neck.

Nuclear medicine. This young, developing, changing branch of medicine got a foothold when RADIOISOTOPES produced in nuclear reactors became available on a large scale. Radioisotopes of an element "decay" spontaneously—ultimately revert to a stable atom—and in the process give off energy in the form of radiation which is detectable by very sensitive devices. Thus, substances "tagged" or labeled with radioisotopes (for example, radioactive iodine, phosphorus, chromium) can be followed in their course through the body, giving information about chemical processes of life. Drugs can be tagged to gain new knowledge of how they work. There are now about 120 different tests and 60 clinical procedures that can be performed with radioactive materials. Recently developed *scintillation cameras* translate isotope emissions into dots on film, giving a pattern of radiation within a patient's body. Certain tissues are selective for certain elements; the thyroid gland, for instance, is avid for iodine. Radioisotopes which tend to concentrate in such tissues may be given with the object of destroying or reducing the functioning of cells. Diagnostically, radioisotopes help to measure the functional abilities of certain tissues, are useful in evaluating some blood disorders, and in locating and marking the boundaries of tumors.

Basically, radioisotope diagnosticians attempt to evaluate the fate of a carefully measured dose of radiation in the body. This evaluation may give important information about the functioning capacity of an organ. Or by "scans"—film or paper records of dots corresponding to different concentrations of radioisotopes in tissues—an abnormality, such as a tumor, may be distinguished from adjacent normal tissues (see PHOTOSCANNER).

Major radioisotopes and some of the tests they are used for are as follows:

Test	Radioisotope
Blood plasma volume	Iodine I_{131}
Red blood cell mass or volume	Chromium Cr_{51}
Exchangeable body sodium	Sodium Na_{22}
Total body water	Tritium H_3
Thyroid function	Iodine I_{131}
Kidney function	Iodine I_{131}
	Mercury Hg_{197}

Nucleus

Test	Radioisotope
Liver function	Iodine I_{131}
Red blood cell survival	Chromium C_{51}
Gastrointestinal absorption	Cobalt Co_{57} / Iodine I_{131}
Brain scan	Mercury Hg_{197} / Technetium Tc_{99M}
Thyroid scan	Iodine I_{131} / Iodine I_{125} / Technetium Tc_{99M}
Parathyroid scan	Selenium Se_{75}
Lung scan	Iodine I_{131}
Heart muscle scan	Cesium Cs_{137}
Heart cavity scan	Iodine I_{131}
Liver scan	Gold Au_{198} / Iodine I_{131}
Kidney scan	Mercury Hg_{197}
Eye scan (for melanomas)	Phosphorus P_{32}
Placental location	Iodine I_{131}

Nucleus. The rounded central body of a cell, surrounded by cytoplasm. It contains the CHROMOSOMES and mechanisms of cell division and heredity.

Nummular eczema. Dry skin with coin-shaped plaques on the back of the hands and outer surfaces of the arms, legs, and thighs (178).

Nullipara. A woman who has never borne a child.

Nyctalopia. See NIGHT BLINDNESS.

Nymphomania. Insatiable sexual desire of a female (332).

Nystagmus. Involuntary, rhythmic oscillation of the eyeballs, horizontal, vertical, or rotary. Most persons experience nystagmus if the body is whirled to produce dizziness and an attempt is made to fix the gaze on a stationary object. Simple forms of nystagmus can result from eye strain or refractive errors (537). Nystagmus may be a symptom of inner ear disturbance or disorder of the central nervous system.

O

Obesity operations. Occasionally, a surgeon may deem it feasible to remove a huge apron of fat from an obese person. More drastic and controversial is the "intestinal bypass" operation for weight reduction. In principle, the operation permits an obese person to eat all he wants but still lose weight by preventing the assimilation of substantial amounts of food (and calories). This is accomplished by connecting a short part of the small intestine to the colon, leaving behind a non-functioning loop of the small intestine, thus bypassing a considerable area in which food assimilation normally occurs. A variation of the operation consists of cutting out a part of the small intestine, without leaving a bypassed loop. These procedures do lead to weight reduction by leaving the patient incapable of absorbing some of the food he eats, but there is risk of early and late complications. Liver degeneration, anemia, malnutrition, congestive heart failure and a variety of metabolic disturbances have been reported to have occurred sometime after a bypass operation. Until further study reveals why such complications occur and how they can be prevented, the bypass operation must be considered to be somewhat risky.

Obstetric forceps. Two curved flat blades (right and left) which are separately placed with great care around the head of the fetus in the birth passage; the handles are then interlocked (363). Used to assist extraction of the baby in difficult deliveries.

Occiput. The back part of the head.

Occlusion. Closure or shutting off, as of a blood vessel; also, the meeting position of upper and lower teeth when closed (509).

Occult. Hidden, not evident to the naked eye; as, occult blood in feces.

Ocular. Pertaining to the eye.

Ocular muscle imbalance. Disharmony of muscles which move the eyeball (528). Associated with such conditions as cross-eye, wall-eye, poor fusion of images, amblyopia (542).

Oculist. Same as OPHTHALMOLOGIST.

"Oil" pneumonia. See ASPIRATION PNEUMONIA.

Olecranon. A curved part of one of the forearm bones (*ulna*) at the elbow end. It is what we lean on when we rest an elbow on a table.

Olfactory bulb. A structure just above the thin bone which separates the top of the nasal cavity from the brain. It receives nerve fibers that pass upward through small holes in the bone from the "smell area" of the nose (580).

Oligomenorrhea. Scanty menstrual flow, or abnormally long time between menstrual periods.

Oligophrenia. Mental deficiency, feeble-mindedness.

Oligospermia. Abnormally few SPERMATOZOA in the semen.

Oliguria. Scanty secretion of urine; abnormal infrequency of urination.

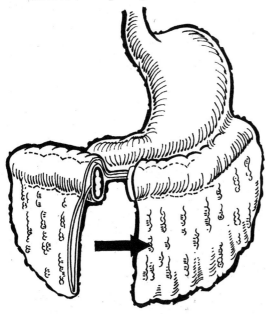

Omentum.

Omentum. A layer of tissue, a fold of the peritoneum, that hangs from the stomach and transverse colon and covers the underlying organs like an apron. It forms a fat pad on the front of the abdomen, sometimes conspicuously thick.

Omphalic. Pertaining to the navel.

Omphalotomy. Cutting of the umbilical cord; for most people, their first surgical experience.

Onchocerciasis. A form of FILARIASIS occurring in tropical areas. Infection with threadlike worms produces tumors in the skin and sometimes blinding disease of the eyes.

Oncology. The science of tumors, new growths.

Onychia. Inflammation of the bed of a nail, often resulting in loss of the nail.

Onychophagy. Nail-biting.

Ophthalmia. Inflammation of the eye, especially with involvement of the conjunctiva (545).

Ophthalmologist. A doctor of medicine specializing in medical and surgical care of the eyes (535).

Ophthalmoscope. An instrument which gives a magnified view of structures of the eye (536).

Opiates. Narcotics derived from or related to opium; for example, morphine, heroin, codeine, paregoric, laudanum. In a broad sense the word applies to any sense-dulling, stupor-inducing drug.

Opisthotonos. A position of the body in which the head and lower legs are bent backward and the trunk arched forward, due to convulsive spasm of muscles of the back, such as is produced by strychnine poisoning.

Optic atrophy. Irreversible degeneration of optic nerve fibers.

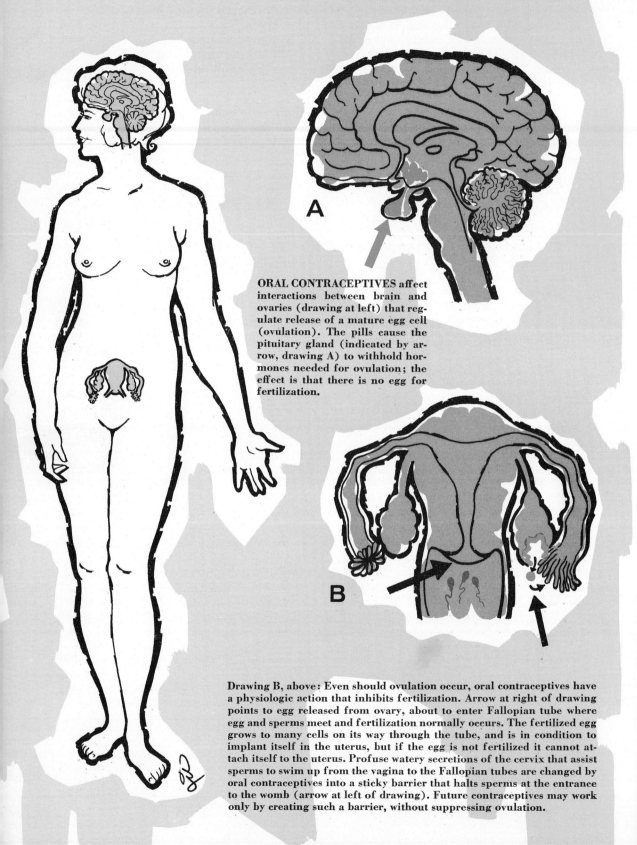

ORAL CONTRACEPTIVES affect interactions between brain and ovaries (drawing at left) that regulate release of a mature egg cell (ovulation). The pills cause the pituitary gland (indicated by arrow, drawing A) to withhold hormones needed for ovulation; the effect is that there is no egg for fertilization.

A

B

Drawing B, above: Even should ovulation occur, oral contraceptives have a physiologic action that inhibits fertilization. Arrow at right of drawing points to egg released from ovary, about to enter Fallopian tube where egg and sperms meet and fertilization normally occurs. The fertilized egg grows to many cells on its way through the tube, and is in condition to implant itself in the uterus, but if the egg is not fertilized it cannot attach itself to the uterus. Profuse watery secretions of the cervix that assist sperms to swim up from the vagina to the Fallopian tubes are changed by oral contraceptives into a sticky barrier that halts sperms at the entrance to the womb (arrow at left of drawing). Future contraceptives may work only by creating such a barrier, without suppressing ovulation.

Optic chiasm. An arrangement of nerve fibers in which the optic nerves of both eyes cross at a junction near the pituitary gland (533).

Optic disk. The area at the back of the eye where all the nerve fibers of the retina merge with the optic nerve (555). Because light is not perceived at the point where the optic nerve enters the eye, the area is a normal BLIND SPOT.

Optician. A skilled technician who fills the prescription of an ophthalmologist or optometrist for glasses or contact lenses; a manufacturer or designer of optical equipment.

Optic nerve. A bundle of a million or so nerve fibers which transmits impulses from the RETINA to the occipital lobe at the back of the head where they are transformed into vision.

Optometrist. An expert qualified to fit and prescribe glasses and contact lenses and give non-medical care of the eyes (535).

Oral contraceptives. STEROID compounds taken by mouth by women to prevent conception; "the pill" (331). The tablets contain combinations of estrogen-progestogen or they may be "sequential," furnishing estrogen alone on certain days of the cycle, followed by combined estrogen-progestogen. Regularity of dosage as the doctor directs is very important. The Committee on Human Reproduction of the American Medical Association concludes that the pills are virtually 100 per cent effective if taken properly under medical direction. The pills prevent conception by suppressing OVULATION; the effect is that there is no egg to be fertilized. The compounds suppress ovulation by depressing the pituitary gland's production of *follicle-stimulating hormone* and *luteinizing hormone* (327). See opposite page.

Orbit. The bony socket that contains the eyeball (527).

Orchidectomy. Castration; surgical removal of the testicles. The operation leaves the patient sterile.

Orchitis. Inflammation of the testicles. It may be a complication of mumps.

Organ of Corti. The center of the sense of hearing in the inner ear. It contains feathery cells which oscillate in response to pulsating fluids, stimulating nerve endings which merge into the nerve of hearing that carries impulses to receiving centers in the brain.

Organic disease. Disease that has a physical cause, a lesion, disorder of an organ, as opposed to FUNCTIONAL DISEASE.

Orgasm. The climax of the sexual act, terminating in ejaculation of semen by the male and release of tension in the female (410).

Oriental sore (*cutaneous Leishmaniasis*). Single or multiple skin ulcers produced by infection with organisms transmitted by sandflies (71).

Orifice. The opening, entrance, or outlet of a body cavity or passage.

Ornithosis (*parrot fever, psittacosis*). A pneumonia-like disease produced by viruses from infected birds (56).

Orthodontics. "Tooth straightening"; the branch of dental science concerned with prevention and correction of irregularities of the teeth and jaws (519).

Orthopedics. The surgical and medical specialty concerned with correction of deformities, diseases, accidents and disorders of body parts that move us about—limbs, bones, joints, muscles, tendons, etc.

Orthopnea. The need to sit upright in order to breathe comfortably, manifested by persons with congestive heart failure (96).

Orthopsychiatry. A division of psychiatry concerned with "straightening out" disorders of behavior and personality, especially in children.

Orthoptics. Teaching, training, and exercise programs for improving the fusion of images from both eyes (as in cross-eyes), putting a "lazy eye" back to work, and generally making visual mechanisms more efficient (543, 557).

Orthostatic. Induced or intensified by standing upright; for example, *orthostatic hypotension,* a lowering of blood pressure brought on by changing from a lying-down to an upright position.

Osgood-Schlatter disease. Degeneration of a natural protuberance on the knee-end of the TIBIA, the long bone of the lower leg. A form of OSTEOCHONDRITIS, most frequent in young persons.

Osmosis. The phenomenon of transfer of materials through a semipermeable membrane that separates two solutions, or between a solvent and a solution, tending to equalize their concentrations. *Osmotic pressure* is that exerted by the movement of a solvent through a semipermeable membrane into a more concentrated solution on the other side. This pressure is the driving force that causes diffusion of particles in solution to move from one place to another. Walls of living cells are semipermeable membranes and much of the activity of the cells depends upon osmosis.

Osseous. Composed of bone or resembling bone; bony.

Ossicle. One of the three tiny bones of the middle ear (*malleus, incus, stapes*) which conduct sound vibrations to the inner ear (560).

Ossification. The process of forming bone. CARTILAGE is made into bone by the process of ossification. Calcium and phosphorus are deposited in the cartilage, changing it into bone.

Osteitis. Inflammation of bone.

Osteitis deformans. A chronic process of bone overgrowth, destruction, and new bone formation, ultimately producing deformities; PAGET'S DISEASE (625). The skull and weight-bearing bones are most commonly affected.

Osteochondritis. Inflammation of both bone and CARTILAGE. *Osteochondritis dissecans* is a fairly common condition of late adolescence in which there is local death of a section of the joint surface of a bone (usually of the knee) and its overlying cartilage (617). *Osteochondritis deformans juvenilis* (Perthe's disease) is a degenerative condition of the upper end of the thigh bone in children three to eight years of age, which eventually heals but may leave some deformity of the hip joint (614).

Osteogenesis imperfecta. A rare hereditary condition of defective formation of bony tissues, resulting in brittle bones which fracture easily.

Osteomalacia. Adult RICKETS; softening of bone, abnormal flexibility, brittleness, loss of calcium salts. Usually due to vitamin D deficiency or impaired absorption of nutrients; rare in the U. S. (624).

Osteomyelitis. Infection of bone and marrow due to growth of germs within the bone. Infection may reach the bone through the bloodstream or direct injury (38, 600).

Osteoporosis. Enlargement of canals or spaces in bone, giving a porous, thinned appearance. The weakened bone is fragile and may be broken by some minor injury or may fracture spontaneously. The condition is relatively common in women after the menopause and occurs to some degree in all aging persons (624). Recent evidence indicates that drinking water with adequate fluoride content helps to prevent the condition; see FLUORIDES.

Osteotome. An instrument for cutting bone.

Otalgia. Earache.

Otitis. Inflammation of the ear. *Otitis externa* is a bacterial or fungal infection of the ear canal (570). *Otitis media* is an infection of the middle ear (571).

Otoplasty. Plastic surgery for correction of malformed ears. See PROTRUDING EARS.

Otorhinolaryngologist. A medical specialist in diseases of the ear, nose, and throat. An *otologist* confines himself to the ear.

Otorrhea. Chronic, malodorous discharge from the ear (571).

Otosclerosis. Overgrowth in parts of the middle ear of spongy bone which "freezes" sound-conducting mechanisms to some degree, dampens vibrations, and impairs hearing (565). This type of hearing loss is often correctible by surgery which restores the vibration-transmitting system to good working order (567).

Otoscope. A funnel-ended instrument with a light source for inspecting the ear canal and eardrum (571).

Oval window. A membrane-covered opening to the inner-ear, to which the footplate of the STAPES is attached (560). Sounds conducted by the chain of bones in the middle ear are "hammered" against the oval window and transmitted to fluids behind it and thence to the inner ear.

Ovarian cyst. A sac containing fluid or mucoid material arising in the ovary (414, 707). A cyst with a stem may become twisted and produce sudden severe pain in the lower abdomen.

Ovariectomy. Surgical removal of one or both ovaries (707). Also called *oophorectomy.*

Oviducts. The tubes through which the egg cell is transported to the uterus, and in which fertilization usually occurs (350). Same as *Fallopian tubes.*

Ovulation. Release of a mature egg cell from the follicle in the ovary in which it develops (327). This is the time during the menstrual cycle when conception can occur. There are no infallible signs of ovulation that a woman can unfailingly recognize, but there are suggestive signs. Ovulation usually occurs about midway between menstrual periods in a normal menstrual cycle of approximately 28 days. Body temperature tends to rise sharply, though to small degree, at the time of ovulation. Abdominal pain and a pinkish discharge from the vagina may also occur at the time of ovulation; see INTERMENSTRUAL PAIN, "SHOW" and MITTELSCHMERZ.

Ovum. The female reproductive cell; an egg. The ovum is the largest human cell but it is barely discernible by the naked eye. It is about one-fourth the size of the period at the end of this sentence. It is a round cell with a clear shell-like capsule, with the consistency of stiff jelly, weighing about a 50-billionth of an ounce—the "original weight" of every human being (the weight of the much smaller fertilizing sperm scarcely counts). Like the sperm, the ovum contains only 23 CHROMOSOMES, which at conception "pair off" with those of the sperm to give the embryo a normal complement of 46 chromosomes. Although the ovum is about 85,000 times larger than the sperm, both contain the same number of GENES. The relatively huge size of the ovum is partly accounted for by its content of nutrient yolk globules. Only about 400 ova ripen to maturity and are released by ovulation during a woman's reproductive lifetime; of these, only a very few are fertilized.

Outpatient. A patient who comes to a hospital for treatment but does not reside there.

Oxyhemoglobin. HEMOGLOBIN carrying a full load of oxygen; the hemoglobin in bright red arterial blood.

Oxytocin. A hormone of the pituitary gland which stimulates the uterus to contract. It is frequently administered by slow drip into a vein to stimulate labor and insure effective contractions (363).

Oxyuriasis. Pinworm infection (69).

Ozena. A chronic disease of mucous membranes of the nose, giving off a very foul-smelling odor or discharge.

P

Pacemaker. A small knot of tissue in the right auricle of the heart which triggers the heartbeat (77). In certain heart disorders, battery-powered devices connected to the heart can take over the pacemaking function. See CARDIAC PACEMAKER.

Pachydermatous. Thick skinned.

Paget's disease. Two diseases bear this name. *Paget's disease of the breast* is manifested by thickened, eczema-like scaliness of the area around the nipple, with fissuring, oozing, and destruction of the nipple as the underlying disease (cancer of the central ducts of the breast) advances. The other Paget's disease, also known as *osteitis deformans,* is a chronic disease of bone metabolism. The skull, pelvis, spine, and long bones are especially affected. Calcium is lost from the bones, which become soft and bend easily. Irregular replacement of calcium causes thickening and deformity. Bone pain, impaired hearing, and muscle cramps are frequent symptoms. The disease progresses slowly and after many years may lead to chronic invalidism.

Painful menstruation, exercises. Primary dysmenorrhea (332) is characterized by pain, cramps, or mild to severe discomfort occurring at the onset of menstrual periods, in the absence of any organic disorder. Physical exercises may help to banish distress. Any exercise which involves systematic twisting, bending, and extending of the trunk is helpful. The following simple exercises can be performed in ordinary clothing without equipment: 1. Stand upright, arms raised sideward at shoulders, trunk turned to left. Keep the knees straight, twist and bend the trunk downward, touch left foot with right hand, try to touch outside of heel of right foot. Repeat with trunk turned to right— each side as a unit. 2. Stand upright, arms at sides, feet parallel. Swing both arms upward and forward, at the same time raising one leg vigorously backward. Repeat with other leg. Do the exercises three times a day, exercising each side several times at each session.

Painful shoulder syndrome. Limitation of motion and pain about the shoulder may arise from injury, calcium deposits, bursitis, osteoarthritis, degeneration of tissues, diseases of the chest, coronary heart disease. The predominant symptom is severe pain in the shoulder area and inability to raise the arm because of pain and weakness (628).

Painter's colic. LEAD POISONING.

Palliative. Relieving pain, suffering, or distressing symptoms of disease but without any curative action.

Palpation. A method of obtaining information about a patient's condition by manipulating or feeling a part of the body with the hand.

Palpebral. Pertaining to the eyelid.

Palpitation. Throbbing, "pounding," rapid or fluttery heartbeat, sufficiently out of the ordinary to make the patient aware of it. More often than not the condition is temporary and not of serious import, but there are many causes and if the symptom is repeated or alarming it should be investigated (104).

Palsy. Slight or moderate paralysis.

Pancreatitis. Inflammation of the pancreas gland. It occurs in acute and chronic forms (459).

Pandemic. A super-epidemic, one that occurs on a large scale over a very wide area of a country or of the world.

Panhypopituitarism. Severe loss of function of the anterior pituitary gland (308). See SIMMONDS' DISEASE; SHEEHAN'S DISEASE.

Panniculus. A layer of fat beneath the skin; the layer on the front of the abdomen sometimes expands the waistline.

Panophthalmitis. Pus-producing inflammation of all the tissues of the eye, threatening total and permanent blindness.

Papanicolaou smear (*"Pap test"*). A screening test for cancer of the cervix and the uterus, employing CYTOLOGIC DIAGNOSIS. Cell scrapings obtained painlessly from the surface of the cervix are spread on glass slides, stained, and examined under a microscope. Detection of cancer cells in the specimen, and confirmation of cancer of the cervix by other diagnostic measures, leads to prompt treatment of a form of cancer which in its early stages is almost invariably curable (418). (See illustration, page 962).

Papilla. A small conical or nipple-shaped elevation, like a pimple. Papillae give the front of the tongue its velvety appearance, and orderly lines of papillae projecting into the upper skin layer give us our fingerprints.

Papilledema (*choked disk*). Non-inflammatory swelling of the optic nerve where it enters the eye, due to increased pressures within the skull or interference with flow of blood from veins of the eye. It occurs most frequently in patients with brain tumor, brain abscess, or meningitis; concussion or hemorrhage may also be responsible. Vision is good in early stages but gradually deteriorates. Treatment depends on detection of the underlying cause.

Papilloma. A tumor of surface-lining tissues—skin, mucous membranes, glandular ducts—composed of epithelial cells covering supporting papillae. It is usually benign.

Papule. A small solid elevation on the skin; a solid pimple containing no pus or fluid.

Paracentesis. Surgical puncture of a body cavity to withdraw fluid.

Paraffin packs. A way of heating body parts, especially painful arthritic hands, giving sustained deep penetration of heat. The hands are dipped into melted paraffin until a thick heat-retaining layer is built up (29).

Paralytic ileus. Intestinal obstruction resulting from decreased peristaltic activity of the bowel (461).

Paranoia. A form of mental illness characterized by suspiciousness, delusions, feelings of being persecuted, spied upon, endangered. The patient's delusions are so systematized and seemingly logical that they can be quite convincing to others, especially since the paranoid patient often seems quite sane and reasonable except on one or a few subjects. Mild paranoid trends are not uncommon in suspicious people who think others "have it in for them," put obstacles in their way, and are responsible for their failures, but the extreme paranoid, who may do violence to his supposed persecutors, has a severe mental illness (681).

Paraplegia. Paralysis of both legs, usually due to injury or disease of the spinal cord. The bladder, bowels and other organs may be paralyzed as well

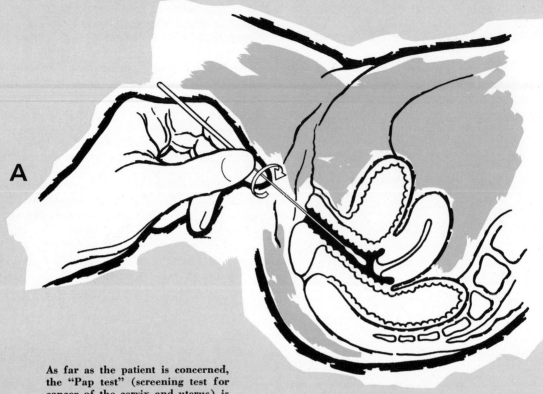

A

As far as the patient is concerned, the "Pap test" (screening test for cancer of the cervix and uterus) is simple, painless, and takes but a few moments during routine physical examination. Above, a swab is gently rotated to collect secretions from the vagina and cervix.

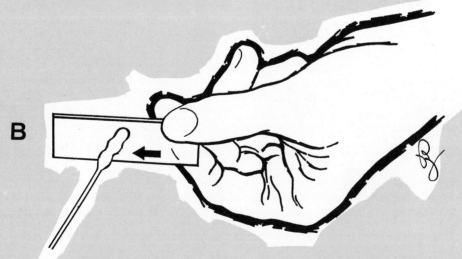

B

Secretions containing cast-off cells are transferred to a glass slide, stained, and examined under a microscope by cytologists trained to recognize normal and abnormal cells. If some cells appear to be malignant, other tests are done to rule out or confirm the presence of cancer in the genital tract.

as the legs, depending on the controlling part of the nervous system that is injured. Rehabilitation training and devices may restore a good measure of self-sufficiency to the paraplegic patient.

Parathyroid glands. Four bead-size glands embedded superficially on the back and side surfaces of both lobes of the thyroid gland. The glands secrete hormones which maintain a stable concentration of calcium in the blood. Either an excess or deficiency produces mild to serious bodily disturbances (316).

Paratyphoid. An acute infectious disease which resembles typhoid fever but is less severe. It is caused by *Salmonella* bacteria transmitted directly or indirectly from feces and urine of infected persons (400).

Parenchyma. The functioning, specialized, "working part" of an organ, as distinguished from connective tissue that supports it.

Parenteral. Outside of the alimentary tract. The word commonly refers to substances given by injection or infusion instead of by mouth.

Paresis. Slight or incomplete paralysis. Also, a term for general paralysis of the insane, resulting from syphilis, rare since the advent of antibiotics.

Paresthesia. Abnormal sensations of crawling, burning, and tingling of the skin, due to neuritis or lesions of the nervous system.

Parietal. Pertaining to the wall of a cavity; especially, the bones of the skull at the top and sides of the head behind the frontal bones (594).

Parkinson's disease (*parkinsonism*). A chronic progressive disease of which the chief symptoms are tremor, stiffness, and slowness of movement, resulting from disturbance of a small center at the base of the brain (241).

Paronychia. Pus-producing infection of tissues around the nails, caused by yeasts (190) or bacteria. Acute bacterial paronychia is usually treated by hot saline soaks and antibiotics administered by the physician. Surgical drainage may be necessary. Chronic bacterial paronychia may require prolonged treatment with hot soaks, drainage, and local application of an antibiotic ointment. During treatment the involved finger or fingers should be kept as dry as possible.

Parotid gland. One of the saliva-producing glands, located in the angle of the jaw in front of and below the ear (430).

Parotitis. Mumps; inflammation of the parotid gland. A new MUMPS VACCINE gives long-lasting immunity; a skin test detects susceptibility.

Paroxysmal tachycardia. Periodic attacks of extremely rapid beating of the heart, as many as 300 beats per minute. Attacks may last only a few seconds or as long as several hours (105).

Parrot fever. See PSITTACOSIS.

Parturition. Childbirth.

Passive transfer. An indirect method of testing for skin allergies. Serum of the patient is introduced into areas of the skin of another person, and a couple of days later these sites are tested for reactions to suspected allergens (657). The other person acts as a guinea pig, demonstrating skin reactions to substances to which he himself is not allergic.

Patch test. A method of identifying allergic sensitivities by applying suspected material to the skin, leaving it uncovered, or more often covering it with a bandage (657).

Patella. The kneecap (513).

Patent. Wide open.

Paternity tests. Blood groups (139) are determined by unvarying laws of HEREDITY. This is the basis of tests for excluding paternity. If a child's red blood cells contain substances called "factors" which are incompatible with the blood groups of its presumed parents, one of the couple cannot be the father or the other cannot be the mother. A person with AB blood cannot have a child of group O; a person of group O cannot have a child of group AB; a person of group M cannot have a child of group N. Presence or absence of a number of other factors follows the same hereditary rules. The blood factors of the mother, child, and putative father are determined by sensitive tests using antiserums and red blood cells known to contain A, B, O, M or N factors. If the factor tested for is present, the red cells clump together; if it is absent they do not. Tests cannot prove that a man *is* the father of a certain child. They can only prove that he cannot be, and they cannot always do that because by coincidence his blood may contain the same factors as the actual father. The chance that non-paternity can be proved is a little better than 50 per cent. Only three blood groups (ABO, MN, Rh-Hr) are used for medicolegal purposes, but several other factors are known and it is theoretically possible to distinguish 50,000 different blood group combinations. Indeed, it is believed that blood is as individual as fingerprints, a testament of personal uniqueness, and when its subtle chemical markers are more fully revealed it may become possible to determine that a child is the offspring of a particular couple.

Pathogenic. Having the capacity to produce disease. Many bacteria are harmless and even beneficial to man, but the vicious sorts that cause disease are pathogenic organisms.

Pathology. The science and study of the nature of disease: its processes, effects, causes, manifestations; changes from normal in structure and function. Pathology does not mean "disease," but its study. The word is often misused. Even the reports of some doctors, who mean to say that an examined patient is free from disease, state that "no pathology was found." *Pathologists* examine stained cells and tissues, do autopsies, and employ chemical and laboratory methods to assist in diagnosis of disease in a particular patient and to add to scientific knowledge of disease processes in general.

Pectoral. Pertaining to the chest.

Pedicle graft. A flap of a patient's own skin attached to the body by a stalk or pedicle containing intact blood vessels that supply nourishment while the flap is "taking hold" in an area to which it is grafted (742).

Pediculosis. Infestation with body lice (191).

Pellagra. A DEFICIENCY DISEASE manifested by rough skin, sore mouth and tongue, sometimes mental disturbance (480).

Pelvimetry. Measurement of the dimensions of the bony pelvis, usually done to determine whether the outlet between the two bones that rim the birth passage is of sufficient size to permit the fetus to pass into the world (344).

Pelvis. A basin-shaped cavity, especially that formed by bones in the hip region. The bony pelvis supports the spinal column, rests on the legs, and contains structures of the lower end of the trunk (595). The *kidney pelvis* is a cavity which collects urine from the organ's filtration units and funnels the urine to the ureter and thence to the bladder (273). The female bony pelvis is slightly different and distinguishable from that of the male.

Pemphigus. An uncommon but serious disease manifested by crops of large blisters which rupture and leave raw surfaces (188).

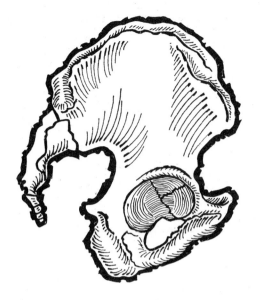

Side view of left half of the bony pelvis; the "tailbone" is at extreme lower left of drawing.

Penicillin reactions. The major single cause of systemic reactions to drugs is penicillin. Reactions occur in persons previously sensitized to the drug by therapeutic doses, or sometimes by indirect contact, as in milk products. The most serious and fortunately the most rare reaction is ANAPHYLAXIS; its most common pattern is acute breathing difficulty, swelling of the larynx threatening suffocation, profound shock. This reaction occurs within seconds or minutes after administration of penicillin to sensitized patients. Far more common and less serious, but distressing, are skin reactions such as rash, hives and itching. SCRATCH TESTS on persons with no previous history of penicillin sensitization may be performed before administering the drug, but if patients with past histories of penicillin sensitivity are to be tested, emergency treatment facilities should be available.

Penis. The male sex organ.

Pepsin. A protein-digesting enzyme in gastric juices. It is active only in an acid environment, which the stomach provides (342).

Peptic ulcer. An ulcer associated with the digestive action of acid juices; it may be located in the stomach or duodenum, or at the site of surgical joining of the stomach and jejunum. The most frequent form is duodenal ulcer (453).

Percomorph. Refers to fish of the perch family. Percomorph oil, prepared from the livers of such fish, is a concentrated source of Vitamin D.

Percussion. A method of physical diagnosis. Short firm blows are tapped upon a body surface by a finger or small hammer to produce sounds or vibrations. Solid, fluid-filled, tense, empty, or congested organs have different resonances, just as an empty barrel sounds different when tapped than a barrel full of water. Percussion is most often applied to the chest and back.

Perennial allergic rhinitis. A condition similar to hay fever but running a more or less continuous course without seasonal variations (663).

Perforated eardrum. The eardrum may be punctured by direct injury (never stick hairpins or toothpicks into the ear canal!) or by infections of the middle ear which break through the drum. A punctured eardrum may heal itself, close the openings, but if not, a route of invasion of infectious material from the outside world is wide open. A person with a punctured eardrum should not dive or swim or get the head under water because of danger that infectious material may be forced into internal ear parts. Ear plugs do not give dependable protection. A perforated eardrum can be closed by an operation known as *tympanoplasty* (573).

Perianal. Situated around the anus.

Pericarditis. Inflammation of the PERICARDIUM from causes such as rheumatic fever or extension of infections from neighboring parts (100).

Pericardium. The sac of tough tissue that encloses the heart (78). It secretes lubricating fluids that permit free-sliding movements of the expanding, contracting heart.

Perimeter. An instrument for mapping the limits of the field of vision (536).

Perineum. The area between the anus and scrotum in the male, and the anus and the vulva in the female.

Periodontal disease. Inflammation of membranes that cover the roots of the teeth (508); laymen commonly call it PYORRHEA.

Periosteum. The tough, membranous covering of nearly all bone surfaces (598).

Peripheral. At or near an outer surface; for example, peripheral blood vessels, near skin surfaces.

Peristalsis. Wavelike movements of constriction and relaxation which propel materials along the digestive tube. Encircling muscle contracts to squeeze material forward while muscles in front of the material relax; the latter muscles constrict in their turn, and so on (430).

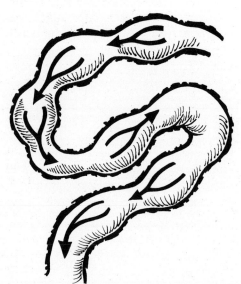

Peristalsis.

Peritoneum. The strong, smooth, colorless membrane which lines the abdominal wall and contains the abdominal organs.

Peritonitis. Inflammation of the PERITONEUM; the most frequent cause is a ruptured appendix, but infection can occur from other routes (464).

Perleche. Cracks at the side of the mouth, thickened, covered with whitish material. The condition is classically associated with deficiency of a vitamin, riboflavin, but this is rare in the U. S. Usually the patient has excessive folding of the skin at the corners of the mouth—perhaps congenital, or the result of missing teeth or poorly fitting dentures—and the moist opposing surfaces rub together, resulting in maceration, inflammation, possible infection. The patient licks the cracks, fostering further maceration; spicy or acid foods may be irritating. Perleche must be distinguished by a physician from other lesions that may resemble it. An ointment may be prescribed, together with appropriate measures to keep the area dry—correction of malocclusion, poorly fitting dentures, abstention from smoking, chewing gum, and chewing tobacco.

Perspiration. The refined person's sweat (170).

Perthe's disease. Degeneration of the upper end of the thighbone in young children (615).

Pertussis. Whooping cough (402).

Pessary. One of many devices of metal, rubber, or plastic, of different shapes and sizes, placed in the vagina or the uterus or parts of it to support sagging, tipped, slipping, or otherwise displaced pelvic structures.

Petechiae. Tiny pinpoint hemorrhages under the skin (151).

Petit mal. A relatively mild form of epileptic attack, consisting of sudden loss

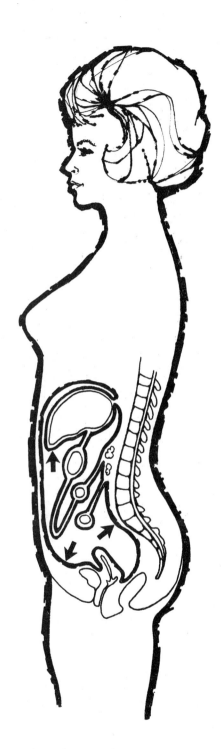

Peritoneum. As the small arrows indicate, the membrane is a continuous lining of the abdominal cavity and covers most of the organs contained in it.

of consciousness lasting only a few seconds (262).

Pets. See HOUSEHOLD PETS.

pH. Technically, a symbol expressing hydrogen ion concentration; practically, a scale of the acidity or alkalinity of substances. The neutral point is pH 7. Below 7, acidity increases. Above 7, alkalinity increases.

Phagocyte. A white blood cell which has the engaging property of engulfing, digesting, and generally eating up invading bacteria or other foreign particles (134).

Phalanx. One of the bones of the fingers or toes (593). The plural is *phalanges*.

Pharmacopoeia. An authoritative collection of formulas and methods of preparing and using drugs, which sets minimum standards of purity, safety, and potency. Some manufacturers exceed the standards. The U. S. Pharmacopoeia is recognized as the standard in this country. It is revised every few years, dropping some old drugs and adding new ones. A medicine with the initials "U.S.P." on the label conforms to Pharmacopoeia standards.

Phantom limb. The illusion that a limb which has been amputated is still attached to the body and feels pain and other sensations.

Pharyngitis. Sore throat.

Pharyngeal tonsils. Lymphoid tissue better known as *adenoids* (583).

Pharynx. The membrane-lined tube at the back of the nose, mouth, and larynx; the place where a sore throat hurts (583).

Phenylalanine. An essential AMINO ACID, present in protein foods.

Phenylketonuria (*PKU*). Hereditary inability to metabolize phenylalanine, an essential amino acid, because of a genetically determined lack of a necessary enzyme; an inherited "error of metabolism." Breakdown products of incompletely metabolized phenylalanine accumulate in the infant's body and impair brain function. The *Guthrie* test of an infant's blood gives evidence of the condition soon after birth (766). Institution of a diet of special foods, very low in phenylalanine, lessens the threat of damage to the developing nervous system.

Pheochromocytoma. A tumor, usually arising in the inner part of the adrenal gland, which secretes excessive amounts of hormones, producing such symptoms as tremor, cramps, palpitations, headache, nausea, and high blood pressure. Treatment is surgical removal (322).

Philadelphia chromosome. An abnormal CHROMOSOME which can be found in nearly 95 per cent of patients with chronic myelogenous leukemia (158). Its association with leukemia supports the hypothesis that specific GENE mutations may induce a high frequency of chromosome "breakage" and that chromosome rearrangements may be a common pathway through which cancer-inducing factors are expressed.

Phimosis. Elongation and tightening of the foreskin of the PENIS, preventing retraction over the head of the organ.

Phlebitis. Inflammation of the walls of a vein, which may lead to formation of a clot, *thrombophlebitis* (130).

Phlebothrombosis. Formation of a clot in a vein (130).

Phlebotomy. "Bloodletting" by cutting into a vein; venesection. Irrational bloodletting for almost any state of ill health—the aspirin of its day—was practiced wholesale in the seventeenth and eighteenth centuries. The practice undoubtedly weakened and hastened the death of thousands of patients, including George Washington, and fell into highly deserved disrepute as a panacea. But there are some conditions for which bloodletting is recognized as a part of modern treatment; see HEMOCHROMATOSIS and POLYCYTHEMIA (145).

Phlegmasia alba dolens. See MILK LEG.

Phobia. An abnormal, excessive dread or fear. There are scores of specific phobias, each with its own medical name. Some of the more common are:

Phobia	Fear of
acrophobia	heights
agoraphobia	open places
aichmophobia	sharp objects
ailurophobia	cats
algophobia	pain
androphobia	men
bacteriophobia	germs
ballistophobia	missiles
belonephobia	needles, pins
claustrophobia	confined spaces
cynophobia	dogs
dipsophobia	drink
erythrophobia	blushing
genophobia	sex
gymnophobia	nakedness
hemophobia	blood
hypnophobia	falling asleep
lalophobia	talking
lyssophobia	becoming insane
melissophobia	bees
mysophobia	dirt, contamination
ochlophobia	crowds
osmophobia	odors
pedophobia	children
photophobia	light
pyrophobia	fire
siderodromophobia	railroads
sitophobia	eating
tocophobia	childbirth
triskaidekaphobia	number 13
xenophobia	strangers

Phocomelia. A type of congenital malformation in which the upper and lower limbs are absent or grossly underdeveloped but the hands and feet are present.

Photophobia. Intolerance of light or morbid fear of light.

Photoscanner. An instrument which measures the concentration of radioisotopes (measured doses of radiation) in a patient's body. It has a scintillator crystal which, when struck by radiation, energizes an amplified stream of high-speed electrons from a photomultiplier tube. This burst is employed in the simultaneous production of two records of the concentration of radioactivity. One record consists of dots produced on a moving sheet of paper; the more concentrated the radioactivity, the more concentrated the dots. The other record is produced on an x-ray film; here the increased concentration of radioactivity produces increased blackness of dots as well as an increase in the number of dots. The complete system enables doctors to differentiate areas of tissue with as little as 15 to 25 per cent more radiation than their surroundings. The instrument can scan a patient's body at a rate of 200 inches per minute and record diagnostic information in as little as ten minutes. See NUCLEAR MEDICINE.

Photosensitivity. A number of disorders are triggered or made worse by exposure to sunlight. Photosensitive reactions may result from certain drugs taken internally, from materials in cosmetics or substances applied to the skin, from contact with certain plants (parsnips, celery, carrots, dill, parsley), or from underlying disease which increases the sensitivity of the skin to sunlight. A clue to photosensitive reactions is the presence of lesions on exposed areas of the forehead, nose, rims of the ears and backs of the hands, while areas under the jaw not exposed to sunlight are not affected. Patients with *lupus erythematosus* (185, 640) are very sensitive to sunlight.

Phototherapy. Treatment with light rays, including invisible ultraviolet and infrared wave lengths.

Phrenic nerve. The principal nerve of breathing which activates the great muscle of respiration, the *diaphragm* (204). The nerve also serves the PERICARDIUM and PLEURA.

Phthisis. An old term for pulmonary tuberculosis.

Physical allergy. Allergic reactions induced by purely physical factors such as heat, cold, or light (675).

Phytobezoar. A compact ball of vegetable matter in the stomach.

Pia mater. The innermost of the three membranes that cover the brain and spinal cord (253).

Pica. A craving to eat strange foods or unnatural substances—wood, clay, coal, dirt, chalk, starch, etc. Clay-eating is not uncommon in some parts of the country; it may lead to anemia and other ailments. Pica is particularly dangerous in children who swallow lead-containing flakes of paint or plaster, leading to LEAD POISONING.

Pigeon-breeder's lung. A recently recognized respiratory disease occurring in pigeon breeders or others in close contact with pigeons. Chills, fever, cough and shortness of breath develop a few hours after inhaling dusts in an environment of pigeons. The disease is not a bacterial or viral infection, but appears to be a hypersensitivity reaction to ANTIGENS in pigeon feathers and droppings, an allergic lung disease similar to FARMER'S LUNG.

Pigeon toe. Inward turning of the feet and toes when walking. Children in the early stages of walking are often pigeon-toed but usually outgrow the condition (621).

Piles. See HEMORRHOIDS.

"Pill rolling." Involuntary movement of thumb and fingers, as if a pill were being rolled, characteristic of Parkinson's disease (241).

Pilonidal cyst. A congenital hair-containing sac under the skin overlying the tailbone (*coccyx*, 595) at the top of the buttock crease. There may be only a dimpling of the skin or a hairy overlying tuft to mark the presence of the cyst until it becomes infected, swollen and painful, and perhaps develops a FISTULA through which fluids are excreted. Surgical removal of the cyst is usually necessary for a permanent cure.

Pimple. The ordinary term for what doctors call a *papule* or *pustule*.

Pineal gland. A cone-shaped structure about a quarter of an inch long which lies very nearly in the center of the brain. For centuries physiologists were unable to ascribe any function to it. Now there is evidence that the pineal is a sort of "biological clock" which sends out "ticks" to influence the activities of hormones. Experiments with animals indicate that in some way the pineal regulates the sex glands. Whether visible light, acting upon the pineal, is in some way translated into hormonal triggers of the human menstrual cycle is a speculation that challenges investigators.

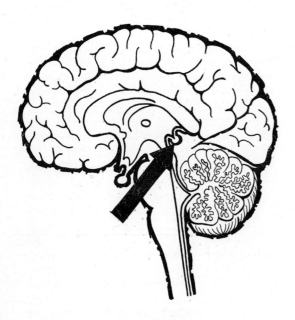

Pineal gland.

"Pink eye." Acute *conjunctivitis*, a highly contagious infection of the eye (544). Discharges contain the infectious organisms.

Pinna. The external ear; the obvious, protruding part of the hearing mechanism.

Pinta. An infectious disease, most frequent in tropical America, characterized by white, blue, brown or red spots on the skin, produced by a *spirochete* very similar to the organism of syphilis (50).

Pinworm infection. Oxyuriasis (69).

Pityriasis rosea. A non-infectious, non-contagious skin disease of young adults, characterized by scaly spots which disappear in two or three months (182).

Placebo. An inert substance such as a sugar pill, without drug effect, given to please the patient. Oddly, seeming therapeutic benefits from placebos are not uncommon. This phenomenon, called the "placebo effect," has to be taken account of in treatment and experiment.

Placenta. The organ on the wall of the uterus through which the fetus receives nourishment and eliminates wastes (341). Structures of the implanted embryo grow into the uterine wall and the placenta develops until it occupies about half the area of the uterus at the fourth month of pregnancy. The fetus and placenta are connected by the UMBILICAL CORD. The placenta has a definite life span and is a senile organ by the time labor pains begin. It is expelled as the AFTERBIRTH shortly after the baby is born. The placenta gets its name from a Latin word for "a flat cake." It somewhat resembles a cake about an inch thick and six or seven inches in diameter. Complications of pregnancy may be caused by a mislocated placenta (*placenta previa*, 355) or by premature detachment.

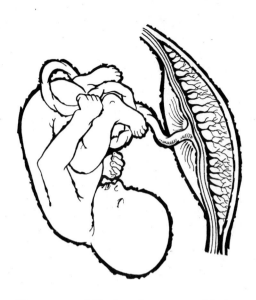

Placenta; umbilical cord connects with fetus.

Plague. An acute feverish disease caused by bacilli (*Pasteurella pestis*). It is primarily a disease of rats and other rodents, which tend to be inhabited by fleas, which can transmit the plague organisms to man (46). *Bubonic plague* is characterized by swellings (*buboes*) which may break down into bleeding ulcers. *Pneumonic plague* affects the lungs and has a high fatality rate. The black plague, or black death, which decimated Europe in the fourteenth century, was a form of bubonic plague with a high incidence of hemorrhage.

Plantar. Pertaining to the soles of the feet. The most frequent affliction of this area is *plantar warts* which usually form at points of pressure on the ball of the foot (182).

Plaque. Tiny patches or unnatural formations on tissues such as on tooth surfaces and on inner arterial walls. *Atheroma,* plaques that are found in walls of arteries, contain some LIPIDS and some connective or scar tissue. They contribute to stiffening of blood vessel walls, closing of arteries, choking of circulation, and ruptured arteries.

Plasma. The fluid part of the blood, minus the blood cells and clotting elements (132).

Plasma cell. A type of white blood cell closely related to *lymphocytes* (165). MULTIPLE MYELOMA and a form of leukemia are associated with plasma cell abnormalities.

Plasmodium. The genus of parasites that cause malaria, transmitted by mosquitoes (70).

Platelets (*thrombocytes*). Tiny, colorless formed elements of the blood, about one-fourth the size of a red blood cell, which help to initiate blood clotting (135). They are formed in the bone marrow. Platelets are quite fragile and short-lived outside of the circulation, and there are various methods of salvaging and transfusing them. *Platelet transfusions* may be necessary in some bleeding disorders such as *purpura* (151). Platelet transfusions may be of fresh whole blood, or of recently stored blood collected in specially treated glass containers or plastic bags. Since it is the platelets themselves rather than whole blood which the patient usually requires, a recently developed procedure promises to be less wasteful of hospital blood bank supplies. Platelets for transfusion are separated from blood given by a donor, and the donor's blood, minus the platelets, is returned to his circulation after a short wait in the collection room.

Pleura. The thin, glistening membrane attached to the outer surface of the lungs and the inner surface of the chest wall (198). The opposed fluid-lubricated surfaces glide over each other as the lung contracts and expands, so that breathing is a painless function.

Pleurisy. Inflammation of the pleura, heralded by knifelike pains aggravated by a deep breath or coughing. There are "wet" and "dry" forms of pleurisy (221).

Pleurodynia. Excruciatingly sharp pain in the muscles between the ribs. It is characteristic of DEVIL'S GRIP, an acute virus-caused epidemic disease, also called *epidemic pleudorynia* and *Bornholm disease.*

Plumbism. LEAD POISONING.

Pneumoconiosis. Chronic inflammation of the lungs due to long-continued inhalation of various kinds of mineral dusts (225).

Pneumoencephalogram. An x-ray film of the brain made after replacing the CEREBROSPINAL FLUID of the brain cavities with air or gas.

Pneumonectomy. Removal of an entire lung (712).

Pneumonia. Inflammation of the lungs caused by various organisms (35). In the past it was customary to classify pneumonias according to the part of the lung affected—*lobar pneumonia* if a lobe or lobes were involved (199), *bronchopneumonia* if infection was localized to air sacs connecting with bronchi. Now the trend is to classify pneumonia according to the organism that causes it. The terms *viral pneumonia* and *primary atypical pneumonia* came into vogue after World War II to describe pneumonias not caused by recognized bacteria. Viruses may be implicated, but it is now known that most cases of atypical pneumonia are caused by *mycoplasma*. These are strange organisms, like bacteria with their skins off. They lack the stiff outer covering that holds conventional bacteria in shape and are enveloped only in a flexible membrane. During the progress of research the organisms have been called *Eaton's agent* and *pleuropneumonia-like organisms* (PPLO), the latter because they resemble organisms which cause a respiratory disease of cattle called pleuropneumonia. They have recently been given a category of their own, the genus *mycoplasma*. Respiratory infection caused by these germs comes on gradually, producing fever, chills and cough. The patient does not appear to be very ill, and often does not consult a doctor, although he may stay home from work for a few days with a "bad cold." The organisms are sensitive to tetracycline, an antibiotic. Another form of pneumonia, of which the cause may not be immediately suspected, is parrot fever (*ornithosis, psittacosis*), an infection transmitted by parrots and other birds. Other unusual pneumonias may result from foreign material that gets into the lungs; see ASPIRATION PNEUMONIA.

Pneumothorax. Collapse of a lung due to air in the pleural cavity (223).

Podagra. Gout.

Podalic version. The maneuver of turning the fetus in the uterus to bring the feet through the birth canal for feet-first delivery.

Polyphagia. Voracious eating.

Poisonous plants. Any plant that is not a familiar food plant is poisonous if parts of it are eaten. That is the safest rule to follow, even though parts of some strange or common plants may be harmless. Children are particularly attracted by berries which look good to eat but may be highly poisonous. They should be taught never to chew or eat unknown berries, leaves, roots or barks. Many highly toxic plants are cultivated in gardens; others grow wild.

A partial list of toxic plants includes many cultivated for their beauty: foxglove leaves and seeds, poinsettia leaves, oleander leaves and branches, iris roots, larkspur and delphinium, lily of the valley, monkshood, yew, daphne, Christmas rose, bittersweet. Bulbs of hyacinth, narcissus and daffodil are toxic; as purchased, plant bulbs may be treated with toxic chemicals. Bloodroot, castor beans, Jimson weed, rhubarb leaves (the stalks are edible), Wisteria seeds, any part of laurels, rhododendrons and azaleas can produce serious poisoning. Play safe by never putting any part of a growing plant into the mouth. Immediate treatment of plant poisoning is emptying of the stomach by inducing vomiting, unless the victim is unconscious or convulsing, and calling a doctor who will know the specific antidote if the plant can be identified.

Pollen counts. Measurements of the number of pollen particles in the air at a given time, made by counting the number of particles adhering to a glass slide covered with sticky material.

Pollinosis. A state of allergic reaction to inhaled plant pollens; for example, hay fever, bronchial asthma (649).

Polyarteritis. A rare disease characterized by inflammation and nodular swellings of artery walls, sometimes leading to local death of tissues. Also called *periarteritis nodosa* and *polyarteritis nodosa*. The cause is not known. Frequently there is an allergic background.

Polycystic kidney. A kidney filled with multiple bubble-like cysts; a congenital condition (278).

Polycythemia. Too many red cells in the blood (145).

Polydactyly. More than the normal number of five fingers or toes.

Polydipsia. Enormous thirst, characteristic of *diabetes insipidus* (304).

Polyps. Smooth outgrowths or tumors of mucous membranes which line body cavities. Usually the polyp hangs from a stem or stalk. Polyps occur most commonly in mucous tissues of the nose (585), uterus (413), and colon (468). They rarely cause symptoms, but nasal polyps may be associated with allergies, and some polyps, as of the colon, may be precancerous and are best removed when discovered. Surgical removal is relatively simple.

Rectal polyp indicated by arrow; in circle, surgical removal.

Polyunsaturated fats. Much interest has been aroused by well-publicized knowledge that high levels of CHOLESTEROL in the blood may be reduced by increasing the proportion of polyunsaturated fats in the diet. The hope is that reduction of blood cholesterol may slow the process of *atherosclerosis* (82) which leads to heart attacks. It is not possible to speak with complete assurance about prevention of an extremely complex and incompletely understood process, but most authorities agree that it is unwise to flood the body with large amounts of saturated fats (85). "Saturated" is a technical word referring to bonds between carbon atoms of fatty acids which combine with glycerol to form fats and oils. These bonds in *saturated fats* contain all the hydrogen atoms they can hold. *Unsaturated* and *polyunsaturated* fatty acids have additional bonds between carbon atoms and can take on additional hydrogen atoms; thus they are more chemically active. Most of the animal fats and some of the vegetable oils (for example, coconut oil) are formed from fatty acids which are highly saturated. Fish oils, corn oil, safflower oil, cottonseed oil, and some other vegetable oils are highly unsaturated. The polyunsaturated fatty acid of principal nutritional importance is *linoleic acid*. Most of the fat stored in the adult human body is relatively unsaturated. The average human body contains about two pounds of linoleic acid in its fat storehouse.

Polyuria. Excessive output of urine.

Popliteal. Pertaining to the hind part of the knee joint.

Portuguese man-of-war. Creatures that people call "jellyfish" sometimes depopulate beaches in a hurry. The most formidable, not exactly a jellyfish, is the Portuguese man-of-war, a creature—actually composed of many separate organisms—which floats on the surface like an overturned toy boat and drapes scores of tentacles into the depths. The tentacles, as long as 50 feet, contain venom-injecting surfaces for killing prey. The "stingers" feel like a hot iron to the bather who comes in contact with them. There is immediate pain, burning, feeling of tightness in the chest, and nausea after a minute or so. The muscles cramp and it feels that every muscle of the body is contracted. The stung areas should be flushed with water while medical help is on the way. The skin may be rubbed with a cloth, or better yet, lathered and shaved with a safety razor to remove venomous particles. Antihistamine drugs seem to give the most rapid relief of pain, cramping and spasm. Persons with weak hearts may be dangerously affected by the toxin and should have prompt medical care.

Postpartum. After childbirth.

Postprandial. After a meal. *Postcibal* has the same meaning.

Postural drainage. Use of gravity to assist in draining secretions from the lungs and chest. The patient lies face down over the edge of a bed or table, his head, shoulders and chest hanging down lower than the waist. In this position, gravity helps to drain secretions. Hawking, coughing, and thumping the back encourage drainage.

Postural drainage.

PPLO. Pleuropneumonia-like organisms. See PNEUMONIA.

Precordial. Pertaining to the area of the chest overlying the heart, approximately under the tip of the breastbone. Precordial pain may or may not come from the heart; there are many structures in this area.

Precursor. Forerunner; something that precedes. In biology, a compound that can be used by the body to form another compound. For example, the body converts *carotene* into Vitamin A.

Prematurity. Birth weight of 5½ lbs. is customarily and rather arbitrarily taken as the borderline between a premature and a mature baby.

Premenstrual tension. Cyclic occurrence of emotional symptoms associated with body changes about a week before onset of a menstrual period. Most women are aware of some change in disposition during the premenstrual week and learn to live with it, but some have sufficient distress to seek medical attention. Nervous symptoms such as irascibility, tension, fatigue, moodiness, weepiness, severe enough to upset domestic tranquillity, are not "all in the mind" but reflect subtle changes. Physical symptoms such as abdominal bloating, weight gain, puffing of the hands and swelling and tenderness of the breasts, indicate that the fundamental disturbance which provokes emotional irritability is cyclic EDEMA—transitory retention of fluids, which exert pressure on internal organs and have far-flung effects. The tension state ends quite abruptly at the onset of menstruation. A physician may prescribe diuretic medicines, sedatives, stimulants, or other measures according to individual need. Explanation that premenstrual tension is not abnormal is reassuring.

Prenatal. Before birth.

Prepuce. A fold of skin covering the glans (head) of the PENIS or CLITORIS; the foreskin; the part that is removed in circumcision.

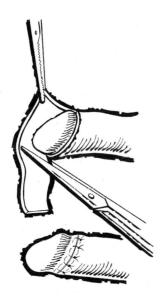

Circumcision.

Presbycusis. Normal diminution of acuteness of hearing that comes with increasing age (564). Mainly, sensitivity to the highest sound frequencies is reduced while sensitivity to lower frequencies—those most important in conversation and daily affairs—remains good.

Presbyopia. "Old sight"; not always so very old—it begins to come on in middle life when the crystalline lens of the eye loses some of its elasticity and power of ACCOMMODATION. Near objects have to be held farther away to see them distinctly. In a culture that puts a premium on reading, close vision, and paperwork, corrective glasses are a kindness and an aid to efficiency.

Priapism. Abnormal, painful, sustained erection of the PENIS, unrelated to sexual stimuli. It may result from obstruction of vessels that drain the organ, from injury to nerve centers, or from triggering stimuli such as bladder stones or PROSTATITIS.

Prickly heat. See MILIARIA.

Primary irritants. Caustic, acid, corrosive, or otherwise irritating substances which are harmful to anyone's skin on first exposure in sufficient concentration; no allergic reaction is involved (655).

Proctitis. Inflammation of membranes of the rectum (468).

Proctologist. A medical specialist in diseases of the anus and rectum.

Proctoscope. A tubular instrument with a light source which permits the inner lining of the bowel to be viewed directly (442).

Prodromal. Premonitory; early warning signs of an oncoming condition before overt symptoms appear.

Progeria. Premature aging; a child so afflicted looks like a very old little man.

Prognosis. A doctor's forecast of the course and duration of an illness based on the best information available to him.

Projectile vomiting. Ejection of stomach contents so forcefully as to hurl material a foot or two from the body (376).

Prolactin. A hormone of the pituitary gland which stimulates milk production (305, 308).

Prolapse. A falling downward of a part from its normal position; for example, *prolapsed uterus* (415).

Prophylaxis. Prevention of the spread or development of disease. A specific form of prophylaxis is the mechanical removal of tartar and debris from the teeth by a dentist.

Prostatectomy. Removal of all or part of the *prostate gland* by one of several surgical techniques (295, 719).

Prostatitis. Inflammation of the *prostate gland* (294).

Prosthesis. An artificial substitute for a missing part of the body; for example, artificial eye, limb, or denture.

Prosthodontics. The branch of dentistry that pertains to the replacement of missing teeth and oral structures by artificial devices.

Proteins. Large complex molecules built up of long chains of simpler AMINO ACIDS. Skin, hair, nails, most of us that is visible to the public, is largely protein. It is the characteristic stuff of life (the word means "of first importance"). Enzymes which trigger multitudes of living chemical processes of the body are proteins. About one half of the dry weight of the body is protein. Protein constituents of foods are broken down into their constituent amino acids by digestion, assimilated, and the separated parts are reassembled by body cells into specific and unique personal proteins (see GENES, HEREDITY). Incessant bodily synthesis of proteins is essential not only for growth and repair of tissues but for the continuance of the multitudes of chemical processes we live by. Protein elements of foods can be burned for energy if necessary, but carbohydrates and fats are superior energy providers and spare protein.

Prothrombin. A plasma PROTEIN, one of many elements necessary in the complicated step-by-step processes of blood coagulation. Tests of "prothrombin time" are used in patients having a tendency to hemorrhage and as a guide to treatment of patients receiving anticoagulant drugs (769).

Protoplasm. Living matter; the viscid, translucent material which is the essential stuff of living cells, never found in the inanimate world. The word was meaningful years ago when the best that scientists could do was to analyze the cell constituents—carbohydrates, proteins, fats, salts, water, etc.—of what they considered to be a homogeneous mixture. Today, many of the structures and activities of specific elements of protoplasm are known—mechanisms of heredity, protein synthesis, energy transformations, chemical directives of life—and the word is outliving its usefulness except as a very general term for living matter.

Protruding ears. Plastic surgery to correct protruding, flattened, or deformed ears is usually performed on children but is just as suitable for adults. The operation (*otoplasty*) is performed by means of incisions behind the ears. The procedure takes from an hour to an hour and a half. The patient may be discharged from the hospital as soon as 24 hours after surgery. A bandage is worn over the ears for about one week after surgery, and the ear is further protected during sleeping for another two weeks.

Protozoa. Single-celled organisms of the animal kingdom. Most protozoa do not cause disease, but those that do are responsible for malaria, amebic dysentery, and a number of other serious diseases (69).

Proud flesh. An excess of GRANULATION TISSUE.

Prurigo. A chronic skin ailment characterized by small, deep-seated, solid pimples that itch intensely.

Pruritus. Severe itching.

Psilocybin. See HALLUCINOGENIC DRUGS.

Psittacosis (*ornithosis, parrot fever*). A pneumonia-like disease transmitted by infected birds (56). The disease not only affects birds of the parrot family, but pigeons, chickens, ducks, turkeys and other birds.

Psoriasis. A chronic disease of the skin, of unknown cause, usually persisting for years with periods of remission and recurrence (180). It is characterized by elevated lesions in various parts of the body—elbows, knees, scalp, nails, lower back—covered with dry silvery scales that drop off. General health is rarely affected, although *psoriatic arthritis,* a destructive form of arthritis in the fingers and toes, may develop in some patients.

Psychedelic. The word means "mind manifesting," from Greek words for "mind" and "clear." See HALLUCINOGENIC DRUGS.

Psychoanalysis. A system of mental therapy created by Sigmund Freud, originally as a research method to gain insight into mental processes. Essentially, the patient bares his soul to the psychoanalyst by speaking of whatever comes to mind, during a long series of half-hour to hour-long sessions which usually total several hundred hours for a complete analysis. Unconscious conflicts expressed through dreams, slips of the tongue, symbolism, etc., are interpreted by the psychoanalyst with the object of giving the patient insight into his conflicts and thus lessening their trauma. The therapeutic value of psychoanalysis is somewhat controversial (689).

Psychomotor seizure. A relatively mild form of epileptic attack which the patient never remembers (262). The person does not fall but may stagger, make restless movements and strange sounds, lose contact with his environment for a minute or two.

Psychoneurosis. Relatively mild, emotionally based disturbance of the personality, often severe enough to be handicapping, generally a defensive reaction to psychic threats and conflicts (684).

Psychosomatic disease. Disability, sometimes but not always without accompanying physical causes, in which disturbing emotions of the patient play an important part in inciting, worsening, or continuing the disability (684).

Psychosis. Serious mental illness, disabling, usually requiring treatment in a hospital for a period of time. Some psychoses have organic causes and others primarily psychological causes or possibly metabolic disturbances too subtle to be identifiable (685).

Psychosurgery. Operations on parts of the brain to improve a patient's mental state (690). *Prefrontal lobotomy,* an operation in which the frontal lobes of the brain are cut into, at one time had many advocates. Unmanageable, assaultive, manic patients subjected to this procedure usually became tractable and even amiable, but too often there was gross deterioration of personality to a vegetative level. Psychosurgery is less resorted to since the advent of tranquillizing drugs.

Psychotherapy. Treatment of emotional and mental disorders by psychological methods as opposed to physical methods (687).

Pterygium. A triangular growth of the conjunctiva in the corner of the eye nearest the nose, due to a degenerative process caused by long-continued irritation, as from exposure to wind and dust.

Ptomaines. Putrid substances produced by decay of dead animal matter. Food poisoning is not caused by ptomaines, which are too repulsive for anyone to ingest. Food poisoning is commonly caused by salmonella or staphylococcus organisms.

Ptyalin. An enzyme in saliva which initiates the digestion of starch (444). It is what gives a sweetish taste to a piece of cracker held in the mouth for a while. *Ptyalism* is a condition of profuse drooling of saliva; salivation.

Puberty. The age at which the reproductive organs become functionally active. It occurs when a person is between 12 and 17 years old and is indicated in the girl by the beginning of menstruation and in the boy by seminal discharge and change of voice.

Pudenda. The external sex organs.

Puerperium. The time between childbirth and return of the uterus to its pre-pregnancy size and state, about six weeks (365).

Purpura. A disorder of blood coagulation; tiny blood vessels bleed into the skin and mucous membranes and cause purplish patches or pinpoint hemorrhages (151).

Purulent. Containing, exuding, or producing pus.

Pustule. A small elevation of the skin containing pus.

Pyelogram. An x-ray film of the pelvis of the kidney and the ureter, visualizing the entire urinary tract.

Pyelonephritis. Infection of the kidney and its urine-collecting pelvis (280).

Pyemia. Pus in the blood.

Pyloric stenosis. Congenital obstruction of the outlet of the stomach due to abnormal thickening of the pyloric muscle that encircles it. The condition is completely relieved by an operation which cuts some of the muscle fibers (396, 452).

Pylorospasm. Spasm of the circular muscle at the outlet of the stomach, manifested by PROJECTILE VOMITING of an infant shortly after birth (396). Usually the condition can be corrected by medication which relaxes the spastic muscle and permits normal passage of food.

Pyogenic. Pus-producing.

Pyorrhea. Flow of pus; a common term for *periodontoclasia,* inflammation and gradual destruction of supporting tissues of the teeth. Pockets form and enlarge between the gum surface and tooth, bacteria and debris fill the pockets, pus forms, bone is resorbed, eventually the tooth becomes loose in its socket and is lost from lack of support. The condition can be arrested but lost tissue cannot be restored (508).

Pyrexia. Fever.

Pyridoxine. One of the B vitamins, commonly designated as Vitamin B_6.

Pyrosis. Heartburn.

Pyuria. Pus in the urine (280).

Q

Q fever. A self-limited RICKETTSIAL DISEASE resembling pneumonia, often mild and unrecognized (64).

Q.i.d. Four times a day.

Quadriceps. The large muscle which extends the thigh.

Quadriplegia. Paralysis of both arms and both legs.

Quartan. Occurring every fourth day, as, the fever of *quartan malaria.*

Quartipara. A woman who has borne four children. A *quadripara* is bearing or has borne her fourth child.

Queasiness. Nausea.

Quick. A tender, vital part, as the bed of a fingernail.

Quickening. The time around the middle of pregnancy when bumps, kicks and flutters within the uterus give unmistakable proof that lively life is present (354). Father may be invited to "meet" the baby via its abdominally communicated contortions.

Quincke's edema. ANGIONEUROTIC EDEMA (667).

Quinsy. An abscess in and around a tonsil, causing a very sore throat (38).

Quotidian. Recurring every day.

R

Rabbit fever (*tularemia*). An infection acquired from handling diseased rabbits or from the bites of ticks (46).

Rabbit test. A biologic test for pregnancy (342).

Rabies (*hydrophobia*). A lethal disease caused by viruses which have an affinity for brain and nervous tissue (57). The virus is transmitted to man by the bite of an infected (rabid) animal. Mere contact of saliva of an infected animal with abraded or scratched skin can transmit the disease. "Mad dogs" are not the only sources of rabies. A considerable reservoir exists in wildlife of the U.S. Bats, foxes, squirrels, raccoons, skunks and other rabid animals can transmit the disease directly by biting people or indirectly by infecting domestic animals which in turn can transmit the disease by their bites or saliva. This chain of transmission is broken if the family dog is properly immunized against rabies. The disease is invariably fatal but has an incubation period of a month to a year or more. The incubation period is shortest if bites are inflicted on the head, face, neck or arms, and are severe and numerous. Prompt "Pasteur treatment"—daily injection of rabies vaccine for two weeks—usually prevents rabies from taking hold. The treatments are painful and the type of vaccine cultivated in animal nerve tissue sometimes has bad side effects. A newer type of duck-embryo rabies vaccine greatly reduces the serious problem of nervous system reactions. Immediate preventive injections may not be necessary if the biting animal can be caught and kept under observation. If killed, the animal's body and particularly the head should be kept for laboratory studies which can determine whether or not the animal was rabid by the presence or absence of NEGRI BODIES in the brain tissue. If injections have been started, and the animal proves not to be rabid, they can be discontinued. The problem of what to do about the bite of a possibly rabid animal should be turned over immediately to the family physician and local health department.

Rachitic rosary. A beadlike row of nodules on the ribs of children with rickets, strung along the junctions of ribs and cartilage.

Radiation sickness. Illness resulting from intense or less intense but accumulative exposure to sources of radiation. Exposure to massive doses of radiation, as in the neighborhood of a nuclear explosion, is very rare, which is fortunate because an overwhelming dose of radiation is extremely serious if not fatal. Necessary therapeutic use of x-rays may sometimes be followed by mild radiation sickness—lassitude, nausea, vomiting—which usually disappears rather quickly and can be coped with effectively by the physician or radiologist. There is virtually no threat of radiation sickness from the use of diagnostic x-rays by an experienced physician or radiologist (759).

Radiculitis. Inflammation of a spinal nerve root.

Radiograph. An x-ray photo.

Radioisotopes. See NUCLEAR MEDICINE.

Radiologist. A physician who specializes in the making and interpretation of x-ray studies and in therapeutic and diagnostic application of radiation (749).

Radiopaque. Not transparent to x-rays. Radiopaque substances (for example, BARIUM MEAL) are introduced into parts of the body to give clear delineation of structures which otherwise would not show up distinctly on an x-ray film or fluoroscopic screen.

Radiosensitivity. The capacity of tissues to react with different degrees of intensity to radiation. Radiosensitive tumors and cells are more susceptible to destruction by radiation than less sensitive ones.

Radiotherapy. Treatment of disease by x-rays, radium, radioisotopes, and other forms of ionizing radiation (756).

Radon. A colorless radioactive gas given off by the decay of radium. *Radon seeds* are tiny radon-containing tubes of gold or glass for implantation into tumors (756). The gas decays at a steady rate and after a week or so loses all of its radioactive power, so no harm is done if radon seeds are lost in tissues.

Rales. Abnormal sounds from the lungs or air passageways, heard over the chest. The sounds, described as coarse, medium, fine, wet, dry, etc., are not specific for specific diseases but help the trained ear to judge the condition of the patient.

Ratbite fever. Two varieties of infectious disease transmitted by the bites of rats (50). A type caused by bacteria (*Haverhill fever*) is sudden in onset, marked by a skin rash of arms and legs, headache, fever and joint pains. The other type, caused by spirochetes, is characterized by a relapsing type of fever, dusky skin rash, a hard ulcer and enlarged lymph nodes at the site of the bite. A bite by a rat or any other rodent should have prompt treatment by a physician.

Raynaud's disease. Intermittent blanching and reddening of the skin, especially of the fingers and toes, brought on by exposure to cold. Blood vessels first constrict, causing pallor and numbness, then expand and the affected area tingles and becomes very red or reddish-purple as large amounts of blood return. An attack may last for minutes or hours. The condition may be secondary to other diseases, but more often the peculiar blood vessel spasms occur without apparent cause; 90 per cent of patients are women. There is some evidence that affected persons may be unusually susceptible to collagen diseases such as SCLERODERMA in later life, but in itself Raynaud's disease is more of a nuisance than a serious condition. Patients are usually instructed to protect themselves well against cold, as by wearing lined gloves and overshoes, because a certain amount of exposure to cold is necessary to trigger attacks. Smoking, which tends to constrict superficial vessels, is forbidden. In its most extreme and rare form, Raynaud's disease may eventually lead to dry GANGRENE of fingers or toes. Surgical severing of nerve branches which serve blood vessels of affected areas may be resorted to in patients with severe symptoms.

Rectalgia. Pain in the rectum.

Rectocele. A bulging of the rectum through the rear wall of the vagina (416, 708).

Rectum. The terminal part of the bowel, about six inches long, ending in the narrow muscular anal canal and anus (437).

Red palms (palmar erythema). The palms often become deeply pink or reddish, like a sustained blush, during pregnancy. The reddening, caused by a high level of circulating hormones, fades after delivery and needs no treatment. A similar phenomenon occurs in some patients with cirrhosis of the liver.

Referred pain. Pain that doesn't originate where it hurts. For instance, pain due to an acting-up gallbladder may be felt in the back under the shoulder blade.

Reflex. An action in response to a stimulus, occurring without conscious effort or thinking about it (234) ; for example, dilation or contraction of the pupil in response to different intensities of light. Some 300 different reflexes have been catalogued. They are useful in helping to diagnose or locate the sites of certain disorders of the nervous system.

Refraction. Bending of light waves from a straight line in passing through lenses or transparent structures of different densities. In ophthalmology, the measurement and correction by lenses of defects of the eye (*near-sightedness, far-sightedness, astigmatism*) which prevent light waves from being brought to sharp focus exactly on the retina (537).

Regional ileitis (*regional enteritis*). Inflammatory disease of the lower portion of the small bowel (462). The disease may be principally inflammatory, obstructive, or diffuse, with varied symptoms. Total recovery may be made after a single attack and there may be no symptoms for many years although abnormalities of the small bowel still exist. Medical treatment usually is effective but complications may require surgery.

Regurgitation. Effortless casting up of food from the stomach soon after eating; "spitting up" of food. Babies are adept at it (376). Not to be mistaken for vomiting. The word also means backflow of blood through a leaky heart valve (101).

Reiter's syndrome. A form of arthritis with inflammation of the mucous membrane of the eyes and of the urethra. It resembles rheumatoid arthritis but is less crippling and is self-limited.

Relapsing fever. Episodes of fever which subside spontaneously, then recur. Specifically, an acute infectious disease spread by lice and ticks (50).

Remedial reading. See DYSLEXIA.

Renal. Pertaining to the kidneys.

Renal insufficiency. Incapacity of the kidneys to filter toxins adequately from the blood (280).

Renin. A kidney protein capable of raising blood pressure by activating *angiotensin,* a powerful pressure-elevating agent (110).

Resect. To cut out a part of an organ or tissue.

Residual urine. Significant amount of urine left in the bladder after urination. The symptom in the male may be associated with prostate trouble; in the female, with CYSTOCELE or pressure of tumors of the uterus.

Respiratory distress syndrome. See HYALINE MEMBRANE DISEASE.

Respirator. An "iron lung"; a mechanical breathing device for patients whose breathing muscles are paralyzed.

Resuscitation. Artificial respiration applied to a person threatened with death by asphyxia (773).

Reticulo-endothelial system. Pervasive mechanisms woven like a meshwork through the body, which defend against foreign invaders and carry oxygen and carbon dioxide to and from every cranny of the body (131).

Retina. The tissue-thin light-receiving structure at the back of the eye, composed of several specialized layers (531). Hundreds of thousands of nerve endings in the retina merge into the optic nerve which conveys impulses to the seeing part of the brain at the back of the head.

Retinal detachment. See DETACHED RETINA.

Retinitis pigmentosa. Hereditary degeneration and atrophy of the retina.

Retinoblastoma. A malignant tumor of the retina; a congenital form of cancer occurring in infants and young children. An early sign is a white pupil; this sign in an infant or young child has serious import and immediate medical diagnosis is imperative. Retinoblastoma is life-threatening, but improved methods of treatment, given as soon as the tumor is discovered, usually save life though sometimes at the cost of partial or total blindness. If only one eye is affected, it is usually removed. If both eyes are involved the more seriously affected one is usually removed and the other is treated in hope of destroying the tumor and preserving as much vision as possible. X-rays, radioactive applicators, photocoagulation and other measures may be used in an effort to save the eye. The disease is thought to be inherited as a dominant trait; see HEREDITY.

Retinopathy. Any abnormal condition of the retina.

Retractors. Instruments of varied design, to hold or pull back the edges of an incision or wound.

Retrobulbar. Behind the eyeball.

Retroflexion. Condition of being bent backward.

Retrolental fibroplasia. An ocular disease in which a mass of fibrous tissue forms in back of the lens of the eye, blocking vision; associated with premature birth and excessive oxygen in incubators (556).

Retroversion. A backward-tilted position of an organ, as a retroverted uterus (415).

"Rh disease." See ERYTHROBLASTOSIS.

Rheumatism. A general term for distressing, painful, disabling conditions affecting the joints and their surrounding structures (627).

Rheumatoid factor. An abnormal PROTEIN in the blood of about 70 per cent of patients with classic *rheumatoid arthritis* (634, 642). The rheumatoid factor acts like an ANTIBODY against one of the patient's own normal body proteins, with resulting inflammation and damage to tissue. This is much like an acquired allergy to a part of one's self. Mechanisms which produce the rheumatoid factor have not been proved to be a cause of rheumatoid arthritis, but better knowledge about the factor may throw light on the fundamental nature of the disease. Tests for the factor are commonly given in diagnosing a suspected case of rheumatoid arthritis.

Rhinal. Pertaining to the nose.

Rhinitis. Inflammation of mucous membranes of the nose. It may arise from something as common as the common cold or from infections or allergies (663).

Rhinophyma. Gross overgrowth of blood vessels, sebaceous glands, connective tissue, and skin of the nose, giving the enlarged organ a knobby, reddish, conspicuously bulbous appearance (587). The condition is sometimes associated with over-spirited indulgence in spirits. Correction is surgical.

Rhinoplasty. Plastic surgery of the nose, for cosmetic purposes or correction of deformities (587).

Rhinorrhea. Runny nose.

Rhinoviruses. A family of 30 or more viruses which are major causes of the common cold.

Rhodopsin. A purple pigment in rods of the retina. It is bleached on exposure to light and requires Vitamin A for regeneration.

Rhythm method (*calendar method*). A method of avoiding conception which relies on abstinence from sexual intercourse during the fertile phase of the menstrual cycle (331). OVULATION occurs around the mid-point of the menstrual cycle (327); the "fertile period" of about one week is assumed to span this midpoint, during which abstinence is practiced. If the menstrual cycle is regularly 28 days in length, the fertile period can be counted as beginning 11 days after onset of menstruation and continuing through the 18th day (or for extra assurance, beginning on day 10 and continuing through day 20). Menstrual cycles are rarely of exactly the same duration month after month. Calendar records may give a reasonably good average over several months, but if swings are great the accuracy of calculations is lessened. Some subjective signs suggest but do not positively prove that an egg has been released and that conception is possible; see OVULATION. In general, for couples who adopt the rhythm method, the "safest" safe period when conception is unlikely is the few days just before and just after menstruation.

Rice diet. A diet furnishing about 10 ounces of boiled rice a day, with fruit juices and sugar, introduced in 1949 as an adjunct in treatment of patients with severe high blood pressure. Benefits of the diet have been attributed largely to its very low sodium (salt) content. Many physicians feel that low-sodium diets which offer a greater variety of foods (32), and restrict calories if weight loss is desirable, are just as effective and better tolerated than a monotonous rice diet. Since the introduction of anti-hypertensive and diuretic drugs, it is usually no longer necessary to restrict salt intake extremely (114).

Rickets. A vitamin DEFICIENCY DISEASE of infants, resulting from insufficient dietary vitamin D or insufficient exposure to sunshine which creates vitamin D from substances in the skin (479). Infantile rickets is manifested by distortion, softening, and bending of incompletely mineralized bones, and sometimes by nodules strung like beads over the ribs (*rachitic rosary*). Infantile rickets is rare in the U.S. because of vitamin D fortification of milk and prescription of vitamin supplements by a pediatrician if he deems it necessary. *Renal rickets* is not a deficiency disease but a congenital incapacity of the kidneys to reabsorb phosphate salts necessary for sturdy bone structure.

Rickettsiae. Disease-causing microbes smaller than bacteria but larger than viruses (62). They are transmitted to man via the biting activities of obnoxious fleas, ticks, and lice. Among the diseases they cause are *typhus, Rocky Mountain spotted fever, trench fever, Q fever, and rickettsialpox.*

Rickettsialpox. A mild non-fatal infection characterized by fever, chills, lymph node enlargement, headache, and chickenpox-like rash (64). It is caused by the bites of mites harbored by mice or small rodents.

Ringworm. Not a worm at all, but infection by various fungi of "dead" tissues of the skin, hair, nails and scalp (189). The troubles they cause have a general medical name, DERMATOPHYTOSIS, and a general word, *tinea*, linked with a name for the affected area, as *tinea capitis, tinea barbae, tinea pedis* (the latter better known as "athlete's foot").

R.N. Registered nurse.

Rocky Mountain spotted fever. A feverish, eruptive infection transmitted by ticks, not limited to western parts of the country (64).

Rodent ulcer. A form of skin cancer (*basal cell epithelioma*, 184) which does not spread to other areas of the body but which, if long neglected, tends to penetrate deeply and erode soft tissues and bones. The ulcers usually occur on sun-exposed areas of the face, especially at margins of the eyes, lips, nose, and ear. The edges of the ulcer have a rolled appearance. The lesion usually begins as a single pinhead to pea-sized nodule, waxy or pearly, which slowly enlarges by development of other waxy nodules near it and coalescence with them. In early stages before undermining of skin and bones begins, surgical removal or x-ray treatment is effective and leaves little or no scarring.

Rods. Cylindrical nerve structures in the retina, about 100,000,000 to each eye (532). The rods see only shades of gray but are extremely sensitive to faint light and are responsible for most of what we see in dim surroundings. Rods cover most of the cup-shaped RETINA and discern movements which we don't look at directly but perceive from the "corner of the eye." There are no rods in the small round spot near the center of the retina (*fovea*) where all color vision and fine discriminating seeing takes place. The fovea is composed of different, close-packed nerve structures called CONES.

Roentgen (*r*). A quantitative unit of x-radiation, used in calculating intensity of exposure.

Roentgenogram. An x-ray photo.

Rohrschach test. See INKBLOT TEST.

Rongeur. A type of forceps for cutting bone, shaped somewhat like pliers with sharp cupped edges.

Root canal. A small channel in the root of a tooth, continuous with the pulp chamber above it (498). A tooth dead or dying from injury to its pulp ("nerve") may sometimes be saved by root filling or root resection procedures (514).

Rosacea. See ACNE ROSACEA.

Rose fever. A form of hay fever due to sensitivity to rose pollens.

Roseola. Any rose-colored eruption of the skin. *Roseola infantum* is a viral infection of young children producing a fever which lasts three or four days, after which temperature drops to normal, a skin rash appears, and the child is well (400).

Roughage. Indigestible food residues in the intestinal tract, mostly composed of cellulose. A reasonable amount of bulky material is a mechanical aid to intestinal functioning.

Roundworms. Several varieties of opprobrious worms that invade the human body if given a chance, gaining entrance via their eggs or larvae in contaminated soil or by hand-to-mouth transmission. The giant of the species is *Ascaris lumbricoides* (68); roundworms of lesser size, but just as repugnant, are HOOKWORMS, WHIPWORMS, PINWORMS. Good sanitation, shoe-wearing, handwashing, hygiene, and cooking are preventive measures.

"Royal jelly." A substance from the salivary glands of bees, fed by the worker bees to the queen bee. No important nutrient has been reported to be present in "royal jelly" that cannot be obtained readily from ordinary foods in our regular food supplies.

Rubefacient. Any agent that makes the skin red.

Rubella. See GERMAN MEASLES.

Rubeola. Measles. Preventable by measles vaccine.

Rubin test. A test of female fertility; also called *tubal insufflation*. It determines whether the OVIDUCTS through which egg cells are transported to the uterus are open or obstructed. A gas, usually carbon dioxide, is introduced through the cervix under pressure. An instrument records significant changes in pressure as the gas flows through. If the oviducts are open, bubbles of gas pass into the abdominal cavity and the patient experiences shoulder pain when she sits upright. The procedure takes but a few minutes and there is little discomfort (330).

Rugae. Wrinkles, folds, elevations, ridges of tissue, as of the linings of the stomach and vagina.

Runaround. Inflammation all around a nail; PARONYCHIA.

Rupture. See HERNIA.

Ruptured disk. Protrusion of the pulpy, cushioning pad between vertebrae through a rent in surrounding ligament (603).

S

Sabin vaccine. Oral poliovirus vaccine (OPV) for immunization against polio. It contains weakened live polio viruses which produce an inapparent infection that establishes long-lasting immunity, possibly for a lifetime. The American Academy of Pediatrics recommends the vaccine for routine immunization in infancy, as the most effective procedure for the prevention of polio.

Sac. A pouch or baglike covering of an organ or tissue; for example, the pericardial sac of the heart, the sac of a cyst or hernia or tumor.

Saccular. Sac-shaped.

Sacro-iliac trouble. Backache in the region of the sacro-iliac joints. The large sciatic nerve traverses this area (254) and ligaments and muscles are subject to injury. Many mechanisms can produce low back pain; correction depends upon determination of the cause (602).

Sacrum. A large, triangular, curved bone of the lower back, just above the tailbone, composed of five vertebrae that have fused together (594). The sacrum forms the back wall of the bony pelvis, is close to the surface, and

can be just about covered by a hand placed on the back between the hips a little below the belt line. On either side of the sacrum is the big hipbone, the *ilium,* and their junction constitutes the sometimes winceful *sacro-iliac joint.*

"Safe period." The days during the midpoint of menstrual cycle when conception is not likely to occur. See RHYTHM METHOD.

St. Anthony's fire. Erysipelas (38).

St. Louis encephalitis. A mosquito-transmitted infection producing feverish illness, headache, stiff neck, sleepiness, mental confusion (59).

St. Vitus' dance. See CHOREA.

Salicylism. A toxic condition produced by overdosage with drugs of the aspirin family (salicylates), causing ringing in the ears, rapid breathing, nausea.

Salivary glands. The three saliva-producing glands on each side of the face: the *parotid* gland in front of and below the ear (the one that is affected in mumps); the *sublingual* gland under the tongue; and the nearby *submaxillary* or *submandibular* gland (430).

Salivation. Excessive secretion of saliva. Ordinary MOTION SICKNESS, irritation of the nervous system, poisoning, local inflammations, certain infectious diseases, and disturbances of the stomach or liver can produce it.

Salk vaccine. A killed-virus vaccine for establishing immunity to polio. It is given in spaced injections; booster doses are recommended every two years. Oral polio vaccine (see SABIN VACCINE) is considered by the American Academy of Pediatrics to have clearcut superiority "from the point of view of ease of administration, immunogenic effectiveness, protective capacity, and potential for the eradication of poliomyelitis."

Salmonella. A family of bacteria which cause gastrointestinal infections (43). They are the most common causes of FOOD POISONING. There are some 400 varieties of Salmonella; one type produces typhoid fever. Most cases of Salmonella food poisoning are not definitely identified. The U. S. Public Health Service estimates that there are up to 2,000,000 cases a year and that the incidence is increasing. The most frequent symptom is gastroenteritis, ranging from a few cramps to fulminating diarrhea. A small percentage of recovered patients become carriers of the infection. The organisms are widely distributed in eggs, poultry, and other animal products. Thorough heating (above 165 degrees) destroys the organisms.

Salpingitis. Inflammation of one or both OVIDUCTS (Fallopian tubes). Symptoms are pain in the lower abdomen, tenderness, discharge from the cervix. The word also applies to inflammation of the Eustachian tube which connects the middle ear and the throat.

San Joaquin fever. *Coccidioidiomycosis* (72).

Sarcoidosis. A non-contagious disease of unknown cause, somewhat resembling tuberculosis. Small lumpy tumors arise in almost any tissue, but particularly in the lungs, skin, bones, eyes, lymphatic system, liver, muscle (226). The nodules may persist more or less unchanged for years or they may heal and recur. Symptoms vary with the organs affected. There is no specific treatment.

Sarcoma. A form of cancer arising mainly from connective tissue. *Osteogenic* sarcoma is a bone tumor, usually requiring amputation of the part. *Ewing's* sarcoma of children and young adults affects the shafts of long bones; the prognosis is poor. A somewhat similar tumor, *reticulum cell* sarcoma, is sensitive to x-rays and treatment by irradiation or amputation offers a good chance of survival.

Saturated fat. See POLYUNSATURATED FATS.

Satyriasis. Excessive sexual desire in the male.

Scabies. "The itch"; infestation with female mites that burrow tiny tunnels in the top layer of the skin and lay eggs in them (191).

Scaphoid. A small boat-shaped bone of the wrist (611) or ankle.

Scapula. The shoulder blade (593).

Scheuermann's disease. Wedge-shaped deformation of parts of certain vertebrae; a relatively common cause of backache in adolescents (604).

Schick test. A skin test for immunity to diphtheria, performed by injecting a minute amount of diluted diphtheria toxin into the skin. If the injected area becomes red and swollen within a week, it indicates that the individual is not immune to diphtheria and should have protective shots (398).

Schistosomiasis (*bilharzia*). A parasitic disease of the tropics acquired by wading in fresh water where free-swimming forms of a blood fluke hook onto the skin and migrate to various organs via the bloodstream. Snails in which eggs of the parasite develop into free-swimming larvae are reservoirs of the disease (66).

Schlemm's canal. A small channel at the junction of the white of the eye and the cornea through which fluids drain from the chamber of the eye in front of the lens. Narrowing or blocking of the drainage channel builds up destructive pressures within the eye (*glaucoma*, 549).

Sciatica. Not a disease, but a symptom: pain in the back of the thigh and leg along the course of the sciatic nerve (254). Sciatica may be a form of neuritis (253) or severe forms may result from "disk trouble" (603).

Scirrhous. Hard.

Sclera. The strong, elastic outer coat of the eye, visible in front as the white of the eye (528).

Scleroderma. "Hidebound skin"; a connective tissue disease (634) of unknown cause. The first signs usually appear in skin of the hands and feet, in patchy areas which gradually involve more and more of the body. The skin slowly becomes hard, thickened, stiff, smooth and shiny. The face may become masklike because of loss of flexibility. Internal organs—lungs, heart, digestive tract, kidneys—are progressively affected. There is no specific treatment but measures to deal with manifestations in various organs are valuable.

Sclerosing agents. Substances injected to harden and obliterate vessels, as in varicose veins and hemorrhoids.

Sclerosis. Hardening of tissue, especially by overgrowth of fibrous tissue. The sclerosing process affects many kinds of tissues; for example, nerve tissue (*multiple sclerosis*) and linings of the arteries (*arteriosclerosis*). What iniates and perpetuates the process is not known.

Scoliosis. Sidewise curvature of the spine (604).

Scorbutus. SCURVY.

Scotoma A dark spot, blind, or partially blind area in the field of vision, indicating some change in the optic nerve or retina requiring examination by an ophthalmologist. *Scintillating scotomas,* frequently colored, which have saw-toothed shimmering edges and spread out from a small spot to a large area and disappear in a few minutes, are often migraine-like phenomena.

Scratch test. A skin test for allergic sensitivity, especially to inhaled and contacted substances, done by scratching test materials lightly into the skin without drawing blood (656). If the patient is sensitive to the substance, a positive reaction appears within 15 minutes.

Scrub typhus (*tsutsugamushi fever*). A feverish disease of eastern Asiatic regions, transmitted by mites (64).

Scrofula. Tuberculosis of lymph glands of the neck. The affliction was once common but has almost vanished since the advent of modern methods of treating tuberculosis. A popular treatment used to be the "laying on" of a king's hands, and monarchs honored this regal obligation in ceremonies hopefully attended by the afflicted. One of the last patients to be treated in this manner in England was Dr. Samuel Johnson, the famous subject of Boswell's biography, who as a small child had a laying on of hands by Queen Anne—to no avail. He carried scars of the disease for the rest of his life.

Scrotum. The pouch covering the testicles (300).

Scuba diving. Diving with Self-Contained Underwater Breathing Apparatus. A physical examination once a year is essential to minimize the hazards of this popular sport. Persons with PERFORATED EARDRUM or acute or chronic infections of the respiratory tract should not dive. Increase and decrease in pressure associated with ascent and descent in diving can turn a simple cold into a serious ear, sinus, or lung infection. The teeth should be in good condition; a pressure-caused gas pocket in a tooth can be excruciating. Physical examination should give special attention to the ears, heart, and respiratory system and should include a chest x-ray. Scuba divers should be aware of the hazards of AIR EMBOLISM and CAISSON DISEASE.

Scurvy. A DEFICIENCY DISEASE due to lack of Vitamin C (479), easily preventable and curable by replacement of the vitamin. Advanced scurvy with its classic symptoms of spongy, bleeding gums, loose teeth, and hemorrhages under the skin is rare in this country, but mild scurvy due to monotonous diets, food aversions, or inadequate supplementation of infant foods is still encountered occasionally.

Seasickness. See MOTION SICKNESS.

Seatworms. Pinworms (69).

Sebaceous cyst. A wen; a skin tumor produced by obstruction of the outlet of an oil-secreting gland (196).

Sebaceous glands. "Oil wells" of the skin which secrete *sebum* or skin oil; usually associated with hair follicles (170).

Seborrhea. Overproduction or change in quality of skin oil secreted by sebaceous glands, producing "oily skin," crusts or scales; associated with acne, dandruff, seborrheic dermatitis (178).

Secundines. The placenta, umbilical cord, and membranes expelled from the uterus after a baby is born.

Sedimentation rate. The rate at which red blood cells settle out of a prepared specimen of blood under laboratory conditions; useful in diagnosis of certain diseases.

Self-limited. A disease that comes to an end all by itself in a limited time, such as an uncomplicated cold.

Semen. The viscid, whitish, mucoid secretion containing SPERMATOZOA which is ejaculated by the male during orgasm. It is a mixture of secretions of testicular organs and of the prostate gland which contributes most of it.

Semicircular canals. Three interconnecting, partially fluid-filled canals of the inner ear which lie in planes at right angles to each other (563). Our sense of balance is located here. Fluid in the canals responds to movements and sends information over nerve pathways to the brain.

Semilunar. Halfmoon-shaped, as the *semilunar valve* of the heart (76).

Seminal vesicles. Accessory glands of the male reproductive system, continuous with the prostate gland (293, 298). The two pouchlike vesicles lie behind the bladder and rectum. Each consists of a single tube much coiled upon itself. The vesicles are storage organs for spermatozoa and secrete a fluid which is added to secretions of the testes.

Seminoma. A tumor of the testicle.

Sepsis. Fever, chills, and other reactions of the body to bacteria or their toxins in the bloodstream; the thing that antisepsis is against.

Septal defects. Abnormal openings between chambers of the heart which permit blood to "leak" from one side of the heart to the other (93, 717).

Septicemia. "Blood poisoning"; fever, prostration, reactions to living, growing bacteria in the blood. Septicemia is much less common, and much more controllable when it does occur, since doctors have had antibiotics to combat and prevent it.

Septum. A partition or wall between two compartments or cavities; for instance, the nasal septum which divides the nose.

Sequestrum. A small piece of dead bone which has become detached from its normal position; for example, "joint mice" (617).

Serum. The amber-colored fluid of blood that remains after the blood has coagulated and the clot has shrunk. It contains disease-fighting ANTIBODIES of the host. This is the basis of serums and antitoxins for treatment of disease. Animals, commonly horses, are inoculated with gradually increasing doses of bacteria or toxins until they build up large amounts of corresponding antibodies. The animal's serum is withdrawn, purified, and injected to increase a person's resistance to a particular disease.

Serum sickness. A reaction to drugs (674). The most common symptom is HIVES. Some patients break out with a skin rash; some have fever, pain in the joints, enlarged lymph nodes. Serum sickness is closely related to ANAPHYLAXIS but much milder and symptoms do not appear until several days after contact with the offending drug.

Sessile. Broad-based; said of a tumor that does not have a stem or stalk.

Sex determination. Although sex is almost always self-evident at birth, there are borderline cases where anomalies of development make the true sex difficult to determine (see HERMAPHRODITE). A guide to determination of genetic sex has been found to be the presence or absence in the subject's body cells of minute particles called *chromatin bodies,* which are visible under a microscope. Female cells contain chromatin bodies. Male cells do not, although the chromatin may be undetectable rather than absent. The sex chromatin method has been used to predict the sex of an infant before birth, by study of cells obtained from amniotic fluid which surrounds the fetus.

Sex-linked heredity. Certain traits such as COLOR BLINDNESS and HEMOPHILIA show a form of inheritance called *sex-linkage.* For example, mothers who do not themselves exhibit a trait may transmit it to their sons, who do exhibit it, but not to their daughters. However, the daughters may "carry" the trait, which is in turn manifested in their sons. There are many technical and complex differences in sex-linked transmission lines, but the general principle is fairly simple: sex-linked traits occur because the GENES for expressing them are located in the pair of sex CHROMOSOMES which all normal persons possess. A female has two X chromosomes, one from her mother and one from her father, in her pair (XX). A male has an X chromosome from his mother and a Y chromosome from his father (XY). The Y chromosome is smaller and contains fewer genes. Many genes in the X chromosome have no counterpart in the Y. If there is a defective gene in one X chromosome of a woman, she has another X which is likely to be normal and to suppress the defective gene trait (although she still carries it). But the same defective gene in a man's X chromosome is paired with a Y which has no complementary gene to neutralize the trait, which therefore is fully expressed.

Sheehan's disease. Much the same as SIMMOND'S DISEASE, but resulting from local deficiency of blood supply to the pituitary gland because of severe postpartum hemorrhage (308).

Shigellosis. See BACILLARY DYSENTERY.

Shingles (*herpes zoster*). A virus infection of nerve endings, manifested in the skin by crops of small blisters which follow nerve pathways (55). The chest, face, and upper abdomen are most often affected. Red patches appear and develop into fluid-filled blisters which become dry and scabby in four or five days and eventually heal. The skin should be kept clean and dry and a doctor can prescribe measures to relieve distress. Infection of a facial nerve may reach the eye and threaten to leave scars on the *cornea;* competent care by an eye physician is important. In older people, shingles is sometimes followed by painful, stubborn, long-lasting *neuralgia* that is difficult to treat. Viruses that cause shingles and chickenpox are thought to be identical. Some adults exposed to chickenpox have "come down" with a case of shingles.

Shoe dermatitis. Not all cases of dermatitis of the feet are "athlete's foot." Some cases which may be mistaken for common fungus infection of the feet are instances of shoe dermatitis —sensitization and reaction to rubber, leather, dyes, adhesives, and innumerable substances used in the manufacture of shoes. The affected skin may be dry and scaly, or it may be red and itchy and crops of little blisters may develop. Sweating and maceration of the skin promote sensitization by leaching irritant substances from the shoes and more or less bathing the feet in them. Shoe dermatitis may first be suspected when treatments for supposed "athlete's foot" do not give any benefit. Unlike fungus infection of the feet, shoe dermatitis does not affect the webs of the toes or cause crumbling of the nails. Shoe dermatitis may be suspected if both feet are affected in the same symmetrical pattern, which may correspond with the design of the shoes. If the irritation subsides when a particular pair of shoes is not worn, and flares up when they are worn again, some irritant in that pair of shoes may be suspected. Shoes are made of dozens of different materials and scores of different chemicals are used in processing these materials. Identification of a specific irritant depends upon a PATCH TEST done with samples taken from the patient's shoes. The only remedy is to cease wearing a particular pair of shoes that gives trouble.

Shoe fluoroscopes. Radiation devices in some shoe stores make the bones of the feet visible, ostensibly for better fitting of shoes. Unfortunately, some of the devices, or their excessive use by children for the fun of it, can deliver substantial amounts of quite unnecessary radiation. Many states and municipalities have outlawed the use of shoe-fitting fluoroscopes, and the American Medical Association and the American College of Radiology have condemned their use as hazardous (760).

"Show." A small amount of reddish or pink discharge from the vagina indicating the onset of labor (359).

Sickle cell anemia (*sicklemia*). An hereditary abnormality transmitted as a dominant trait (see HEREDITY). The peculiar defect is an abnormal form of HEMOGLOBIN, differing only slightly from normal hemoglobin but sufficiently to cause red blood cells to take a crescent or sickle shape. The misshapen cells tend to thicken the blood, to clot abnormally and obstruct vessels, and large numbers of the fragile cells break down, causing anemia. Crises marked by fever and attacks of pain occur (149).

Siderosis. A form of *pneumoconiosis* (225); chronic lung inflammation due to long inhalation of iron-containing dusts.

Sigmoid. S-shaped; especially, the *sigmoid flexure*, in the part of the colon above the rectum.

Silicosis. Lung inflammation caused by inhalation of very fine particles of silicon dioxide over a long period of time (225).

Simmond's disease. A severe form of *panhypopituitarism* (308); major damage of the anterior pituitary gland with loss of its function, due to atrophy, necrosis, or tumor. Simmond's disease in women is characterized by shrinkage of breasts and genital organs, loss of sexual hair, weakness, poor appetite, premature aging. Symptoms vary somewhat with the degree of secondary disturbance of the thyroid and adrenal glands.

Sims-Huhner test. A test of semen in the vaginal canal for viability of SPERMATOZOA, employed in diagnosis of infertility (330).

Singer's nodes. Nodules like calluses on the vocal cords of singers, orators, teachers and others who use the voice to excess.

Singultus. HICCUPS.

Sinus. A hollow space, cavity, recess, pocket, dilated channel, suppurating tract. Of the scores of medically designated sinuses, the *paranasal sinuses*—"holes in the head," membrane-lined cavities in bones around the nose—are most familiar to laymen (582). *Sinusitis* (inflammation of the sinuses) is experienced to some degree by everyone who has a head cold, and more excruciatingly if drainage channels become blocked and infection sets in.

Sippy diet. Originally, a diet for patients with acute peptic ulcer, providing a mixture of milk and cream every hour for three days, then gradually adding cereal and egg, and after ten days, other bland foods to replace the milk-cream mixture, until at the end of four weeks the patient is graduated to a low-residue diet. Modifications of the Sippy diet may alternate antacid powders with the milk-cream mixture at the beginning and after a few days add foods of a bland diet (32).

Situs inversus. Transposition of all the organs of the chest and abdomen from the "normal" side of the body to the opposite side. For example, the liver is on the left side instead of the right; organs are in mirror-image positions. Total transposition does not necessarily impair general health.

Sitz bath. Application of wet heat to relieve pain, congestion, spasm, etc., in the pelvic area, by sitting in a tub of warm water (110 degrees or a little more) which covers only the hips and buttocks.

Skene's glands. Two glands with ducts just inside the opening of the female urethra. *Skenitis* is an inflammation of the glands, which may involve the bladder and cause urgency of urination; the most common cause is gonorrhea.

Skin writing. See DERMOGRAPHIA.

Skipped beat. See EXTRASYSTOLE.

Sleep. New insights into patterns of sleep have come from studies with the ELECTROENCEPHALOGRAPH, but no researcher can yet say precisely what sleep "is." Brain waves of hundreds of experimental subjects show that we fall asleep in four stages, from Stage 1 (light sleep) to Stage 4 (deepest sleep), and awaken in reverse order. It takes about an hour and a half to go from light sleep to deep sleep and back again. There are about five such cycles in an average uninterrupted night's sleep of approximately eight hours. At the top or light sleep phase of each cycle, we are close to waking, and may even awaken and go back to sleep without remembering it. Perhaps this is the most critical time for insomniacs who fall asleep easily enough but wake in a little while and can't get to sleep again. The discovery that dreaming is accompanied by a peculiar but characteristic kind of rapid eye movements has given some new information about dreams. Hundreds of studies confirm that we generally have the first dream of the night after we ascend to light sleep from the first deep sleep. The average sleeper spends about two hours a night in dreams which occur in four or five cycles corresponding to light sleep. Experimenters believe that everybody dreams repeatedly every night but that dreams are almost immediately forgotten, remembered only unless we awaken while a dream is in progress, and then not usually remembered long.

Sleeping pills. See BARBITURATES.

Sleeping sickness. Untimely attacks of sleepiness do not necessarily imply organic disease (see NARCOLEPSY). "Sleeping sickness" usually refers to a symptom resulting from various injuries, infections, or inflammations of the brain, especially *encephalitis lethargica* (59). *African sleeping sickness* is a specific disease transmitted by the bite of an infected fly (71).

Sleepwalking (*somnambulism*). Parents are often concerned about sleepwalking in children; the condition is more rare in adults. Sleepwalkers may perform dangerous feats, but they may also injure themselves by falling out of windows or crashing against objects. Anxiety and tensions are often strong components of sleepwalking, and investigation of such factors is desirable if sleepwalking persists. The belief that it is dangerous to awaken a sleepwalker has no basis in fact. It is better to awaken him, to prevent injury to himself or others.

Slipped disk. See RUPTURED DISK.

Slit lamp. An instrument for examining structures of the front part of the eye. It produces a slender beam of light and has a microscope which magnifies structures.

Slough. A mass of dead tissue cast off from or contained in living tissue.

Smallpox vaccination. See VACCINIA.

Smears. Secretions or blood spread on a glass slide for examination under a microscope. Smears are often stained with various dyes to bring out fine details.

Smegma. Thick, cheesy material that sometimes accumulates under the PREPUCE in men and around the CLITORIS in women (405).

Smell patch. A small area of tissue about a half inch square at the top of the nasal cavity, where receiving ends of nerves of the sense of smell are located (579).

Snellen chart. The familiar eye test chart consisting of block letters in diminishing sizes (537).

Snoring. If snoring is a "disease," it is one that does no injury to the snorer, only to those within earshot. A snorer almost never knows that he is snoring, even though he may occasionally be awakened by an especially vigorous snort. He knows of his affliction only through the testimony of others. The sounds of snoring—gasps, whistles, gurgles, buzzes, hisses—are produced by vibrations of air passing in and out over the soft palate and other soft structures. Symphonic variations are modified by the force of air flow, frequency of vibration, and the size, density, and elasticity of affected tissues. Sleeping on one's back is conducive to snoring, but some virtuosos can perform while sleeping on their sides. A few causes of snoring may be correctable; it is worth consulting a physician to find out. Most cases of snoring in children are associated with enlarged tonsils and adenoids. Snoring is often associated with mouthbreathing, and if blocked nasal passages or predisposing conditions are treatable there is hope of relief. Nasal polyps are readily removed, a deviated septum can be corrected, blockages associated with infections and allergies are treatable. However, many snorers have native skills that cannot be exorcised and often the best that can be done is to keep them from sleeping on their backs by sewing a rubber ball, or something else uncomfortable, into the back of their pajamas. The most practical remedy, useless to the snorer but of great value to his auditors, is ear plugs.

Solar urticaria. HIVES produced by exposure to sunlight.

Solitary kidney. A rare congenital condition; only one kidney is present.

Somatic. Pertaining to the body.

Somatotype. Body build, constitutional type. Somatotyping procedures most widely used today were developed by Dr. William H. Sheldon whose terms, *endomorph, mesomorph,* and *ectomorph* have entered the common language. Constitution-classifying is based on the three primitive cell layers of the embryo from which particular organs and systems develop. Skin and nervous system derive from the outside layer, the *ectoderm*. Bones, muscles and vascular system derive from the middle layer, the *mesoderm*. The lining of the gut derives from the inner layer, the *endoderm*. Everyone has all three components, but in varying proportions. The circus weight lifter, fat man, and living skeleton are extreme constitutional types. An extreme mesomorph has a predominance of muscle and bone and a hard, square build. An extreme endomorph has superb digestive tract, soft roundness of body, and great facility for getting fat. An extreme ectomorph with a preponderance of skin and nervous tissue has a slender "beanpole" build and great alertness to what is going on around him. Accurate somatotyping requires accurate measurements and photographing of the nude body.

Somniferous. Producing sleep.

Somniloquy (talking in sleep). It is quite common for children to talk in their sleep. Even some adults worry that they may babble secrets when sleeping. Words spoken in sleep are usually fragmentary, mumbled, even ludicrous, and probably indicate participation in dreams or remembered events of the previous day. Talking during sleep probably reflects decreased depth of sleep and is nothing to be alarmed about. See SLEEP.

Spasm. Sudden, severe, involuntary contraction of muscles, interfering with function and often causing pain. If tightening of muscle is steady and persistent, as in leg cramps, it is called *tonic* spasm. If contractions alternate with relaxations, causing jerky movements, the spasms are called *clonic*. Both voluntary and involuntary muscles can be affected, causing a variety of *spastic* conditions. Spasms of involuntary muscle may involve the bronchial tubes (ASTHMA), intestines, blood vessels (RAYNAUD'S DISEASE), and sphincters of the gallbladder and urethra, to mention a few conditions. Antispasmodic drugs such as bella-

donna may be prescribed to ease spastic conditions of involuntary muscle, such as spastic colon (464).

Speculum. An instrument for viewing the interior of a passage or body cavity; for instance, the vagina, rectum, nose, ear.

Spermatocele. A swelling of the SCROTUM caused by cystic dilation (fluid-filled sac) of the sperm-conducting tubules of the testicle (300). Surgical removal of the cyst is usually desirable.

Spermatocide. An agent that kills SPERMATOZOA.

Spermatozoa. Male germ cells; sperm (329). The sperm is the smallest human cell, and the only one capable of independent locomotion, by virtue of its tail which acts as a propeller. Sperms are produced in enormous numbers in the seminiferous tubules of the testicle. Primitive cells in the lining of the tubules develop into maturing sperms which fall off and are carried into a coiled tube, the *epididymis,* and thence into a straighter tube, the *vas deferens* (299, 323). The trip takes about two weeks, during which the sperms continue to mature. They do not move under their own power until they are suspended in SEMEN at the time of ejaculation. Sperm production is a continuous process from puberty to old age. The average man produces some 400,000 *billion* sperms in his lifetime, a number too vast to be comprehensible. The average ejaculate contains from 200 to 250 million sperms. An individual sperm has a head, neck, midpiece and tail (329). The head carries the nucleus which contains 23 CHROMOSOMES, one of which is a sex chromosome—either an X (female-determining) or a Y (male-determining) chromosome. The sex chromosome of the human egg is always an X. Hence, it is the sperm that determines the sex of offspring. If the sperm contains a Y chromosome to pair with the X chromosome of the egg, the XY combination produces a boy. If the sperm contains an X chromosome to pair with the X of the egg, the combination produces a girl.

Sperm count. A laboratory procedure for calculating the numbers of SPERMATOZOA in a specimen of semen, useful in assessing male fertility. Although a count of 40,000,000 sperms per cubic centimeter of ejaculate is generally considered normal (counts two to three times greater are not unusual), conception can occur with a relatively low sperm population. Vigorous activity of sperms, and relative lack of abnormal forms, may be more significant to fertility than a relatively low sperm count. If sperms are vigorous and well-shaped, a sperm count of 20,000,000 per cubic centimeter is generally considered adequate for fertility. The volume of ejaculated semen ranges from two to six cubic centimeters.

Sphenoid. Wedge-shaped; especially, the *sphenoid sinuses* of the bone which lies behind the upper part of the nasal cavity (583).

Sphincter. A "purse string" muscle which surrounds and closes a natural orifice; for example, the anal sphincter.

Sphygmomanometer. The instrument that measures arterial blood pressure when a physician puts a rubber cuff around your arm and inflates it.

Spider (arterial). Dilation of small blood vessels in the skin, branching somewhat like the legs of a spider. "Spider bursts" may be associated with liver disease, pregnancy, varicose veins and other conditions but may also occur in normal persons.

Spider bite. The Black Widow spider (810) has been thought to be the only common American spider capable of inflicting an excruciating bite. A relative newcomer, the Brown Recluse spider, is now known to be even more

venomous and to be expanding its habitat into many states. It is a shy brown spider that tries to stay away from people, but hides in shoes, blankets, rolled-up newspapers and similar haunts that people are always disturbing. When a brown spider bites, the victim may feel a mild sting or nothing at all. Pain soon occurs, followed by swelling, blistering, even hemorrhage and ulceration. A severe bite may require hospitalization. There is no specific treatment, but prompt injection of cortisone-like drugs, followed by two or three injections on alternate days, is recommended by some investigators. The brown spider's venom is more potent than cobra and other snake venoms, but fortunately the creature can inject only a small amount.

Spina bifida. A congenital malformation of the spine in which some of the vertebrae fail to fuse, so that a sac containing the covers of the spinal cord and even the spinal cord itself may protrude under the skin (260).

Spinal cord. The soft, fluted column of nerve tissue enclosed in the bony vertebral column (236, 593). *Spinal nerves* (all the nerves of the body except the 12 pairs of cranial nerves) enter or leave the spinal cord through openings in the vertebrae.

Spinal tap. Withdrawal of CEREBROSPINAL FLUID through a needle; used in diagnosis of diseases such as meningitis, tumors, polio.

Spinal tap.

Spirochete. A microbe shaped like a corkscrew (47). Many kinds of spirochetes are quite harmless, but the more malicious ones cause syphilis, yaws, relapsing fever, tropical ulcer, ratbite fever, and a few other infections.

Splenomegaly. Enlargement of the spleen.

Split graft. A flap of skin from which the deeper layers have been cut away, leaving the outer layers for grafting (742).

Spondylitis. Inflammation of vertebrae (640).

Spondylolisthesis. Deformation of the lower spine, due to a slipping forward of a lumbar vertebra (603).

Spoon nail. A nail with a concave outer surface instead of the normal convexity.

Spore. An inactive form of a micro-organism that is resistant to destruction and capable of becoming active again. For example, TETANUS spores.

Sporotrichosis. Infection by a kind of fungus that is parasitic on plants. The disease produces nodules along the course of lymphatic vessels which enlarge, ulcerate, and discharge pus. Nurserymen, farmers, and persons in contact with plants and woods are most susceptible. The infection is stubborn and may persist for months but usually responds to treatment.

Spotting. A slight show of blood in the vaginal discharge at times other than menstruation. Slight spotting is not uncommon at the approximate time of OVULATION between menstrual periods. Spotting in pregnancy (348) or after the menopause (420) should be reported promptly to a doctor.

Sprain. Tearing or laceration of ligaments that hold bones together at a joint, a result of severe wrenching.

Sprains are sometimes difficult to distinguish from fractures; both may result from the same injury (800). Diagnosis should be left to physician.

Sprue. See MALABSORPTION SYNDROME.

Squint (*strabismus*). Failure of the two eyes to direct their gaze simultaneously at the same object because of muscle imbalance (542).

Staghorn calculus. A large stone which more or less fills the cavity of the kidney and has irregular projecting surfaces somewhat resembling antlers (277).

Stamp grafts. Small pieces of skin about the size of a postage stamp, used for grafting (742).

Stapes. A tiny, stirrup-shaped bone of the middle ear (560). "Freezing" of the footplate of the stapes by bone growing around it (*otosclerosis*) prevents free conduction of sound to the inner ear. Several types of operations aim to correct this form of hearing loss (568, 727). *Stapes mobilization* is a procedure to "unfreeze" the stirrup bone from its surroundings and restore free vibratory movements. In *stapedectomy*, the stirrup bone is removed and replaced by a plastic substitute.

Staphylococci. Spherical bacteria which tend to grow in clumps like a bunch of grapes (34). They are common inhabitants of the skin and nasal passages (13).

Stasis. Stagnation; slowing of normal flow of body fluids, blood, intestinal contents. *Stasis dermatitis* is an eczematous condition of the leg, common in elderly persons (194).

Status. A severe, refractory condition. *Status asthmaticus:* intractable asthma, extreme difficulty in breathing, cyanosis, exhaustion, lasting a few days to a week or longer (659). *Status epilepticus:* epileptic attacks coming in rapid succession, during which the patient does not regain consciousness.

Steapsin. An enzyme produced in the pancreas gland that aids in digesting fats.

Steatorrhea. Stools containing large amounts of undigested fats.

Stein-Leventhal syndrome. A rare condition of sterility, absence of menstruation, and hairiness, in women having enlarged ovaries with many cysts. Treatment is surgical removal of a wedge-shaped section from each ovary.

Stenosis. Narrowing or constriction of a duct or aperture of the body.

Sterilization, human. Any procedure which leaves a man or woman incapable of having children; usually, a surgical procedure. See TUBAL LIGATION and VASECTOMY. Voluntary sterilization is legal in all 50 states and there are no restrictions on the purposes of the operation except in Connecticut and Utah, where it may be performed only for reasons of "medical necessity."

Sternum. The breastbone (593).

Sternutation. Sneezing.

Steroids. Natural hormones or synthetic drugs whose molecules share a common skeleton of four rings of carbon atoms (the steroid nucleus) but which have different actions according to the attachment of other atoms. Natural steroids include the male and female sex hormones and cortisone-like hormones of the cortex of the adrenal glands (318). Oral contraceptives ("the pill") are steroids. Many synthetic steroids developed by pharmaceutical research increase potency, enhance desired effects, minimize side effects or otherwise "improve" the actions of a molecule by shifting, attaching, or disattaching a few atoms.

Stethoscope. An instrument which conducts bodily sounds, especially those of the heart, but of other organs as well, to the ears of the examiner. It is the device that interns carry around their necks in television shows about the travails of doctors. A piece of paper rolled into a cylinder, one end of which is placed on the chest of the patient and the other at the ear of the listener, demonstrates the principle. The stethoscope was invented by Rene Laennec, a French physician, who was called upon to examine a young woman and found a way to listen to her chest sounds without offending her modesty.

Still's disease. A disease of children, like rheumatoid arthritis, affecting many joints.

Stingray injuries. Stings inflicted by stingrays (it happens to about 750 people a year along our coasts) inject venom. Immediate treatment is to immerse the part in hot water, as hot as the patient can stand, and to keep it immersed for about an hour. Heat detoxifies the venom. This is an immediate first aid measure; afterward, the wound requires medical attention.

"Stomach flu." A term more current among griping patients than physicians. Usually the complaint is of queasiness, vomiting, and diarrhea, which run their course in a couple of days or even 24 hours and have nothing to do with influenza. Gastrointestinal viruses may cause such upsets but it is practically never possible to identify the viruses. Many cases of self-diagnosed "stomach-flu" may be instances of unsuspected FOOD POISONING.

Stomatitis. Inflammation of soft tissues of the mouth. The inflammation may be limited to the mouth or it may be a symptom of some systemic disease. Viruses, bacteria, or fungi may infect mouth tissues, membranes may be sensitized to certain materials, some drugs may produce oral inflammation.

Stomatitis may be an aspect of blood disorders, vitamin deficiencies, mechanical injuries from jagged teeth or ill-fitting dentures, and skin diseases. Treatment is as varied as the causes.

Stool. The bowel evacuation; feces.

Strabismus. Cross-eyedness (542).

Stratum corneum. The topmost horny layer of the outer skin or epidermis, composed of dead cells that are shed and replaced from below (168).

Strawberry mark. A birthmark comprised of superficial blood vessels, present at birth or developing shortly thereafter, which has a tendency to disappear spontaneously in the course of time (184).

Strawberry tongue. A bright red tongue seen especially in scarlet fever; the blood-engorged papillae are enlarged and prominent.

Streptococci. Sphere-shaped bacteria which tend to grow like chains of little balls (34). They are responsible for scarlet fever, "strep throat," and many other infections.

Stria (pl. *striae*). A streak, line, stripe, narrow band. Whitish striations of the abdomen may appear as the skin is stretched during pregnancy and in the breasts after milk production ceases. Obesity or an excess of cortisone-like hormones (320) may produce "stretch marks" on the abdomen. Striations may appear temporarily in adolescent girls as hormone balances of sexual maturity are becoming established.

Stricture. Narrowing or tightening of the passageway of a duct or hollow organ; may result from inflammation, contraction, injury, scarring, or obtrusion of tissue.

Stroke. Apoplexy, cerebrovascular accident, paralytic stroke (117).

Stroma. The supporting tissue of an organ, as opposed to its active "producing" tissue.

Struma. Goiter.

Stupe. A cloth wrung out of hot water and applied to the skin; turpentine is sometimes sprinkled in the water as a counter-irritant.

Subacute. An almost acute condition; intermediate between chronic and acute illness.

Subclinical disease. A disease, usually mild, that has no definite symptoms or signs which can be recognized by the usual visual or clinical means.

Subcutaneous. Beneath the skin, as a hypodermic injection.

Subluxation. Partial or incomplete dislocation, sprain.

Substernal. Underneath the breastbone.

Sudorific. Sweat-inducing.

"Summer itch." A North American form of SCHISTOSOMIASIS, quite different from the serious tropical variety. It sometimes afflicts swimmers in northern fresh water lakes. Larvae which are parasites of snails in the lakes get into the skin, cause a prickling sensation, and itchy red spots and pimples develop (66). The condition clears up by itself but in the meantime, lotions to decrease itching are comforting.

Sunburn, Suntan. Too long exposure to intense sunlight will, as practically everyone has learned, cause sunburn, which is in every sense a burn. What most people want to acquire is a suntan, not a burn. The amount of sun that individuals can stand varies with thickness, pigmentation, and personal structure of the skin. For most of North America the sun usually is intense enough to affect the skin between 9:30 a.m. and 2:30 p.m. from

April through August. To develop a tan without a burn, the skin should be exposed gradually, starting with an exposure of no more than 20 minutes the first day, increasing exposure by about one-third each successive day. After a week the skin should have been conditioned sufficiently to permit a moderate amount of sunbathing through the summer. Suntan is produced by the darkening and moving toward the surface of melanin granules made by cells in deeper skin layers. Exposure to sun not only darkens the skin, but thickens it. The extra thickness gives much of the protection against sunlight. The extra thickness lasts only six weeks or so after exposure has ceased. Unlimited exposure to burning rays of the sun has undesirable long-term effects. Continued exposure ages the skin prematurely, thickens, wrinkles, and leatherizes it. This aging is irreversible, the delayed price of overexuberant tanning.

Superfluous hair. Hirsutism; especially, excessive hairiness of the lips, cheek, chin or legs of women. There may be an underlying endocrine disorder (328), a family tendency to hairiness, or hair may be unduly conspicuous in an area where it is normally present. Electrolysis performed by a skilled operator employs electric current to destroy the hair root permanently, but its application is tedious. Chemical depilatories remove hair satisfactorily but directions must be followed carefully to avoid skin irritation. A bleach may mask the condition if hair growth is fine.

Supernumerary. More than a normal number, as a sixth finger or toe.

Suppuration. Formation of pus.

Suprarenal glands. Adrenal glands (318).

Supraspinatus syndrome. A term for disorders of the shoulder region which make it painful or impossible to lift the arm completely (606).

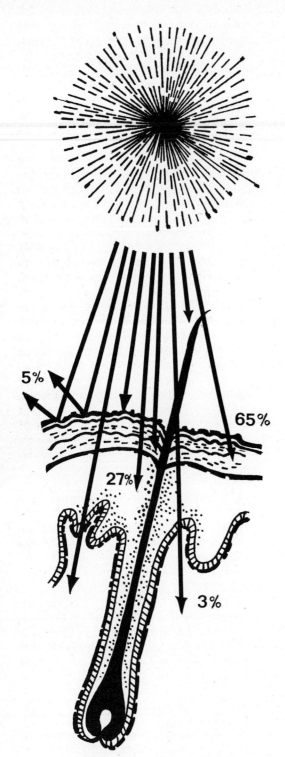

5%

65%

27%

3%

Suntan-sunburn: 5% of ultraviolet rays reflected off skin surface, 65% absorbed by horny layers of skin, 27% absorbed by rest of epidermis, 3% reach dermis ("true skin").

Surfer's knots. Soft-tissue swellings on the instep and just below the knee, produced by continued kneeling on a surfboard. After a year or two of steady surfing the knots become hard and firm. Large knots over a joint may cause changes in small bones of the feet. The knots may be painful and sometimes require treatment. If surfing is discontinued the knots tend to disappear in a few months, but knots of several years' duration may disappear only partially after the sport is given up. Probably no greater permanent disability will be suffered than mild deformity or arthritis of the foot.

Sympathectomy. Surgical removal of fibers of the sympathetic nervous system (238). The object is to modify for the better the activity of organs regulated by sympathetic nerve trunks, as in sympathectomy for reduction of high blood pressure (114).

Sympathetic ophthalmia. Inflammation of one eye due to injury of the other eye. Prompt treatment of an injured eye is important to prevent involvement of the other eye and possible blindness.

Symphysis. The junction of originally distinct bones which have grown together; for example, the lines of fusion of the sacrum and the coccyx, and of the pubic bones (595).

Suture. To sew up a wound, or the threadlike materials used for this purpose; catgut, linen, silk, wire, cotton, etc. *Absorbable* sutures such as catgut (actually, sheep's intestines) are often used to close wounds in deep tissues. Sutures used to sew surface tissues are usually non-absorbable and removable, to the considerable anguish of the patient.

Swimmer's ear. "Athlete's foot" of the ear canal; water incompletely drained from the ear sets up moist and soggy conditions favorable to fungus infection (570).

Swimming pool granuloma. A rare infection of the skin caused by acid-fast bacteria related to tuberculosis germs. The organisms apparently gain lodgment in cracks, fissures and rough surfaces of some swimming pools. The first sign of infection is the appearance of a group of small, red, tender pimples on the skin. Later the pimples merge to form a plaque or nodule which occasionally contains pus. The elbows are the most common site of infection. Lesions may also appear on the knees and feet. These are body areas most likely to be banged or scraped against rough pool surfaces. Pressure or rubbing against parts of a pool where germs are present apparently gives them entrance to the skin, although there may be no obvious sign of abrasion or injury. The infection is chronic and may persist for many weeks. Patients with swimming pool granuloma given TUBERCULIN TESTS commonly have a positive reaction. Adequate chlorination of the water and repair of broken tiles or concrete to produce smooth surfaces protect against outbreaks of the infection. It is not known where the germs come from or why they are peculiarly associated with swimming pools.

Sycosis. Inflammatory disease of the hair follicles, especially of the beard. Usually a STAPHYLOCOCCUS infection, characterized by pus-filled pimples perforated by hairs.

Sydenham's chorea. See CHOREA.

Synapse. A point of communication between processes of nerve cells which come close together but do not actually touch; a sort of "spark gap" for nerve impulses to jump (233).

Syncope. Fainting.

Syndactyly. Webbed or fused fingers or toes.

Syndrome. A set of symptoms which occur together and collectively characterize a disease.

Synovial fluid. The clear viscid fluid, resembling the white of an egg, which lubricates the movements of tendons and joints.

Systemic disease. One which affects the body as a whole, not limited to a particular part; for example, an infection spread through the bloodstream.

Systole. The period of blood-pumping contraction of the heart. Systolic pressure is the higher of the two figures (such as 120/80) by which doctors express blood pressure readings. See DIASTOLE.

Saphenous veins. Two large veins of the leg near the skin surface which sometimes become varicosed (127).

T

Tarry stools. Stools resembling tar in color and consistency; usually an indication of bleeding into the intestinal tract. Iron and other medications can produce similar stools.

Tachycardia. Rapid heart beat (104).

Talipes. Foot deformity; clubfoot (621).

Tarsus. The instep of the foot (619).

Tampon. A plug of absorbent material inserted into a body cavity, such as a vaginal tampon to absorb menstrual flow.

Taenia. TAPEWORM.

Tapeworm. A ribbonlike flatworm which may invade the intestines of consumers of undercooked beef, fish, or pork (66).

Tartar (*dental calculus*). Hard, mineralized deposits on surfaces of teeth, irritating to the gums and underlying bone (508). Toothbrushing helps to prevent the deposits when they are in a soft state, but they solidify quickly. Periodic removal by a dentist or dental hygienist is good insurance against disease of supporting tissues of the teeth.

Tattooing. Insertion of permanent colors into the skin through punctures, as by a needle. "Tattoo parlors" whose operators decorate the skin with garish designs and sentiments have no relation to medicine, unless a customer who is emblazoned with the name of a girl friend he wants to forget asks a physician about the possibilities of erasure. Unclean tattoo needles can transmit viral HEPATITIS and other diseases, and for that reason many municipalities have banished the old-time tattoo artist. In competent medical hands, tattooing has recognized but limited value, primarily for minimizing skin discolorations. *Portwine stain*, a bluish-red birthmark (184), may be made less conspicuous by tattooing skin-colored pigments into the area.

Tapping. Emptying fluids from a body cavity by surgical puncture; resorted to when accumulated fluids embarrass the functioning of the heart, lungs, abdomen, cranium, and other organs.

Tabes dorsalis. See ATAXIA.

Tay-Sachs disease. See AMAUROTIC FAMILIAL IDIOCY.

Tear gas. Increasing sale of tear gas pens, pencils, and gas shells causes some concern about possible burns or injuries of the eyes. The tear gas most commonly used (chloracetophenone) is ejected by a black powder propellant covered by wadding. If the gun is exploded so close to the eye that liquid or solid particles strike it directly, the eye may be seriously injured. Otherwise, there is little or no danger of permanent damage. Exposure to a fine spray or cloud of tear gas causes tears to flow copiously and the eyelids to close spasmodically. In fresh air these symptoms disappear and only a slight redness of the conjunctiva may remain for a short time.

Teflon. A coating applied to skillets to keep foods from sticking. The material is perfectly safe. Teflon does not decompose except at temperatures far greater than can be attained by any cooking procedure.

Temporal bone banks. This is a program by means of which persons with impaired hearing or other forms of ear disorders (head noises, Meniere's disease, etc.) can bequeath their inner ear structures for medical research. Temporal bones are those which contain the inner ear and its nerve structures inside the head. These cannot be examined directly during life and research into causes and prevention of deafness is severely handicapped. By relating a patient's history of ear disease to abnormalities observed in his bequeathed temporal bones, the Temporal Bone Banks Program aims to obtain information of scientific value in assessing the effectiveness of medical and surgical treatments and in the prevention and correction of ear disorders. Four regional Temporal Bone Banks Centers are located at the University of California, San Francisco; the University of Chicago; Johns Hopkins Hospital, Baltimore; and Baylor University, Houston. Information can be obtained from the Deafness Research Foundation, 366 Madison Ave., New York, N. Y. 10017.

Tenaculum. A long, slender type of forceps like tongs, with scissors handles, having teeth or hooks at the end to grasp a part, such as the cervix of the uterus. It is used especially in gynecologic surgery.

Tendon. A band of tough white fibrous tissue that connects a muscle to a bone. Muscle fibers merge into one end of a tendon, the other end of which is attached to a bone. Sometimes a tendon conveys muscle action over a considerable distance, as in the back of the leg, where a long tendon inserted into the rear of the ankle transmits the pull of calf muscles above it. This makes it unnecessary to have a huge mass of muscle around the ankle itself. Most tendons are covered by sheaths which secrete lubricating fluids for easy sliding. Tendons and their sheaths are subject to injury by tearing, stretching, twisting stresses ("pulled tendon" is a common athletic injury) and to inflammations, for which there are technical names such as *tenosynovitis* and *tenovaginitis*.

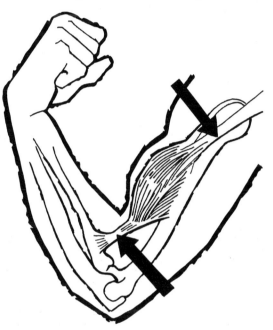

Tendons connecting biceps muscle to bones.

Tenesmus. Painful straining to empty the bowel or bladder, without success.

Tennis elbow. This painful condition of the outer side of the elbow joint can affect anyone who overvigorously uses a screwdriver as well as a tennis racquet. It is a form of BURSITIS produced by violent extension of the wrist with the palm downward or vigorous rotary movement of the forearm against resistance, putting severe stress on the elbow joint (609).

Tendinitis. Inflammation of tendons and their attachments.

Telangiectasis. Dilation of groups of small blood vessels, appearing as fine lines on the skin, sometimes associated with diseases of the skin, cirrhosis of the liver, and other disorders. The dilations may form hard, red, wartlike spots the size of a pinhead or pea. In *hereditary hemorrhagic telangiectasis,* a rare form, the dilated vessels become thin and fragile, rupture spontaneously, and bleed into the skin, intestines, or other parts of the body. It is inherited as a dominant trait; see HEREDITY.

Temperomandibular joint. The joint in front of the ear in which the hinge of the lower jaw fits into a socket in the base of the skull. Its close relationship to the teeth may bring about changes not common in other joints. Uneven bite, tooth-clenching habits, poorly fitting dentures or tooth restorations, may throw the joint out of joint, limit sidewise motion, limit the opening of the mouth, cause pain, soreness, clicking noises, and even headaches (521).

Testosterone. The male hormone, a STEROID hormone produced by cells of the testicle independent from cells which produce SPERMATOZOA.

Testicle, testis. The primary male sex glands or gonads; paired organs, enclosed in the pouch of the SCROTUM, together with accessory structures (323).

Teratology. The branch of science concerned with the study of malformations and monstrosities. A *teratoma* is a tumor containing hair, teeth, bones, or other material not normal to the part in which it grows.

Term (at term). The end of the normal period of gestation or pregnancy when birth occurs.

"Test tube babies." Popular term for offspring of ARTIFICIAL INSEMINATION.

Tetanus (*lockjaw*). A grave, often fatal infection caused by toxins of tetanus organisms which get into the body through perforating, penetrating, or deep wounds and thrive in the absence of oxygen (42, 798). The disease is easily prevented by harmless *tetanus toxoid* "shots." These are routinely given to infants and should be just as routine for adults who are as likely to suffer accidents as anybody (400).

Tetany. Painful muscle twitchings, spasms, especially of wrists and feet; sometimes convulsions. Insufficient calcium in the blood causes the muscular irritability and consequent symptoms. Insufficiency of circulating calcium may result from vitamin D deficiency or underactivity of the parathyroid glands (317). Treatment is with calcium salts, orally or by infusion if the condition is severe. Do not confuse with *tetanus.*

Tetralogy of Fallot. Congenital malformation of the heart, exhibiting four defects: aorta turned to the right, ventricular septal defect, constriction of the pulmonary artery or valve, hypertrophy of the right ventricle.

Thalassemia. Cooley's anemia (149).

Thelarche. Precocious growth of the female breast (307).

Thenar. Pertaining to the palm of the hand; especially, the padded thenar eminence that bulges at the base of the thumb.

Therapy. Treatment of disease. Anything that is therapeutic is designed to help or heal.

Thermography. Body surfaces emit slightly different amounts of heat because of local differences in underlying blood supply. This is the principle of thermography, which employs sensitive instruments to scan body areas and record slight heat differentials on sensitized paper. Thermography has been used to detect and localize very small breast tumors, to investigate blood vessel obstructions, and to localize the site of the placenta. It is a young technique, limited to a few medical centers.

Thoracentesis. Puncture of the chest wall with a hollow needle for withdrawal of fluids.

Thoracoplasty. Removal of several rib segments to collapse the chest wall and lung (211). A treatment for tuberculosis that has become less common since the development of effective anti-tuberculosis drugs.

Thorax. The chest.

Threadworms. Roundworms which in larval form can enter the body through the skin, usually of the feet, and migrate to the intestines, causing diarrhea and pain in the pit of the stomach (67).

Thrombin. An enzyme present in blood oozing from a wound, but not in circulating blood. It acts upon a blood protein to produce *fibrin,* which is the essential portion of a blood clot.

Thromboangiitis obliterans. See BUERGER'S DISEASE.

Thrombocytes. Blood PLATELETS which help to initiate blood clotting.

Thrombocytopenia. Deficiency of platelets necessary for blood coagulation, resulting in bleeding from tiny blood vessels into the skin and mucous membranes, known as PURPURA (151).

Thrombophlebitis. Presence of a blood clot (THROMBUS) in a vein, with inflammation; *venous thrombosis* (130). Veins of the leg are most commonly affected. If superficial, the affected vein may be felt as a very tender cord. Thrombosis of deep veins is serious because blood clots may break off and be carried in the bloodstream until they become "stuck" and plug vital vessels. A large particle (EMBOLUS) may reach the heart or lungs and cause death. The tendency of clots to form in slightly injured veins is greatly increased by physical inactivity such as prolonged bed rest. Getting the patient out of bed soon after surgery or childbirth, and encouraging bedridden patients to carry out frequent movements of the legs, are preventive measures. Treatment of active deep venous thrombosis includes such measures as elevation of the foot of the bed, warmth, and anticoagulant drugs which retard blood clotting.

Thrombosis. Formation of a clot in a blood vessel, and the partial or complete plugging of the vessel that ensues. The most familiar example is *coronary thrombosis* (84), but the process can occur in many vessels besides those which supply the heart.

Thrombus. A clot which forms in a blood vessel and remains at the site of attachment. If a fragment or the entire clot breaks off and is carried through the bloodstream, it is called an EMBOLUS.

Thrush. A fungus infection of the mouth, occurring in young infants. Whitish spots in the mouth become painful shallow sores (397).

Thymus gland. An organ in the chest (301) which for years puzzled anatomists who could find no function for it. Recent research has shown that immediately after birth, the thymus begins to activate the body's defenses against infections. The thymus is a self-starter which produces and sends out millions of tiny *lymphocytes* (137) to the spleen and lymph nodes, where they synthesize ANTIBODIES. Once these seedbeds are established with the aid of a hormone from the thymus, production of lymphocytes in lymphoid tissues continues throughout life. The thymus, having got things going, shrinks and retires. In infants the thymus is a large organ, relative to body size. It continues to grow for eight to ten years. By that time the body's immunity systems are running smoothly and the thymus which ignited them is no longer necessary. The gland begins to shrink and in adults is very small. At one time it was thought that an enlarged thymus was a cause of sudden unexplained deaths of infants, because the thymus of infants dead from infections was much smaller than the thymus of infants who died suddenly from unknown causes. It is now realized that the thymus of infants who die from infections is abnormally small because the gland shrinks rapidly in the presence of infections and stresses, and that a relatively large thymus is normal in infancy. There is some evidence that the thymus may play a part in the inception of AUTO-IMMUNE DISEASES.

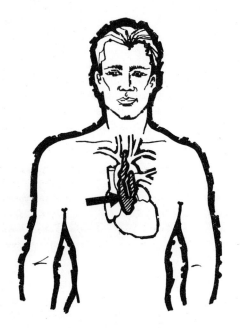

Thymus gland.

Thyroglobulin. An iodine-protein substance, the form in which thyroid hormone is stored in the gland (303).

Thyroid. The shield-shaped gland in the neck, covering the sides and front of the windpipe (303). It is a "governor" of metabolism, regulator of the rate at which body fires burn.

Thyroidectomy. Surgical removal of part of the thyroid gland (311, 723).

Thyroiditis. Acute or chronic inflammation of the thyroid gland (314).

Thyrotoxicosis. Hyperthyroidism; a toxic condition due to excessive activity of the thyroid gland, or to a tumor of the gland (310).

Thyroxine. The hormone released from the thyroid gland (309).

Tibia. The shinbone.

Tic douloureux (*trigeminal neuralgia*). Stabbing, excruciating pain in one side of the face along pathways of a cranial nerve, set off by touching a "trigger" area (255).

Tick paralysis. Muscular weakness, incoordination, or paralysis, beginning in the legs and ascending, caused by toxins which enter the blood through bites of woodticks or dog ticks. Symptoms give warning to search carefully for an imbedded tick which may be hidden in hairy parts of the body. Prompt removal of the tick (809) is usually followed by gradual disappearance of symptoms.

Tics. Habit spasms; quick, twitchy, repetitive movements of certain muscle groups, always in the same manner: pouting the lips, batting the eyelids, wrinkling the nose, making faces, shaking the head, shrugging a shoulder, tilting the neck, etc. The nervous habits develop most commonly in children and often disappear in the course of time if the child isn't constantly nagged about them. Usually the "ticky" youngster is pretty tense and tightened up inside to begin with; he may be a target of demands, expectations, and pressures that might make anyone twitchy if bottled up inside. A little loosening of the reins by those who hold them may help to relax a child who, after all, does not consciously decide to indulge in tics. Nervous habits should be distinguished from purposeless movements associated with some physical disorder. Genuine tics never appear during sleep.

T.i.d. Three times a day.

Timetable of fetal development. See pages 1006-7.

Tinea. Ringworm; fungus infection of the skin (189).

Tine test. A form of TUBERCULIN TEST. A small disposable stainless steel disk with four prongs covered with dried *tuberculin* is pressed into the skin (209). The unit is used on only one patient, is never reused. The technique is advantageous in screening large population groups of school children and susceptible young adults for tuberculosis.

Tinnitus. Head noises; ringing, roaring, clicking or hissing sounds in the ears (573).

Tipped uterus. Forward, backward, or other displacement of the uterus from its theoretically ideal position (415).

Tissue culture. A method of growing cells in a suitable nutrient in flasks or test tubes outside of the body, and of propagating viruses in the cells. Polio viruses and some others are grown in tissue culture for manufacture of vaccines. Viruses can be identified by tissue-culture reactions under laboratory conditions. More than 100 "new" viruses have been isolated and identified by tissue culture techniques in the past decade and some have been associated with diseases.

Toad venom. Ordinary toads are harmless. But a giant tropical variety (*Bufus marinus*) which has invaded the Florida coast in the Miami Beach area exudes venom similar to a cobra's. Some small animals that have tangled with the toads have died from the venom's effects. The giant toad, weighing a pound or more, is yellowish brown with black markings. Its milk-colored venom is exuded from glands behind the eyes. The creatures breed in ponds and lakes but often come out on dry land at night to hunt insects. The giant toads should not be picked up or touched.

Tolerance. Ability to withstand abnormally large doses of a drug, induced by its continual use.

Tomograms. X-ray films of layers or planes of the body, like a layer cake. A tomogram shows a plane of the body about a half inch thick. The layer shows in fine detail but structures above and below it are fuzzy (752).

Tonometer. An instrument for measuring internal pressures of the eyeball, used in screening for *glaucoma* (553).

Tophi. Masses of urate deposits in the external ear, joints, and other structures composed largely of CARTILAGE; characteristic of *gout* (631).

Torticollis (*wry neck*). A condition in which muscles of one side of the neck are in a state of more or less continuous spasm, pulling the head into an unnatural position (258, 606).

Torulosis. A serious systemic fungus infection, occurring in eastern and southern parts of the U. S.; *cryptococcosis* (72). The infection most frequently attacks the central nervous system but may invade the bones, lungs, and skin.

Tourist's diarrhea. Mild to severe attacks of vomiting, nausea, diarrhea, afflicting unacclimatized visitors to foreign lands. Although popularly blamed on the water, spicy foods, oils, exotic cuisine, and the like, the specific causes remain a mystery. Common bacteria seem not to be responsible. Other forms of dysentery having specific causes should be ruled out. There is no certain preventive, but sensible eating helps. Eat two meals a day of familiar foods that you are accustomed to at home, if you can get them, and limit yourself to one meal a day of strange foreign foods until you become adapted. Go easy on sauces, gravies, salad oils containing mixtures of unknown ingredients. Cooked foods are safest to eat in unfamiliar places. If an attack comes on, take

TIMETABLE OF FETAL DEVELOPMENT

Only a few of the landmarks of growth of a new life in the womb can be given in the list below. Organs do not grow at uniform rates but surge forward, lag behind, come together, interact, change positions, and evince their earliest presence in the form of microscopic bulges and cell clusters that only an expert can recognize as the shape of things to come. Normally, conception occurs at the fimbriated end of the Fallopian tube (351) and it takes 3 or 4 days for the fertilized egg to reach the uterus.

AGE AFTER FERTILIZATION	STAGES OF GROWTH
5-9 DAYS	Remains free in uterine cavity.
10-11 DAYS	Attaches to and begins to become imbedded in the hormone-prepared lining of the uterus. Differentiation of embryonic germ layers (*ectoderm, mesoderm, endoderm*) from which specialized tissues will develop is well under way.
14 DAYS	Irregular, bloblike oval body with a faint longitudinal depression (*primitive streak*) from which cells are pushed continuously into enlarging body.
18-21 DAYS	Thickening of *neural plate*, forerunner of the central nervous system. The primitive heart is a simple tube. There are primitive lung buds. Two faint depressions are the sites of eyes. The embryo begins to curve head-to-tail to fit its environment.
4th WEEK	Beginning of gallbladder and liver tubules. Parts of brain begin differentiation. Local dilation indicates beginning of stomach. Heart tube becomes slightly bent with local bulges and constrictions. Nose parts suggested by pair of thickened bulges. There is a tiny liver prominence and belly stalk. Primitive head parts—mouth, brain, eyes, ears—are forming. Opening from mouth to gut breaks through; a little later, opening of anus. Primitive thyroid cells at floor of throat. Tiny rounded outgrowth suggests windpipe and larynx. The heart is under the chin. Its divisions are recognizable but it still operates as a simple tube. First heartbeats occur. Blood corpuscles form, circulation begins.
5th WEEK	Nasal pit, buds that will be arms and legs, cells that will develop into pancreas gland, tiny thickenings that will be tongue appear. The gut elongates. Primitive blood vessels function. Beginnings of eye lens, cranial nerves, retinal layer.
6th WEEK	Arm and leg buds lengthen, faint grooves suggest toes and fingers. Regional divisions of brain recognizable. Lung buds bifurcate. Primitive kidney parts established. Eyes far to either side of head. Epithelium and primitive ear parts begin to form. Nasal pits recognizable as nostrils. Stomach suggests adult form. Salivary glands identifiable. "Milk lines" from armpits to groin appear as slight thickening

from which breasts will later develop. Pre-cartilage cells laid down for parts of skeleton. Germ cells of gonads recognizable. First evidence of lymphatic system. Heart at critical stage of development; parts grow and fuse, its 4 chambers form.

7th WEEK Distinct beginnings of fingers, toes, eyelids, delicate fibrils that will be muscles, autonomic nervous system. Nasal openings break through, optic nerve fibers extend, gallbladder elongates. Adrenal gland cells accumulate, thyroid cells start to move into position.

8th WEEK Centers of bone growth established, formation of deeper lying bony structures begins, collar bone well ossified. Thumb and big toe begin to diverge. Local buds destined to be teeth appear. Rapid growth of nose and upper jaw. Bilateral parts of lips and palate meet and fuse. Human facial characteristics quite recognizable. Ears set very low on head. Externally, most of the changes from a minute oval body to a structure of recognizable human form (but not adult proportions) have been laid down.

3rd MONTH Eyelids meet and fuse, eyes remain "closed" until seventh month. Bony parts of skull develop from base of skull upward. Ossification centers of jaws, nasal bones, ossicles of middle ear, occiput, are active. Inner ear structure almost completed. Eye lens formation proceeding rapidly. Primitive hair follicles and deeper-lying skin layers become distinct. External genitals evidenced by swellings; sex not obvious but distinguishable by an expert. Spots where nails will develop take shape. Buds of tear glands appear. Main lymphatic channels quite well marked. Vocal cords begin to take shape.

4th MONTH Brain a recognizable miniature of adult brain; large bulge of forebrain distinguishable from cerebellum and brain stem. Paranasal sinuses have appeared. Buds of what will be sweat glands appear first on palms and soles. Bladder wall develops. Outer skin thickens into distinctive layers.

5th MONTH Structures of testes and windpipe well established. Branching structures will become collecting tubules of kidney.

6th MONTH Eyebrows, eyelashes begin to become visible. Fetus is coated with downy hair (*lanugo*). Skin ridges form on palms and soles, the lifelong basis of fingerprints and sole prints. The bronchial tree branches out actively, continues to do so after birth.

7th MONTH Eyelids unfuse, that babies may be born with eyes open. Testes begin descent through inguinal ring to scrotum. Fat begins to be deposited under translucent skin layers and the fetus becomes plumper and plumper until birth.

A seven-month baby often is sufficiently well developed to survive. All of its vital systems have been established; what is lacking is the "finishing off" period of growth and maturation that normally occurs in the womb, but in the case of a premature infant has to take place in the outside world, requiring extra care. Every additional week in the womb, up to normal term, is a plus value for the baby.

fluids to combat dehydration; plain warm tea is excellent. Applesauce, boiled rice, boiled chicken, and bland soups are good. Add other simple plain foods until recovery. Drugs do not attack the unknown cause of tourist's diarrhea but some help to control the symptoms.

Toxemia. A "poisoned" condition due to absorption into the blood of toxic substances produced by bacteria or body cells, but without the presence of bacteria in the blood. *Toxemia of pregnancy* is a disturbance of metabolism which in severe form (rare if the patient has good prenatal care) is attended by fever, headache, convulsions and rapid rise in blood pressure (356).

Toxic goiter. THYROTOXICOSIS, hyperthyroidism (310).

Toxin. A poisonous substance originating in cells of microbes, animals, or plants. Injection of a specific toxin into an animal stimulates the production of specific ANTIBODIES. This is the basis for pharmaceutical preparation of an antitoxin that neutralizes a particular toxin, for example: *botulinus, tetanus, diphtheria, snake venom.*

Toxoid. Resembling a toxin; a substance prepared by treating a toxin with agents which produce a *toxoid* that has the same immunity-stimulating ability as the toxin but is itself harmless and non-toxic. Tetanus and diphtheria toxoids are widely used in routine immunization.

Toxoplasmosis. A disease caused by infection with protozoan organisms (71). Inapparent infection of a pregnant woman may cause severe abnormalities in her baby.

Tracer elements. See RADIOISOTOPES.

Trachea. The windpipe.

Tracheobronchitis. Inflammation of the windpipe and bronchial tubes (386).

Tracheotomy. Cutting an artificial hole in the windpipe to bypass an obstruction and permit air to flow under it into the lungs (725).

Trachoma. A contagious disease of the eyes, caused by viruses which attack the lining membranes of the lids and eyes (546). Raspberry-like elevations on the inner eyelids rub against the CORNEA, leading to ulcers and blindness.

Tragus. The small lid of CARTILAGE over the external opening of the ear.

Tranquilizers. A popular, non-medical term for a variety of drugs which more or less selectively depress the central nervous system to produce calming, sedative effects but which do not dull consciousness or induce sleep, in proper doses. "Tranquilizer" is a broad term that includes many drugs of somewhat different individual actions, taken account of by a physician in prescribing a particular agent. The drugs are often categorized as *major* and *minor* tranquilizers.

The major tranquilizers, most of which belong to chemical families known as *phenothiazines* and *piperazines*, have their greatest use in treating severely disturbed psychotic patients. They tend to reduce agitation, excitement, panic, hostility and to quiet the wild, assaultive, destructive behavior associated with those emotional states, and there may be a reduction of psychotic symptoms such as hallucinations and delusions. This often makes the calmed patient more reachable by other forms of therapy. Many can be discharged from hospitals and returned to their communities relatively soon. Many patients must continue on the drugs for varying lengths of time, but this often can be supervised by the family physician, and recovery tends to be assisted by a comfortable environment of home and family.

The major tranquilizers are sometimes used in non-psychiatric patients for their secondary actions in pre-

Hypothetical mode of action of tranquilizing drugs. Drawing A shows *limbic system*, a border around the brain stem. The limbic cortex, hypothalamus, and associated structures are concerned with "non-thinking" activities of internal environment and of self-preservation, provocative of emotions—fear, rage, anxiety, agitation, sexual and defensive reactions. In a sense, emotions go round-and-round in the limbic system and are diffusely projected to other parts of the nervous system. Excessive, persistent reverberations of emotions are thought to be factors in neuroses, phychosomatic ailments, mental illnesses. Tranquilizing drugs are thought to dampen the stresses of disturbed emotions by disconnecting or interrupting reverberative circuits. Below, interacting structures of the limbic system. Colored lines suggest circuits, arrows suggest outward pathways of nerve impulses; actual pathways not known.

1. Limbic cortex.
2. Corpus callosum
3. Fornix system.
4. Thalamus.
5. Hypothalamus.
6. Amygdaloid nucleus.
7. Hippocampus.

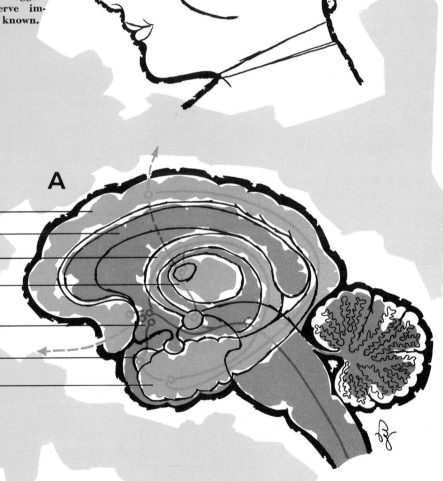

A

venting or arresting nausea and vomiting, and for intensifying the actions of anesthetics and pain-relievers so that smaller doses of the latter can be given.

The minor tranquilizers (sometimes called *atarctics* or "peace of mind" drugs) are mainly used to suppress mild to moderate manifestations of anxiety and tension in psychoneurotic patients as well as in normal persons who react tensely to stresses of their environment. Their action is quite similar to, and probably not superior to, that of the barbiturates in easing anxiety-tension states. However, the classic sedatives cause some drowsiness and loss of alertness; in correct doses, the minor tranquilizers produce mild sedation without dulling consciousness or impairing performance. Some of them have moderate muscle-relaxing action. The minor tranquilizers have considerably greater margin of safety than potent sedatives and massive overdosage is less likely to be serious or fatal, although huge overdoses, taken with suicidal intent, can lead to coma, shock, and even death. Patients who take excessive amounts of the drugs for long periods may become dependent upon them and suffer withdrawal reactions when they are discontinued.

Transillumination. Examination of a cavity or structure by means of light passing through it; for example, examination of nasal sinuses with the aid of a light in the patient's mouth.

Transplantation. Surgical techniques for transplanting an organ from one person to another are well advanced. The best known procedure is kidney transplantation (286), but the heart, lung, liver, and spleen have been transplanted in a very few human beings, demonstrating that surgical techniques of transplantation have been mastered. The major obstacle to permanent transplantation is the body's ultimate rejection of a donated organ as foreign tissue. This is due to ANTIGENS in the donated organ which provoke the patient's immune mechanisms to reject the organ as a foreign agent. Two promising ways of prolonging the "take" of transplanted organs are the objectives of much research: development of better methods of selecting compatible donors, and refinements of "immunosuppressive" techniques which subdue the body's natural antagonism to foreign tissue. Kidney transplantation is most successful when the donor is an identical twin, less successful if the donor is a close relative, least successful if the donor is unrelated. Yet unrelated donors may have tissue compatibility approximating that of twins. The problem is to identify them. It is easy to determine that prospective donors and recipients have the same blood groups (139), which is important, but the red blood cells do not carry the antigens which cause tissue rejection. So-called *transplantation antigens* are carried by white blood cells known as *lymphocytes* (134). It is hoped that improved *tissue-typing* techniques may identify donors with hostile antigens and eliminate reaction problems by very accurate matching of donor and recipient. Drugs, x-rays or combinations of both are currently used to suppress the body's antagonism to foreign tissue. These agents stop the multiplication of lymphoid cells and reduce their capacity to recognize foreign tissue. Unfortunately, they also reduce the patient's resistance to infection and it is very difficult to strike a razor-edge balance between desirable and undesirable effects. The ideal agent which is safe, effective, and induces permanent acceptance of foreign tissue as the body's own, remains to be found. It is to be expected that the future of organ transplantation rests more upon knowledge and control of tissue responses than upon improved surgical techniques.

Trauma. Injury, wound.

Transvestism. Perverted desire to wear the clothes of the opposite sex; a person who does so is a *transvestite*.

Tremor. Involuntary quivering and trembling of muscle groups, other than from obvious causes such as shivering in the cold. Tremor is a symptom which may give information about a constitutional disease. A doctor may ask a patient to hold out the arms at shoulder level with palms down and fingers stretched; fine, rapid tremor of the fingers may suggest hyperthyroidism. There are fine, coarse, slow and rapid tremors; harmless but annoying hereditary tremors; tremors that appear when at rest; and "intention tremors" that appear when voluntary movement of a part is attempted. Tremors may or may not indicate a disorder of the nervous system; there are hysterical tremors that have no organic basis at all.

Trench fever. A louse-borne, typhus-like, non-fatal RICKETTSIAL INFECTION. Many cases occurred in World Wars I and II but the disease has since gone into hiding (64).

Trench mouth (*Vincent's infection*). Painful, swollen, malodorous inflammation of the mouth and gums (37, 511). The disease is not considered to be contagious. Susceptibility is increased by debilitating disease, malnutrition, poor mouth hygiene, and heavy smoking.

Trepanning. Cutting a button of bone out of the skull with a *trephine*, a circular instrument with sawlike edges.

Treponema. A tribe of spiral microbes responsible for a number of infectious diseases, including syphilis (47).

Triceps. The muscle that extends the forearm.

Trichinosis (*trichiniasis*). A parasitic disease due to ingestion of encysted larvae of worms present in raw or undercooked pork (67).

Trichobezoar. A ball of hair in the stomach.

Trichomoniasis. A quite common infestation of the vagina with minute pear-shaped creatures which have tiny propellers for getting about (412). Their presence produces vaginal irritation and a thin, white, watery, offensive discharge. Men may be affected too but often have no symptoms. Local methods of treatment by insufflation of powders, medicated douches, etc., give relief but the organisms are hard to eradicate. Infection may be re-transmitted by marital partners and for total eradication, both partners may be treated. A new oral drug, *metronidazole*, is highly effective in eradicating the infection.

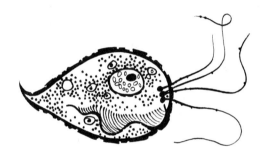

Trichomonad, the causative organism of trichomoniasis.

Trichophytosis. Ringworm of the scalp (189). The causative fungi fluoresce when exposed to a WOOD'S LIGHT. The condition, which is contagious, occurs in children before puberty.

Trichotillomania. A neurotic habit of pulling out one's own hair.

Tricuspid valve. A valve with three triangular-shaped leaflets through which blood moves from auricle to ventricle in the right side of the heart (76, 99).

Trigeminal neuralgia. See TIC DOULOUREUX.

Trigger finger. A condition in which efforts to unbend a finger are at first unsuccessful, but it is soon straightened with a snap or a jerk, like the release of a trigger. It is caused by a constriction which prevents free movement of a tendon in its sheath (612).

Trimester. Three months, or one-third of the nine months of pregnancy. The nine months of pregnancy are divided into the first, second, and third trimester.

Trismus. Spasmodic tightening of muscles of the jaw, as in lockjaw.

Trocar. A perforating instrument for puncturing a cavity to release fluid; it fits inside a *cannula.*

Tropical ulcer. Chronic, tissue-destroying ulceration of the lower leg or foot, caused by a spirochete (50).

Trypanosomiasis. African sleeping sickness, produced by organisms transmitted to the blood by the bite of an infected insect (71).

TSH. Thyroid-stimulating hormone (305).

Truss. A device, usually a pad attached to a belt, designed to hold in place a HERNIA or internal organ which tends to protrude through the skin.

Trypsin. A protein-digesting enzyme produced by the pancreas gland.

Tryptophan. One of the essential AMINO ACIDS. It is frequently inadequate in food protein of plant origin.

Tsutsugamushi disease. See SCRUB TYPHUS.

Tubal ligation (*salpingectomy*). An operation for sterilization of women. The surgeon makes a small incision in the abdomen and cuts and ties the OVIDUCTS (350). This prevents the meeting of sperm and egg and makes conception impossible. The procedure is comparable to an appendix operation and is always performed in a hospital. It is frequently performed a few hours

after delivery of a baby but can be done at any time for a non-pregnant woman. Tubal ligation does not interfere with menstruation or sexual capacity; the ovaries continue to produce hormones. The operation should not be undertaken unless permanent sterility is desired, for although fertility has been restored in some cases by rejoining the tubes, successful reversal cannot be assured.

Tubal pregnancy. Implantation of a fertilized egg in the walls of the Fallopian tube instead of in the uterus; the most common form of ECTOPIC PREGNANCY (353).

Tubercle. A small nodule or prominence; especially, a mass of small spherical cells produced by tubercle bacilli that is characteristic of tuberculosis. The word also means a rough, rounded prominence on a bone.

Tuberculin test. A skin test for tuberculosis (209). There are several modifications of the test; the MANTOUX TEST is usually employed in routine case-finding. Tuberculin in various forms is a sterile fluid containing substances extracted from dead tuberculosis germs. Tissues of a person with tuberculous infection are hypersensitive to products of tubercle bacilli. Injection of a small amount of tuberculin under the skin gives a positive or negative reaction. A positive reaction, indicated by redness and swelling of the injected area within a few hours, indicates the presence of tuberculous infection but does not tell whether the infection is active or inactive. It merely indicates that tuberculous infection was acquired at some time, and appropriate measures can be taken.

Tubule. A little tube; any minute tubular structure, such as the kidney tubules or the semeniferous tubules of the testes.

Tularemia. Rabbit fever (46).

Tumefaction. Swelling.

Turbinates. Scroll-shaped bones of the outer sidewalls of the nasal cavity, covered by spongy tissue which moistens and "air conditions" inhaled air (577).

Turner's syndrome. A congenital condition in which the ovaries do not mature or produce egg cells (328). The affected girl develops along female lines but breast enlargement and menstruation do not occur at puberty, unless the condition is recognized early and treated with female hormones; however, the patient is permanently sterile. A woman with Turner's syndrome has only 45 instead of the normal 46 CHROMOSOMES. One sex chromosome is missing. A normal woman has two XX (female-determining) chromosones; in Turner's syndrome, one X chromosome is lacking. Its absence results in ovaries lacking egg-producing follicles, and there is retardation of body growth; ultimate stature is usually less than five feet. With judicious hormone therapy the affected woman can live a reasonably normal life but can never bear children.

Tussis. A cough.

Twins. See MULTIPLE BIRTHS.

Tympanites. Taut distention of the abdomen by intestinal gases or fluids; bloating.

Tympanoplasty. Plastic surgery of the middle ear, to close a punctured eardrum (573) or to clean out and reconstruct the cavity (727).

Tympanum. The middle ear and the eardrum, the *tympanic membrane* (559).

Typhoid fever. Acute feverish illness caused by germs of the Salmonella family, contained in the feces of infected patients and unknowing carriers; usually transmitted by contaminated water or food or poor personal hygiene (43). Modern sanitation, alert health departments, and medical prog-

ress have made typhoid fever a rare disease in the U.S. where it was once common, feared, disabling, and often deadly. An antibiotic, chloramphenicol, is very effective in treating typhoid fever. Vaccination against the disease (three inoculations a week or more apart, and an annual booster dose if one remains in an infected area) is recommended for travelers to regions where typhoid fever is endemic, but not for the general population in this country (400).

Typhus. A RICKETTSIAL DISEASE transmitted to man by infected lice and fleas, with rats and mice as intermediaries. There are several varieties of typhus (63). The disease has not existed in the U.S. for many years, but is endemic in parts of Asia, the near East, India, and other areas. Vaccination is recommended for travelers to such areas (51).

U

Ulcer. An open sore with an inflamed base; local disintegration of tissues of the skin or mucous membranes, leaving a raw, sometimes running surface. The cause may be infection, pressure (as in BEDSORES), erosive irritation (PEPTIC ULCER), varicosities, systemic disease, impaired circulation.

Ulcerative colitis. Inflammation of the colon and rectum, characterized by sores or ulcers inside the tube and bloody diarrhea. The disease may be mild and responsive to medical treatment or so severe as to require surgical removal of the affected part of the colon (468, 703).

Ulceromembranous stomatitis. TRENCH MOUTH.

Ulna. The bone on the side of the forearm opposite to the thumb; its companion bone is the RADIUS (593).

Ultrasound. Sound waves of high frequencies above the range of human hearing. Ultrasonic devices of various and changing design have several medical uses. Instruments which register the "echoes" of ultrasound have been used to locate and define brain tumors, to locate the position of the placenta and fetus, and to identify the site and severity of arterial obstruction by registering the rate of blood flow in deep vessels. Therapeutically, ultrasonic equipment is used to clean tartar from teeth, to treat bursitis, and an ultrasound "probe" has had some success in destroying nerve endings in the inner ear, without damage to hearing and the sense of equilibrium, in patients with MENIERE'S DISEASE (257, 728) who have not responded to medical treatment.

Ultraviolet rays. Wavelengths of radiation too short to be seen as visible light. They lie between the wavelengths of visible light and x-rays. The spectrum of visible light runs from short violet rays to long red rays. The sequence of colors in a rainbow or sunlight scattered by a prism is incorporated in a memory-aiding word, VIBGYOR: violet, indigo, blue, green, yellow, orange, red. Beyond red lie the long, invisible and hot *infra-red rays*, emanated by special lamps sometimes used to deliver dry heat to parts of the body. Ultraviolet rays contained in sunshine or produced by ultraviolet lamps (sunlamps) act upon substances in the skin to make vitamin D. They also produce a skin tan (see SUNBURN). These are the only known benefits of ultraviolet rays in moderation. Excessive exposure to natural or artificial ultraviolet radiation can produce severe burns and age the skin prematurely. It is wise to ask for and follow a physician's advice about the use of sunlamps.

Umbilical cord. The long flexible tube which is attached to the PLACENTA at one end and to the abdomen of the fetus at the other (341). It is the lifeline of the fetus. Through vessels of the cord the fetus receives nutrients and disposes of wastes without effort. The cord allows considerable freedom of movement in the dark fluid cavern of the womb. The cord continues to function until it is tied and severed at birth. After that the newborn human being is on his own.

Umbilical hernia. A protrusion of the intestines through a weakness in the abdominal wall in the region of the navel, not uncommon in infants (391).

Umbilicated. Depressed like a navel.

Umbilicus. The navel, belly-button; a depressed round scar in the middle of the abdomen, permanent memorial to umbilical vessels that nourished the fetus via the placenta.

Uncinaria. HOOKWORMS (67).

Underweight. Body weight 10 per cent less than desirable weight (481) is usually considered to be underweight. However, healthy people vary in bone and muscle proportions and rates of energy expenditure. Underweight may be a symptom of some disease process and should be evaluated by a doctor; sudden unexplained loss of weight requires medical investigation. What is thought to be underweight may be only a mother's expectation that a child ought to eat more and be chubbier. Simple underweight should respond to an increase in food calories (487). In addition to calories, plenty of rest, relaxation, and easing of tensions may be necessary in energetic, restless, overcommitted, hard-driving underweight people who burn their candles at both ends.

Undescended testicles. See CRYPTORCHIDISM (299, 324).

Undulant fever. See BRUCELLOSIS.

Ungual. Pertaining to the nails.

Unguentum. An ointment.

Uniovular. Pertaining to or originating from a single egg, as identical twins.

Universal donor. A person with Type O blood does not have "factors" which would antagonize blood of Types A, B, or AB, and hence is presumably compatible with all blood types. However, there are many blood factors besides the ABO group (Rh, M, N, Lewis, Kell, Duffy, Lutheran, and others) which may make the blood of a Type O donor antagonistic to a recipient. A universal donor's blood may be given in an emergency, but cross-matching of blood is necessary for greatest safety in transfusions (140).

Unsaturated fats. See POLYUNSATURATED FATS.

Upper respiratory infection. Infection of nasal passages or throat above the lungs. An infection may extend from the original site of symptoms. See page 1016.

Urea. A nitrogen-containing substance in blood and urine, formed mainly from nitrogen groups removed in the liver from the AMINO ACIDS of protein foods. Some is formed from nitrogen released by the wear and tear of body tissues. Increasing the protein portion of the diet increases the output of urea in the urine. The *urea clearance test* of blood is a test of kidney function.

Uremia. Presence in the blood of toxic substances due to incapacity of the kidney to filter and excrete them in urine; *uremic poisoning* (280, 283). Symptoms may develop in a few hours or over a period of weeks: headache, dimness of vision, drowsiness, restlessness; later, diarrhea and vomiting, difficult breathing during the night, convulsions, coma, death. It is the way in which serious kidney disease usually terminates. It is this condition of dammed-up toxins that the ARTIFICIAL KIDNEY is designed to overcome (284).

Ureter. The narrow tube through which urine from the kidneys passes into the bladder (273). Urine is not drawn down the tube by gravity nor does it descend in a steady flow. The ureter has walls of smooth muscle which contract in waves (PERISTALSIS) to move urine into the bladder in jets which occur from one to five times a minute.

Urethra. The canal from the neck of the bladder to the outside through which urine is passed. The female urethra is about an inch and a half long; the male urethra, eight to nine inches (269). Voiding of urine is regulated by circularly arranged sphincter muscles which in the adult are largely under voluntary control.

Urethritis. Inflammation of the URETHRA.

Uric acid. A nitrogen-containing compound present in normal blood and urine. It is derived from substances in the nuclei of cells called *purines,* in which liver, sweetbreads, kidney and other glandular meats are particularly rich. An excess of uric acid products is characteristic of GOUT (631), a disorder in which tiny, spiky urate crystals tend to be deposited in cartilage with "red hot" intimations of their presence.

Uricemia. Excessive URIC ACID in the blood.

Urinalysis. Inspection and chemical analysis of urine. The extent of analysis depends on what the doctor wants to find out. At the minimum, observations of color, clarity, specific gravity, acidity, sugar, and ALBUMIN content are usually made. More extensive microscopic or chemical analysis of possible constituents—pus, bile, blood cells, protein, crystals, casts—may be necessary to throw light on what is going on in the body (274).

Urine. The amber-colored, slightly acid fluid secreted by the kidneys. It is mostly water but normally contains about four per cent of dissolved materials such as salt, ammonia, urea, uric acid, hormones or their breakdown products. Excessive or deficient

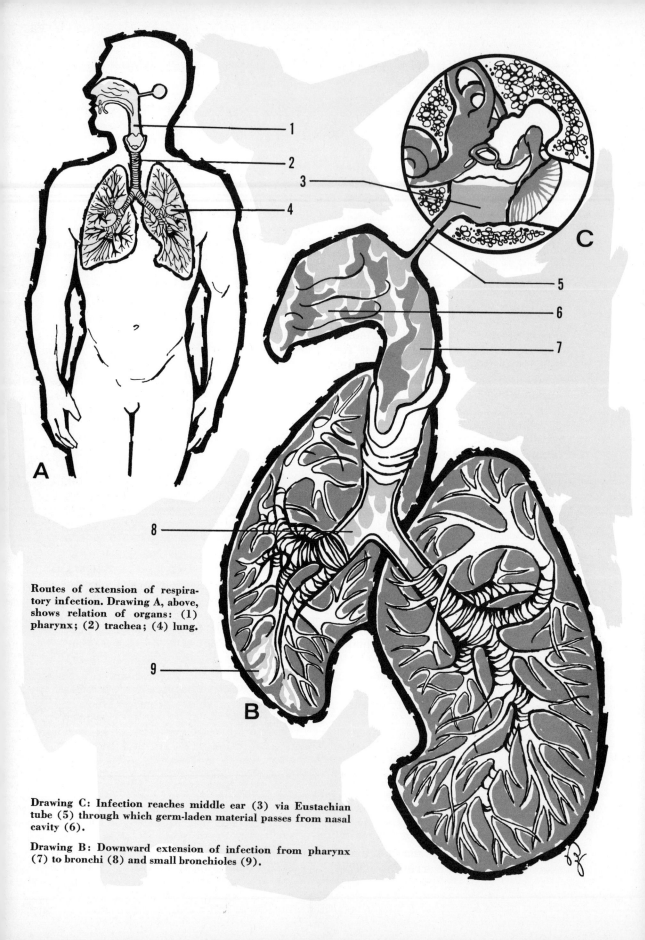

Routes of extension of respiratory infection. Drawing A, above, shows relation of organs: (1) pharynx; (2) trachea; (4) lung.

Drawing C: Infection reaches middle ear (3) via Eustachian tube (5) through which germ-laden material passes from nasal cavity (6).

Drawing B: Downward extension of infection from pharynx (7) to bronchi (8) and small bronchioles (9).

amounts of normal constituents may indicate disease, and abnormal constituents—fat, blood, pus, bacteria, spermatozoa, bile—almost always do. Acidity of the urine varies with the diet. Most fruits reduce the acidity of the diet; starvation or a high protein diet increases it. Acidity of the urine indicates that the kidneys are doing their job of maintaining the slight alkalinity of the blood (see ACID-BASE BALANCE). The average adult forms about three pints of urine a day. The volume of urine is reduced in hot weather, by strenuous muscular exercise or scanty fluid intake, and is greater on a high than a low protein diet. The most concentrated urine is passed after getting up in the morning. Doctors have good reason for specifying that a sample of urine should be taken at a certain time. Formation of urine is decreased during sleep; decided and persistent increase of volume of night urine, with many gettings-up, may be a sign of chronic kidney or other disease. The yellow pigment that gives urine its color is called *urochrome.*

Urogenital. Pertaining to the urinary and genital organs.

Urogram. X-ray visualization of the urinary tract made after injecting a radiopaque substance.

Urologist. A medical specialist in diseases of the urinary tract in females and of the urogenital tract in males.

Uroscopy. Examination of urine.

Urticaria (*hives, nettlerash*). Whitish, intensely itching elevations of the skin, wheals or welts, resembling mosquito bites but usually larger, sometimes covering patches as large as the palm (666). An attack may be a solitary event, never again experienced, subsiding in a few days, but in some instances urticaria is miserably repeated and persistent. Frequently the condition is an allergic reaction to certain foods (strawberries, shellfish, etc.), to drugs (674), to cold (675), to heat or sunlight (676).

Urushiol. The despicable oil in poison ivy and poison oak that causes skin eruptions.

U.S.P. United States Pharmacopoeia.

Uterine displacements. "Tipped uterus"; backward, forward, or sideward shift of the uterus, or a "fallen womb" protruding into the vagina (415).

Uterine tubes. The Fallopian tubes; OVIDUCTS.

Uterosalpingography. X-rays of the uterus and tubes, following injection of iodized oil into the uterus, to determine whether the tubes are open (330).

Uterus. The womb; the pear-shaped, muscular, hollow, distensible nesting-place of the fetus in pregnancy (341). In the adult non-pregnant woman the uterus is about three inches long, two and a half inches wide near the top, tapering to a neck (*cervix*) about an inch wide, which occupies the upper part of the vagina. It has walls of smooth muscle like thick felt with a lining of mucous membrane (ENDOMETRIUM). Its triangular cavity, a mere slit, is continuous with a narrow canal through its neck which affords an entrance for SPERMATOZOA and an exit for menstrual discharges. The uterus lies between the bladder and the rectum, tilted forward, its upper part resting on the bladder. It is rather loosely supported by eight LIGAMENTS which allow freedom of motion and position in adjusting to pressures of surrounding organs and enlargement of pregnancy. The organ enlarges slightly during menstruation, enormously during pregnancy, and after childbirth returns almost to its previous size but its cavity is larger than before.

Uvea. Pigmentary layers of the eye: the IRIS, CILIARY BODY, and CHOROID coat, composed largely of interlaced blood vessels vital to the eye's nutrition (529).

Uveitis. Non-pus forming inflammation of the UVEA, the IRIS and associated eye structures (547). It is a serious condition that can cause blindness. It may be associated with systemic diseases (TOXOPLASMOSIS, HISTOPLASMOSIS, LEPTOSPIROSIS), but there are many types of uveal inflammation for which no specific cause can be found. One form is thought to be an AUTOIMMUNE DISEASE resulting from a patient's sensitization to tissues of the lens of his own eyes.

Uvula. The blob of tissue hanging like a big tear from the soft palate at the back of the mouth. You can see it with a mirror by opening your mouth wide and depressing the tongue (403). It rarely causes any trouble, except that it may be implicated in snoring, but generally that does not trouble the snorer.

V

Vaccine. The word derives from the Latin word for "cow," the source of cowpox virus used to vaccinate against smallpox. It has come to mean any bacterial or viral material for inoculation against a specific disease. Virus vaccines are of two types, *live virus* or *killed virus* vaccines. Live virus vaccines contain living viruses, so weakened that they cannot cause significant disease, but still can stimulate the body powerfully to make protective ANTIBODIES against a particular disease. For example, SABIN VACCINE contains live viruses, so weakened in the laboratory that they produce only unnoticeable infection but stimulate antibody production that persists for a long time, perhaps a lifetime. Killed virus vaccines contain viruses treated by physical or chemical means to kill or inactivate them so they cannot cause disease but nevertheless can stimulate immunity-producing mecha-

nisms of the body. SALK VACCINE is of this type. In general, live virus vaccines are more potent and create longer lasting immunity than killed virus vaccines.

Vaccinia. Cowpox; a disease of cattle caused by viruses which, inoculated into man, create immunity to smallpox. Babies should be vaccinated against smallpox before they are a year old unless there is a medical reason for postponing it (infants with eczema, impetigo, or skin rashes should not be vaccinated until the condition clears up, nor should they be in close contact with others who have just been vaccinated). About three days after smallpox vaccination a red pimple appears at the site of inoculation, enlarges, gets blistery, and is surrounded by a reddened area about the size of a quarter. The lesion begins to dry in a week to ten days. It forms a scab which falls off by the end of the third week or sooner, leaving a flat whitish vaccination mark which some persons prefer to have elsewhere than on the arm. Reaction to one's first smallpox vaccination is a "primary take." Reactions in persons who have been vaccinated previously are milder, but if there is no reaction at all it does not mean that one is naturally immune, but that the vaccine was weak or did not get through the skin.

Vacuole. A clear space in tissue.

Vacuum extractor. A cuplike device within which a partial vacuum is created when it is placed over the presenting part of a baby's head during childbirth. The adherent cup with its handle facilitates extraction of the baby and the device is sometimes used in delivery as a substitute for obstetric forceps.

Vagina. A sheath; the female organ of copulation, a muscular canal lined with mucous membrane which opens at the surface of the body and extends inward to the cervix of the uterus (406, 415).

Vaginal diaphragm. A contraceptive device consisting of a spring-rimmed rubber dome inserted into the vagina to cover the cervix.

Vaginal hysterectomy. Surgical removal of the uterus through the vagina (707).

Vaginismus. Painful, spastic constriction of female pelvic muscles, making sexual intercourse difficult or impossible (411).

Vaginitis. Inflammation of the vagina, characterized by discharge and discomfort; see MONILIASIS and TRICHOMONIASIS (412). A form occurring after menopause is called *atrophic* or *senile vaginitis*.

Vagotomy. Cutting of certain branches of the VAGUS nerve which communicates with many organs in the chest and abdomen. The object is to diminish the flow of nerve impulses, such as those which stimulate the stomach to produce acids (699).

Vagus. The "wandering" cranial nerve which arises in the brain and extends its fibers to the pacemaker of the heart, to the bronchi, esophagus, gallbladder, pancreas, small intestine and secretory glands of the stomach.

Valsalva maneuver. Originally a technique devised by an Italian anatomist for pushing air into the middle ear by exhaling forcibly while keeping the glottis closed, so that air cannot escape from the throat. A similar condition is produced by coughing or straining at the toilet. The maneuver is used by cardiologists as a diagnostic test of congestive heart failure. Buildup of pressure within the chest and abdomen prevents the return flow of blood from the head, hands, and feet. Heart output decreases and venous blood pressure increases. When the effort is ended, a surge of venous blood into the right side of the heart causes temporary overloading of the heart chambers. The mechanism explains why some persons feel light-headed or dizzy during bowel movements or while coughing.

Valve. A structure that prevents backflow of fluids. There are valves in the heart (100), in many veins, at the stomach outlet, and at junctions along many tubular communication lines, to keep blood or fluid materials moving in the right direction.

van den Bergh test. A qualitative test of blood serum, useful in determining the origin of different types of JAUNDICE and measurements of liver function.

Varicella. Chickenpox (398).

Varices. VARICOSE VEINS.

Varicocele. Varicosed, dilated, twisted veins of the spermatic cord; a soft mass in the SCROTUM that feels like a bag of worms. The condition occurs most frequently in adolescence and tends to disappear with maturity. Usually it is a minor affliction, often undetected, causing no discomfort, or sometimes a slight draggy feeling relieved by wearing a suspensory. Varicocele does not significantly affect the health of the testes or lead to impotence or sterility. Only the most distressing cases warrant surgery.

Varicose veins. Swollen, dilated, knotted, tortuous veins (126). The sites most frequently affected are the legs and anus (HEMORRHOIDS). Varicose veins frequently develop during or are aggravated by pregnancy (347).

Variola. Smallpox.

Variola minor (*alastrim*). A mild form of smallpox. Symptoms are similar to those of virulent smallpox (400) but much less severe; fatalities are very rare. Standard smallpox vaccination protects also against this mild form of the disease.

Vas. A tube or vessel, usually but not always a blood or lymphatic vessel.

Vascular. Pertaining to or abundant in vessels, especially blood vessels. Well-vascularized tissues have abundant blood supply; *avascular* tissues such as the CORNEA have none at all.

Vas deferens. The duct through which SPERMATOZOA are transported from the testicle to the seminal vesicles and urethra (298).

Vasectomy. A relatively simple surgical procedure for sterilization of the male. The excretory duct of the testis (*vas deferens*, 298-99) is severed or a portion cut out of it to prevent SPERMATOZOA from entering into the SEMEN. The structures are close to the surface and the operation is usually done in the doctor's office under local anesthesia. There is no interference with sexual capacity since the hormone-producing tissues of the testicle are not affected. It is prudent to regard the sterilization as permanent, although in a few cases the severed ends of the ducts have been rejoined, with restoration of fertility.

Vasoconstrictor. A drug or natural body substance or mechanism that clamps down on small blood vessels, narrows their caliber and reduces the volume of blood flowing through them. This action, rather like that of myriads of tiny tourniquets, increases the amount of blood in the reservoirs of big expansible arteries and increases blood pressure until matters come into balance.

Vasodilator. An agent that dilates small blood vessels so that more blood flows through them; blood pressure is usually lowered. If it happens locally, one blushes. The opposite of VASOCONSTRICTOR.

Vasomotor. Pertaining to mechanisms that control dilation or constriction of walls of blood vessels, and thus the volume of blood flowing through them. Impulses from centers in the brain go to muscle fibers in walls of blood vessels over nerves of opposite action: constriction or dilation. Feedback mechanisms of the vasomotor system are exceedingly intricate. In hemorrhage, for instance, the fall in blood pressure caused by loss of blood triggers the vasomotor machinery to constrict blood vessels and speed the heart, which tends to restore blood pressure to normal.

VDRL test. A screening test for syphilis using blood serum (Venereal Disease Research Laboratory).

Vector. A carrier, spreader of disease; especially, an insect or animal host that carries disease germs that infect people.

Veins. Thin-walled, strong, low-pressure vessels that collect dark "used" blood from tissues and carry it to the heart to be pumped through the lungs, where the blood dumps a load of carbon dioxide and takes on a load of oxygen. Blood from capillaries is collected into *venules* (very tiny veins) which

VEIN CHART →
1. axillary
2. superior vena cava
3. right atrium (heart)
4. inferior vena cava
5. hepatic
6. portal
7. pancreaticoduodenal
8. superior mesenteric
9. hypogastric
10. femoral
11. anterior tibial
12. peroneal
13. superior sagittal sinus
14. external carotid
15. internal carotid
16. subclavian
17. innominate
18. pulmonary veins
19. gastric
20. splenic
21. ulnar
22. radial
23. inferior mesenteric
24. median
25. external iliac
26. great saphenous
27. popliteal
28. posterior tibial
29. marginal
30. cephalic
31. brachial
32. basilic

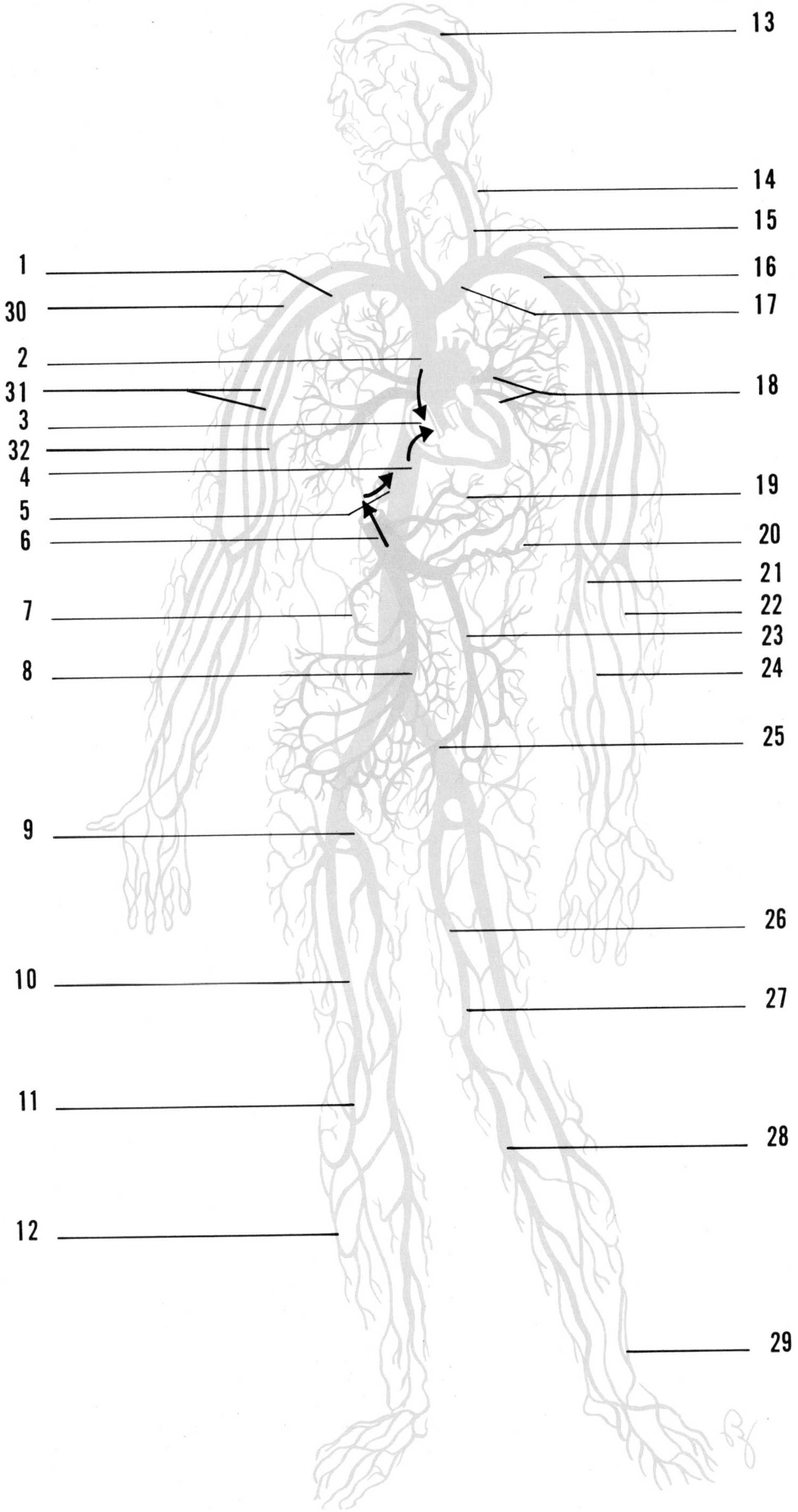
1
30
2
31
3
32
4
5
6
7
8
9
10
11
12
13
14
15
16
17
18
19
20
21
22
23
24
25
26
27
28
29

enter into larger veins and finally into the *vena cava* which opens into the right auricle of the heart (75). When a vein is cut the blood wells out in a steady flow with no evident pressure. Veins are capable of great dilation and can hold large reservoirs of blood.

Venereal warts. CONDYLOMA ACUMINATA.

Venesection. Bloodletting; same as PHLEBOTOMY.

Venoclysis. Injection of fluids by vein. A vein of the wrist is preferred but is sometimes too small, inaccessible, or shrunken, and a vein of the leg, foot, or thigh may be used.

Ventral. The belly side; the aspect of a part directed toward the belly.

Ventricle. A small cavity or chamber; especially, the ventricles of the heart and brain. The lower part of the heart has a right ventricle which receives venous blood and pumps it to the lungs, and a left ventricle which receives oxygenated blood from the lungs and pumps it to the body (74). The brain has several ventricles filled with CEREBROSPINAL FLUID (259). Increased volume and pressure of fluid in brain ventricles, due to impaired drainage, results in HYDROCEPHALUS (260).

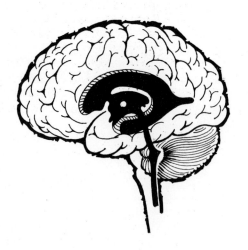

Ventricles of the brain.

Ventriculogram. An x-ray of the brain taken after introducing air or a contrast medium into certain ventricles.

Venules. The smallest veins, communicating with capillaries.

Vermiform. Worm-shaped.

Vermifuge. An agent that kills or expels intestinal worms.

Vernix caseosa. A greasy, cheesy substance that covers the skin of the fetus.

Verruca. A wart.

Version. Turning, manipulation of the fetus in the uterus to attain a better position for delivery, as PODALIC VERSION.

Vertebra (pl., *vertebrae*). One of the 33 bones which constitute the backbone (593). Vertebrae are flat, roughly circular bones with knobs for muscle attachments and a hole in the middle for passage of the great nerve trunk, the spinal cord. Individual vertebrae, except the four which are fused to form the COCCYX, are separated by pads of elastic cartilage (*intervertebral disks*) which absorb shocks and give flexibility.

Vertex. The highest point of the skull, the topmost part of the head.

Vertigo. See DIZZINESS.

Vesicant. An agent that produces blisters.

Vesicle. A small sac containing fluid; a tiny bladder, like a skin blister.

Viable. Capable of living.

Vibrissae. Hairs in the nose. Also, a cat's whiskers.

Villi. Minute fingerlike projections from the surface of a mucous membrane. The small intestine contains millions of villi which increase the surface area in contact with foods and give the lining of the tract a velvety feel (434).

Vincent's infection. TRENCH MOUTH (37, 511).

Virilism. Development in a female of masculine characteristics (beard growth, deep voice, etc.), usually due to a masculinizing tumor of the ovary, overactivity of the cortex of the adrenal glands, or administration of androgenic hormones (328).

Viruses. Molecules that cause disease (52).

Visceroptosis. Sagging of abdominal organs from their normal position.

Viscid. Sticky, adhesive.

Viscus (pl., *viscera*). An internal organ, especially one of the large ones in the abdominal cavity.

Visual field. The area of physical space seen when the gaze is fixed straight ahead (534, 536).

Visual purple. A pigment produced by RODS of the RETINA, essential for good vision in dim light. The purplish pigment bleaches to yellow when exposed to light. A product of its breakdown is vitamin A, which is also needed for its regeneration. Severe deficiency of vitamin A causes night blindness because of inability of visual purple to regenerate adequately.

Visual radiations. Nerve fibers which fray out to the rear of the brain where what we see is actually seen (533).

Vitiligo (*leukoderma*). Piebald skin; irregular white patches of skin, sometimes streaks of white or gray hair, due to lack of pigment. Often there is a family tendency to develop the condition. The white patches are most conspicuous when surrounded by deeply tanned skin. No infallible way of inducing repigmentation of the spotty patches is known, but in some instances the taking of an oral drug, *methoxypsoralen*, followed by controlled exposure to sunlight, may produce some deposit of pigment. However, results are uncertain and the treatment may cause some irritation of affected areas and excessive pigmentation of surrounding skin. Vitiligo is not a systemic disease but a purely cosmetic defect which, if distressing, can usually be covered satisfactorily with a tinted preparation.

Vitreous humor. Transparent, colorless, soft gelatinous material which fills the eyeball behind the lens (527).

Volvulus. Twisting or knotting of the bowel, leading to intestinal obstruction and GANGRENE of the part (461).

Vomiting. Forcible ejection of stomach contents, triggered by a vomiting center in the brain; a protective mechanism for getting rid of toxic or irritating materials. Rats do not have a vomiting center and consequently may be poisoned by substances which vomiting mammals get rid of with ease. Ordinarily, vomiting is a transient event of no great significance in itself, provoked by gastric indiscretion, motion sickness, or some infectious illness accompanied by other symptoms. Simple vomiting from minor intestinal upsets can be managed rather simply (376). However, PROJECTILE VOMITING or COFFEE-GROUND VOMIT is a symptom requiring immediate investigation. Intractable, long-continued vomiting (or diarrhea) can seriously deplete body fluids and ELECTROLYTES, especially in infants who have small reserves. Common causes of "ordinary" infant vomiting are stomach dilation from *overfeeding* (too frequent feedings or too much at a time) or *underfeeding*, leading to hunger, crying, lots of air-swallowing and distention. Too hot feedings may induce vomiting. Formulas at room temperature are quite acceptable, and sometimes vomiting may be controlled by ice-cold feedings.

von Gierke's disease. GLYCOGEN STORAGE DISEASE with liver and kidney involvement.

von Recklinghausen's disease. See NEUROFIBROMATOSIS.

Vulva. The external female sex parts.

Vulvovaginitis. Inflammation of both the VULVA and VAGINA. A rare but severe gonorrheal form occasionally is transmitted to female infants and children by careless hygiene. See TRICHOMONIASIS and MONILIASIS.

W

Wall-eye. Outward turning of an eye; divergent squint, a condition of ocular muscle imbalance (542).

Warts. Harmless but unsightly small growths from the skin (181). Common warts of the hands, face, and feet, most frequent in children, are caused by viruses, are contagious, and the sufferer can re-inoculate himself over and over again. Common warts can be removed by a great variety of methods, including hocus-pocus, and they tend to disappear in time with no treatment at all. An isolated wart is probably best left alone, unless it is very disfiguring or painful, or is enlarging or changing its appearance, or is in a part of the body subject to constant irritation.

Warts at the edges of fingernails or underneath them are hard to treat; applications of cold—dry ice or liquid nitrogen—are commonly used. Warts in the scalp or beard area are especially troublesome because shaving and combing the hair tend to spread them. A man with warts in the beard area should use an electric shaver.

Wassermann test. The original blood test for syphilis. It is not specific for syphilis; "false positive" reactions may be produced by malaria, hepatitis, mononucleosis, and other unrelated diseases. Many newer tests (sometimes used in conjunction with Wassermann-type tests) have been developed: Kline, Kahn, Mazzini, Hinton, VDRL, Eagle, and others. One of the most specific tests for syphilis is the *treponema immobilization test* (TPI). Blood tests required by many states for issuance of a marriage license employ one or another of these procedures.

Waterhouse-Friderichsen syndrome. Overwhelming meningococcal infection in children, characterized by convulsions, collapse of the circulatory system, and bleeding into the adrenal glands.

Water on the brain. HYDROCEPHALUS (259).

Wax epilation. A method of removing superfluous hair, usually of the legs or lips. A waxy compound is warmed to make it fluid and a layer is applied in the direction in which the hair lies. After the layer has hardened, the sheet is pulled sharply against the direction of hair growth. Imbedded hairs are pulled out by the roots. The hair follicle is not permanently destroyed, as it is in ELECTROLYSIS. Fine hair tips reappear in two or three weeks, but wax epilation does not leave a stubble as shaving does. Repeated wax epilation tends to damage some follicles and in time to reduce the number of hairs. Slight irritation lasts for a few hours after wax epilation. The treatment is considered to be safe in competent hands, but the skin of some women will not tolerate it.

W.B.C. White blood cell count.

Webbed fingers. Connection of adjacent fingers (or toes) by a thin fold of skin between them (621).

Weber test. A hearing test to determine which ear hears better by bone conduction. It is performed by touching a vibrating tuning fork to various parts of the head.

Weil's disease. An acute feverish illness caused by spirochetes (50), also called *infectious jaundice*. A severe form of LEPTOSPIROSIS.

Wen. A sebaceous cyst, a skin tumor ranging up to the size of a marble or larger, filled with cheesy material; movable, firm, rarely painful (196). Wens usually occur on the scalp, face, or back, and result from obstruction of an oil-secreting gland.

Wetzel grid. A chart for plotting, comparing, and projecting the height, weight, and other growth aspects of children.

Wheals. Hives; temporary skin swellings resembling mosquito bites, but often much larger (666). Wheals may result from allergies, drugs, irritants, or injection of substances in skin tests of sensitivities.

Whiplash injury. A popular term for injury sustained when the head is suddenly thrown forward and jerked backward, as in cracking a whip (606). The injury is something like a "sprained neck"; muscles and ligaments may be strained and torn but bones and nerves are rarely damaged.

Whipple's disease. A rare progressive disease of unknown cause characterized by multiple arthritis, fever, fatty stools, lymph gland enlargement, diarrhea, loss of weight and strength, and abnormalities of the small intestine. Antibiotic treatment continued for many months may reverse the course of the disease, which may possibly be of bacterial origin.

Whipworms. Slender worms which inhabit the CECUM of dogs, pigs, sheep and goats. Their eggs can be transmitted to man by contact with contaminated soil (67). The infection may be symptomless or it may produce diarrhea or acute appendicitis.

Whites. Vaginal discharge; see LEUKORRHEA.

Whitlow. See PARONYCHIA.

Whooping cough (*pertussis*). A serious but preventable disease of childhood, especially dangerous and sometimes fatal in young infants whom it readily attacks (402). Active immunization of all infants with an effective vaccine (often combined with *diphtheria* and *tetanus* toxoids) should be started between six and 12 weeks of age.

Widal test. An ANTIBODY test of blood for diagnosis of typhoid fever.

Wilms tumor. A malignant tumor of the kidney occurring in children (283). The tumor may first be noticed as an abdominal mass by mothers in caring for their babies. Early discovery and immediate treatment (surgery and radiation) give the best hope of permanent cure. Simultaneous administration of *dactinomycin,* an antibiotic which causes the tumor to regress, has recently been shown to improve the chances of cure.

Wilson's disease (*hepatolenticular degeneration*). A disease inherited as a recessive trait (see HEREDITY). Abnormal deposits of copper in many tissues, especially the brain, eyes, kidneys, and liver, cause damage producing various symptoms as the disease progresses: tremor, clumsiness, psychic disturbances, weakness, emaciation, blue half-moons of the nails, retraction of the upper lip exposing the upper teeth. Treatment is directed to decreasing the intake of copper-rich foods (chocolate, molasses, shellfish, kale, liver, peas, nuts, corn, whole-grain cereals, dried beans, mushrooms, lamb, pork, dark meat of chicken), and use of drugs to prevent absorption of copper and speed its excretion (488).

Witch's milk. A milk-like secretion, resembling COLOSTRUM, exuded from the breasts of newborn infants of either sex. If left alone, the secretion dwindles and disappears in a few days. Temporary enlargement of the breasts of newborn infants is not uncommon. In some instances the structure of the infant's breast closely resembles that of the lactating adult breast. In the uterus the fetus receives some estrogen (female hormone) from the mother. Withdrawal of this estrogen supply after birth presumably stimulates the production of witch's milk for a brief time.

Withdrawal symptoms. Physical reactions to withdrawal of certain drugs (narcotics, barbiturates) from persons addicted to them, who have established physical dependence on the drug. The patient has nausea, diarrhea, a runny nose, watery eyes, chills, waves of gooseflesh. His arms and legs ache, muscles twitch, he perspires and even in hot weather may cover himself with a heavy blanket. Usually the worst of the withdrawal symptoms are over within a week although complete recovery may take as long as six months.

Womb. The UTERUS.

Wood's light. A device used in diagnosing ringworm of the scalp. Light passed through a special glass filter causes certain fungi to fluoresce.

Wool-sorter's disease. So named because of its occurrence in persons who handle raw animal hides and hairs; *anthrax* (47).

Wrist drop. Drooping of the hand at the wrist, inability to lift or extend it, due to paralysis or injury of muscles or tendons which extend the fingers and hands.

X

Xanthelasma. A form of XANTHOMA occurring as soft yellow-colored plaques on the eyelids (183).

Xanthoma. "Yellow tumor"; a yellowish nodule or slightly raised patch in the skin.

Xanthomatosis. A generalized condition attended by many deposits of yellowish fatty material in tissues, due to some disturbance of CHOLESTEROL and LIPID metabolism (164). An hereditary form characterized by masses of yellowish deposits around tendons, especially in the elbows, wrists, and ankles, may appear early in life. It is transmitted as a dominant trait (see HEREDITY). In this condition (*familial hypercholesterolemia*) blood levels of cholesterol are very high and patients have a tendency to develop premature hardening of the arteries. The inborn trait cannot be corrected but blood cholesterol levels may be lowered by stringent dietary restriction of saturated fats.

Xanthopsia. "Yellow vision," a condition in which objects look yellow. It sometimes accompanies JAUNDICE.

Xanthosis. Yellow discoloration of the skin, due to eating excessive amounts of carrots, squash, sweet potatoes and yellow vegetables which contain pigments (*carotenoids*) that are deposited in the skin. The condition clears up when yellow vegetable intake is restrained.

X chromosome. The female sex-determining chromosome: females have two of them, males only one. See CHROMOSOMES. The X chromosome is larger than the Y chromosome and contains some GENES for which there are no complements on the Y chromosome.

X disease. An epidemic form of encephalitis, first recognized in Australia, now called *Murray Valley encephalitis* (59).

Xeroderma. Dry skin; a mild form of "fish skin disease" (196). A rare form, *xeroderma pigmentosum*, begins in childhood. Pigmented spots, made worse by sunlight, appear in the skin, and there is scattered TELANGIECTASIS. The skin contracts and the lesions progress to warty growths which become malignant.

Xerophthalmia. Extreme dryness of membranes which line the eyelids and front of the eye. Lack of tears may cause infection and ulceration of the CORNEA. The condition is associated with NIGHT BLINDNESS and severe deficiency of vitamin A. Specific treatment consists of prescribed daily doses of the vitamin.

Xerostomia. Dryness of the mouth, due to deficient salivary secretion, drugs, dehydration, or secondary to fevers or other diseases.

Xiphoid. Shaped like a sword; applies to the structure at the lower tip of the breastbone.

X-rays (*roentgen rays*). Electromagnetic radiation of shorter wavelength than visible light. X-rays can penetrate "solid" substances, produce shadows of structures of different densities on film, and destroy living tissues (756). Some living cells, said to be RADIOSENSITIVE, are more easily destroyed by x-rays than others; this is the basis for therapeutic use of x-rays in cancer.

Y

Yaws. A tropical disease caused by *spirochetes* resembling syphilis organisms (40). It is non-venereal, possibly is transmitted by insect bites. It is characterized by fever, rheumatic pains, red skin eruptions, and destruction of skin and bones of the nose if not treated.

Yellow fever. An acute, infectious, feverish disease caused by viruses transmitted by the bites of mosquitoes (55). The disease does not exist in the U. S. but travelers to tropical America where yellow fever is endemic should be protected by a vaccine which is highly effective.

Yellow spot. The *macula lutea,* the small spot near the center of the RETINA which is the focus of all finely detailed seeing (532).

Y chromosome. The male sex-determining chromosome. See CHROMOSOME.

Yogurt. A milk product formed by the action of acid-producing bacteria. It has the same food value as the milk from which it is made. When made from partially skimmed milk, as it often is, yogurt is lower in fat, Vitamin A, and calories than when it is made from whole milk. Yogurt is good source of the other nutrients obtained from milk, however, especially calcium, riboflavin, and protein.

Z

Zonules. Tiny slinglike processes which suspend the crystalline lens of the eye (529). *Zonulysis* is a technique of dissolving the zonules with a specific enzyme to loosen the lens for extraction in selected cases of CATARACT surgery.

Zoonoses. Diseases of animals transmissible to man.

Zoster, zona. SHINGLES.

Zygoma. The cheekbone.

Zyloprim (*allopurinol*). A drug which reduces the body's production of URIC ACID, used in treatment of GOUT.

Zygote. The fertilized egg cell before it starts to divide.

Module 3 • Set 2 • Transportation

CONTENTS

This book belongs to

. . . .

GREAT MINDS™

Great Minds® is the creator of *Eureka Math*®, *Wit & Wisdom*®, *Alexandria Plan*™, and *PhD Science*®.

Geodes® are published by Great Minds PBC in association with Wilson Language Training, publisher of Fundations®.

Credits
- *Call a Cab*: p. 14, (top left) PhotoQuest/Archive Photos/Getty Images, (top right) George Eastman House/Premium Archive/Getty Images, (center left) Glasshouse Images/Alamy Stock Photo, (center right) Motoring Picture Library/Alamy Stock Photo, (bottom left) John McKenna/Alamy Stock Photo, (bottom right) Education & Exploration 2/Alamy Stock Photo; More page, Kodda/Shutterstock.com
- *The First Car to Get That Far*: p. 9 (both), Courtesy UVM Libraries; p. 14, National Automotive History Collection, Detroit Public Library; More page, Library of Congress, Prints & Photographs Division, [LC-DIG-ggbain-03065]
- *The Golden Gate*: Title page, pp. 2–3, 5, 10, © Underwood Archives/age footstock; p. 4, © tci/Marka/age footstock; pp. 8, 12, San Francisco History Center, San Francisco Public Library; p. 14, Peter Dean/Shutterstock.com; More page, dbimages/Alamy Stock Photo
- *Fly, Amelia, Fly*: More page, Everett Historical/Shutterstock.com

Copyright © 2020 Great Minds PBC:
Call a Cab
The First Car to Get That Far
The Golden Gate
Fly, Amelia, Fly

greatminds.org

ISBN 978-1-64497-810-8

Printed in the USA

1 2 3 4 5 6 7 8 9 10 CCR 25 24 23 22 21

Call a Cab

written by
Emily Goodson

illustrated by
A. Richard Allen

▲ Child

● Adult

▲ Run.

Jog.

Lug a bag.

● This city is big.
How do you get
to the shop and back?

HANSOM CAB
1869

▲Hop in a cab!

2

But back then,
the horse had to lug a cab.

3

▲It was a big job.

It was a lot to lug.

● It was too much work
for a horse.

▲But a car?

It can lug a lot.

The cab is a car!

CHECKER CAB 1920

▲ Hop on in.

8

This cab can get you to the shop.

9

DESOTO SKYVIEW CAB
1944

▲Get your bag.

10

CHECKER CAB
1950

• Get cash to pay.
Then sit back.

11

▲ Let the cab do the job.

TAXICABS TODAY

- From then to now.
  From this place to that.

  Hip, hip, hooray
  for the taxicab!

13

ABOUT TAXICABS:
THEN & NOW

1900s

1900s

1940s

1920s

1970s

Today

MORE

In many American cities, yellow cabs are a common sight. Not all taxis are yellow, though, and at first yellow was not the most common color. Some were red. Others were black or green. Then, Albert Rockwell decided to paint his cabs yellow. He chose his wife's favorite color. He hoped his yellow cabs would stand out in traffic. They did. Rockwell's company grew to have one of the biggest taxi fleets in New York City.

John Hertz owned a fleet of cabs in Chicago. He painted them yellow after reading that it was the easiest color to see from far away. Hertz's company also grew, and soon there were yellow cabs in cities around the country.

MÁS

En muchas ciudades de Estados Unidos, es muy común ver taxis amarillos. Pero los taxis no siempre fueron amarillos. Al principio, eran de muchos colores. Algunos eran rojos. Otros eran negros o verdes. Un día, Albert Rockwell decidió pintar sus taxis de amarillo. Escogió el color preferido de su esposa con la esperanza de que sus taxis se destacaran entre todo el tránsito. Y así fue. La compañía de Rockwell creció de tal manera que llegó a tener una de las flotas de taxis más grandes de la ciudad de Nueva York.

John Hertz era el propietario de una flota de taxis en Chicago. Los pintó de amarillo después de leer que este era el color que se veía de lejos más fácilmente. La compañía de Hertz también creció y pronto hubo taxis amarillos en ciudades de todo el país.

THE FIRST CAR TO GET THAT FAR

words by Michelle Warner

illustrations by Christopher Cyr

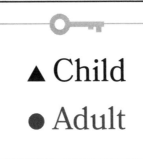

▲ Child

● Adult

On May 23, 1903, Horatio Jackson and Sewall Crocker left San Francisco to drive to New York City.

▲ The 2 men got set.

● They had a wish—
to cross the U.S. in a car.

Could they be the first?

▲ *Zig,*

zag,

zip.

● They had to rush!

But the path
had a lot of bumps.

▲ *POP!*

It was a flat!

● They had to fix it.

5

▲ *DIP!*

It was a pit!

● They had to tug
to get out of the mud.

▲ *Pip,*

pip,

pip . . .

The gas!

8

● They had to stop . . .

a lot.

9

▲ The men met
Bud the dog!

● And they met a lot of helpers.

▲ On and on and on,
   in fog
      and mud
         and sun.

● *Chug, chug, chug.*

They did not quit.

 13

▲ And . . . they did it!

● It was the first car
to get that far.

Jackson, Crocker, and Bud arrived in
New York City on July 26, 1903.

More

In 1903, Horatio Nelson Jackson and Sewall Crocker became the first men to drive across the United States. They drove from San Francisco, California, to New York City in 63 days. Six years later, Alice Ramsey became the first woman to drive across the country. Three female friends joined her. They drove from New York City to San Francisco in just 59 days.

Alice Ramsey drove a big green car. None of the other women could drive, so Alice drove the whole way. Along the way, Alice and her friends had many challenges. They got flat tires. They ran out of gas. They drove on very rough roads and even got lost. But the women met each challenge and finally made it to San Francisco.

Alice Ramsey

Más

En 1903, Horatio Nelson Jackson y Sewal Crocker se convirtieron en los primeros hombres en atravesar Estados Unidos en automóvil. Manejaron desde San Francisco, California, hasta Nueva York en 63 días. Seis años después, Alice Ramsey se convirtió en la primera mujer en atravesar el país en automóvil. La acompañaron tres amigas. Condujeron desde la ciudad de Nueva York hasta San Francisco en solo 59 días.

Alice Ramsey condujo un automóvil verde grande. Ninguna de las otras mujeres sabía conducir, así que Alice condujo todo el tiempo. Alice y sus amigas se enfrentaron a muchos desafíos en el camino. Se les pincharon llantas. Se quedaron sin gasolina. Condujeron por carreteras en muy mal estado y hasta se perdieron. Pero las mujeres superaron todos los desafíos y finalmente llegaron a San Francisco.

THE GOLDEN GATE

written by
Lior Klirs

illustrations by
Molly O'Halloran

▲ The men sit
up in the fog.

● Bit by bit,
they are building a bridge.
It will cross the big gap.

1

▲It is wet at the top,
but the men
tap and hum.

2

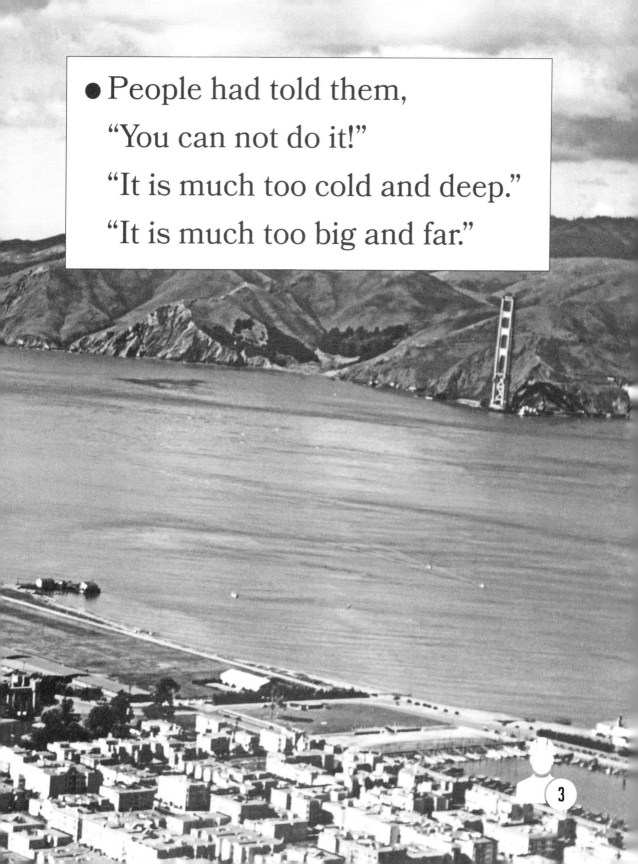

● People had told them,
"You can not do it!"
"It is much too cold and deep."
"It is much too big and far."

▲ "The job
is not too big
for us.
Let us hop to it!"

The men dash up.

5

▲ Blow it up!
Dig it up!

● The men blast the rock.
Then they dig a big pit.

▲ Mix it up!
Stack it up!

8

● Up goes the tower.

▲ Rig it up!

● The thick wires
hold up the bridge.

▲Set it up!

● The ropes hold up the road.
The men have a net
to nab them if they fall.

13

▲ The men did it.

● The Golden Gate bridge is up.

14

MORE

The Golden Gate Bridge is a suspension bridge in California. Heavy steel cables hold it up. People can walk, bike, or drive over a full mile of water on this bridge.

Not all bridges are suspension bridges. The Causeway Bridge in Louisiana crosses the wide Lake Pontchartrain. The bridge is actually more than 2,000 beam bridges linked together. Each piece is made from a special kind of concrete that is both strong and flexible. This concrete is used for very long bridges. The Causeway Bridge is 24 miles long. It is the longest bridge in the United States.

MÁS

El puente Golden Gate es un puente colgante en California. Lo suspenden fuertes cables de acero. Se lo puede atravesar en bicicleta, a pie o en automóvil por encima de una milla de agua.

No todos los puentes son colgantes. El puente Causeway de Louisiana cruza el ancho lago Pontchartrain. El puente está hecho en realidad de más de 2000 puentes de vigas conectados entre sí. Cada parte está construida con un tipo especial de hormigón que es fuerte y a la vez flexible. Este hormigón se utiliza para puentes muy largos. El puente Causeway tiene 24 millas de largo. Es el puente más largo de Estados Unidos.

Fly, Amelia, Fly

words by Tree Liberatore
illustrations by Eric Puybaret

▲ Child

● Adult

▲ The sun was up.

It was the big day.

● It was 1932.

This was Amelia.

▲ Hop in!

It was not a big jet.

But it was *her* red plane.
And she was the pilot.

3

▲ Up, up, up!

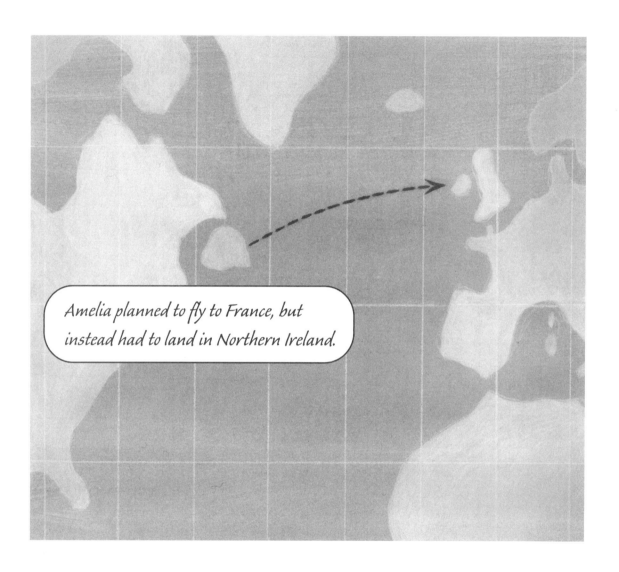

Amelia planned to fly to France, but instead had to land in Northern Ireland.

● She had a map.
She was set to fly
across the sea.

▲ Yes! It was fun.

● It was such a rush
to sit on top
of the world.

▲ Wet. Fog.

Not a bit of sun.

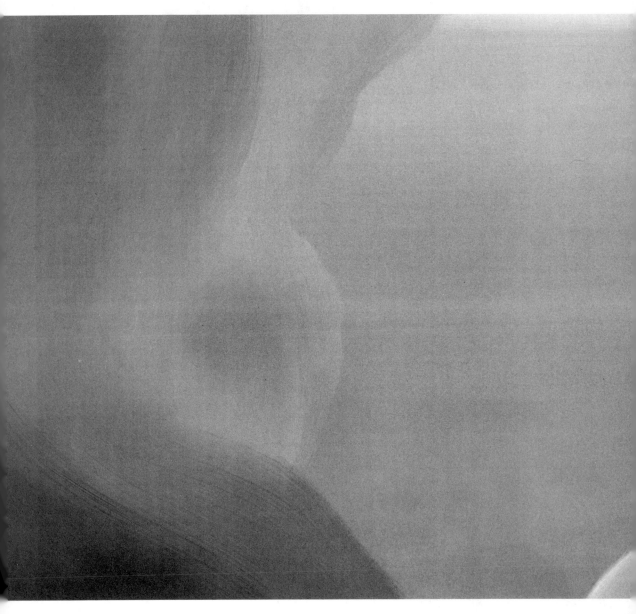

• She hit bad weather.

▲ A big dip.

A zig and a zag.

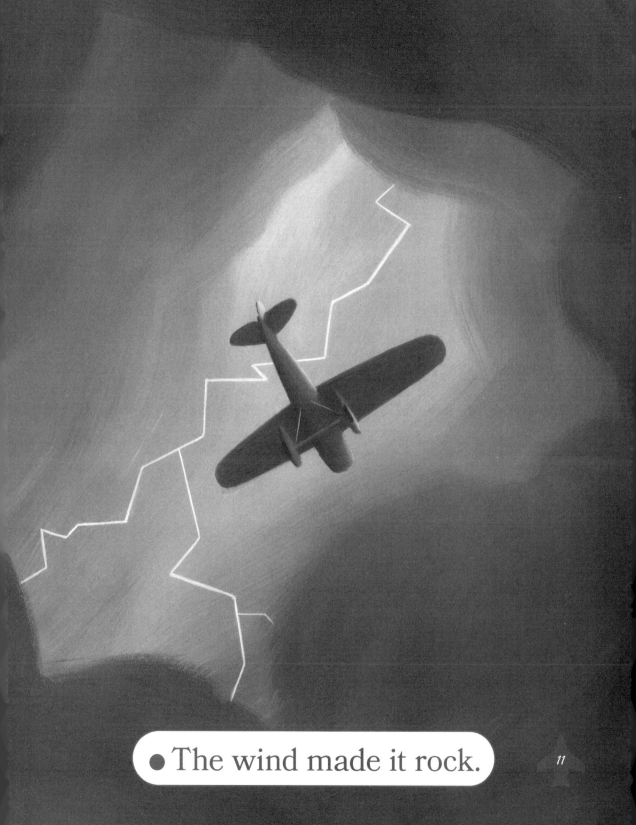

● The wind made it rock.

11

▲ But then the sun was up.

● In a bit, she saw
a dot of land.

13

▲ A tap and a big thud.

● Amelia did it!

14

More

Amelia Earhart took her first airplane ride in 1920 and loved it. She learned to fly and bought her own plane. As a pilot, Earhart set many records. She was the first woman to fly alone across the Atlantic Ocean.

This accomplishment was important, but Earhart had more goals. She wanted to be the first woman to fly around the world. Her world trip began in the United States. She flew nearly 22,000 miles, stopping in South America, Africa, India, and New Guinea. On July 2, 1937, Earhart took off from an island in the Pacific Ocean to continue her flight. She did not make it to her next stop, and her disappearance continues to be a mystery.

Más

Amelia Earhart viajó por primera vez en avión en 1920 y le encantó. Aprendió a pilotear aviones y se compró su primer avión. Como piloto, Earhart estableció muchos récords. Fue la primera mujer en cruzar sola el océano Atlántico en avión.

Este logro fue importante, pero Earhart tenía muchas otras metas. Quería ser la primera mujer en dar la vuelta al mundo en avión. Su viaje alrededor del mundo comenzó en Estados Unidos. Voló casi 22000 millas, haciendo paradas en Sudamérica, África, India y Nueva Guinea. El 2 de julio de 1937, Earhart despegó de una isla en el océano Pacífico para continuar con su vuelo. No llegó a la siguiente parada y su desaparición continúa siendo un misterio.